D0552298

READING HISTORY

General Editor: Michael Biddiss
Professor of History, University of Reading

And because time in itselfe... can receive no alteration, the hallowing... must consist in the shape or countenance which we put upon the affaires that are incident in these days.

Richard Hooker (*c.* 1554–1600)

For my students of Paper 96

STALIN'S RUSSIA

CHRIS WARD
Lecturer in the Department of Slavonic Studies
and Fellow of Robinson College
University of Cambridge

Edward Arnold
A division of Hodder & Stoughton
LONDON NEW YORK MELBOURNE AUCKLAND

© 1993 Chris Ward

First published in Great Britain 1993

Distributed in the USA by Routledge, Chapman and Hall, Inc.
29 West 35th Street, New York, NY 10001

British Library Cataloguing in Publication Data
Ward, Chris
  Stalin's Russia. – (Reading History Series)
  I. Title II. Series
  947.0842

  ISBN 0-340-54464-3

Library of Congress Cataloging-in-Publication Data
Ward, Chris.
  Stalin's Russia / Chris Ward.
    p. cm.—(Reading history)
  Includes bibliographical references and index.
  ISBN 0-340-54464-3 : $15.95
  1. Soviet Union—History—1925–1953. I. Title. II. Series.
DK267.W357 1993
947.084'2—dc20   93-3565
                                                       CIP

Typeset in Times Roman by Wearset, Bolton, Tyne and Wear
Printed and bound in Great Britain for Edward Arnold,
a division of Hodder and Stoughton Limited,
Mill Road, Dunton Green, Sevenoaks, Kent TN13 2YA
by Biddles Limited, Guildford and King's Lynn

CONTENTS

ACKNOWLEDGEMENTS

Historians plough a lone furrow, but they till a common field. Knowingly or unknowingly many people helped to steer the plough in this particular field; not only my teachers and colleagues at the Universities of London, Lancaster, Essex, Birmingham and Cambridge who stimulated my interest in Russian history over two decades, but also my students at Cambridge's Slavonic Studies Department – their ability to ask awkward questions often sent me scurrying to the library and makes me wonder if I have not learned more from them than they did from me.

Six people, however, should be singled out for a special thank-you. Between them Dr John Barber (King's College), Jo Clay (late of Clare College), and Dr Simon Franklin (Clare College), carefully scrutinized all the chapters and caused me to pause and think again. Professor R. W. Davies (Birmingham) kindly read the finished manuscript and corrected many mistakes and misconceptions. I owe a very particular debt to my good friend Professor Steve Smith (Essex), who laboured over several drafts, encouraged me to press on and saved me from numerous errors and infelicities. It goes without saying that the remaining defects are mine alone. Finally, I must thank Gladis Garcia for putting up with *Stalin's Russia* for two years.

A book like this which surveys a vast range of specialist literature within a relatively narrow compass places a heavy responsibility on the author. Several historians might raise their eyebrows at finding themselves slotted into this or that category. Others might find their positions inadequately summarized or wrongly expressed. Some might object on both grounds. I can only reply that this is how things seem to me, and that I have done my best to render as accurately as I can my understanding of their views.

Cambridge, January 1993.

GENERAL EDITOR'S PREFACE

The aim of this series is to provide for students, especially at under-graduate level, a number of volumes devoted to major historical issues. Each of the selected topics is of such importance and complexity as to have produced the kind of scholarly controversy which not only sharpens our understanding of the particular problem in hand but also illuminates more generally the nature of history as a developing discipline. The authors have certainly been asked to examine the present state of knowledge and debate in their chosen fields, and to outline and justify their own current interpretations. But they have also been set two other important objectives. One has been that of quite explicitly alerting readers to the nature, range, and variety of the primary sources most germane to their topics, and to the kind of difficulties (about, say, the completeness, authenticity, or reliability of such materials) which the scholar then faces in using them as evidence. The second task has been to indicate how and why, even before our own time, the course of the particular scholarly controversy at issue actually developed in the way that it did – through, for example, enlargements in the scale of the available pri-mary sources, or changes in historical philosophy or technique, or alterations in the social and political environment within which the debaters have been structuring their questions and devising their answers. Each author in the series has been left to determine the spe-cific framework by means of which such aims might best be fulfilled within any single volume. However, all of us involved in 'Reading History' are united in our hope that the resulting books will be wide-ly welcomed as up-to-date accounts worthy of recommendation to students who need not only reliable introductory guides to the sub-jects chosen but also texts that will help to enhance their more gener-al appreciation of the contribution which historical scholarship and debate can make towards the strengthening of a critical and sceptical habit of mind.

MICHAEL BIDDISS

Professor of History
University of Reading

NOTES ON THE TEXT

Organization of the book
The Introduction alerts the reader to the broad technical problems encountered when studying Stalin's Russia. Chapters 1 to 6 cover the main features of the Stalin period which have attracted scholarly attention. Each is divided into three sections. *Narrative* introduces the events under review; *interpretations* surveys the diverse ways in which historians try to understand these events; *evaluations* represents my own views and my attempts to adjudicate between the contending interpretations. The Conclusion summarizes what seem to me to be the successes and failures of historical research. I have tried to make each chapter free-standing – busy students should be able to turn to the chapter on collectivization, for example, and make sense of it without having read the rest of the book, although it is obviously advantageous to read the whole text.

Footnotes and bibliographies
No attempt has been made to use footnotes as a checking apparatus for every statement advanced in the *narrative* sections. Footnotes are intended primarily to bring to the reader's attention a range of published works representative of the various points of view discussed in the *interpretations* sections. I have made them as comprehensive as seems practicable. In every chapter the title of each work referred to appears first in its full form, thereafter in a shortened form. Each chapter concludes with *suggestions for further reading*, a brief selection of what I hope are easily available books and articles of particular interest and most likely to be useful to students. These lists take the place of a full bibliography. Those who wish to delve further are encouraged to refer back to the footnotes or to follow the paths mapped out in the notes and bibliographies of the suggested works.

Dates
Until 31 January 1918 Russia used the Julian calendar, then thirteen days behind the Gregorian calendar used in the rest of Europe. Thereafter Russia adopted the Gregorian calendar. The next day was therefore 14 February. All Russian dates up to and including 31 January 1918 are given in the Julian calendar, all others in the Gregorian calendar.

The Soviet 'agricultural year' ran from 1 July to 30 June of the succeeding year. Until 1 January 1931 the régime's 'economic year' ran from 1 October to 30 September of the succeeding year. After a 'special quarter' (October–December 1930) the economic and calendar years coincided. Dates pertaining to economic years prior to 1931 are indicated by the use of an oblique stroke (e.g. 1927/28), whereas a hyphen (e.g. 1927–8, 1936–7) means the two calendar years.

Terminology

According to Soviet thinking October 1917 signalled the beginning of the *dictatorship of the proletariat* in Russia – the overthrow of the bourgeoisie and the seizure of the state by the working class. The *transition to socialism* occurred over the following nineteen years. 'Exploiting' and 'antagonistic' classes (e.g. kulaks, nepmeny) continued to exist during the *NEP*. Although most Western historians view collectivization and the first piatiletka as the final end of the NEP, to Soviet minds this *Great Breakthrough* into *socialist construction* marked a further transitional stage. Officially, the NEP ended and *socialism* obtained when the 1936 constitution declared that exploiting and antagonistic classes had disappeared. The USSR never reached the *communist* stage, characterized by the 'withering away' of the state. In this book the terms *dictatorship of the proletariat*, *Great Breakthrough*, *socialism*, *socialist construction* and *transition to socialism* are used in the official Soviet sense, *NEP* in the Western sense. *Communist* is used only in relation to the party.

Transliteration

Russian words have been transliterated according to the Library of Congress scheme except where alternative spellings have become well established (e.g. Maxim Gorky not Maksim Gor'kii, Trotsky not Trotskii). Russian terms and words shown in the Glossary have not been italicized in the text.

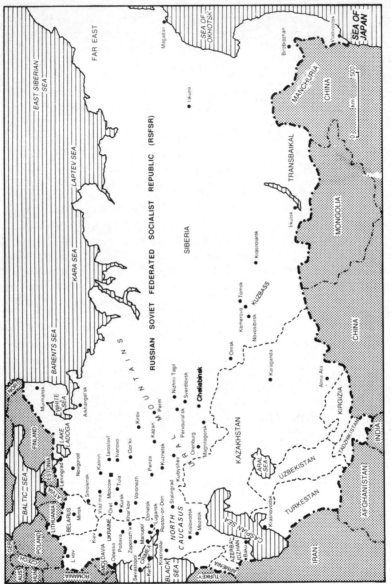

1. The USSR in the mid-1930s.

2. The borders of the western USSR 1941–2.

GLOSSARY

Russian and Soviet history is bedevilled by a plethora of abbreviations, acronyms and technical terms. Listed below are the ones used in this book. Russian words in common use (e.g. kulak, soviet) have been pluralized as English words. Items in square brackets indicate alternative forms sometimes found in other books.

Apparatchik (*pl.* apparatchiki)	'Apparatus man'. Functionary in the administrative apparatus of the party-state (q.v.).
Artel' (*pl.* arteli)	In industry and construction a traditional work group in which wages were earned collectively and divided amongst the workers. In agriculture the predominant form of collective farm in which peasants retained some livestock and a family plot.
Autonomous District/ Autonomous Region	Sub-division of an SSR (q.v.), usually an ethnic minority's officially designated 'national homeland'.
Bedniak (*pl.* bedniaki)	A poor peasant.
Brigade	Work group in a kolkhoz (q.v.) or factory.
Cadres	Key party members. More generally core members of any organization; skilled workers, for example.
Central committee	[CC, TsK] Elected by the party congress (q.v.). In addition each SSR (q.v.) had its own central committee subordinate to the main central committee. The central committee was the party's governing body between congresses, though in practice the Politburo (q.v.) came to dominate both institutions.
Central control commission	[TsKK] A department of the central committee (q.v.) which investigated complaints by party members against the party apparatus (1920–34).

Cheka	[VCHEKA] Extraordinary Commission for Combating Counter-Revolution, Sabotage, Speculation and Misconduct in Office (secret police 1917–22).
Chinovnik (*pl.* chinovniki)	'Petty clerk'. Deprecatory term describing a functionary of the tsarist administrative apparatus.
Chistka (*pl.* chistki)	'Cleansing'. Loosely a party purge. More accurately the expulsion of inactive or undesirable members.
Council of Ministers	Successor to Sovnarkom (q.v.) (1946 onwards).
Ezhovshchina	'The time of Ezhov' (pejorative). The 'Great Purge' of the 1930s named after Nikolai Ezhov, then head of the NKVD (q.v.).
Former people	[Byvshie liudi] A term current in the 1920s and 1930s used to describe the remnants of tsarist social classes deemed neutral or hostile to the régime.
Fraction	A party cell operating in a non-party organization.
GARF	Central State Archive of the Russian Federation. Successor to TsGAOR (q.v.).
Glavlit	Chief Administration for Literary and Publishing Affairs (censorship 1922 onwards).
Goelro	[GOELRO] State Commission for the Electrification of Russia (1920–35). Subordinated to Gosplan (q.v.) in 1921.
GOKO	[GKO] Committee for State Defence (supreme governmental body 1941–5).
Gosplan	State General Planning Commission, based in Moscow (1921 onwards). In addition each SSR (q.v.) had its own Gosplan subordinate to the central Gosplan as well as the SSR.

GPU — State Political Administration (secret police 1922–3).

Great Fatherland War — Soviet term for the Russo-German War (1941–5).

Group A — Soviet term for capital goods industry and the defence sector.

Group B — Soviet term for the consumer industries.

Gulag — [GULag] Chief Administration for Corrective Labour Camps (1930 onwards). In popular parlance the Soviet labour camp system in general.

Istpart — Bureau of Party History.

KGB — Committee for State Security (secret police 1953 onwards).

Kolkhoz (*pl.* kolkhozy) — A collective farm in which the produce was divided between kolkhozniki (q.v.) after obligatory deliveries had been made to the state and the MTS (q.v.).

Kolkhoznik (*pl.* kolkhozniki) — Peasant in a kolkhoz (q.v.).

Kominform — [Cominform] Communist Information Bureau. Successor to the Komintern (q.v.) (1947 onwards).

Komintern — [Comintern] Communist or Third International. The organization of foreign communist parties based in Moscow (1919–43).

Komsomol — [Comsomol] Young Communist League. The party's youth wing (1918 onwards).

Kulak — A rich peasant.

Likbez — 'Liquidation of illiteracy'; adult literacy campaign.

MGB	Ministry of State Security (secret police 1946–53).
Mir	[Commune, obshchina] Loosely the village community. More accurately the ancient organization of peasant self-government responsible for running the village's day-to-day social and economic affairs.
MTS	Machine Tractor Station. A depot which hired out machines to kolkhozy (q.v.) and sovkhozy (q.v.).
Muzhik (*pl.* muzhiki)	A peasant (slightly pejorative).
MVD	Ministry of Internal Affairs (interior ministry 1946 onwards, combined interior ministry and secret police 1953). Also the tsarist interior ministry.
Narkomnats	People's Commissariat for Nationalities (1917–23).
Narkompros	People's Commissariat for Enlightenment (Russian education ministry 1917–46).
NEP	New Economic Policy (1921–c.1927/28).
Nepmen (*pl.* nepmeny)	Private entrepreneur or trader during the NEP (q.v.).
NKGB	People's Commissariat for State Security (secret police 1943–6).
NKVD	People's Commissariat for Internal Affairs (interior commissariat 1917–34, combined secret police and interior commissariat 1934–43, interior commissariat 1943–6).
Nomenklatura system	A portmanteau term covering (a) the party's list of key state and party posts; (b) the party's files on people who might fill these posts; (c) the nation-wide system of appointment arising from the interaction of (a) and (b) controlled by the Secretariat (q.v.).

Obmen

The 'exchange of party cards' (1936), or 'exchange' in general.

OGPU

United State Political Administration (secret police 1923–34).

Oprichnina

Proto-security police established by Ivan the Terrible (Ivan IV or Ivan Grozny, 1530–84).

Orgburo

Organizational Bureau. The body elected by the central committee (q.v.) responsible for liaison with local party organizations (1919–52). In addition each SSR (q.v.) had its own Orgburo subordinate to the central Orgburo.

Party

[CPSU, KPSS, RKP(b), RSDRP(b), VKP(b)] The Bolshevik Party, formed in 1912 from a faction of the RSDRP (q.v.) and named the All-Russian Social Democratic Workers' Party (bolsheviks). Renamed the Russian Communist Party (bolsheviks) in 1918, the All-Union Communist Party (bolsheviks) in 1925 and the Communist Party of the Soviet Union in 1952.

Party conference

A meeting of party delegates. Constitutionally inferior to the party congress (q.v.).

Party congress

Theoretically the party's sovereign body. Delegates elected by party members.

Party control
    commission

Successor to the central control commission (q.v). A department of the central committee (q.v.) responsible for checking the fulfilment of central decisions (1934 onwards).

Party-state

A term coined by Western historians to describe the *de facto* government after 1917.

People's Commissar	Minister of the Soviet government (1917–46).
Piatiletka	'Five yearer'; a five-year plan.
Platform	The organized expression of a political view inside the party.
Plenum	A full meeting of an organization.
Politburo	Political Bureau. The body elected by the central committee (q.v.) responsible for making political decisions on behalf of the central committee and the party congress (q.v.) (1917 and 1919–52). In addition each SSR (q.v.) had its own Politburo subordinate to the central Politburo.
Political Commissar	Officer responsible for political work amongst military personnel and answerable to the party.
Presidium	Successor to the Politburo (q.v.) and Orgburo (q.v.) (1952 onwards).
Proverka	The 'verification' of party documents (1935).
Rabfak (*pl.* rabfaki)	Workers' Educational Faculty. A body which prepared workers for higher education (1919–38).
Rabkrin	[RKI] People's Commissariat of the Workers' and Peasants' Inspectorate (1920–34).
Rada	The Ukrainian Central Council. Revolutionary government of the Ukraine, based in Kiev (1917–18).
RAPP	Russian Association of Proletarian Writers (1928–32).

RSDRP	[RSDLP, RSDWP] Russian Social-Democratic Workers' Party. The forerunner of the Bolshevik, Menshevik and several other Marxist parties operating in the territory of the Tsarist Empire before and after 1917.
RSFSR	Russian Soviet Federated Socialist Republic. The Russian state (1918 onwards).
RTsKhIDNI	Russian Centre for the Preservation and Study of Recent Documents. Successor to TsPA IML (q.v.).
Secretariat	The body elected by the central committee (q.v.) responsible for drawing up agendas for the Politburo (q.v.) and the general management of lower party organizations (1919 onwards). In addition each SSR (q.v.) had its own Secretariat subordinate to the central Secretariat.
Sel'sovet (*pl.* sel'sovety)	The village soviet established in 1918 which eventually took over the functions of the mir (q.v.).
Seredniak (*pl.* seredniaki)	A 'middle' peasant; neither a bedniak (q.v.) nor a kulak (q.v.).
Smychka	The economic link between town and village, the *leitmotif* of the NEP (q.v.).
Soviet	A council. The primary organ of elective government after October 1917. The soviet system culminated in the All-Russian Congress of Soviets (1917–22), the All-Union Congress of Soviets (1922–36) and the Supreme Soviet (1937 onwards). Theoretically, the All-Russian Congress and its successors controlled Sovnarkom (q.v.). In practice the party controlled soviets at all levels.
Soviet control commission	Successor to Rabkrin (q.v.) (1934 onwards).

Sovkhoz (*pl.* sovkhozy)   A farm run by the state in which the workforce received a wage.

Sovkhoznik
(*pl.* sovkhozniki)   Worker in a sovkhoz (q.v.).

Sovnarkom   [SNK] Council of People's Commissars, based in the capital. The apex of the formal government of the RSFSR (q.v.) and subsequently the USSR (q.v.) between 1917–41 and 1945–6. In addition each SSR (q.v.) had its own Sovnarkom subordinate to the central Sovnarkom.

Spets-baiting   [Spetseedstvo] Attacks on technical specialists, engineers and managers by disgruntled workers.

SSR   Soviet Socialist Republic. Constituent republic of the RSFSR (q.v.) or USSR (q.v.).

Stavka   General Headquarters of the Supreme Command (supreme military command 1941–5).

TOZ (*pl.* TOZy)   Association for the Joint Cultivation of Land. A loose form of collective farm pre-dating the 1929 collectivization drive.

Trudoden'
(*pl.* trudodni)   'Labour day unit'. Measure of remuneration for a kolkhoznik (q.v.).

TsGAOR   Central State Archive of the October Revolution. The chief repository of primary sources pertaining to the state in the Soviet period.

TsPA IML   Central Archive of the Institute of Marxism–Leninism attached to the Central Committee of the Communist Party of the Soviet Union. The chief repository of primary sources pertaining to the party in the Soviet period.

Uchraspred	The 'records and assignments' section of the Secretariat (q.v.), responsible for distributing personnel amongst local party organizations.
USSR	[SSSR] Union of Soviet Socialist Republics. The Soviet state (1922 onwards).
Vesenkha	[VSNKh] Supreme Council of the National Economy (1917–32), responsible for state industry.
Vozhd'	'Leader', 'chief' or 'boss'. A term applied, unofficially, to Stalin.
Vydvizhenie	Promotion of workers 'from the bench' into positions of responsibility.
Vydvizhentsy	Beneficiaries of vydvizhenie (q.v.); the 'upwardly socially mobile'.
War Communism	The political economy of the Civil War period (1918–20), characterized by wholesale nationalization, grain seizures and the militarization of the party.
Zhdanovshchina	'The time of Zhdanov' (pejorative). The drive for ideological purity following the Great Fatherland War (q.v.) named after Andrei Zhdanov, then a secretary of the central committee (q.v.).
Zveno (*pl.* zven'ia)	Kolkhoz (q.v.) work team roughly equivalent in size to the peasant's extended family. In use during the Great Fatherland War (q.v.).

INTRODUCTION: RECOVERING STALIN'S RUSSIA

A document is a witness, and like most witnesses it rarely speaks until one begins to question it.

Marc Bloch.

Building history

For civil engineers, old buildings are stones and wood bonded and braced in a particular configuration. For town planners, villages and narrow winding streets present problems to be overcome. Farmers see landscapes as arenas of economic potential. To the chemist, photographs and films are examples of the effects of light on certain compounds; documents and books show the reaction of other compounds when laid on paper or parchment.

History is a different way of looking at things, a way of thinking about their vanished meanings. But it does not follow that we can never know what it felt like to live in the past. The association of words, places and ideas, or the context of body language and speech, as they appeared to denizens of another world, are lost to us forever. If we interview someone who was there, watch a film, visit a building, gaze at a photograph or pore over a document we are no better off: memory fades and distorts, materials reveal nothing without the exercise of disciplined imagination, and in any event all our efforts are refracted through our own times and personality.

It follows that whilst there can be definitive descriptions of things (this document or that photograph belongs to such and such a date), there can be no definitive history; only meditations on things – artifacts seen from a variety of angles, a never-ending debate on the significance which can be ascribed to the 'evidence' or the 'sources', the trail of debris left behind by the dead. The historian's mind creates and sustains the past moment by moment through the process of cognition. If all the historians in the world were struck by amnesia there would be no history, because history does not exist independently of, or anterior to, the historian's mind.

If the act of narrating history, of conjuring up the past, is inseparable from interpretation, the act of interpretation is bounded by the evidence – the cardinal rule of the historian's craft. Our first task, therefore, before we discuss narratives and interpretations, is to glance at the kind of materials available to historians of Stalin's Russia.

The pre-glasnost' source base

The basic sources most frequently used by Western academics are Stalin's collected works and the national press: *Pravda* ('Truth' – the central committee's newspaper which published most party resolutions), *Izvestiia TsK* ('News of the Central Committee') and *Bol'shevik* (the party's theoretical journal, later renamed *Kommunist*).[1] Government publications supplement these party materials: *Izvestiia* ('News' – the Soviet state's newspaper which reported Soviet decrees), *Za industrializatsiiu* ('For Industrialization' – the industrial newspaper which carried resolutions promulgated by Vesenkha and the economic commissariats), *Sotsialisticheskoe zemledelie* ('Socialist Agriculture') and *Trud* ('Work' – the organ of the Central Council of Trades Unions). All are housed in St Petersburg's and Moscow's main libraries or in foreign universities.[2]

Archival holdings pertaining to the period – once the property of the Soviet régime or the Communist Party but now distributed between the USSR's various successor states – are enormous. The chief repository for materials relating to the state was TsGAOR (now GARF), based in Moscow. Other important central archives existed for the national economy, the army, the navy, literature, the arts and the various Soviet academies of sciences. In addition there was a mass of republican and local archives. The party's archives paralleled those of the state, from central to republican, regional and local level. According to figures released in the 1960s the Moscow party organization's holdings exceeded one million storage units, Leningrad's 3.6 million. But these were dwarfed by the vast piles of documents stacked in TsPA IML (now RTsKhIDNI) – the party's equivalent to TsGAOR.

By 1930 almost no family papers remained in private hands and there were no organizations or newspapers free of government control. Even the Orthodox Church – nominally independent – was ruled from the Kremlin. The most important determinant of the pre-glasnost' source base, therefore, was the Soviet state.

The party's newspapers were strictly censored. In fact, they were not newspapers at all, but propaganda sheets which reported party campaigns as news. They paid scant attention to failures or shortcomings – except as an aspect of another campaign.[3] Sometimes, however, they were Aesopian references to 'real' events. In 1932–3

---

[1] Although many party resolutions and instructions were issued in the name of the central committee during Stalin's time, it is worth bearing in mind that they were, in fact, often promulgated by the Politburo or Presidium.

[2] Though a major fire at St Petersburg's Library of the Academy of Sciences in the early 1990s destroyed many irreplaceable newspaper runs.

[3] The industrial press, on the other hand, was often more forthcoming as regards failures and setbacks.

for instance, the press carried stories of famines in Europe and Asia. Since there were no serious famines outside the USSR at that time these could only have been intended as allusions to matters closer to home, perhaps to convince the Soviet people that life was no better elsewhere. More frequently editors rehashed the 'news' as policy changed. In 1936–8, at the height of the purges, they reported the arrest and trial of 'enemies'. In 1938–9 they related stories of unjust accusations and trumpeted abroad the rehabilitation of innocents. Nothing in the Stalinist press is what it seems to be, and researches have to be extraordinarily sensitive to hidden meanings. A new turn of phrase or a slight change in emphasis is rarely accidental and a rash of readers' letters signals the opening of a new campaign rather than a shift in public opinion.[4]

Published accounts of local party, soviet or non-party meetings tend to be less heavily censored – if only because much was considered too trivial to be worth bothering with. These are a valuable resource for social historians looking at the everyday realities of Soviet life. Stenographic records of party congresses and conferences are useful for other reasons. In the first place they often range over a wide variety of topics. Secondly, because they were intended for party audiences, matters were sometimes discussed relatively openly. But Soviet statistics are notoriously unreliable, and those published between 1930 and the early 1950s the most unreliable of all. Industrial data was routinely falsified and even the most basic social information is difficult to recover.[5] Only two nation-wide censuses were carried out in Stalin's time. The first, in 1937, was immediately suppressed. The second, finished two years later, was issued only in the most abbreviated form – a two-page spread in the newspapers. Researches therefore had to make complicated extrapolations from the 1926 and 1959 censuses in order to establish simple facts like gross population or age and gender distributions.[6]

For the reasons rehearsed above TsPA IML, TsGAOR and their local branches were of crucial importance. Archival access, however, was a major problem for *all* scholars, Soviets as well as Westerners. Only party members could work in party archives, and then only if they were recommended by someone important and subsequently cleared by the secret police. This excluded virtually all foreigners and

[4] The Soviet equivalent of *Who's Who*, the *Bol'shaia sovetskaia entsiklopedia* (The Great Soviet Encyclopedia), suffers from similar defects – basic information changed from edition to edition, a reflection of political changes.
[5] In addition, much basic statistical data was never collected. Figures relating to kolkhozy, for instance, are usually concerned only with production, and overall there was a marked decline in record keeping in the late 1930s and early 1940s: the Ezhovshchina (see pp. 119–21) and the German invasion wreaked havoc throughout the USSR.
[6] The 1937 and 1939 census have now become available.

the vast mass of native historians from the key range of primary sources.[7] Entry to TsGAOR and the other state repositories was strictly monitored. Western historians were never permitted to browse through the catalogues, or even to see them:[8] instead they informed archivists of their interests, and the archivists then selected files for their perusal, or refused to hand over particular documents. Access to district newspapers and provincial state archives was no less problematic. Because visa regulations restricted foreigners' movements to within forty kilometres of their specified place of residence, republican or local materials were often unavailable. In 1983 this author tried to visit two old textile towns (Iaroslavl' and Ivanovo) with newspaper runs not duplicated in Leningrad or Moscow. Since both were 'closed' for military reasons (perhaps because their cotton mills made parachutes), permission was never granted.

The Western academic community's response to the niggardliness and bias of officially approved materials was to turn to elsewhere. Until the end of the Second World War this meant reading accounts of life in Stalin's Russia published by émigrés resident in the USA or Western Europe. After the war, however, two valuable sources became available: the Trotsky papers and the Smolensk Archive.

Trotsky left his papers to Harvard University. They were lodged in the Houghton Library and divided into two parts: the 'open' section, which could be consulted immediately, and the 'closed' section (sometimes called the 'exile papers') which could not be examined until 1980. The exile papers were found to comprise thousands of letters to family, friends and political associates. Though they relate mainly to Trotsky's political activities in emigration they also cast some light on opposition to Stalin inside the USSR in the early 1930s.

The Smolensk Archive is much more important. Abandoned by the Soviet authorities to the invading Nazis in June 1941 the Archive was shipped to Germany, seized by United States forces in 1945, lodged in Washington DC, microfilmed, and sold to libraries around the world. It was found to contain 536 files comprising more than 200,000 pages covering the years 1917–41. Most files – 278 – relate to the period 1929–41. Like all archives it has its strengths and failings.[9]

---

[7]   After 1960 a few document collections were published. The problem, of course, is the criteria for selection.

[8]   Indeed, few catalogues were ever published. In consequence Western scholars proceeded by reading Soviet monographs and noting down archival 'call numbers' from their footnotes.

[9]   Some letters sent out by the central committee are not in the Archive, even though it is clear that the material was discussed by local apparatchiki. This is because sensitive documents had to be returned to Moscow. They are probably stored in RTsKhIDNI.

It is particularly good on politics, the purges, agriculture, education, propaganda, women and youth. It is weak on industry, industrial planning, urban affairs, the police and other non-party organizations. Moreover, no one has a clear idea of exactly what was removed by the Russians, Germans or Americans, nor are scholars sure of just how typical it is of other party archives. But it has profoundly influenced our understanding of the party's structure, the chain of command and relations between Moscow and the provinces.

The post-glasnost' source base

Gorbachev's appointment as General Secretary in March 1985 signalled an end to silence on many questions concerning Russia's past. Newspapers and journals – party, literary, popular and professional – vied with each other in publishing disclosures about Stalin and Stalinism.[10] But these revelations, interesting in themselves, are too haphazard to constitute the basis for a new history. Glasnost' broke many taboos, but no systematic study of previously secret materials has so far been undertaken, though several agencies are currently engaged in refashioning and recataloguing the old régime's archival holdings. No one, therefore, yet knows quite what the post-glasnost' source base for the study of the Stalinist period will look like. Following the Soviet Union's collapse, however, the party's archives and the various republican archives now held by the USSR's successor states are much more freely available to Western and native historians.

Suggestions for further reading

R. W. Davies, *Soviet History in the Gorbachev Revolution* (Macmillan, London, 1989). A fine work surveying the ways in which glasnost' impacted on professional and popular history inside Russia and changed Soviet views of the past.

P. K. Grimstead, *Archives and Manuscript Repositories in the USSR: Moscow and Leningrad* (Princeton University Press, 1972). A cru-

---

[10] The most important newspapers were *Izvestiia*, *Literaturnaia gazeta* (Literary Newspaper), *Moscow News* and *Pravda*. Of the literary and popular journals in the forefront of glasnost' *Ogonek* (Fire), *Novyi mir* (New World) and *Znamia* (Banner) were particularly significant. Party journals – *Izvestiia TsK KPSS* (News of the Central Committee of the Communist Party of the Soviet Union) and *Kommunist* – started to print materials from the archives. Furious debate later spread to the pages of professional historical journals – *Istoriia SSSR* (History of the USSR), *Voenno-istoricheskii zhurnal* (Journal of Military History), *Voprosy istorii* (Questions of History) and *Voprosy istorii KPSS* (Questions of the History of the Communist Party of the Soviet Union).

cial finding aid for Western scholars who travelled to the Soviet Union. Others in same series exist for the Ukraine, Moldavia, Belarus and the Baltic republics.

W. Laqueur, *Stalin: The Glasnost Revelations* (Unwin Hyman, London, 1990). A biography of Stalin which draws almost exclusively on glasnost' materials published in the Soviet Union. Useful for Soviet views of Stalin in the USSR's last days.

S. Fitzpatrick & L. Viola, eds., *A Researcher's Guide to Sources on Soviet Social History in the 1930s* (Sharpe, New York, 1990). An invaluable publication. Includes contributions from Sheila Fitzpatrick (newspapers and journals), John Arch Getty (Smolensk Archive), Patricia Grimstead (archival resources), Hiroaki Kuromiya (memoirs), Lewis Siegelbaum (industrialization), Lynne Viola (collectivization) and Stephen Wheatcroft (statistics).

1 THE RISE OF STALIN

*What do you think, that we got together in the Politburo so as to
exchange compliments with each other?*

Stalin, 1928.

Narrative

Stalin to 1922

Iosif Stalin – real name Iosif Vissarionovich Dzhugashvili – was born
in Gori, Georgia, on 9 December 1879, six weeks after Trotsky and
nine years after Lenin. He died on 5 March 1953. His father was a
cobbler, his mother a domestic servant. He went to Tbilisi Seminary
in 1894 and joined the RSDRP in 1898.[1] Expelled the following year
for neglecting his studies he worked briefly at the city's meteor-
ological observatory. Over the next decade or so 'Koba', as he styled
himself, became a prominent local revolutionary; helping strikers,
publishing illegal broadsheets and serving several prison terms. He
soon committed himself to Bolshevism. He first met Lenin in 1905,
organized bank raids to boost party funds, travelled to Vienna,
Cracow, Stockholm and London at Lenin's behest and was co-opted
onto the party's central committee in 1912. With Lenin's blessing he
briefly edited *Pravda* until he was arrested again in 1913.

Stalin arrived in Petrograd from Siberia in February 1917. After an
undistinguished rôle in the October Revolution he became
Commissar for Narkomnats, the government department responsible
for the Republic's non-Russian peoples.[2] In June 1918 he left for
Tsaritsyn to organize food supplies for Petrograd and Moscow.
Within a few months two other appointments followed – chief of the
North Caucasus military district and membership of the Council for
Workers' and Peasants' Defence.[3] There were yet more appoint-
ments in 1919: from April he was Commissar for Rabkrin, the body
set up to root out corruption and inefficiency in the central govern-

[1] Stalin's early life was subsequently so overlaid with mythology that it is difficult for
historians to be absolutely sure of even these basic facts. Robert Conquest, for example, draws attention to confusions over birth dates and parentage. R. Conquest, *Stalin:
Breaker of Nations* (Weidenfeld & Nicolson, London, 1991) chs. 1–2.
[2] Narkomnats was abolished after the ratification of the USSR constitution in July
1923.
[3] The Council for Workers' and Peasants' Defence, later the Council for Labour and
Defence, organized supplies and manpower during the Civil War. Tsaritsyn was
renamed Stalingrad in 1928.

ment machine,[4] and from May the Cheka's 'Special Department' was ordered to report direct to Stalin once a week.[5] By virtue of his posts in Narkomnats and Rabkrin Stalin was also a member of Sovnarkom, the Soviet 'cabinet'.

To these state posts were added offices in the rapidly expanding party bureaucracy. Re-elected to the central committee in April 1917 he was appointed to the Orgburo and Politburo,[6] both created by the eighth party congress in March 1919. The five-man Politburo, drawn from the central committee and instructed to deal with urgent political matters, reported back to the central committee and ultimately to congress, the party's governing body. The five members of the Orgburo were similarly answerable to congress and the central committee: their tasks were to make party appointments and oversee general organizational work. The congress also established a 'Secretariat of the central committee' to draw up the Politburo's agendas and liaise with the Orgburo and the multitude of local party bodies spreading across the land.[7] When the eleventh party congress reorganized and strengthened this latter institution in April 1922 Stalin, assisted by Valerian Kuibyshev and Viacheslav Molotov,[8]

---

[4]   Stalin resigned as head of Rabkrin after his appointment as General Secretary.

[5]   The Special Department was founded in January 1919 and assumed responsibility for Red Army security, counter-espionage and counter-subversion. For the early history of the Soviet secret police see G. H. Leggett, *The Cheka: Lenin's Political Police* (Oxford University Press, 1981).

[6]   In addition to Stalin the Politburo comprised Lev Kamenev, Nikolai Krestinskii, Lenin and Trotsky. Nikolai Bukharin, Mikhail Kalinin and Grigorii Zinoviev were elected 'candidate' or junior members. Krestinskii (1883–1938) was first elected to the central committee in April 1917. Kamenev (real name Rozenfeld) was born into a skilled working-class family in 1883. He studied law at Moscow University, met Lenin in Paris in 1902 and joined the RSDRP. He was married to Trotsky's sister, Ol'ga. Zinoviev (real name Radomylskii) was born in 1883 of Jewish petty bourgeois parents and joined the RSDRP at the turn of the century. He was a close confidant of Lenin's in 1917. Kalinin, born of peasant stock in 1875 and later a worker, joined the RSDRP in the year of its foundation (1898) and was active in the Caucasian underground. For brilliant cameos of Kamenev and other party leaders of the 1920s see E. H. Carr, *Socialism in One Country 1924–1926* (Vol. 1, Macmillan, London, 1958) ch. 4. For a sympathetic portrait of Trotsky see Isaac Deutscher's magnificent trilogy: *The Prophet Armed. Trotsky: 1879–1921* (Oxford University Press, 1954); *The Prophet Unarmed: Trotsky: 1921–1929* (Oxford University Press, 1959); *The Prophet Outcast. Trotsky: 1929–1940* (Oxford University Press, 1963). For Bukharin's life see S. F. Cohen, *Bukharin and the Bolshevik Revolution: A Political Biography 1888–1938* (Wildwood House, London, 1971). Stalin was also a member of a short-lived Politburo formed in October 1917. There is no evidence that it ever functioned.

[7]   The formation of the Orgburo and the Secretariat was due in part to the sudden death of Iakov Sverdlov (b.1885), an indefatigable organizer, on the eve of the congress.

[8]   Kuibyshev (1888–1935) joined the RSDRP in 1904 and was elected to the central committee in 1920. Molotov (1890–1986, real name Skriabin) joined the RSDRP in 1906. He edited *Pravda* in 1912 and became a close associate of Stalin's in 1917. He was known behind his back as 'stony-arse' due to his ability to sit at a desk all day.

became the party's first General Secretary.

By the time Lenin suffered his first stroke a month later, therefore, and ten years after his first appearance on the Bolshevik central committee, Stalin had risen high in the party bureaucracy. He was the only leader who was simultaneously a member of the Politburo, Orgburo, Secretariat and central committee. In addition, he could look back on almost seven years' experience of military commissions and jobs in the state's embryonic administrative apparatus.

The leaders in power

The Bolshevik leaders in power were no happy band of comrades united by a common resolve. Immediately after the October Revolution, five central committee members left in protest over Lenin's refusal to entertain coalition with the other socialist parties. More dissension accompanied the search for peace; the decision to sign the Treaty of Brest-Litovsk with the Central Powers early in 1918 provoked a clutch of resignations and strengthened the hand of the first post-revolutionary Bolshevik faction, the 'Left Communists' led by Bukharin.[9] As hopes of a European revolution waned, and the régime became embroiled in the frantic struggle to defeat the Whites and their foreign backers, arguments erupted over strategy and tactics. In October 1918 Trotsky, appointed Commissar for War in March, removed Stalin from his army command for disobedience. The following year the 'Military Opposition' berated Trotsky for accepting the professional services of ex-tsarist officers. There was further uproar over labour policy. Trotsky's schemes to revive the shattered economy, by converting the soldiery into 'labour armies' and militarizing the entire civilian workforce, were vehemently opposed at the ninth party congress in March 1920. Many delegates, deeply suspicious of his dictatorial methods, were equally alarmed by Lenin's determination to turn trade unions into state agencies and impose one-man management throughout industry. Eight months later Lenin, Zinoviev and Mikhail Tomskii rounded on Trotsky for antagonizing the unions.[10] An incipient 'Worker's Opposition' headed by Aleksandra Kollontai and Aleksandr Shliapnikov went further, demanding union control of industry.[11]

[9] The ratification of the treaty spurred the publication of *Kommunist*, the Left Communists' journal.

[10] Tomskii, a lithographer by trade, was born in 1880. Active in the metalworkers' union he joined the RSDRP in 1904 and became chairman of the Central Council of Trade Unions in 1918.

[11] Born of aristocratic parents, Kollontai (1872–1952) helped organize the party's women's section. Her radical views on sexual matters scandalized Lenin. Shliapnikov (1884–1937), chairman of the metalworkers' union, a founder member of the Bolsheviks' Petrograd Committee of February 1917 and the régime's first Commissar for Labour, came from a solid proletarian background.

The pent-up frustrations over labour policy exploded at the tenth party congress in March 1921 and fused with disquiet over numerous other matters: eight platforms with differing views on the rôle of the unions emerged; Zinoviev attacked Trotsky's management of the railways; the erstwhile 'Democratic Centralists' (a group which two years earlier took Lenin to task for by-passing the central committee) joined the Workers' Opposition in warning against bureaucratism, the suppression of debate and the Cheka's growing power.[12] Lenin, fearful lest the party disintegrate into a mass of warring factions in the face of the Kronstadt revolt, the Tambov rising and the highly contentious decision to introduce the NEP,[13] made it clear that all dissent would be crushed. At a thinly attended session held on the congress's final evening he bludgeoned through two important resolutions. The first – 'On party unity' – ordered the immediate end to all factional activity on pain of expulsion. The second – 'On the anarcho-syndicalist deviation in our party' – specifically condemned the views of the Workers' Opposition as incompatible with Bolshevism.

To add to the party's problems, from the autumn of 1922 tension increased between Lenin and Stalin, in particular over the treatment of Stalin's homeland and the Secretariat's ever growing influence. Georgia, independent after 1917, was forced into a Transcaucasian Federation in March 1922, a harbinger of the USSR, sponsored by Stalin and formed on 30 December.[14] Lenin, having returned to Moscow in October after recuperating from his first stroke, suffered a further stroke in December which left him partially paralysed. By now profoundly disturbed by Stalin's arbitrariness he wrote a fierce memo on the national question, reproaching the General Secretary for tactlessness. Immediately afterwards he dictated the famous 'testament' adding, early in the new year, a recommendation that Stalin should be removed from the General Secretary's office because of his 'rudeness' and insensitive use of power. Two months later, in March 1923, notes of support were sent to the Georgian Bolsheviks and Trotsky was asked to speak in their defence at the forthcoming twelfth party congress. Trotsky handed Lenin's materials on Georgia

---

[12] Trotsky used his control of the railways to try out his ideas on the militarization of labour.
[13] The Kronstadt naval base rose against the Bolshevik régime while the congress was in session. The rising was brutally crushed by the Red Army and the Cheka. The Tambov revolt was the largest of a number of peasant risings triggered by the government's policy of seizing grain.
[14] The USSR originally comprised the RSFSR and the Belarusian, Ukrainian and Transcaucasian SSRs. Central Asian republics were added in 1925 and 1936 and Finnish, Baltic and Moldavian republics in 1940. See S. Becker, *Russia's Protectorates in Central Asia: Bukhara and Khiva 1865–1924* (Harvard University Press, 1968) and below pp. 153, 195.

to the Politburo. A few days later Lenin's third stroke rendered him virtually helpless.[15] Consigned to the care of doctors under Stalin's supervision he took no further part in politics and died on 21 January 1924. Meanwhile, despite Bukharin's and Zinoviev's uneasiness over the reappearance of 'Great Russian chauvinism', Stalin and his allies easily won the day on the Georgian question when the twelfth party congress met in April 1923.[16]

The triumvirate

In Lenin's absence the congress witnessed the birth of an unofficial Politburo 'triumvirate', comprising Kamenev, Stalin and Zinoviev, dedicated to preventing Trotsky from assuming the dying leader's mantle.[17] In October the War Commissar countered with a letter to the central committee deprecating economic policy and bureaucratic degeneration inside the party. A week later forty-six senior Bolsheviks wrote to the Politburo along similar lines. The central committee and the central control commission responded by condemning Trotsky and the 'platform of the forty-six' for 'political errors'.[18] A joint resolution – 'The new course' – signed by Kamenev, Stalin and Trotsky in December 1923 failed to restore unity. As the month progressed Trotsky stigmatized the 'old guard' for stifling debate, Bukharin and Stalin accused Trotsky of factionalism and organizing a 'bloc' with former Democratic Centralists and Left Communists while Zinoviev – the first to identify 'Trotskyism' as a 'definite tendency in the Russian workers' movement' – used his position as president of the Komintern to strengthen the triumvirate's hold over the Bolsheviks' sister parties abroad.

The struggle was waged with increasing vituperation throughout 1924. Trotsky's supporters in the military were systematically removed from their posts and 'Oppositionists' were denied access to

[15] The correspondence of Lenin, Stalin and Trotsky and others concerned with the Georgian question and Stalin's accumulation of power was published by the party's central committee in the last days of the Soviet Union. See 'K voprosu ob otnoshenii V. I. Lenina k I. V. Stalinu v poslednii period zhizni Vladimira Il'icha', *Izvestiia TsK KPSS* (12, 1989); 'Vokrug stat'i V. I. Lenina "K voprosu o natsional'nostiakh ili ob avtonomizatsii"', *Izvestiia TsK KPSS* (9, 1990).

[16] Trotsky remained silent on the Georgian question but seconded Zinoviev's onslaught against two Bolshevik factions opposed to the NEP, 'Workers' Truth' and 'Workers' Group'.

[17] Zinoviev became a full member of the Politburo in March 1921. The triumvirate could therefore always be sure of a majority at the apex of the party machine.

[18] The furore over Trotsky's letter and the platform of the forty–six were published by the central committee in 1990. See 'Vnutripartiinaia diskussiia 1923 g', *Izvestiia TsK KPSS* (10, 1990).

the press.[19] In January Stalin hinted at the possibility of Trotsky's expulsion from the central committee for factionalism. Zinoviev repeated the charge of factionalism at the thirteenth party congress in May (the 'Bolshevization congress') and called on Trotsky to 'recant'. Narrowly re-elected to an enlarged central committee, Trotsky found himself completely isolated in the new Politburo, Stalin having survived a half-hearted attempt by Lenin's widow, Nadezhda Krupskaia, to dislodge him from the Secretariat.[20] Thereafter the battle shifted to the Komintern. In summer, after a brief struggle, Trotsky and his friend Karl Radek were dropped from the executive committee.[21]

These organizational machinations were accompanied by a full-scale assault on 'Trotskyism', the theory of 'permanent revolution', and vigorous attempts to besmirch Trotsky's rôle in the social-democratic movement.[22] It was this complex web of history and ideology that Stalin attacked in a series of lectures ('On the foundations of Leninism') published in *Pravda* in April and May 1924. Six months later Trotsky's 'Lessons of October', scathing of Zinoviev's and Kamenev's waverings in 1917,[23] was condemned by Bukharin, an opening shot in a press campaign against the War Commissar. Kamenev continued the offensive by publicizing disparaging remarks

[19] In January the central control commission ruled that *Pravda*, as the organ of the central committee, was obliged to follow the party line. Four months later Bukharin, editor of *Pravda* since October 1917, became editor of a new journal. According to the émigré Trotskyist Boris Souvarine *Bol'shevik* was founded specifically to counter the challenge posed by the Opposition. See B. Souvarine, *Stalin: A Critical Survey of Bolshevism* (Secker & Warburg, London, 1939) ch. 8. It was later renamed *Kommunist* (not to be confused with the earlier Left Communist journal).
[20] Krupskaia (1869–1939) married Lenin in 1898. She gave a copy of Lenin's testament to the central committee in mid-May 1924. Kamenev and Zinoviev successfully argued against Stalin's removal.
[21] Radek (b.1885, real name Sobelsohn), a prominent Trotsky supporter and a high-ranking party member, started his career in the Polish social-democratic movement and participated in the 1919 German Revolution. He was elected secretary to the Komintern whilst still in a German jail.
[22] Trotsky elaborated the theory of permanent revolution during and after the 1905 Revolution. According to Trotsky the indigenous bourgeoisie was too weak to overthrow tsarist absolutism, consequently the next insurrection would be led by the proletariat. The Russian revolution would be 'permanent' in the sense that it would pass effortlessly from the 'bourgeois' to the 'socialist' stage – the seizure of power by the workers and the establishment of a dictatorship of the proletariat. The second element of the theory was as follows: since the country's backward socio-economic structures made it impossible to contemplate the transition to socialism, a Russian socialist republic could only survive with the help of successful revolutions in the advanced Western European states – socialist revolution would have to be 'permanent' in the geographical sense too. For a full treatment see B. Knei-Paz, *The Social and Political Thought of Leon Trotsky* (Oxford University Press, 1978).
[23] In October 1917 Kamenev and Zinoviev opposed Lenin's decision to launch the insurrection.

made by Lenin in emigration, and by accusing Trotsky of Menshevism, of errors over Brest-Litovsk, economic and labour policy, and of neglecting the importance of the peasantry. Stalin unearthed more unflattering comments made by the dead leader and introduced a fanciful account of the October Revolution which downgraded Trotsky's pivotal rôle whilst promoting himself as chief protagonist.[24] In December Bukharin denounced Evgenii Preobrazhenskii's theory of 'primitive socialist accumulation' as a distortion of Leninism and declared that Trotsky's views on the smychka – the economic link between the town and the countryside and the cornerstone of the NEP – ran contrary to Lenin's.[25] The year closed with the publication by *Pravda* and *Izvestiia* of Stalin's first foray into the world of Marxist exegetics. 'October and Comrade Trotsky's theory of permanent revolution' popularized the notion of 'socialism in one country'. Rejecting Trotsky's formulation as unduly pessimistic, Stalin asserted that socialist construction in backward Russia was possible, even if final victory was impossible without international revolution.

The War Commissar's attempts to deny the existence of Trotskyism and minimize the significance of past disagreements with Lenin came to nothing. Though for the time being he kept his posts on the Politburo and central committee, he was replaced by Mikhail Frunze at the War Commissariat in January 1925 and given charge of two minor government departments four months later.[26]

The defeat of the Left

The triumvirate did not long survive Trotsky's humiliation. Bukharin's enthusiastic espousal of rural entrepreneurship and the peasant's rôle in socialist construction was immediately attacked by the nascent 'Left Opposition':[27] at the fourteenth party conference in April 1925, Iurii Larin spoke out against the NEP's agrarian bias while Zinoviev – head of the Leningrad party organization as well as president of the Komintern – resisted measures designed to increase peasant representation in the party.[28] There were more signs of ten-

---

[24] In Stalin's completely fabricated tale a Petrograd 'military-revolutionary centre' organized the insurrection. For Stalin's actual rôle see R. M. Slusser, *Stalin in October: The Man Who Missed the Revolution* (John Hopkins University Press, Baltimore, 1987).

[25] Preobrazhenskii (1886–193?) joined the party in 1903. A Trotsky supporter for many years, he first came to prominence in 1917 and was one of the instigators of the platform of the forty-six. For primitive socialist accumulation see pp. 55, 56, 73.

[26] Frunze (1885–1925) joined the party in 1904. He distinguished himself in the Civil War, became deputy Commissar for War in March 1924 and Commander-in-Chief of the Red Army a month later. He quarrelled with Trotsky over military matters in 1919. The disagreements were exploited by Stalin and Zinoviev.

[27] See pp. 74–5.

[28] Larin (1882–1932, real name Lurie) was a specialist in agricultural affairs.

sion five months later. Kamenev called for limitations on village enterprise and joined Krupskaia, Grigorii Sokol'nikov and Zinoviev in signing the 'platform of the four', a document which almost certainly expressed concern over Stalin's influence, the pro-peasant line and socialism in one country.[29] Disagreements burst into the open when the fourteenth party congress assembled in December: Zinoviev disparaged Bukharin's peasant orientation, Kamenev warned against the General Secretary's vast reserves of power, Kalinin appealed to the Leningrad delegates to disavow Zinoviev's 'New Opposition' while Stalin, presenting the main report for the first time, stated that the party would go forward with or without his co-leaders and described criticism as a 'deviation' which threatened the régime's very existence.

By the end of 1925 Zinoviev's star was waning. Under pressure from Bukharin and Stalin in the Komintern, most of his associates in the central committee (enlarged yet again) were demoted and new editors appointed to run *Leningradskaia pravda*. Following Molotov's purge of the local party he lost his chairmanship of the city's soviet in January 1926. Simultaneously Kamenev was reduced to the status of Politburo candidate. He surrendered the chair of Moscow's soviet three months later, having already been displaced as head of the capital's party machine in the autumn of 1924.

It was against this background that the 'United Opposition' materialized. In July 1926 Kamenev, Krupskaia, Trotsky, Zinoviev and nine others drew up the 'declaration of the thirteen', a ringing denunciation of 'rightist' economic policy and the suppression of free debate which, according to the signatories, foreshadowed the degeneration of the Revolution. As a result the central committee removed Kamenev from his remaining government post and Zinoviev from the Politburo.[30] Matters came to a head when the Opposition then took their campaign to the factories. At a tempestuous Politburo session held late in October Trotsky, along with Kamenev, was sacked after branding Stalin 'the grave-digger of the Revolution'. Grigorii Piatakov was the first to return from the meeting, recalled Victor Serge,

[29] Currently the document is still unpublished. For assessments of its likely contents see E. H. Carr, *Socialism in One Country 1924–1926* (Vol. 2, Macmillan, London, 1959) pp. 66–8; C. Merridale, *Moscow Politics and the Rise of Stalin: The Communist Party in the Capital 1925–32* (Macmillan, London, 1990) pp. 31–2. Sokol'nikov (1888–1939) joined the party in 1905 and became a candidate member of the Politburo in June 1924.
[30] Zinoviev's downfall was occasioned by Mikhail Lashevich (1884–1928), the deputy Commissar for War and a Zinoviev supporter who addressed a secret Oppositionist meeting in a forest near Moscow in June. Zinoviev was held responsible for his 'illegal' and 'conspiratorial' actions.

He was very pale and shaken. He poured out a glass of water, gulped it down and said: 'You know, I have smelt gunpowder, but I have never seen anything like this! This was worse than anything! And why, why, did Lev Davidovich say this? Stalin will never forgive him until the third and fourth generation!' Piatakov was so upset that he was unable to relate clearly what had happened. When Lev Davidovich at last entered the dining-room, Piatakov rushed at him asking: 'But why, why have you said this?' With a wave of his hand Lev Davidovich brushed the question aside. He was exhausted but calm. He had shouted at Stalin: 'Grave-digger of the revolution'... we understood that the breach was irreparable.[31]

After violent speeches by Bukharin and Stalin, delegates to the fifteenth party conference in October–November unanimously condemned the Opposition.[32] Delivering his last address in front of the Soviet party Trotsky was heard in silence. Kamenev was persistently interrupted and Zinoviev derisively heckled. The denouement was played out in the Komintern immediately afterwards when Bukharin replaced Zinoviev as president.

The rout of the United Opposition was completed over the next two years. Kamenev was sent abroad in January 1927 and Trotsky's loud fusillades against the Komintern's Chinese policy served only to increase his isolation.[33] Arraigned with Zinoviev before the central control commission in the summer, ejected from the International in the autumn, he only just avoided expulsion from the Bolshevik central committee. In September, when thirteen Opposition leaders demanded the full publication of their pamphlet – 'The real situation in Russia' – (*Pravda* carried only an edited version) the OGPU seized their duplicating machine and expelled Preobrazhenskii and sixteen others. Trotsky and Zinoviev were finally hounded out of the central committee in October 1927 when the former circulated his 'Letter to Istpart'.[34] After a forlorn attempt to mount a public

---

[31] Cited Deutscher, *Trotsky 1921–29*, p. 297. Trotsky seems to have first uttered this phrase in September. Born in 1890, Piatakov joined the Bolsheviks in 1910, took part in the Revolution and Civil War and became a leading industrial administrator during the NEP. Serge (real name Kibalchich) was born of Russian émigré parents in Belgium, also in 1890. A committed revolutionary, he became a Soviet citizen after 1917 but left Russia on the eve of the Second World War. Thereafter he lived in Europe and Mexico and died in great poverty in Spain in 1947.
[32] The Opposition had only consultative votes at the congress.
[33] The Komintern, by now completely dominated by the Bolsheviks, ordered the Chinese communists to co-operate with the 'left wing' of the Kuomintang, the nationalist party. In April 1927 the Kuomintang bloodily suppressed workers' organizations in Shanghai.
[34] Trotsky's letter exposed the General Secretary's fabricated version of the October Revolution and detailed Lenin's rift with Stalin in 1922–3.

demonstration in Red Square on 7 November both lost their party cards. The following month the fifteenth party congress expelled a further seventy-five Oppositionists – including Kamenev, Radek and twenty-three former Democratic Centralists – and instructed the central control commission to purge the party of 'Trotskyists'.[35]

The end came in the new year. On 17 January 1928 the hero of the October Revolution and founder of the Red Army was forcibly entrained for Alma-Ata, a remote city on the Chinese border. Radek was exiled to Tomsk, Zinoviev and Kamenev to Kaluga. After refusing to obey police regulations forbidding political activity Trotsky was deported on 10 February 1929. He died in Mexico on 21 August 1940 of wounds inflicted by an NKVD agent.

The defeat of the Right

The destruction of the United Opposition was compounded by mass desertions of its supporters. After repudiating their 'errors' Kamenev and Zinoviev were readmitted to the party in June 1928; two of the 3,098 Bolsheviks who recanted in the six months following the fifteenth party congress. Many defectors were persuaded that collectivization and forced industrialization signalled a 'left turn' by the leadership,[36] but disagreements soon arose within the ruling clique. At a central committee plenum, held a month after the partial rehabilitation of Stalin's former triumvirate partners, Bukharin – the General Secretary's chief ally in the struggle against the Left – spoke angrily against the subversion of the NEP.[37] Inside the Politburo his sentiments were echoed by Tomskii and Aleksei Rykov and seconded by candidate member Nikolai Uglanov.[38] Stalin, however, could count on the support of the other five full members (Kalinin, Kuibyshev, Molotov, Ian Rudzutak and Klimentii Voroshilov) and all the remaining candidates (Andrei Andreev, Vlas Chubar', Lazar Kaganovich, Sergei Kirov, Stanislav Kosior, Anastas Mikoian and Grigorii Petrovskii).[39] Castigated for 'rightist errors' Bukharin

[35] Over the next few months more than two thousand party members were expelled.
[36] Notably Piatakov, who recanted in 1928, and Preobrazhenskii and Radek, who broke with the Opposition in July 1929.
[37] See pp. 41, 78.
[38] Rykov was born into a peasant family in 1881, became chairman of Vesenkha in 1918 and Lenin's deputy in Sovnarkom three years later. Uglanov was born in Iaroslavl' in 1886. A St Petersburg metalworker since the age of twelve he joined the RSDRP in 1907.
[39] Voroshilov (1881–1969), an old friend of Stalin's from the pre-revolutionary Caucasian underground, joined the RSDRP in 1903. He first came to prominence during the Civil War as a military commander working with Stalin in Tsaritsyn. Rudzutak was born in 1887 and joined the party in 1905. The candidates were all old Bolsheviks: Andreev, born in 1895, joined the party in 1914; Chubar' (b.1891, joined 1907); Kaganovich (b.1893, joined 1911); Kirov (b.1886, joined 1904); Kosior (b.1889, joined 1907); Mikoian (b.1895, joined 1915). The oldest, Petrovskii (b.1878), was a founder member of the RSDRP.

arranged a clandestine meeting with Kamenev, beseeching him not to help the General Secretary 'cut our throats' and complaining that Stalin 'manœuvers so that we appear as splitters' while 'changing his theories depending on whom he wants to get rid of at the moment'.

Nothing came of Bukharin's appeal to his old enemy. Undermined in the Komintern and the Institute of Red Professors (another Bukharin stronghold),[40] *Pravda* also began to slip from his grasp; though the paper published his 'Notes of an economist' at the end of September, editorials critical of the 'right wing' had been appearing for some weeks.[41] In October 1928, when Stalin appeared before the Moscow party organization and proclaimed the inauguration of a 'decisive struggle' against 'right opportunism', it became clear that Uglanov was losing control of the most important local party machine.[42] This was followed by a stormy week-long Politburo meeting held early next month during which Bukharin, desperate to parry the charge of factionalism, execrated the 'right deviation' and joined Rykov and Tomskii in offering to resign. Shortly afterwards Uglanov was removed from the Moscow party committee and Bukharin's supporters were purged from the Komintern. Tomskii reaffirmed his resignation offer in December when Kuibyshev turned up at the eighth trades union congress and delivered an impassioned plea for rapid industrialization.

Bukharin's meeting with Kamenev, taken together with a speech delivered on the fifth anniversary of Lenin's death ('Lenin's political testament' – its very title a scarcely veiled attack on the General Secretary), presaged his overthrow. When Stalin convened a joint session of the central committee and the central control commission in January 1929 and accused him of factionalism, he replied with a passionate indictment of Stalin's policies and a defence of the principle of collective leadership. The charge of factionalism was confirmed in February. Tomskii and Rykov suffered the same fate for concealing their knowledge of the 'clandestine meeting' while Bukharin and Tomskii were impugned for refusing to rescind their Politburo resignations.[43] After the three abstained from voting on a Politburo resolution in April endorsing the 'optimum variant' of the first piatiletka, the central committee and the central control commission assembled once more.[44] Stalin rehearsed Bukharin's past disagreements with Lenin and alleged that he conspired with the Left

---

[40] The Institute of Red Professors was created in February 1921 to train Marxist scholars for posts in higher education. Bukharin was its first director.
[41] See pp. 42, 78.
[42] Uglanov became first secretary of the Moscow party organization in January 1925.
[43] Rykov appears to have withdrawn his resignation offer almost immediately after he made it.
[44] See p. 79.

Socialist Revolutionaries during the Brest-Litovsk imbroglio.[45] Bukharin's argument that Stalin had 'capitulated to Trotskyism' by wrecking the NEP was unavailing; his views were declared inconsistent with the party line. Uglanov was dismissed from his remaining party posts, Tomskii from the Central Council of Trade Unions and Bukharin from the editorship of *Pravda* and the Komintern presidency. The latter two were warned that further violations of party discipline would lead to expulsion from the Politburo.

On 17 November 1929, ten days after Stalin's 'The year of the Great Breakthrough' extolled the 'socialist offensive' in town and countryside, Bukharin was ousted from the Politburo for leading the 'right deviation'.[46] The following month saw the beginning of the 'cult of personality': celebrating Stalin's fiftieth birthday with an avalanche of tributes to his leadership, *Pravda* called on the party and the people to unite around 'Lenin's most faithful and dedicated pupil and associate'.

Interpretations

Why Stalin? Ever since the General Secretary defeated his rivals the question has taxed the imagination, not only of all those who study Russia or were involved in the drama in one way or another, but also of every thinking person interested in twentieth-century history. In consequence the range and scope of the literature on Stalin's rise is formidable. A steady flow of material, originating in the late 1920s and growing in volume as the years passed had, by the 1980s, accumulated into a sea of memoirs, commentaries, articles and monographs. Recent events – glasnost', the final repudiation of Stalinism and the collapse of the USSR – have only added to the flood.

It is no easy matter to navigate these waters. Much remains obscure, the prospect facing the historian varies considerably in terms of quality and plausibility, while the cross-currents of explanation are treacherous enough to perplex even the most adept voyager; no single tide of opinion can be identified and the drift of one assessment mingles ambiguously with another. Nevertheless, within this confused vortex it is possible to discern six broad interpretative streams: the 'heroic', 'administrative', 'party history', 'ideological', 'socio-cultural' and 'Trotskyist' approaches.

---

[45] The Left SRs, the Bolsheviks' only coalition partners after 1917, resigned from the government over the treaty, declared a 'revolutionary war' against Bolshevism and 'German Imperialism', killed the German ambassador and staged risings in Moscow and Iaroslavl'.

[46] His recantation appeared with Rykov's and Tomskii's in *Pravda* on 26 November.

The heroic approach

Leonid Krasin, wrote Trotsky in 1940, was the first to call Stalin

> an 'Asiatic'... in saying that he had in mind no problematical
> racial attributes, but rather that blending of grit, shrewdness,
> craftiness and cruelty which has been considered characteristic
> of the statesmen of Asia.[47]

Many have followed where Trotsky led, if not always with such
panache. From the laudatory Soviet accounts of the 1930s, 1940s and
1950s, to the recent offerings of Western, émigré and post-Soviet
Russian historians, the part played by Stalin's ancestry and personality in the struggles of the 1920s has been dissected in numerous
biographies; good, bad and indifferent.[48] On one side the hagiogra-
phers of the 'Stalin school of falsification' point to the General
Secretary's wisdom and foresight in defending socialism from the
wicked schemes of 'Trotskyists' and 'Bukharinists'.[49] On the other
the psychological portraits of Robert Conquest and Robert Tucker
highlight Stalin's duplicity and ruthlessness, averring that he
deceived allies and opponents alike into believing that he took ideas
seriously when in reality he adroitly manipulated the registers of
Bolshevik polemics for his own purposes. Socialism in one country,
the attack on 'Trotskyism', the alliance against the Left Opposition,
the denigration of 'right opportunism' and the proclamation of the
Great Breakthrough were mere rhetorical devices designed to mask

[47] L. Trotsky, *Stalin: An Appraisal of the Man and his Influence* (trans. C. Malamuth,
Hollis & Carter, London, 1947) p. 1. Krasin (b.1870), an engineer active in the
Caucasian underground before the Revolution, was elected to the central committee
in 1912. A friend of Trotsky's since 1905, he died in 1926 whilst on a diplomatic mission to London.

[48] Recent examples include A. Anton-Ovseenko, *Portret tirana* (Khronika, New York,
1980); I. Deutscher, *Stalin: A Political Biography* (2nd ed., Penguin, 1972); A. De
Jonge, *Stalin and the Shaping of the Soviet Union* (Morrow, New York, 1986); R.
Hingley, *Joseph Stalin: Man and Legend* (McGraw-Hill, New York, 1974); R. H.
McNeal, *Stalin: Man and Ruler* (Macmillan, London, 1988); H. Montgomery Hyde,
Stalin: The History of a Dictator (Farrar, Straus & Giroux, New York, 1971); A. B.
Ulam, *Stalin: The Man and His Era* (2nd ed., Beacon Press, Boston, 1989); D.
Volkogonov, *Stalin: Triumph & Tragedy* (trans. H. Shukman, Weidenfeld & Nicolson,
London, 1991). See also B. D. Wolfe, *Three Who Made a Revolution: A Biographical
History* (Penguin, 1974); P. Pomper, *Lenin, Trotsky and Stalin: The Intelligentsia and
Power* (Columbia University Press, 1990).

[49] Two representative samples are G. F. Alexandrov, et al., *Joseph Stalin: A Short
Biography* (Moscow, 1947) – 'Foremost in the attack on the Party were Trotsky, that
arch enemy of Leninism, and his henchmen' (p. 81); and E. Yaroslavsky, *Landmarks
in the Life of Stalin* (Lawrence & Wishart, London, 1942) – 'Right would-be restorers
of capitalism inspired all the enemies of the Soviet Government and the Bolshevik
Party' (p. 146). The latter concludes with a typical panegyric (p. 191), 'Long may he
live and flourish, to the dismay of our enemies and to the joy of all working people –
our own, dear Stalin!'.

the General Secretary's real ambition, to crush his antagonists and make himself dictator of the Soviet Union.[50]

There is broad consensus on the failings of the other main actors. Edward Carr dismisses Zinoviev as little more than an unsavoury careerist and describes Kamenev as bereft of any coherent goal and in need of a strong leader.[51] Bukharin's biographer argues that his passionate belief in the NEP blinded him to the faults of his accomplice in the struggle against the United Opposition.[52] The implication is clear. No one here was a match for the General Secretary. Kamenev and Zinoviev were unceremoniously ditched once they had served their purpose in the triumvirate, Bukharin was abruptly pushed aside once the Politburo and the central committee were firmly under the control of Stalin and his chief cronies – Kalinin, Kuibyshev, Molotov and Voroshilov. As for the rôle of Bolshevism's founder, most historians contend that Lenin, stricken in mind and body and scarcely able to work, realized too late the true nature of his 'wonderful Georgian'.[53] After consistently promoting and protecting a loyal, dull-witted functionary, the scheme to explode 'a bombshell' under Stalin over the Georgian Affair at the twelfth party congress misfired when his health collapsed and Trotsky foolishly referred the matter to the Politburo.[54]

Most specialists record this as only one of Trotsky's mistakes. All acknowledge that he seriously underestimated Stalin; his characterizations of the General Secretary as the 'grey blur' and 'the outstanding mediocrity of our party' enliven the pages of almost every secondary source. Examples of his vaunting self-regard are often incorporated into the story; a soaring intellect and a caustic tongue could pulverize opponents but evinced only the respect, not the affection, of political allies. Anatolii Lunacharskii remarked on Trotsky's 'nonchalant, high and mighty way of speaking to all and sundry' and his 'tremendous imperiousness and a kind of inability or unwillingness to be at all amiable and attentive to people'. 'He made

---

[50] Conquest, *Stalin*; R. C. Tucker, *Stalin as Revolutionary 1879–1929: A Study in History and Personality* (Chatto & Windus, London, 1974). The former is more a sketch than a fully-fledged biography. Similar interpretations are advanced in many of the works cited in p. 19 fn. 48. Specialists are divided on a related matter – the physical elimination of enemies, real or imagined. Trotsky for one suspected that Stalin poisoned Lenin and was involved in Frunze's death in hospital in October 1925, but the weight of opinion leans in the other direction; even those who dwell relentlessly on the General Secretary's responsibility for the horrors of the 1930s are inclined to treat these rumours with extreme caution.

[51] Carr, *1924–26 1*, pp. 155–6, 162.

[52] See Cohen, *Bukharin*, ch. 9.

[53] A phrase used by Lenin in February 1912 in a letter to the writer Maxim Gorky.

[54] See Trotsky, *Stalin*, pp. 361–2; Tucker, *Stalin 1879–1929*, pp. 254– 67. For an excellent analysis of the Georgian Affair and other matters of dispute between Lenin and Stalin after the Civil War see M. Lewin, *Lenin's Last Struggle* (Faber & Faber, London, 1969).

no attempt', adds Carr, 'either to organize his friends or to divide his enemies'.[55] There is general agreement that these were not assets in the febrile corridor politics of the Politburo, the central committee and the congress. The War Commissar's isolation increased while Stalin deftly gathered up the wounded and the disaffected.

The administrative approach

Stalin's accumulation of offices within the party-state machine has long been a focus of historical inquiry, particularly in the 1960s and early 1970s:[56] Carr neatly abbreviated the labours of an entire generation of scholars concerned with state-building and the evolution of Bolshevism's administrative apparatus when he concluded that in the final analysis Stalin's victory 'was a triumph, not of reason, but of organization'.[57]

Many authors describe how Narkomnats endowed Stalin with power and influence over the remote corners of the nascent socialist republic, allowing, by the end of 1922, the construction of the USSR; a centralized polity in which all roads led to the Kremlin. Equal attention is paid to the Workers' and Peasants' Inspectorate – whoever controlled Rabkrin gained an unrivalled insight into the detailed workings of the central government's apparatus. In both instances Stalin could promote friends and demote enemies under the guise of administrative necessity. Inexorably the Soviet Union was made in his own image.[58]

Even more so was the party which, within a few short years, mutated from little more than a peripatetic debating society, comprising a handful of pugnacious intellectuals scattered across half a dozen European cities, into a rambling organization responsible for the governance of one-sixth of the globe's surface. In consequence

[55] Carr, *1924–26 1*, p. 152. Lunacharskii (b.1875) and author of the popular *Revolutionary Silhouettes* published in 1923, was Commissar for Narkompros after October 1917.
[56] See for example E. H. Carr, *The Bolshevik Revolution* (Vols. 1–3, Macmillan, London, 1950–3); id., *The Interregnum 1923–1924* (Macmillan, London, 1954); R. V. Daniels, *The Conscience of the Revolution. Communist Opposition in Soviet Russia* (Harvard University Press, 1960); M. Fainsod, *How Russia is Ruled* (Harvard University Press, 1953); O. A. Narkiewicz, *The Making of the Soviet State Apparatus* (Manchester University Press, 1970); L. Schapiro, *The Communist Party of the Soviet Union* (2nd ed., Eyre & Spottiswoode, London, 1970); id., *The Origins of the Communist Autocracy. Political Opposition in the Soviet State: First Phase 1917–1922* (Praeger, New York, 1965).
[57] Carr, *1924–26 1*, p. 224.
[58] For recent works see J. R. Adelman, 'The development of the Soviet party apparat in the Civil War: center, localities and nationality areas', *Russian History* (1, 1982); G. Gill, 'Stalinism and institutionalization: the nature of Stalin's regional support', in J. W. Strong, ed., *Essays on Revolutionary Culture and Stalinism: Selected Papers from the Third World Congress for Soviet and East European Studies* (Slavica, Columbus, 1990); R. Pipes, *The Formation of the Soviet Union* (Harvard University Press, 1964); T. H. Rigby, 'Early provincial cliques and the rise of Stalin', *Soviet Studies* (1, 1981).

administration began to displace politics. The Politburo might take decisions but it was the Orgburo and the Secretariat which managed things on a daily basis. The staff of this latter body increased from thirty in 1919 to 602 in 1921 and rose again to 767 in 1926, spawning specialist sections along the way and placing the General Secretary at the heart of the 'nomenklatura system', a bureaucratic colossus which assigned swarms of officials to a vast array of jobs and kept the party-state in being.[59]

What grew out of all this, maintains Robert Daniels, was a 'circular flow of power'.[60] Just as local organizations ineluctably became 'Stalinist' (in the sense that their leaders were appointed and controlled by the Secretariat) so did the congress, the central committee, the central control commission and the Politburo. Congress delegates owed their position to Stalin, and they in turn elected the central committee which in turn elected the control commission and the Politburo. When it came to a showdown in the Politburo, therefore, a Trotsky or a Bukharin might win the argument but Stalin invariably won the vote. And while Kamenev and Zinoviev could for a while marshal their own supporters in the central committee (drawn respectively from the Moscow and Leningrad party committees) they were overwhelmed by the ever growing ranks of faceless, apolitical provincial apparatchiki loyal to Stalin. In addition, according to Niels Rosenfeldt, Stalin painstakingly fostered the development of a confidential personal secretariat which gave him exclusive purview of the most sensitive information, especially that concerning the activities of the other leaders, all of which was put to good use in the struggle for power.[61]

But bureaucratization and the hypertrophy of the party-state were not just matters of central prescription. Both were intimately connected with the Revolution's immediate impact. Under the hammer blows of war, civil turmoil and economic disarray the old pre-revolutionary proletariat virtually disappeared. A few workers found jobs in the nomenklatura system, others perished at the front, many more

---

[59] The most important were 'records and assignments' ('Uchraspred', responsible for distributing personnel amongst local party organizations), 'organization–instruction' (chiefly concerned with centre–periphery liaison), and 'agitation–propaganda' (which looked after ideological work). See J. Ali, 'Aspects of the RKP(b) secretariat, March 1919 to April 1922', *Soviet Studies* (3, 1974); R. V. Daniels, 'Evolution of leadership selection in the central committee 1917–1927', in W. M. Pintner & D. K. Rowney, eds., *Russian Officialdom. The Bureaucratization of Russian Society from the Seventeenth to the Twentieth Century* (Macmillan, London, 1980).

[60] R. V. Daniels, 'Soviet politics since Khrushchev', in J. W. Strong, ed., *The Soviet Union Under Brezhnev and Kosygin* (Van Nostrand-Reinhold, New York, 1971) p. 20.

[61] N. E. Rosenfeldt, '"The consistory of the communist church": the origins and development of Stalin's secret chancellery', *Russian History* (2–3, 1982); id., *Knowledge and Power: The Role of Stalin's Secret Chancellery in the Soviet System of Government* (Rosenkilde & Bagger, Copenhagen, 1978).

fled to the countryside in search of food and shelter. These cataclysmic developments had important repercussions for administration. In the first place all manner of popular institutions thrown up by the Revolution – most obviously the soviets – began to atrophy. Secondly, those organizations which continued to show signs of independent life tended to drift away from the party line. The results were several. On the one hand appointment replaced election within the body of the party-state, on the other the Cheka was called in to deal with 'counter-revolutionary' waverings amongst the masses and 'deviations' within Bolshevism. Moreover, since there were never enough qualified workers to staff commissariats, offices and local soviets, the party was obliged to rely on the services of former tsarist bureaucrats, chinovniki who brought with them the habits and customs of the *ancien régime*: lack of initiative, boorishness, a general contempt for the lower ranks and a grovelling respect for authority.[62] These ancient traditions were reinforced by current dilemmas. As the Bolshevik élite looked aghast at the ruined economy, the threat of social and political disintegration and the menace posed by tsarist chinovniki, they adopted many of the old régime's methods and *mores*; regularly purging the apparatus, restricting enterprise and volition, centralizing decision-making and becoming increasingly intolerant of and impatient with the fickle and random aspects of plebeian aspirations. 'As the economic situation deteriorated during 1918–1921', writes William Chase,

> so too did worker–party relations. Animated by a sense of its historic mission and the need to preserve the revolution, the party vainly sought to arrest the economic collapse by asserting increasingly centralized control... Because it had tied itself to a disastrous policy, the party assumed *de facto* responsibility for the crisis... A profound breach separated the former allies and a deep alienation replaced the precocious class consciousness of 1917–1918.[63]

A crushing sense of anxiety and insecurity gave birth to a watchful, suspicious, despotic and arbitrary régime – a 'Caliban state' which reached maturity with Stalin.

---

[62] Tsarist bureaucrats reflected and reproduced the political culture of absolutism. Under the tsars scant space was allowed for autonomous action within society and chinovniki saw themselves as agents of the autocracy, not as servants of society. Like everyone else in the governmental élite they were closely supervised and worked under the threat of arbitrary dismissal or sudden disgrace. No clerk dared criticize his superiors and only the most confident – or foolhardy – would risk drawing attention to himself by overt displays of initiative.

[63] W. J. Chase, *Workers, Society, and the Soviet State: Labor and Life in Moscow 1918–1929* (University of Illinois Press, 1987) pp. 294–5.

The party history approach

The administrative approach overlaps with the party history approach. The scholarly community's attempts to understand the nature of pre-revolutionary Bolshevism rival the efforts made to unravel the puzzle of Stalin's rise to power, but frequently historians are seeking answers to the same question. Did the essence of Bolshevism in some way facilitate Stalin's success? Was Stalin the legitimate heir of Lenin?

As well as countless general histories virtually every specialist monograph iterates the importance of Lenin's pre-revolutionary thinking.[64] In Merle Fainsod's opinion *What is to be Done?*, published in 1902, left 'an ineradicable stamp on the character and future development of the party'.[65] Lenin believed that the working class could never carry through a revolution unaided. Throughout nineteenth-century Europe popular protest always resulted in compromise and restabilization, encouraging the formation of 'trades union consciousness' amongst workers. 'Social-democratic consciousness' (revolutionary intent) would have to be brought to the proletariat 'from without' by a cohort of professional agitators led by Marxist intellectuals. Necessarily, therefore, the 'vanguard party' would have to be tightly controlled: only a strong central committee could prevent the RSDRP's émigré leadership from decomposing into a mêlée of ineffectual coteries and shield the native membership from the unwelcome attentions of the tsar's secret police. Organization, discipline and centralization, according to Lenin, were the keys which would unlock the door to the socialist paradise. Shedding assorted heretics along the way it was over these issues that he finally split the RSDRP in 1912 and constituted the Bolsheviks as a separate party.

The ramifications of these centralizing tendencies after the October Revolution have been repeatedly examined.[66] New rules approved by the eighth party congress in 1919 subjected national

---

[64] In addition to the works cited above, amongst the most notable specialist monographs are N. Harding, *Lenin's Political Thought* (Vols. 1–2, Macmillan, London, 1977–88); J. L. H. Keep, *The Rise of Social Democracy in Russia* (Oxford University Press, 1963); R. H. McNeal, *The Bolshevik Tradition* (Prentice Hall, New Jersey, 1963). A. B. Ulam, *Lenin and the Bolsheviks* (Fontana, London, 1969) is a more popular account.

[65] Fainsod, *How Russia is Ruled*, p. 47.

[66] Recent contributions to this vast literature include G. Gill, *The Origins of the Stalinist Political System* (Cambridge University Press, 1990); T. H. Rigby, 'The origins of the nomenklatura system', in I. Auerbach, et al., eds., *Felder und Vorfelder russischer Geschichte. Studien zu Ehren von Peter Scheibert* (Rombach, Freiburg, 1985); R. Service, *The Bolshevik Party in Revolution: A Study in Organizational Change 1917–1923* (Macmillan, London, 1979). Amongst the journal literature see S. Blank, 'Soviet institutional development during NEP: a prelude to Stalinism', *Russian History* (2–3, 1982); G. Gill, 'Bolshevism and the party form', *Australian Journal of Politics & History* (1, 1988).

branches to the Russian party,[67] instructed provincial communists to take the leading rôle in local soviets (these 'party factions' to be 'unconditionally subordinate' to the next highest party body, and so on up to the central committee and the Politburo) and amplified the principle of 'democratic centralism' – 'the discussion of all disputable questions of party life is completely free until the decision is taken' – a clause which tended to restrict politics to a small band of senior dignitaries. The following year, at the ninth party congress, delegates listened to Lenin's trenchant pleas for 'iron discipline' and 'vertical centralism'. No disputes would be tolerated in the face of economic and social disintegration.

Lenin's anti-democratic sentiments, runs the argument, reached their apogee at the tenth party congress. 'On party unity' and 'On the anarcho-syndicalist deviation in our party' finally extinguished Bolshevism's dissident voices and furnished Stalin with powerful weapons in the succession struggle; disagreement became factionalism, factionalism became treason. The only proper response to defeat in the democratic cockpit of the central committee was silence – or better still recantation. Those who refused to submit to the majority rendered themselves liable to investigation by the Cheka and the central control commission and ultimately to expulsion. One by one Trotsky, Kamenev, Zinoviev and Bukharin fell victim to the very political machine they helped to construct.

The ideological approach

The succession struggle took place, not only in the context of an incipient party-state apparatus, but also in the arena of the NEP. Since the 1960s in particular researchers have been inclined to take seriously leadership disputes over the road to socialism. Carr, Alexander Erlich and Moshe Lewin are foremost amongst several Western scholars who treat the ideological positions adopted by the main protagonists as something other than mere façades disguising personal ambition.[68]

Lenin's 'retreat' into the NEP was an ambiguous bequest. The Left's polemics against revivified capitalism and the 'kulak danger' and vigorous espousal of rapid industrialization, were good Marxism but bad politics. Since the country was overwhelmingly agrarian the only way to promote the proletariat's economic and social well-being

---

[67] The central committees of the Ukrainian, Latvian, and Lithuanian communist parties were declared subordinate to the Russian party's central committee.

[68] Carr, *Interregnum*; id., *1924–26 1–2*; id., *The Russian Revolution from Lenin to Stalin 1917–1929* (Macmillan, London, 1979); A. Erlich, *The Soviet Industrialization Debate 1924–1928* (Harvard University Press, 1960); M. Lewin, *Political Undercurrents in Soviet Economic Debates from Bukharin to the Modern Reformers* (Princeton University Press, 1974). See also R. Day, *Leon Trotsky and the Politics of Economic Isolation* (Cambridge University Press, 1973); Knei-Paz, *Social & Political Thought*.

was by liberating rural enterprise – albeit in a controlled manner. Conversely the Right's championship of the smychka carried conviction only up to a point. Free to sell grain at their own price, peasants would exhibit demand on industry and revitalize Russia's silent factories, but once production ran up against the buffers of under-investment and demand could no longer be satisfied a violent class struggle for scarce products would ensue. The dilemma was straightforward. If adopted too early (or if adopted at all) the Left's prescriptions seemed to risk plunging the country into a bitter conflict between peasants and workers, a conflict which the régime might well not survive. On the other hand the Right's policies, if sanctioned for too long, appeared at best to condemn the Soviet Union to permanent backwardness and, at worst, to restored capitalism or some form of retrogressive 'peasant socialism'.

Situated in the framework of these dilemmas Stalin's manœuvres begin to make sense. Implicit in the ideological approach is the view that the General Secretary was not so much an opportunist as a practical politician balancing between extremes. In the early 1920s he was a Politburo 'moderate' who threw his organizational talents into the fight against the War Commissar, the 'Bonaparte' of the Revolution whose belief that socialism must be international was likely to embroil the fragile Soviet Republic in a series of ruinous foreign adventures leading to the establishment of military dictatorship at home. In the mid-1920s, when Kamenev and Zinoviev changed tack and went over to Trotsky's side, Stalin remained consistent. He now allied with Bukharin, the chief proponent of the 'peasant road to socialism', and expounded the notion of socialism in one country, a theory suited to the demands of the moment.[69] Finally, when the NEP began to break down in the late 1920s, Stalin discovered a way out of the crisis by sponsoring forced collectivization and breakneck industrialization.[70] The struggle against Bukharin, Rykov and Tomskii was only part of a wider struggle against an obsolescent 'right-wing' economic programme, and the General Secretary was supported, not by ciphers of his own fashioning, but by ranking Bolsheviks who found his solutions pragmatic and appealing, many of them erstwhile adherents of the Left and United Oppositions.[71]

[69] Two authorities suggest that socialism in one country was originally intended as a stroke against Zinoviev rather than a counter to permanent revolution. Day, *Leon Trotsky*, pp. 3–4; J. F. Hough & M. Fainsod, *How the Soviet Union is Governed* (Harvard University Press, 1979) p. 140.
[70] These matters are dealt with more fully in chapters 2–3.
[71] M. Reiman, *The Birth of Stalinism: The USSR on the Eve of the 'Second Revolution'* (trans. G. Saunders, I. B. Tauris, London, 1987) asserts that Stalin's 'left turn' was a response to a deep crisis; economic collapse was imminent and the Left may have been planning a *coup d'état*. Reiman's interpretation has been sharply criticized by other specialists. See, for example, John Barber in *The Times Higher Education Supplement* (27 May 1988).

'Machine politics alone did not account for Stalin's triumph', concludes Stephen Cohen, the 'salient political fact' of 1928–9 was 'a growing climate of high party opinion... receptive to Stalin's assiduous cultivation of Bolshevism's heroic tradition'.[72]

The socio-cultural approach

The fifth set of interpretations, generated in the West in 1970s and 1980s, is rather more difficult to summarize. Broadly speaking, however, the socio-cultural approach underscores the importance of society and focuses on a series of cultural factors specific to the post-revolutionary situation, factors which shaped the routines of the embryonic Soviet state while fundamentally altering the nature of Bolshevism.[73]

One aspect concentrates on the Civil War – a 'formative experience' according to Sheila Fitzpatrick.[74] Desperate to defeat the Whites and the invading imperialist powers, the party cast its net far and wide in the search for allies. Members poured in from a variety of backgrounds: adherents of other socialist groups, apolitical specialists looking for a job, opportunists who allied themselves with the winning side,[75] patriots who saw the Red Army as the guarantor of Russia's independence, as well as a vast swath of untutored workers and peasants who were sympathetic to the Revolution but completely ignorant of Marxism or the history and ideology of Leninism. In such conditions authoritarianism, discipline and commandist structures came to the fore and transformed political discourse: images of war, conflict and control displaced those of peace, liberation and initiative. These tendencies strengthened as the NEP took hold.

---

[72] Cohen, *Bukharin*, pp. 327–8.

[73] The following are the most important recent works which, in one way or another, investigate these factors: P. Campeanu, *The Genesis of the Stalinist Social Order* (trans. M. Vale, Sharpe, New York, 1988); S. Fitzpatrick, *Education and Social Mobility in the Soviet Union 1921–1934* (Cambridge University Press, 1979); id., 'The problem of class identity in NEP society', in id., et al., eds., *Russia in the Era of NEP: Explorations in Soviet Society and Culture* (Indiana University Press, 1991); M. Lewin, 'The social background of Stalinism', in R. C. Tucker, ed., *Stalinism: Essays in Historical Interpretation* (Norton, New York, 1977); R. Pethybridge, *One Step Backwards, Two Steps Forward: Soviet Society and Politics under the New Economic Policy* (Oxford University Press, 1990); id., *The Social Prelude to Stalinism* (Macmillan, London, 1974); W. G. Rosenberg, 'Smolensk in the 1920s: party–worker relations and the "vanguard" problem', *Russian Review* (2, 1977). For the views of a Soviet historian sympathetic to Leninism see R. A. Medvedev, *Let History Judge: The Origins and Consequences of Stalinism* (trans. C. Taylor, Knopf, New York, 1971) ch. 9.

[74] S. Fitzpatrick, 'The civil war as a formative experience', in A. Gleason, et al., eds., *Bolshevik Culture: Experiment and Order in the Russian Revolution* (Indiana University Press, 1985).

[75] Popularly known as 'radishes' – red on the outside, white inside.

Specialists were looked upon favourably because they were crucial to economic recovery whilst virtually anyone with some small competence or limited education could easily take out a party card. On the other hand, since most were 'former people' adjudged hostile to the régime, military metaphors – 'struggle', 'front', 'attack' and 'retreat' – became firmly embedded in the leadership's psyche.

A second interpretation highlights social change. Anxious to counter charges that Bolshevism's social base was degenerating, the triumvirate initiated a series of drives to enlist workers 'from the bench', the most spectacular, launched shortly after Lenin's death, being the 'Lenin enrollment' of 1924.[76] But the reconstituted working class, containing large admixtures of former peasants and other *déclassé* elements – the wreckage of the petty bourgeoisie, for instance – was not the proletariat of the Revolution's heroic period. Collective consciousness and political vibrancy were at a discount. 'Transformed in its composition', avers Chase, 'and forced into the daily struggle for individual survival, working-class consciousness gave way to individual strategies hastily fashioned to overcome the immediate situation'.[77] Inside factories proletarians, communists and newly-recruited peasants staged wildcat strikes against tyrannical managers or vented their spleen on specialists struggling to defend the smychka by applying profit and loss accounting to industry.[78]

It was this complex social milieu which expedited bureaucratization and machine politics. In the first instance the ruling élite, faced with the disintegration of the old proletariat, increasingly characterized itself as the metaphysical embodiment of the group it purported to represent, a vanguard superior to the 'really existing' working class – wayward, refractory, unconscious of its historic mission. The 'party masses', divorced from the leadership, became objects of policy rather than partners in decision-making. In consequence, the dictatorship of the proletariat became the Bolshevik dictatorship, and

[76] Figures for the early Soviet period are notoriously unreliable, but party membership, estimated at 23,600 in January 1917, rose to 390,000 in 1918 and nearly doubled over the next two years. Chistki reduced the number to 410,000 in 1922 and 381,000 in 1923 but the figure leapt to over 440,000 by the start of 1925. By then fifty per cent of members were workers by social origin. A second 'Lenin enrollment' brought in 300,000 new members during 1925. Totals for 1926 and 1927 were given as 639,000 and 786,000 respectively. See T. H. Rigby, *Communist Party Membership in the USSR 1917–1967* (Princeton University Press, 1968).

[77] Chase, *Workers, Society*, p. 294.

[78] For a discussion of the régime's (largely unsuccessful) attempts to impose 'commercial accounting' on cotton operatives, the biggest single group of industrial workers in NEP Russia, see C. Ward, *Russia's Cotton Workers and the New Economic Policy: Shop-floor Culture and State Policy 1921–29* (Cambridge University Press, 1990).

increasingly the dictatorship of the leadership.[79] Secondly, a new stratum of middle-ranking party leaders was forged in the crucible of the Civil War. As Bolshevism shed its democratic apparel and put on military dress, soldiers of the class struggle, promoted insofar as they were able to give and take orders without asking questions, rose to positions of power and authority. Obedience replaced debate, skill in command replaced skill in persuasion. Interacting with them were specialists and tsarist chinovniki, reproducing Russia's autocratic culture within the economic and governmental apparatus.

All this placed Stalin centre stage. As the clamour of battle faded away the General Secretary's bureaucratic empire responded to and encouraged the growth of 'administrative methods' – secrecy, centralization, red tape, and a peremptory attitude towards workers and the population at large – factors which crowded out the Revolution's democratic and emancipating impulses and isolated the party from society. Nevertheless, towards the end of the 1920s Stalin could count on some plebeian support. To thousands of workers and ordinary party members Bukharin's prognoses signified only impoverishment: if nothing changed they would continue to shoulder the costs of appeasing the peasantry. The 'attack' on the Right, however, opened up the prospect of a socialist offensive which would obliterate unemployment, reduce the cost of living, destroy the remnants of tsarism and sweep away 'former people'. 'It was in the Moscow districts, at the lowest levels', notes Catherine Merridale,

> that the call for an enquiry into the Right began... Many... believed in the policies Stalin now seemed to be proposing; some had begun to express 'Stalinist' views before Stalin himself thought it politic to do so. Historians may conclude that proletarian support was not 'necessary' at this point, that the leadership was powerful enough to act alone, but at the time an explicitly proletarian mandate was valued by all who planned to take risky and unprecedented steps forward.[80]

Given these conditions Stalin's dictatorship gradually overwhelmed the dictatorship of the leadership and left the other contenders for power, deprived of even this meagre social base, suspended in a political void.

---

[79] For a fine discussion of the ways in which party membership became a matter of securing privileges rather than assuming obligations, thus encouraging the elaboration of control from above, see Carr, *1924–26 1*, ch. 3.

[80] Merridale, *Moscow Politics*, pp. 220–1.

The Trotskyist approach

In many ways Trotsky's approach, elaborated in exile and discussed by numerous historians,[81] is the progenitor of both the ideological and socio-cultural approaches; all three try to locate Stalin within a matrix of socio-economic forces beyond anyone's control, all three are keen to situate the intra-party struggle squarely within the framework of the NEP. There the similarity ends. Trotsky's intention was to articulate a specifically Marxist theory which would explain his own downfall and the success of his arch-rival. By drawing analogies with late eighteenth-century France while at the same time focusing on two factors peculiar to early twentieth-century Europe – Russia's backwardness and the abortive international revolution – Trotsky advanced the notions of 'Thermidorian reaction' and 'bureaucratic degeneration'.

On 27 July 1794 (9 Thermidor in the new revolutionary calendar) when moderates in the National Convention, weary of terror and revolutionary innovations, overthrew Maximilien de Robespierre and the other Jacobin leaders, the French Revolution slid into reaction. Trotsky maintained that these events were paralleled in Russia, but whereas the French Thermidor happened all of a piece the 'Soviet Thermidor' was a slow process. By failing to transcend its native soil the 1917 Revolution gradually began to degenerate. Dispersed and weakened by the experience of war, revolution and famine, the Republic's tiny working class could not transform the gains of October into a fully fledged democratic dictatorship of the proletariat. Instead a bureaucratic Leviathan – the totalitarian party-state machine – lifted itself above society and seized control of politics, administration and the manufacture and distribution of scarce material commodities. Reaction and bureaucratic degeneration were the inevitable corollary of international isolation and socio-economic backwardness. Russia's insubstantial civil society allowed commissars, enterprise bosses, party functionaries, soviet officials – apparatchiki of all kinds responsible for supply and distribution – to

---

[81] Trotsky's ideas are scattered throughout the émigré *Biulleten' oppozitsii* and many pamphlets and books. Of the latter the most important are *My Life* (Charles Scribners' Sons, New York, 1931); *The Revolution Betrayed: What is the Soviet Union and Where is it Going?* (trans. M. Eastman, Harcourt & Brace, New York, 1937); *Stalin*; *Stalinism and Bolshevism* (Pioneer Publishers, New York, 1937). Of the secondary materials see S. Bahne, 'Trotsky on Stalin's Russia', *Survey* (41, 1962); A. Callinicos, *Trotskyism* (Open University Press, 1990); Day, *Leon Trotsky*; Deutscher, *Trotsky 1929–40*; Knei-Paz, *Social & Political Thought*; M. Krygier, '"Bureaucracy" in Trotsky's analysis of Stalinism', in M. Sawer, ed., *Socialism and the New Class: Towards the Analysis of Structural Inequality within Socialist Societies* (APSA Monograph 19, Bedford Park, 1978); D. W. Lovell, *Trotsky's Analysis of Soviet Bureaucratization* (Croom Helm, London, 1985); R. H. McNeal, 'Trotskyist interpretations of Stalinism', in Tucker, *Stalinism*.

mutate into appropriaters of the country's niggardly 'surplus product', people for whom the ideals of October were but a distant and uncomfortable memory: 'lolling in automobiles technically owned by the proletariat', jeered Trotsky, 'on their way to proletarian-owned summer resorts to which only the chosen few were admitted, the bureaucrats guffawed, "What have we been fighting for?"'[82]

Initially the sympathies of this new élite lay with the Right, since only the maintenance of the smychka and the cultivation of rural capitalism could guarantee its privileges. Stalin – the bureaucracy personified – therefore led a merciless struggle against the 'proletarian vanguard' in the shape of the Left and United Oppositions. But, once the Left had been defeated and the contradictions of the NEP became apparent, the bureaucrats forced a change of course. Now Stalin was driven to wage war on the 'kulaks' and their political friends (abruptly transformed into 'right opportunists'), ushering in a 'third period' of Soviet history, collectivization and industrial modernization imposed from above.[83]

To Trotsky's mind, therefore, the decay of socialism was not the result of some original sin committed by Lenin or the Bolshevik party. Nor was it due to the mistakes of the Left and United Oppositions. Rather, it was the product of a unique historical juncture, one which found expression in the character of the General Secretary, a leader selected by 'the dialectics of history' working through human instruments fashioned by the NEP – 'the tired radicals... the bureaucrats... the upstarts, the sneaks... all the worms that are crawling out of the upturned soil of the manured revolution'.[84]

Evaluations

Personality

The rôle of 'Great Men' in shaping events is a basic problem for historians. On one level it would be frivolous to deny that personality plays a part, perhaps a crucial part, in the making of history. Some generals are gifted in the business of warfare, for example, others are not; and even if all historians agreed that a different military outcome would have changed only the details and not the overall

---

[82] Trotsky, *Stalin*, p. 407.
[83] The 'first' and 'second' were the revolutionary period and the period of post-revolutionary stabilization.
[84] Trotsky, *Stalin*, p. 393. Left-wing historians and sociologists have long agonized over the question of whether or not the Soviet bureaucracy should be treated as a social class in some quasi-Marxist sense of the term, or as a social category specific to socialism. A seminal work on this problem is Milovan Djilas's *The New Class* (Thames & Hudson, London, 1957).

scheme of the past, the point remains that the patterns of what is commonly understood to be 'history' would be otherwise.

But this is an unsatisfactory solution. In the absence of any clear ruling from the psychological sciences historians cannot assume personality to be a fixed agent of causality. In the first place, what constitutes the self may be reconstituted many times throughout life. The adolescent Stalin of 1894 might not be the mature revolutionary of 1919 or the General Secretary of 1929.[85] Secondly, the psychological qualities of any individual are apprehended only through the the inconstant eye of the beholder – several of Stalin's associates only 'discovered' his 'dangerous' attributes after they had fallen out with him. Thirdly, and most importantly, personality functions in a social, political and cultural context. There are doubtless numerous people alive today in whom character traits similar to Stalin's lie dormant, but they will not become manifest unless they interact with a specific set of conditions. Stalin's personality cannot be divorced from the world in which he functioned.[86]

Intentionality

By the same token care must be taken in assuming intentionality, in ascribing to Stalin a unique predisposition to manipulate ideas consciously for his own selfish ends. If Stalin was an ambitious man, so were all the other contenders for power. If Stalin changed his mind on key issues of the day, so did the others. Bukharin started his post-revolutionary career as a Left Communist but by the mid-1920s was the Right's champion. Kamenev and Zinoviev appear to have followed no clearly identifiable political line. Like Stalin, the latter tried to pose as the legitimate heir of Lenin. Trotsky was by turns one of Bolshevism's most unforgiving critics, the arch-centralizer of the Civil War years, the passionate advocate of intra-party discipline and the equally trenchant defender of the right to dissent. Lenin's political and ideological gyrations were no less spectacular. Were all these leaders – Stalin included – merely deploying political arguments and ideological formulae in the pursuit of personal power? Even if they were alive today we could never be sure. Hostile witnesses would

---

[85] There was no 'Stalinism' before the 1930s, remarks Lewin, 'and even Stalin himself was not a "Stalinist" in the preceding decade'. M. Lewin, in C. Merridale & C. Ward, eds., *Perestroika: The Historical Perspective* (Edward Arnold, London, 1991) p. 244.

[86] A point implicit in Trotsky's vivid recollections of 1927: 'the official sessions of the Central Committee became truly disgusting spectacles', resembling 'an obscene and rowdy bar-room burlesque... The stage director of all this was Stalin. He would walk up and down at the back of the præsidium, looking now and then at those to whom certain speeches were assigned, and made no attempt to hide his approval when the swearing addressed to some Oppositionist assumed an utterly shameless character... The habits of the Tiflis [Tbilisi] streets were transferred to the Central Committee of the Bolshevik Party'. Trotsky, *Stalin*, pp. 413–4.

endorse such an interpretation, friendly witnesses would demur. Researchers must go beyond biography and 'psycho-history' in their quest for explanations of Stalin's rise to power.

Two legacies

The intra-party struggle was fought out against the background of two important legacies. The first was autocracy. The tsarist empire bequeathed to the post-revolutionary world comparatively few democratic or pluralistic traditions. The halting attempt to erect a bourgeois democracy after 1905 – parliamentarianism, equality before the law, sanctions against arbitrariness – scarcely survived the onslaught of the Stolypin tyranny, and in any event the fragile institutions of the Duma Monarchy were quickly destroyed in the tumults of 1917 and after.[87] Grass roots organizations – soviets, factory committees, communes and workers' associations of various kinds – were no less susceptible to civil commotion and economic disintegration. In such circumstances the reproduction of an authoritarian culture within the infant Soviet Republic's nascent administrative apparatus was hard to resist.

Paradoxically, authoritarianism was given space by the second legacy. The Bolsheviks had a powerful theory of the state but a weakly developed theory of government, a significant lacuna within the liberating intentions of Marxism–Leninism. The state was conceived as an element of the Marxian 'superstructure', a prize seized by the victorious class in any given historical epoch, and the particular form of government imposed on the state was a second order phenomenon, an expression of the ruling class's ideology, itself determined by the workings of the 'base', the economic sub-structure of society. And since only the 'dialectics of history' could adjudicate on state forms appropriate to the dictatorship of the proletariat, attempts to elaborate ideal constitutions were dismissed as hopelessly utopian. Once common ownership of the means of production emerged from the travails of Revolution and Civil War, governmental structures would arise naturally as reflections of the new socioeconomic configuration. All state-building was therefore interim. All instruments of decision-making were no more than *ad hoc* responses to specific exigencies of no particular substance in themselves.

In consequence, administrative methods flourished without institutional checks and in the absence of any coherent theoretical challenge from within Bolshevism. The RSFSR constitution of 1918 made no reference to the rôle of the party and the Cheka, nor did

---

[87] Petr Stolypin (1862–1911) became prime minister in 1906. The 'Stolypin tyranny' refers to the period after 1907 when he successfully rolled back many of the gains of the 1905 Revolution; the 'Duma Monarchy' to the quasi-parliamentary polity established after October 1905.

the USSR constitution of 1923. The Left Opposition could only make sense of Stalin's growing power by pointing to the failure of the international revolution and the Russian proletariat's cultural poverty and numerical insignificance. A few years later, Bukharin was forced to step outside Marxist theory and recall Max Weber's studies of bureaucracy in order to try to understand the dimensions of his own predicament.

Looking for Napoleon

Bolshevism's historicist view of politics had other consequences. Party intellectuals were obsessed with the fate of earlier and initially successful popular insurrections: the English Revolution of the 1640s cut off a king's head but soon collapsed into Cromwell's rule of the major-generals and monarchical restoration; the French Revolution degenerated into Napoleonic adventurism and imperialism; the Paris Commune was quickly overthrown by military leaders terrified of socialism.

In all cases the danger of reaction seemed to come from the remnants of armies loyal to the old régime or from the military apparatus cobbled together in the struggle against the enemy. To guard against such eventualities the central committee insisted on the complete demobilization of the tsarist military machine and the appointment of political commissars to the Red Army, but as the Civil War drew to a close the spectre of 'Bonapartism' continued to haunt the leadership's collective imagination. On the one hand, the introduction of the NEP might open the door to a new round of social and political crises, the results of which would be difficult to foresee; on the other the army was led by a charismatic figure possessed of a messianic internationalist vision who seemed ill-adapted to the humdrum arts of peace. The Russian Bonaparte appeared to be staring the party in the face in the person of Trotsky, not the person of Stalin.

The evolution of the party-state

Indeed, Stalin was distinguished by his trustworthiness and lack of imagination, a faithful servant busy in the backwaters of the administration. Initially Narkomnats and Rabkrin were inconsequential Commissariats. The first, concerned with populations on the edge of the modern world who would take no part in the great events immanent in Western Europe, was given to Stalin because he was Georgian, a fitting representative of Soviet power in the campaign to secure the acquiescence of the non-Russian nationalities in the Civil War. The second, engrossed in the detailed workings of governmental departments – temporary organs of proletarian hegemony destined to wither away as the Revolution strode forward – became Stalin's almost by default. No one else wanted the job. But, as expectations of international revolution subsided and the Soviet

Republic's institutions ossified, their importance increased dramatically. By 1922 'comrade card-index', as he was patronizingly known, found himself at the axis of the state-building enterprise.

Things were much the same inside the party. Even in 1923 Stalin was scarcely visible outside the élite's inner circle and nothing was expected of him in terms of intellectual pyrotechnics.[88] The Orgburo and the Secretariat were appropriate bailiwicks for a man of limited accomplishments (excepting some administrative flair), leaving the other leaders free to get on with the weighty business of high politics and Marxist theorizing. Before the mid-1920s he had little to say on the burning issues of the day: he never resigned; his infrequent contributions to the fervent dispute over Brest-Litovsk were of scant interest; his attitude to the trade union debate was indistinguishable from that of any middle-ranking functionary; he did not figure in the tenth party congress clashes over democracy – even the doctrine of socialism in one country was first mooted by Bukharin as he laboured to come to terms with the 'collapse of our illusions', the stillborn international revolution and the introduction of the NEP.[89]

But as the party crystallized into a governing institution and fused with the state, Stalin could not help but become a powerful figure. The Politburo had to trust the Secretariat to bring to its attention matters worthy of consideration. Thereafter the Politburo passed its decisions to the Orgburo for implementation. Insofar, therefore, as Stalin (or anyone else, for that matter) combined the office of General Secretary with membership of the Orgburo and the Politburo, and worked more or less efficiently, party policy would be transmogrified in the process of execution.

The intra-party struggle

Perhaps this would not have mattered if Stalin had never had any ideas of his own. He was viewed as a junior partner in the struggle against Trotskyism, far less important than Kamenev and Zinoviev and recruited by them primarily because of his ability to deliver votes at congress and central committee meetings. Similarly Bukharin was understood to be the senior theorist in the duumvirate of the NEP years: the General Secretary's main contribution was to complete the organizational ruin of the Left and United Oppositions.

The machine politics of the intra-party struggle, however, were entangled with debates over the future of socialism. All Bolshevik leaders were striving to find their feet in an unfamiliar and unanticipated world, and the doctrine of socialism in one country at least had

---

[88] Lunacharskii did not even bother to include him in his *Revolutionary Silhouettes*.
[89] Socialism in one country was first proposed by Bukharin in 1922–3. See Cohen, *Bukharin*, pp. 147–8.

the merit of describing things as they really were. The Left might rail against the decay of the Revolution but without relying on agriculture, without the peasants' co-operation, the régime was unlikely to survive for long. Even if this involved the risk of stimulating agrarian capitalism, Bukharin and the General Secretary could point to Lenin's last fragment of political advice: rural co-operatives were the road to socialism and on no account should the peasants be antagonized.[90]

The reservations of many historians notwithstanding, there is no compelling reason to think that Stalin's avowal of socialism in one country was anything other than genuine, but his championship of Bukharin's views had important consequences. The theory evoked a sympathetic response from two groups: the new sub-élites advanced by the crises of the immediate post-revolutionary years and workers sickened by the manifold injustices and inequalities of the NEP. The latter were men and women indifferent to factional squabbles and impatient for socialist construction; the former were people with meagre experience of Europe and less knowledge of international socialism, a social ingredient of Trotsky's constituency for Thermidorian reaction for whom the Revolution was primarily a Russian achievement – Soviet patriotism sat easily with enjoyment of the fruits of offices disbursed by the Secretariat. A Stalinist constituency was in the process of formation, and Stalin's 'left turn' brought most of them round to his way of thinking, as well as persuading many former Oppositionists to offer their support.

Why Stalin?

It should be obvious by now that no single factor can satisfactorily explain Stalin's rise. What historians are dealing with is not so much a series of mutually exclusive interpretations as a set of overlapping hypotheses which cannot easily be prioritized. Each of them, moreover, has its own problems. In the absence of clear guidance from psychology the heroic approach lacks plausibility. The administrative approach discounts the temporary intent of many changes: Lenin's 1921 innovations, for instance, look like hasty responses to dire emergencies, not recipes for dictatorship; somehow or other the leadership had to weather the Kronstadt revolt, appease the peasants and hold the central committee together. The party history approach presupposes rigid conformism, a view impossible to sustain in the light of recent research: debate and factionalism were the hallmarks of Bolshevism, before and after 1917.[91] The ideological approach

[90] *On Co-operation*, dictated in January 1923, asserted that 'one or two decades' would be required to transform the peasant into an 'intelligent and literate tradesman', leading to 'a system of civilized co-operators', which in Russian conditions was the nearest approach to a 'system of socialism'.

[91] See E. Acton, *Rethinking the Russian Revolution* (Edward Arnold, London, 1990).

cannot answer the question of intentionality, of whether or not Stalin manipulated ideological registers for other, hidden ends. The socio-cultural approach is open to the charge of reductionism – Stalin and the élite become puppets of abstract forces which they neither controlled nor understood. Finally, the Trotskyist approach assumes prior agreement with Marxist theory, a meta-historical discourse which all too frequently tends towards closure and schematization.

New materials culled from archives free of Soviet control will doubtless refine our knowledge of the intra-party struggle, but barring some cataclysmic revision of how the past is understood, these are likely to remain the categories through which academics try to understand Stalin's rise, and as the decades pass and the actors in the drama accept the constitution of silence and are folded in a single party it becomes easier for historians to see them all as functions of an extraordinary period.

Revolution and civil war gave birth to a 'politics of permanent emergency'. This had two consequences. In the first place militarization conditioned behaviour within the leadership long after the guns fell silent, persuading them that the best way to get results was to utilize the symbols and structures of command and authority. One form of Bolshevism was being selected out by élite perceptions of contemporary realities, and to some extent Stalin's success was due to his adroit use of skills learned in the harsh world of the immediate post-revolutionary years. Secondly, permanent emergency precluded consensus or coalition, within and outside the party. Stalin was only one amongst many – Lenin included – who were intolerant of dissent and eager to brand opponents as deviationists. Before this became apparent he was given administrative jobs by his peers because he was good at them, because no one else wanted them, and because of his loyalty; few others, identified with this or that faction or platform, could be so trusted.

But the difficulties of governing inflated the importance of administration, a factor never envisaged by Bolshevism's founder until the moment of his death. Governing required consensus in and between society and state, but this was in short supply. Ruling required strong and stable channels for the exercise of power, but these had been smashed by revolution and war. Consequently the enigmas of governing and ruling resolved themselves into problems of administration, and these in turn became matters of establishing and servicing a bureaucratic machine. The Soviet régime's power structures thus emerged independently of its constitutional structures – weakly formulated in any case – and Stalin stood at the focal point of this development. Given Lenin's death (which threw the leadership into disarray), a modicum of popular support (evident amongst the metropolitan proletariat in 1928) and his mastery of the apparatus (staffed by the new cohort of sub-élites thrown up after 1917), circumstances ensured that inside the mutating body of the party-state he would succeed and his rivals fail.

Suggestions for further reading

E. H. Carr, *The Russian Revolution from Lenin to Stalin 1917–1929* (Macmillan, London, 1979). An elegantly written analysis from the founding father of Soviet history in Britain. Summarizes the author's *The Russian Revolution 1917–1923* (Vols. 1–3, Macmillan, London, 1950–3), *The Interregnum 1923–1924* (Macmillan, London, 1954), *Socialism in One Country 1924–1926* (Vols. 1–3, Macmillan, London, 1958–64) and *Foundations of a Planned Economy* (Vols. 1–3, Vol. 1 parts 1 & 2 with R. W. Davies, Macmillan, London, 1969–78).

S. Farber, *Before Stalinism: The Rise and Fall of Soviet Democracy* (Polity Press, Cambridge, 1990). Sympathetic account of the tribulations of the party from 1917 to 1924.

G. Gill, *The Origins of the Stalinist Political System* (Cambridge University Press, 1990). A carefully researched monograph detailing the institutional elaboration of the party-state in the context of the intra-party struggles.

A. Gleason, et al., eds., *Bolshevik Culture: Experiment and Order in the Russian Revolution* (Indiana University Press, 1985). Contains Sheila Fitzpatrick's 'The Civil War as a formative experience', a seminal contribution to the 'socio-cultural' approach.

O. A. Narkiewicz, *The Making of the Soviet State Apparatus* (Manchester University Press, 1970). Succinctly describes key aspects of the development of the party-state apparatus.

R. Pethybridge, *The Social Prelude to Stalinism* (Macmillan, London, 1974). A survey of the social ingredients of Stalinism and the social factors conditioning the party's thinking and behaviour in the 1920s.

R. C. Tucker, *Stalin as Revolutionary 1879–1929: A Study in History and Personality* (Chatto & Windus, London, 1974). The best example of the 'heroic' approach to the problem of Stalin's rise to power.

2 COLLECTIVIZATION

'Where?' they ask. *'How?' 'That will never be'. 'Only in a hundred years',* etc. *Such petit bourgeois prejudice must be sternly rejected.*

Zinoviev, 1930.

Narrative

The smychka under strain

Serious economic difficulties faced the régime in 1927. When shortages of consumer goods appeared the previous year the Politburo, fearful of another 'scissors crisis' and determined to check the uncontrolled spread of petty trade,[1] rushed through article 107 of the Criminal Code, unleashed the OGPU against nepmeny and slashed retail prices.[2] Urban buyers quickly snapped up scarce commodities at bargain rates: soap, candles, matches, footwear, crockery – and especially textiles. Unable to turn to nepmeny, and finding little available in the rapidly emptying state shops and co-operative stores, villagers responded by reducing grain sales: there seemed little point in trading for useless rubles.[3] A further complication was the state's control of grain prices. Since these were kept low peasants switched their attention to other agricultural products. To make matters worse a 'war scare' flared up early in 1927,[4] sparking off hoarding and panic buying.

---

[1] In 1923 group B enterprises responded to 'commercial accounting' by raising retail prices. Peasants – free to sell grain after the introduction of the NEP and holding surpluses due to a recent famine (less mouths to feed at home meant more opportunities to sell food) – competed with each other in urban markets. Grain prices fell relative to retail prices and a price 'scissors' opened up between industry and agriculture. Terrified lest peasants retreat into subsistence farming (thereby precipitating unemployment, hunger and urban social unrest), the party hastily reversed retail price increases. The scissors began to close after October 1923.

[2] Article 107 imposed fearsome penalties for speculation. Many nepmeny were rounded up and deported to Siberia.

[3] The textile industry was the biggest single supplier of consumer goods to the peasantry. See C. Ward, *Russia's Cotton Workers and the New Economic Policy: Shopfloor Culture and State Policy 1921–29* (Cambridge University Press, 1990).

[4] The Soviet government feared that Poland, backed by Britain and France, might try to seize Soviet territory. For the details see E. H. Carr, *Foundations of a Planned Economy* (Vol. 3, part 1, Macmillan, London, 1976) ch. 65; S. Fitzpatrick, 'The foreign threat during the first five year plan', *Soviet Union/Union Soviétique* (1, 1978); A. G. Meyer, 'The war scare of 1927', *Soviet Union/Union Soviétique* (1, 1978); J. P. Sontag, 'The Soviet war scare of 1926–27', *Russian Review* (1, 1975).

To the party's chagrin, and particularly the Left's, peasants were no more willing to supply the government. Indeed, ever since Lenin introduced the NEP the smychka between 'socialist' cities and 'capitalist' villages had been a bone of contention. Like ordinary shoppers the régime tried to pay as little as possible for food; as well as subsidizing soldiers and working-class consumers grain was exported in exchange for industrial equipment. 'We must not forget', intoned Preobrazhenskii in reply to Bukharin's criticisms of his economic theories,

> the forced character of our co-operation with private economy. There is co-operation in prison, too. Are we not in a sort of concentration camp along with the capitalist elements of our economy? We are at one and the same time warders and prisoners. We are prisoners because we are separated by the prison-wall of time from the world socialist revolution... We are warders because by the wall of our monopoly of foreign trade... we have separated our private economy from the world private economy.[5]

By the time the fifteenth party congress met in December 1927 grain purchases by state agencies had dropped by half in comparison with 1926, threatening hunger in the expanding towns and a retreat from the industrialization programme. Matters were far from satisfactory, reported Stalin, but he assured delegates that problems could be overcome by strengthening co-operatives, promoting mechanization and fostering the voluntary pooling of land, agricultural implements and buildings – the kolkhoz or collective farm movement. Molotov was less sanguine. Ruminating on the structures of rural life he characterized the mir as the fundamental barrier to reform and exhorted his audience to augment the sel'sovet's powers and impose tougher restrictions on kulaks. In his view 'forward to the large-scale collectivization of agriculture' should be the watchword for the immediate future.

The end of the NEP

The deliberations of the 'collectivization congress', as it became known, marked the beginning of a profound shift in agrarian policy, but as yet there was no clear commitment to socialization or dekulakization.[6] It was only when Stalin's animosity towards the peasantry became evident that the NEP's delicate structures finally began to fall asunder.

---

[5]   E. A. Preobrazhenskii, *The New Economics* (trans. B. Pearce, Oxford University Press, 1965) p. 40. These remarks were made in the second, 1927, edition of his book.
[6]   By and large the congress ignored the grain crisis.

In January 1928 the General Secretary visited Siberia. Despite reports of substantial yields sales to state agencies were dismally low,[7] prompting allusions to nefarious 'kulak gentry' and the looming peril of undersupply. 'You have had a bumper harvest', he told party administrators,

> one might say a record one. Your grain surpluses this year are bigger than ever before. Yet the plan for grain procurements is not being fulfilled. Why? What is the reason?... Look at the kulak farms: their barns and sheds are crammed with grain; grain is lying open under pent roofs for lack of storage space...
>
> You say that the kulaks are unwilling to deliver grain, that they are waiting for prices to rise, and prefer to engage in unbridled speculation. That is true. But the kulaks... are demanding an increase in prices to three times those fixed by the government...
>
> But there is no guarantee that the kulaks will not again sabotage the grain procurements next year. More, it may be said with certainty that so long as there are kulaks, so long will there be sabotage of grain procurements.[8]

Instructed to find more food at the same low prices local officials seized grain, closed down markets and levied fixed-price quotas on each village, leaving peasants to distribute assessments amongst themselves. Those who resisted were branded as kulaks and arrested under article 107. As the exercise was repeated across the country Stalin tightened the screw still further. After the 1928 harvest, what became known as the 'Ural–Siberian method' provoked the first major instances of rural unrest, fears that disturbances might spread to the peasant dominated army, and urban bread shortages as farmers held back stocks in anticipation of better prices or concealed grain to avoid the levy.

As the crisis accelerated ration cards appeared in the provinces and serious divisions wracked the leadership. At the July 1928 central committee meeting Bukharin, frantic to preserve the smychka at all costs, demanded a balanced approach to economic development. Stalin countered by arguing that cheap grain was an essential prerequisite of the first piatiletka: investment funds could not be diverted from industry to appease kulaks. Although the plenum's resolutions endorsed the Right's views – an end to forced measures and

---

[7]   In fact Siberia's harvest was about eleven per cent lower than in 1927, though there were still considerable surpluses.

[8]   J. V. Stalin, *Works* (Vol. 11, Lawrence & Wishart, London, 1955) pp. 3–9. Stalin, apparently, made only fleeting visits to the villages during his sojourn.

increased wholesale prices – naked coercion continued. Thereafter tensions burst into the open: on 30 September 1928 *Pravda* published Bukharin's 'Notes of an economist', an implicit criticism of Stalin's methods and a defence of the NEP's economic prescriptions. Meanwhile the crisis gathered pace. Sales to state agencies, well below expectations in autumn, fell drastically in November and in December the situation became desperate when it transpired that crops had failed in the country's central and south-eastern regions.[9] Free market prices leapt ahead of official prices, deliveries to the government plummeted and rationing swept through metropolitan Russia.[10]

De-kulakization

By 1929 the Ural–Siberian method had been adopted almost everywhere and the smychka lay in ruins.[11] Stalin's thoughts on the matter were published in November: the 'Year of the Great Breakthrough' vigorously extolled the virtues of kolkhozy and called for a 'decisive offensive' against rural capitalists. The following month he told a conference of Marxist agronomists that kulaks would be 'liquidated as a class'. Molotov, speaking at the key November central committee plenum, forecast the socialization of several million households by March 1930 – despite the fact that more than ninety per cent of peasants still lived and worked in traditional communities. Specific proposals quickly followed. In January 1930 the Politburo brushed aside previous targets,[12] earmarking thirty million hectares – about twenty-five per cent of the USSR's total sown area – for socialization by spring. The most important grain districts (the North Caucasus, the Central and Lower Volga) were to be collectivized by the autumn, other areas by the autumn of 1931.

Outright war was declared on kulaks when a decree of 1 February gave local committees powers to apply 'necessary measures' against them. The decree, according to R. W. Davies, was based on a secret

---

[9] When figures for 1928 as a whole appeared collections were found to be two per cent lower than in 1926/27.

[10] Due to rapidly rising free market prices, privately traded grain increased from twelve to twenty-three per cent of total marketings during 1928. Bread rationing spread to Leningrad, Kiev, Khar'kov and Odessa late in 1928 and Moscow in March 1929. Soon afterwards most other foodstuffs and some consumer goods were rationed. Rationing applied only to socialized retail outlets where controlled prices obtained. Scarce goods were still available on the open market but at exorbitant prices.

[11] In September quotas were extended to seredniaki and landless labourers.

[12] Gosplan anticipated that no more than 17.5 per cent of the country's grain lands would be socialized by 1932. The French economic historian Eugène Zaleski points out that initial drafts of the first piatiletka were cautious as regards agriculture. E. Zaleski, *Planning for Economic Growth in the Soviet Union 1918–1932* (trans. M. MacAndrew & G. W. Nutter, University of North Carolina Press, 1971).

central committee resolution – dramatic enough in scope but modest in comparison with what was to follow – which divided kulaks into three classes. Group one comprised around 63,000 'counter-revolutionaries' destined for execution or exile and confiscation of all property. Group two – 150,000 households designated 'exploiters' or 'active opponents' of collectivization – were to be deported to remote regions but allowed to retain some possessions. A residual classification encompassed between 396,000 and 852,000 farmers who would remain in their home districts but on land outside the new collectives.[13] Assisted by the secret police, local authorities were to identify offenders and place them in the appropriate category.

In fact OGPU troops had been rounding up alleged kulaks, quelling rebellions and forcing the recalcitrant into kolkhozy since 1929,[14] but it was only after the February 1930 decree that a full-scale assault was launched against the countryside. Over the next two or three weeks more than a quarter of a million volunteers and conscripts (OGPU units, Red Army personnel, party members and about 25,000 workers organized into 'collectivization brigades') tried to bludgeon twenty-five million families – seredniaki and bedniaki as opposed to kulaks – into collective farms.[15] 'I am off in villages with a group of other brigaders organizing kolkhozy', enthused Nadia, a young Komsomolite, to her American friend,

It is a tremendous job, but we are making amazing progress... our muzhik is yielding to persuasion. He is joining the kolkhozy, and I am confident that in time not a peasant will remain on his own land. We shall yet smash the last vestiges of capitalism and for ever rid ourselves of exploitation... The very air here is afire with a new spirit and a new energy.[16]

[13] R. W. Davies, *The Industrialization of Soviet Russia 1: The Socialist Offensive; The Collectivization of Soviet Agriculture 1929–1930* (Macmillan, London, 1980) pp. 234–6.
[14] In autumn 1929 'special commissions' staffed by local soviets, the procuracy, the OGPU, the Commissariat for Agriculture and the Peasants' and Agricultural Workers' Union seized the herds of the 700 richest families in Kazakhstan. This action served as a model for later expropriations.
[15] These are Davies's estimates. Conquest gives a total of no more than 163,000 in collectivization brigades. Male reproduces Soviet figures of 72,402 urban dwellers organized into 10,422 brigades sent out to service agricultural machinery and conduct propaganda. Medvedev thinks that about one million armed personnel were mobilized to eliminate kulaks. R. Conquest, *The Harvest of Sorrow: Soviet Collectivization and the Terror–Famine* (Hutchinson, London, 1986) pp.146–7; Davies, *Industrialization 1*, p. 205; D. J. Male, *Russian Peasant Organization before Collectivization: A Study of Commune and Gathering 1925–1930* (Cambridge University Press, 1971) p. 201; Z. A. Medvedev, *Soviet Agriculture* (Norton, New York, 1987) p. 77.
[16] M. Hindus, *Red Bread* (Jonathan Cape, London, 1931) p. 13.

Things looked different through peasant eyes; scarcely a single ham-let escaped the terrors of arrest, execution or deportation. A year after the event Katia, a 'barefoot, half-naked bit of humanity', told her story to a young engineer who took her in:

> My father didn't want to join the kolkhoz. All kinds of people argued with him and took him away and beat him but still he wouldn't go in. They shouted he was a kulak agent... At the sta-tion there were many other people like us, from other villages. It seemed like thousands. We were all crushed into a stone barn but they wouldn't let my dog, Volchok, come in though he'd fol-lowed us all the way down the road... After a while we were let out and driven into cattle cars... We all shrieked and prayed to the Holy Virgin. Then the train started. No-one knew where we were going. Some said Siberia but others said no, the Far North or even the hot deserts. Near Khar'kov my sister Shura and I were allowed out to get some water... Not far away were some peasant huts so we ran there as fast as our feet would carry us.[17]

Thereafter Katia and Shura roamed from town to town – sleeping rough, riding the rails, begging and foraging – until they lost each other while evading the police.

'Dizzy with success'

Brigades were told to follow 'methods of mass work' – avoiding com-pulsion while encouraging bedniaki and seredniaki to join kolkhozy – but central prescriptions, clearly articulated by the Politburo in January 1930, clashed with the voluntary principle and fed the fires of enthusiasm smouldering in the breasts of local OGPU operatives, provincial apparatchiki and proletarian brigaders. 'If in some matter you go too far and are arrested', remarked one official to a north Russian collectivization conference, 'remember that you have been arrested for a revolutionary cause'. Sergei Syrtsov told brigades in the Lower Volga to minimize 'the quantitative aspect' and warned against engaging in 'a kind of sporting contest', but on the other hand stressed that 'nothing must hold up the growth of the kolkhoz movement'. Karl Bauman, Moscow province's most ardent collec-tivizer, reflected exuberantly on the effects of 'sporting contests' held close to the capital:

> Ryazan' proposed to collectivize sixty per cent or even seventy-five per cent of peasant households by the time of this spring

[17] V. Kravchenko, *I Chose Freedom: The Personal and Political Life of a Soviet Official* (Robert Hale, London, 1947) pp. 88–9.

sowing... When I was in Tula, I pointed out the successes of Ryazan'. The Tulans are now entering into socialist emulation with the Ryazanians.[18]

These were not the only 'excesses': according to Lynne Viola in Buriat-Mongolia a seredniak was branded with a hot iron, rings were torn from women's ears and collectivizers even tried to pull the gold from people's teeth.[19]

Confronted by local radicals, crusading youngsters and militant workers responding to ambiguous instructions, and alarmed by all manner of rumours (the socialization of women, communal beds for entire villages, special machines to burn up old people) peasant resistance grew rapidly, forcing Moscow into a precipitous retreat. Stalin's 'Dizzy with success: problems of the kolkhoz movement', published in *Pravda* on 2 March, called for the restoration of the voluntary principle, criticized the wholesale socialization of livestock and condemned activists for closing churches and removing their bells.[20] Over-zealous officials fell from grace (notably Bauman) and farmers abandoned kolkhozy in droves: 'News came of a letter which Stalin had written', recalled one foreign observer,

ordering organizers to stop driving people into the kolkhoz. At once people braced up. They rushed to the post offices and the town to buy the newspapers... They paid three, four or five roubles for a copy... that was how eager they were to see the letter with their own eyes. In the market places peasants gathered in groups and read it aloud and discussed it long and violently, and some of them were so overjoyed that they brought all the vodka they could pay for and got drunk. Others... flashing it before the officials and organizers, gave them a piece of their mind. In some places officials and organizers hid themselves, and it was well they did... now that people learned from Stalin himself that this was not what the centre favoured they were so exasperated that they might have done something desperate...[21]

[18] Cited Davies, *Industrialization 1*, p. 215. Syrtsov (1893–c.1937) joined the party in 1913, was elected to the central committee in 1927 and became a Politburo candidate in 1929. Bauman (1892–1937) joined the party in 1906, worked in the central committee apparatus after 1923 and replaced Uglanov as first secretary of Moscow's party committee in 1929.

[19] L. Viola, *The Best Sons of the Fatherland: Workers in the Vanguard of Collectivization* (Oxford University Press, 1987) p. 110.

[20] Bells were stripped out for several reasons. Villagers often sounded the tocsin to warn of approaching brigades, thereby attracting the attention of militant atheists. Others thought the metal might be put to better use in the service of industrialization. See p. 193.

[21] Hindus, *Red Bread*, p. 147.

While the number of collectivized households stood at about two million in October 1929, rose to five million in January 1930 and peaked at roughly fifteen million in March (sixty per cent of all households), by April the aggregate had fallen to under ten million and hovered around six million from May to the end of the year.

Lasting no longer than seven weeks, the first phase of collectivization ended in utter chaos. The mir was in ruins, but despite the havoc wrought by the 'great change' the 1930 harvest was larger than the previous year's. The accident of good weather and the ever intensifying pressure on the remaining individual cultivators temporarily saved the situation.[22] Deliveries from the socialized sector, however, were below plan – collective farms were in no better condition than the mir – and the rise in grain production was more than offset by the cataclysmic deterioration of animal husbandry; one quarter of the Soviet Union's livestock was lost in twelve months as peasants slaughtered and ate their beasts rather than hand them over to kolkhozy or watched them die because there was no fodder.

Gross production (livestock and crops) was therefore slightly lower in 1930 than in 1929, but as these figures trickled into Moscow they were interpreted as evidence of success. When the sixteenth party congress met in June 1930 Stalin declared that the grain crisis was almost over and the kulaks close to extinction, adding that the final victory of the kolkhoz movement awaited the development of large-scale mechanized farming. Although delegates acknowledged a few mistakes, the main thrust of the proceedings was on renewed offensives.[23] Thereafter a 'second collectivization drive' forced those peasants who had abandoned collectives after the March 1930 'great retreat' back into the fold through a combination of outright force, exorbitant taxation and excessively high quotas – the so-called 'hard obligations' which, if unmet, resulted in fines, property sequestrations and deportation to the Gulag.

In August 1931 the central committee duly reported that collectivization was virtually complete in the grain lands of the North Caucasus, the Urals, the Volga and parts of the Ukraine, and that the cotton fields of Central Asia, Kazakhstan and the North Caucasus, together with the sugar beet regions of the Ukraine and the Central Black Earth would follow suit by December. The number of socialized households rose to over fifty per cent of the total by the end of the year, surpassing the Politburo's September 1930 targets. This

---

[22] The influence of weather is detailed in S. G. Wheatcroft, 'The significance of climatic and weather change on Soviet agriculture (with particular reference to the 1920s and 1930s)', *SIPS 11* (Discussion Paper, Centre for Russian & East European Studies, University of Birmingham, 1977).

[23] Some delegates believed that peasants were particularly angered by church closures and admitted that livestock production was declining.

time, however, the grain situation was balanced on a knife-edge. Deliveries to state agencies reached only 22.1 million tons in 1930–1 exceeding the 1929/30 figure by six million tons but below the government's expectations. This left peasants very short of grain and formed the backdrop to the agony which was soon to follow.

The new order

What happened between November 1929 and December 1931 cannot be grasped merely by reciting statistics or referring to the decisions of Stalin, the Politburo, the central committee or the party's congresses. Though many peasants tried to bow to the inevitable by faking collectivization (declaring that the mir had already socialized itself) a socio-economic system in existence for five hundred years vanished forever.[24] But the whirlwind which swept across the countryside destroyed the way of life of the vast majority of the Soviet people, not just the Russians. Kazakh herdsmen were the first to feel the full blast of the storm. Early in 1930, countless individuals and families in entire regions and republics – the Russian, Ukrainian and Caucasian grain districts – were stigmatized as kulaks, driven from their land, forced into collectives, exiled or shot. Central Asian cotton growers and sugar beet farmers in the Central Black Earth region suffered the same fate in 1931.

As before, the state took grain for three reasons: for export, to satisfy urban requirements and to feed the military. Only then would villagers (now transformed into kolkhozniki – collective farm peasants) be permitted to eat. How, given these massive demands, would the threat of hunger be countered? There was no answer to this question. Originally collectivization was thought to make sense only in the context of mechanization. With this in mind, plans for the Stalingrad Tractor Plant were ratified in April 1927, whilst two years later the sixteenth party conference urged the formation of Machine Tractor Stations (MTSs), rural-based depots which would hire out machinery and thus encourage socialization. By late 1929, however, Stalin had come to believe that collectivization would work even without machines or peasant compliance, but the Politburo still had no clear idea as to how the new farms would operate.

The few collectives in existence before autumn 1929 were organized as arteli, or more rarely TOZy; small units where fields and heavy equipment were held in common but all livestock and some implements remained the property of individual peasants and each family kept a plot for its own use.[25] Arteli were the preferred model

---

[24] The mir's origins are lost in the mists of time. By the sixteenth century, however, the practice of periodically redistributing land via a primitive form of village democracy under the landlord's control had become widespread.

[25] Only 1.7 per cent of households were in collectives in June 1928.

of the All-Union Commissariat for Agriculture, established in November 1929,[26] but there was no time to draw up model statutes, and in any event the artel' principle was already being abrogated by local activists. At first 'gigantomania' gripped the party. Peasants were sometimes advised that kolkhozy would incorporate several villages – or even whole districts – without being told how they would function.[27] What the Commissariat did do, in January 1930, was to cancel work on schemes predicated on the continued existence of small-scale cultivation and dismiss those agronomists who, since 1919, had been trying to rationalize the mir.[28] A vital link between government and peasants was therefore broken. Aside from local party organizations, the only central agencies left in the villages were collectivization brigades staffed by soldiers, party members, workers and policemen. Upon them devolved the job of running the new large-scale kolkhozy, but even if they had been competent farmers – which they were not – they faced an impossible task: too few draft animals remained to plough the land and there were not enough tractors to make good the deficiency.[29] Weeds choked the fields and what equipment there was rusted away because no one had thought to provide adequate storage facilities.

Famine

The mayhem and confusion could not last for long without fearful consequences. The first hint of disaster came in October 1931 when Molotov revealed that several million hectares of grain land were afflicted by drought. Famine appeared in the Ukraine the following spring. Matters eased as the summer harvest was gathered in but deteriorated rapidly thereafter; by late spring in 1933 starvation had spread to the North Caucasus (the Kuban district was particularly hard hit), Kazakhstan and the Middle and Lower Volga. After a short-lived recovery in late summer dire food shortages reappeared and dragged on into mid-1934.

Little is known about the 1932–3 famine, but it was without doubt the worst in Russia's history. Despite attempts to suppress the details a few foreign journalists sent back accounts of what they saw; one Englishman wrote of the Ukraine's fertile lands reduced to 'a melancholy desert' inhabited by multitudes of emaciated and starving

[26] The All-Union Commissariat took precedence over various republican commissariats which had previously enjoyed considerable autonomy.

[27] This was before Stalin's 'dizzy with success' article. Afterwards kolkhozy were roughly related to settlement structure.

[28] See G. L. Yaney, 'Agricultural administration in Russia from the Stolypin land reform to forced collectivization: an interpretive study', in J. R. Millar, ed., *The Soviet Rural Community* (University of Illinois Press, 1971).

[29] Only one MTS existed in 1928 'and in 1929 machines provided only 2.8 per cent of agriculture's motive power.

muzhiki.[30] When little Katia's protector arrived in a village on party business late one evening in 1933 his peasant host warned him to expect the worst:

> 'I will not tell you about the dead,' she said, 'I'm sure you know. The half-dead, the nearly dead are even worse. There are hundreds of people in Petrovo bloated with hunger. I don't know how many die every day. Many are so weak that they no longer come out of their houses. A wagon goes round now and then to pick up the corpses. We've eaten everything we could lay our hands on – cats, dogs, field mice, birds. When it's light tomorrow you will see the trees have been stripped of their bark, for that too has been eaten. And the horse manure has been eaten.' I must have looked startled and unbelieving. 'Yes, the horse manure. We fight over it. Sometimes there are whole grains in it.'[31]

Cannibalism appeared in many districts.

All researchers agree that millions died over these two or three years: as we shall see historians differ only in their assessment of the scale of the tragedy. Whatever the true figure this was a man-made disaster, a direct result of forced collectivization. Notwithstanding the warning signals emanating from the countryside, there was no change of policy: at the seventeenth party conference in January 1932 Molotov and Kuibyshev spoke of the need for further assaults on kulaks in order to eliminate the last traces of rural capitalism.[32] Six months later the third Ukrainian party conference, held under the watchful gaze of Kaganovich and Molotov, settled on the absurdly high grain procurement target of 6.6 million tons. Even though total collections for 1932–3 fell by twenty per cent in comparison with the previous year grain exports continued, while towns and the Red Army still received priority over the starving villages.

Indeed, it had been clear for some time that food would be extracted at all costs. Far from being a means of promoting voluntary socialization the 2,500 or so MTSs created between 1929 and 1932 became, along with sel'sovety, the régime's chief method of controlling the hostile countryside and wresting ever more grain from despairing peasants. Farms were obliged to hand over twenty per cent of their produce to pay for the hire of scarce machinery, and OGPU-dominated 'political departments' were attached to each station early in 1933 to ensure that every kolkhoz surrendered its quota

[30] Malcolm Muggeridge, writing in spring 1933.
[31] Kravchenko, *I Chose Freedom*, p. 113.
[32] According to official figures sixty-one per cent of all households had been collectivized by the end of the year.

of foodstuffs.[33] Unauthorized food consumption by kolkhozniki had been criminalized in November 1931. In September 1932 a law 'On the Protection of the Property of State Enterprises, Kolkhozy and Co-operatives' prescribed execution for theft of socialized property, including collectivized livestock and crops (a few ears of corn gleaned from a collective farm's fields was enough to warrant conviction). Should dying kolkhozniki feel themselves inclined to take advantage of decrees dated 6 and 10 May 1932, which allowed them to sell meat or grain to their equally pauperized neighbours, they would have to take cognizance of further decrees of 22 August and 2 December, which imposed sentences of up to ten years' imprisonment for trading before quotas were fulfilled. On 10 November the criminal code was amended to outlaw the purchase and resale of goods. Five days later, yet another law declared that no one who left the kolkhoz could revert to the status of an individual farmer. Families or individuals trapped by these measures who nevertheless determined to flee the famine risked falling foul of the 27 December regulations, which introduced internal passports like those issued by the tsar's interior ministry; since kolkhozniki were denied the new documents they were supposed to remain where they were.[34]

Sovkhozy and kolkhozy

When the seventeenth party congress (the 'congress of victors') assembled in January 1934 agriculture was beginning to recover from the worst of the famine. Stalin reported that the USSR had been transformed from a land of small peasant proprietors into a country of large-scale mechanized collectives. In fact there were still about nine million families working their own farms, but these were slowly and inexorably eliminated via ruinous taxes and impossible quotas; the state seized the property of those who failed to meet their obligations. By December 1934 collectivization encompassed seventy per cent of households. The figure rose to seventy-five per cent in 1935 and ninety per cent in 1936. Thereafter sovkhozy or kolkhozy controlled virtually all Soviet farmland.

Sovkhozy (state farms) concerned themselves almost exclusively with large-scale mechanized monoculture, classed their employees as

---

[33] Despite the construction of the Stalingrad Tractor Plant there was never enough machinery. In May 1931 Kuibyshev announced that agriculture would soon be completely mechanized, but tractor supply had reached only just over half the planned figure by December 1934 – 4.5 million instead of eight million horsepower. Political departments were abolished in November 1934 because of friction with local party organizations. See R. F. Miller, *One Hundred Thousand Tractors: The MTS and the Development of Controls in Soviet Agriculture* (Harvard University Press, 1970).

[34] The following March it became illegal for kolkhozniki to leave without the consent of kolkhoz chairmen. In practice, however, peasants violated or found ways round both regulations.

workers and paid guaranteed minimum wages; two privileges never extended to kolkhozniki. In February 1935 a special congress finally adopted model kolkhoz statutes. Based on the artel' principle and defined as voluntary co-operatives utilizing state-owned land granted rent free in perpetuity, general meetings elected chairmen and boards (functionaries, for the most part, drawn from the ranks of collectivization brigades) which ran and policed the farms.[35] Grain or cash left over after mandatory extractions had been met was divided between kolkhozniki on the basis of trudodni (labour day units). Organized into brigades and assigned specific tasks under the direction of brigade leaders – ploughing or threshing, for example – a kolkhoznik's trudoden' allocation varied according to task assignment; highly-skilled occupations attracted more trudodni than less skilled ones. In addition, families were allowed access to small areas of plotland and permitted to keep a limited amount of livestock.[36]

Kolkhoznik incomes thus hinged on three factors: private plots, the number of trudodni earned and the value of each trudoden' – the second depended on task assignment, the third on how much cash and produce remained after deliveries to procurement agencies and payments to MTSs. Since remuneration for collective work was very poor, and since by 1935 livestock and crops raised on plotland could be sold legally in special kolkhoz markets, households tended to pay more attention to their own 'private economy' than to the collective's fields. Indeed, most of their income (excepting grain) came from these plots. Sovkhozniki, on the other hand, did not have to bear the cost of any losses the enterprise might make. In both instances the system offered peasants little incentive for collective work.

1933–41

By 1941 socialized agriculture accounted for the production of almost all grain and technical crops (cotton, flax, etc.),[37] but grain output recovered from the disasters of 1932–3 only very slowly, reaching seventy-five million tons in 1935 (the first time pre-collectivization levels were exceeded) and falling to 56.1 million tons in 1936 before rising to 97.4 million in 1937. State priorities always overrode other considerations: procurement quotas took no account of harvest variations (figures for 1936–7 were due to weather fluctua-

[35] Kolkhozy were obliged to hand over 'thieves' and 'wreckers' to the OGPU.
[36] Kolkhoz chairmen were allowed to assign no more than a minuscule 0.5 hectares of land to each family.
[37] By the outbreak of the Second World War, according to two specialists, the socialized sector covered eighty-seven per cent of the USSR's total sown area. See P. R. Gregory & R. C. Stuart, *Soviet Economic Structure and Performance* (Harper & Row, New York, 1974) table 14 p. 234.

tions), nor were they allocated with proper regard to differences between kolkhozy – sown area or plotland allocations, for example. Moreover, prices were fixed according to a notional 'biological yield' (expected returns as opposed to the actual yields), a factor which necessarily depressed rates paid to kolkhozy.

As the decade drew to a close the régime stepped up the pressure on the villages. In 1939 the central committee instructed kolkhozy to augment livestock herds at the household's expense and ordered the integration of around 2.5 million hectares of plotland into collectives. Procurements were increased by shifting the measure from actual sown area to total area available for cultivation, and by raising payments to MTSs. The following year farm chairmen became liable to imprisonment if they 'underestimated' harvest yields and kolkhozy were told that surpluses could be distributed only after extra amounts had been set aside for reserves. In consequence less food remained in the villages and average grain payments per trudoden' fell from a record of four kilograms in 1937 to 1.3 kilograms in 1940. Despite these measures most agricultural commodities (excepting grain and technical crops) continued to originate from within muzhik households; by 1940, according to one estimate, peasant families produced forty-three per cent of all marketed wool, fifty-two per cent of vegetables, fifty-seven per cent of fruit, seventy per cent of meat and seventy-one per cent of milk.[38]

The evidence for agriculture's revival after 1933 should not be allowed to obscure the fact that most collective farmers, particularly kolkhozniki, lived harsh lives. Tied to land which was no longer theirs, deprived of even those limited civil rights enjoyed by workers and virtually excluded from the money economy unless they could make a few extra rubles from their tiny plots, they resembled nothing more than their serf ancestors of three-quarters of a century previously.[39] Thousands of other peasants – the less fortunate who had been de-kulakized – were shot: no one knows the exact number. Many more, incarcerated in the Gulag and put to lumbering, mining or building work, expired from cold or malnutrition. For those other multitudes who somehow managed to flee to the towns or find work as labourers on the first piatiletka's giant construction projects, life was sometimes little better. The market price of flour rose twenty-three fold between 1928 and 1932, far outstripping wage increases. In an attempt to close the yawning gap between free and rationed

---

[38] J. Karcz, 'From Stalin to Brezhnev: Soviet agricultural policy in historical perspective', in Millar, *Rural Community*, p. 54.
[39] In the gallows humour of the times one abbreviation for the party, VKP(b), was read as *Vtoroe Krepostnoe Pravo (bol'shevikov)* – 'The Second Imposition of Serfdom (Bolshevik)'. Peasants became liable to corvée in August 1931 – six days a year devoted to road maintenance.

prices controlled prices for most basic foodstuffs soared in the early 1930s. The cost of a loaf of rye bread doubled in 1934, for example,[40] though to a large extent price gaps like these closed after the abolition of rationing a year later.

Collectivization was forced on the country at a staggering human and economic cost. The suffering inflicted on the numberless masses who perished in the Gulag, or died as a result of de-kulakization and famine, beggars description. The wider effect was to pauperize further a rural population which was already amongst the poorest in Europe and to turn rationing and shortages into permanent features of everyday life for almost everyone. By the early 1940s fifty million Soviet citizens were dependent on ration cards for their daily bread (rationing reappeared in 1941 and lasted until 1946). Meat production did not reach pre-collectivization levels until after 1953.

Interpretations

Stalin centre stage

Why was the collectivization drive launched at all? The Stalinist explanation is relatively simple. The NEP generated a powerful class of capitalist farmers – kulaks. By the end of the 1920s they were strong enough to hold the country to ransom. Their rapacious demands for ever higher grain prices foreshadowed the collapse of the industrialization programme and the degeneration of the Revolution. Stalin's decision to 'liquidate the kulaks as a class' and throw the party's weight behind the kolkhoz movement (bedniaki and seredniaki supposedly supported collectivization) rescued the first piatiletka, saved the USSR from military defeat in the Second World War and secured the future of socialism. Stalin's policies, firmly anchored in the scientific doctrine of Marxism–Leninism, were correct, necessary, and inevitable. Collectivization was the Soviet Union's historical destiny.[41]

Predictably, this account has given rise to its opposite. The idea that the General Secretary cold-bloodedly attacked the peasants, driven forward by a dogmatic vision which desired nothing less than the transformation of the entire population into cogs in some vast totalitarian machine, is characteristic of the majority of overtly anti-Stalinist texts published in the Soviet Union after 1985. 'Stalin

---

[40] Since kolkhozniki could market or consume produce from their private plots they were denied ration cards.

[41] There are many forgotten Soviet works published during and after Stalin's rule which repeat this interpretation. The most famous, and the most succinct and easily available, is the central committee's *History of the Communist Party of the Soviet Union (bolsheviks): Short Course* (Moscow, 1939).

decided to eliminate NEP prematurely', declared one Soviet sociologist in 1988,

> using purely administrative measures and direct compulsion; this led, speaking mildly, to pitiable results. Agricultural production was disrupted, in a number of districts of the country famine began. In towns measures against artisans and small producers in practice destroyed a whole sphere of services. The lives of tens of millions of people (I speak not of the servitors in the capital, but of the main population of the country) were filled with incredible deprivations and difficulties, often at the limit of purely biological existence.[42]

Heavily influenced by the Cold War's ideological certainties, many Western authors came to the same conclusion years before glasnost' took hold.[43] Other foreign historians have concentrated on detailed aspects of the policy. In Conquest's opinion the mass starvation of 1932–3 can only be described as a 'terror famine': Stalin was well aware of the extent of the suffering but deliberately blocked the flow of food to the countryside – to the Ukraine in particular – in order to eliminate all traces of nationalist sentiment and destroy the peasant's will to resist.[44] Numerous specialists, frequently émigrés drawn from the Soviet Union's national minorities who restrict their narratives to a single ethnic group, repeat the accusation.[45]

Economic dilemmas

Though they are conceptually far more sophisticated, some Western academics accept that much in the Stalinist analysis is plausible. According to Gregory and Stuart's 1974 monograph, for example,[46]

---

[42] Cited R. W. Davies, *Soviet History in the Gorbachev Revolution* (Macmillan, London, 1989) pp. 49–50. For a trenchant Soviet attack on Stalin's agrarian policies see A. Anton-Ovseenko, *Portret tirana* (Khronika, New York, 1980), and for a powerful glasnost' condemnation see D. Volkogonov, *Stalin: Triumph & Tragedy* (trans. H. Shukman, Weidenfeld & Nicolson, London, 1991).

[43] See, for example, H. Andics, *Rule of Terror* (trans. A. Lieven, Constable, London, 1969); C. J. Friedrich & Z. K. Brzezinski, *Totalitarian Dictatorship and Autocracy* (Harvard University Press, 1956). A more recent – and particularly vituperative – contribution to this historical tradition is R. J. Rummel, *Lethal Politics: Soviet Genocide and Mass Murder since 1917* (Transaction, London, 1990).

[44] Conquest, *Harvest*, part 3. Dalrymple also suggests that the famine was used to stamp out peasant resistance. D. G. Dalrymple, 'The Soviet famine of 1932–1934', *Soviet Studies* (3, 1964).

[45] See, for example, J. Borys, *The Sovietization of the Ukraine* (Canadian Institute of Ukrainian Studies, Edmonton, 1980); H. Kostiuk, *Stalinist Rule in the Ukraine* (Atlantic Books, London, 1960); J. Mace, 'Famine and nationalism in Soviet Ukraine', *Problems of Communism* (3, 1984); M. B. Olcutt, 'The collectivization drive in Kazakhstan', *Russian Review* (2, 1981).

[46] Gregory & Stuart, *Structure & Performance*, chs. 2–4, 12.

the Bolsheviks faced an appalling dilemma: the NEP, launched in response to War Communism's palpable failure, carried with it enormous risks: a partially deregulated peasant economy prefigured class differentiation, the revival of capitalism, the decay of socialism and the disintegration of the party. One answer to the conundrum, elaborated by Preobrazhenskii during and after 1924, was to ensure that the 'socialist sector' (large-scale nationalized industry) grew faster than the 'private sector' (nepmeny and peasant farming). The country's poverty and its exclusion from the international credit system dictated the means necessary to bring this about. Early modern bourgeois régimes engaged in 'primitive capitalist accumulation' – plundering colonies, holding down wages and organizing state loans; all of which hastened the transformation of 'the feudal mode of production into the capitalist mode'. Primitive accumulation would play a similar rôle in Soviet Russia; whilst repudiating 'on principle' the 'forcible methods of capital', Preobrazhenskii held that fiscal exploitation of the mir would provide money for industry and check the growth of a rural bourgeoisie:

> Primitive *socialist accumulation*... means accumulation in the hands of the state of material resources mainly or partly from sources lying outside the complex of state economy... Taxation of the non-socialist forms not only must inevitably take place... it must inevitably play a very great, a directly decisive role in peasant countries such as the Soviet Union.[47]

No other options were available. Since peasants could live in a natural economy (without trading) demand for industry's products was highly inelastic – villagers would not respond to lower retail prices by selling grain in order to purchase more goods.

Preobrazhenskii's Left-wing 'super-industrialization' prognosis was hotly contested by the Right. 'We must constantly keep in mind', wrote Bukharin in 1927,

> that our socialist industrialization must differ from capitalist industrialization in that it is carried out *by the proletariat*, for the goals of *socialism*, that its effect upon the peasant economy is different and distinct in nature, that its 'attitude' towards agriculture generally is different and distinct. Capitalism caused the *debasement* of agriculture. Socialist industrialization is not a par-

---

[47] Preobrazhenskii, *New Economics*, pp. 84, 88. See also id., *The Crisis of Soviet Industrialization. Selected Essays* (ed. D. Filtzer, Macmillan, London, 1980); A. Erlich, 'Preobrazhensky and the economics of Soviet industrialization', *Quarterly Journal of Economics* (1, 1950).

asitic process in relation to the countryside... but the means of its greatest *transformation and uplifting*.[48]

But he agreed with Preobrazhenskii on two important points: in the first place industrialization was essential to the socialist project; secondly, Soviet modernization would necessarily be financed by 'pumping over' resources from agriculture to industry. The key, however, was to expand consumer demand – not to reduce peasant incomes through excessive taxation – and to foster the smychka between town and village, 'a single integrated organism' which could be torn apart only with the most dire results. If socialist accumulation displaced economic symbiosis, warned Bukharin, 'you will have silent factories... you will have a declining peasant economy; you will have a general regression'. Contrary to Preobrazhenskii he believed peasant demand to be elastic: reducing industrial prices would enlarge the volume of sales and thereby increase investment funds for industrialization.

Bukharin's dread that high taxes would prompt farmers to reduce marketings and destroy the smychka was valid in principle but carried little weight after 1926. By then the threat of a kulak renaissance, coupled with the growing danger of war, determined that industrialization should be pursued at all costs. The alternatives were simple and stark: on the one hand foreign invasion and the end of socialism; on the other the triumph of rural capitalism and socialism's collapse from within. When grain producers withdrew from the market (the 1927/28 crisis) the régime had little choice but to resort to coercion. As this in turn sparked off peasant unrest and dramatic falls in sales, options narrowed still further. Stalin cut through the dilemma articulated by the party's Left and Right wings by using force on a massive scale, something which neither Preobrazhenskii nor Bukharin anticipated or desired.

Economic dilemmas revisionized
Over the last thirty-odd years, and particularly in the 1960s and 1970s, several aspects of this interpretation have been challenged. In a seminal debate between James Millar and Alec Nove published in 1976, Millar claims that Preobrazhenskii never envisaged primitive socialist accumulation as an alternative to the NEP; that Bukharin's fear that farmers would withdraw from the market if taxes were raised was misplaced; that the Bolsheviks misunderstood the nature of the 1927/28 grain crisis, and that the Ural–Siberian method –

[48] Cited S. F. Cohen, *Bukharin and the Bolshevik Revolution: A Political Biography 1888–1938* (Wildwood House, London, 1971) p. 171. For Bukharin's views see also A. Nove, 'Some observations on Bukharin and his ideas', in S. Abramsky & B. J. Williams, eds., *Essays in Honour of E. H. Carr* (Macmillan, London, 1974).

which did rupture the smychka – was an unjustified response to a highly complex situation, a fact which Stalin should have been aware of since several specialists had shown that the dynamics of the peasant household were not as straightforward as he imagined.[49] In Millar's view the grain crisis was a temporary phenomenon which could have been overcome simply by manipulating agricultural prices. There was no dilemma and no need for collectivization.

Nove, on the other hand, whilst not denying that there were alternatives to Stalin's policies, believes that the decisions taken late in 1929 must be seen against the background of the Bolshevik *Weltanschauung* and the cultural inheritance bequeathed by tsarist absolutism. An impoverished, isolated and insecure régime, convinced of impending international conflict, beset by all manner of domestic difficulties and run by a party forged in the brutalizing crucible of the Civil War, naturally interpreted the grain crisis in crude ideological terms. 'If there is a genuine alternative for me to eat either a cheese sandwich or a ham sandwich', quipped Nove, 'this is not an alternative for a rabbi'. By the same token the option of manipulating prices was never a genuine alternative for Bolsheviks – Stalin viewed peasant reluctance to market food not as rational economic conduct but as 'kulak sabotage'; something which undermined socialism and threatened the state's survival, to which the state replied with the kind of aggressive measures reminiscent of tsarism. As for the countryside's willingness to respond to fiscal incentives, Nove is far less optimistic than Millar, characterizing Russian agriculture as profoundly backward and the peasant household as deeply conservative. Farmers were unlikely to behave according to the dictates of eighteenth-century classical economic theory and maximize their marketings, choosing instead to eat more or work less. Given all this collectivization was 'necessary', if not 'desirable'.

Viktor Danilov, one of the few Russian historians of the late Soviet period who studied the mir seriously, accepts that the NEP was no longer viable but contests the view that kulaks were numerous enough to constitute a class, nor does he believe that they were mutating into greedy rural capitalists. In his judgement collectivization was necessary and inevitable, but should have been advanced gradually and with the village's consent. Referring to evidence which suggests that peasant households were capable of spontaneously

---

[49] J. R. Millar & A. Nove, 'A debate on collectivization: was Stalin really necessary?', *Problems of Communism* (4, 1976). According to Millar, instead of retreating into self-sufficiency when faced with falling prices villagers reacted by increasing their marketings. Peasants did not exist in some primordial state of nature but were closely integrated into the industrial economy through a complex series of market relations, buying farm equipment and consumer goods they could not produce at home. Millar's views mirrored those of Larin. See p. 58 fn. 50.

transforming themselves into TOZy, he contends that Lenin's notes on co-operation pointed the way forward. Collectivization was premature in all senses – economically, socially, culturally and politically.[50] A similar interpretation is offered by the émigré Russian historian Zhores Medvedev. Medvedev agrees that agricultural reforms were unavoidable in the long run, that a more cautious approach should have been followed, that Stalin's policies were disastrous, and that left to their own devices villagers, assisted by properly funded and equipped MTSs, would have switched to more intensive farming techniques in due course. Unlike Danilov, however, he argues that change could have been effected within the parameters of the NEP.[51]

A further group of researchers have examined a range of factors which modify what might loosely be termed pro- and anti-collectivization interpretations. Jerzy Karcz claimed that Stalin acted on false premises. Agricultural statistics were defective and the state itself induced the crisis by lowering payments for grain and allowing meat prices to rise, encouraging peasants to switch from arable to livestock farming.[52] Conquest maintains that things were not as bad as Stalin imagined, and that in any event nothing warranted the use of coercion; the levies destroyed confidence in the NEP and triggered the smychka's collapse.[53] Lewin, on the other hand, insists that 1928 was a year of real crisis: collections were so low that the régime was obliged to spend scarce foreign currency on grain imports,[54] a circumstance which, in the leadership's mind, pointed inexorably towards collectivization.[55] Despite alarms on the 'grain front' and the spread of the Ural–Siberian method, Carr thinks that Stalin was

---

[50] V. P. Danilov, *Rural Russia under the New Regime* (trans. O. Figes, Hutchinson, London, 1988) pp. 304–5; id., 'K kharakteristike obshchestvenno-politicheskoi obstanovki v sovetskoi derevne nakanune kollektivizatsii', *Istoricheskie zapiski* (79, 1966); id., *Sovetskaia dokolkhoznaia derevnia: sotsial'naia struktura, sotsial'nye otnosheniia* (Moscow, 1979) p. 347; id., 'Zemel'nye otnosheniia v sovetskoi dokolkhoznoi derevne', *Istoriia SSSR* (3, 1958).

[51] Medvedev, *Agriculture*, pp. 95–6.

[52] J. Karcz, 'Thoughts on the grain problem', *Soviet Studies* (4, 1967). In the 1920s Larin held that peasants were rational economic actors, trading off the advantages of arable or livestock farming. When grain prices fell, for example, farmers fed more to their beasts; conversely, when prices rose they switched back to marketing grain. Iu. Larin, *Sovetskaia derevnia* (Moscow, 1925) p. 217.

[53] Conquest, *Harvest*, pp. 88–9.

[54] M. Lewin, *Russian Peasants and Soviet Power: A Study of Collectivization* (trans. I. Nove & J. Biggart, George Allen & Unwin, London, 1968) pp. 242–3.

[55] Most other contributions to the late 1960s and early 1970s 'grain problem' controversy can be found in *Soviet Studies*. See R. W. Davies, 'A note on grain statistics', (3, 1970); J. Karcz, 'Back on the grain front', (2, 1970); M. Lewin, 'The immediate background of Soviet collectivization', (2, 1965); O. A. Narkiewicz, 'Soviet administration and the grain crisis of 1927–28', (2, 1968). A more recent contribution is Y. Taniuchi, 'A note on the Ural–Siberian method', (4, 1981).

undecided even in 1929. He interprets elections to rural soviets, in progress since January 1929, as a last ditch attempt to promote voluntary socialization, but by summer the Politburo had come to believe that too many soviets were dominated by kulaks, a factor which tipped the balance in favour of a direct assault on the peasants.[56] Donald Male adds that the state's aggressive line served only to unite all villagers – bedniaki, seredniaki and kulaks – against the régime.[57]

Finally, in 1980 Davies placed the decisions taken at the key November 1929 central committee plenum in the context of three interlocking factors, two negative and one positive. On the one hand fear of war and worries about industrialization accentuated the general mood of apprehension; on the other the euphoria engendered by the accelerating rate of 'voluntary' collectivization amongst seredniaki and bedniaki (pushed forward by local activists with a minimum of coercion) was interpreted as evidence of 'sharpening class conflict' in the villages, persuading Stalin that drastic measures would meet with little resistance.[58]

Popular support

The interpretations offered so far assume that a despotic régime, heavily influenced by Russia's pre-revolutionary political culture and possessed of a narrow ideology which blocked out alternative visions of the world, acted upon a recalcitrant population without any social support whatsoever. But some historians, including several of those mentioned above, have suggested that Stalin enjoyed a degree of popular backing.[59] Viola's recent monograph on the 'twenty-five thousanders' – the workers who volunteered for the collectivization brigades – shows that many town dwellers welcomed socialization. They viewed the 'great change' as a renewal of the Revolution. They saw the promotion of kolkhozy and sovkhozy as a patriotic duty, part and parcel of the country's modernization programme. They resented competing with peasant migrants for jobs. They demonized wealthy muzhiki as the root cause of expensive food and they perceived de-kulakization as a way of escaping from urban poverty.[60] Chase and Merridale have demonstrated that such sentiments were

[56] Carr, *Foundations 3-1*, pp. 282–9.
[57] Male, *Peasant Organization*, p. 211.
[58] Davies, *Industrialization 1*, pp. 109, 157–82, 397–402. The number of individuals in kolkhozy rose from 286,000 to 1,008,000 between October 1927 and June 1929.
[59] See, for example, Davies, *Industrialization 1*, pp. 204–28, where a comparison is made with the populist 'to the people' movement of the 1870s – a time when many young revolutionaries went to the villages to make contact with peasants, and Lewin, *Russian Peasants*, pp. 482–3.
[60] Viola, *Best Sons*, pp. 210–18.

particularly strong in the capital and especially amongst the young: the political culture of Moscow's working class fortuitously aided the Stalinists in their struggle against the city's Right-dominated party organizations and bolstered the confidence of middle-ranking activists – Karl Bauman, for instance – enamoured of collectivization.[61]

For its part the Stalinist leadership appealed to rank-and-file enthusiasts, in order to circumvent obstructionist bureaucrats unconvinced of the virtues of current policies, and mobilized collectivization brigades to hobble rural organizations unable or unwilling to cope with the new situation.[62] 'These communists', scolded a 1928 investigation, which found that ten per cent of party members in one district were well-to-do peasants,

> not only do not fulfil party decisions, not only do they not appear as examples for the broad peasant masses in the transformation of small, individual peasant holdings into large collectives, but become a hindrance on the path to collectivization and represent a clear expression of the Right deviation.[63]

Stalin and the Politburo were merely one set of actors – albeit the most significant – in a complex and evolving scenario in which 'centre' (the Moscow leadership) and 'periphery' (collectivization brigades, soviets and local party cells) reacted on each other in a confused and contradictory manner.

Human costs

If historians differ over causation they are equally divided when they turn to the human consequences of collectivization. Nearly thirty years ago Dana Dalrymple guessed that deaths resulting from the 1932–3 famine totalled somewhere around five million.[64] In 1975 two Soviet authors stated that 115,000 and 265,800 kulak families were sent to the Gulag in 1930 and 1931 respectively,[65] figures much higher than previous Soviet estimates. Four years later Roy Medvedev, on the basis of the 1975 Soviet figure and assuming an average of six or seven individuals per household, calculated that 2.5 million peas-

[61] W. J. Chase, *Workers, Society, and the Soviet State: Labor and Life in Moscow 1918–1929* (University of Illinois Press, 1987) pp. 301–4; C. Merridale, *Moscow Politics and the Rise of Stalin: The Communist Party in the Capital 1925–32* (Macmillan, London, 1990) pp. 218–27.
[62] See Viola, *Best Sons*, p. 211.
[63] Cited D. Thorniley, *The Rise and Fall of the Soviet Rural Communist Party 1927–39* (Macmillan, London, 1988) p. 18.
[64] Dalrymple, *Soviet Studies* (3, 1964).
[65] B. A. Abramov & T. K. Kocharli, 'Ob oshibakh v odnoi knige', *Voprosy istorii KPSS* (5, 1975).

ants were exiled in 1930–1, but suspected that he was underestimating the true dimensions of the tragedy.[66]

The famine controversy intensified in the 1980s and became entangled with a furious debate on the technicalities of the 'population shortfall' (the total number of premature deaths plus the number of unborn children). Wheatcroft's opinion that aggregate fatalities specifically caused by famine did not exceed three to four million was challenged by Conquest, Rosefielde and Medvedev. Conquest reckoned up to five million deaths in the Ukraine alone, with a further one million in the North Caucasus and one million elsewhere – a grand total of seven million. Rosefielde and Medvedev gave figures of 4.2 and six million respectively. Turning to the absolute number of 'excess deaths' attributable to collectivization, Wheatcroft advanced a figure no higher than six million for 1926–39. Conquest ascribed 6.5 million to de-kulakization in the period 1930–7 and Rosefielde insisted on a figure of 20.1 million between 1929 and 1938, broken down as follows: 4.2 million in the famine; 4.3 million in the Gulag; 5.8 million due to the 1929–32 collectivization drive; 3.6 million resulting from 'terror' and a further 2.6 million assigned to 'miscellaneous' factors. Medvedev calculates that of the ten million peasants dispossessed between 1929 and 1932 somewhere between two and three million lost their lives.[67] The General Secretary's thoughts on the matter were recorded when he met Churchill in August 1942: many of the country's kulaks 'agreed to come in with us... but the great bulk were very unpopular and were wiped out by their labourers'.[68]

Economic results

The tumult continues when historians consider collectivization's economic consequences. No one challenges the view that grain deliveries to the state rose after 1928. Rather, controversy centres on the sources of increased procurements and agriculture's contribution to the five-year plans. There are two schools of thought. One believes that socialization provided the wherewithal for rapid industrialization: kolkhozy and sovkhozy supplied cheap grain for export and fed

[66] R. A. Medvedev, *On Stalin and Stalinism* (trans. E. de Kadt, Oxford University Press, 1979) p. 74.

[67] Conquest, *Harvest*, p. 306; *Moscow News* (27 November 1988); S. Rosefielde, 'Excess collectivization deaths 1932–1933', *Slavic Review* (1, 1985); id., 'New demographic evidence on collectivization deaths: a rejoinder to Stephen Wheatcroft', *Slavic Review* (3, 1985); id., 'Incriminating evidence: excess deaths and forced labour under Stalin: a final reply to critics', *Soviet Studies* (2, 1987); S. G. Wheatcroft, 'New demographic evidence on excess collectivization deaths', *Slavic Review* (3, 1985). For a recent contribution to the debate see M. Ellman, 'A note on the number of 1933 famine victims', *Soviet Studies* (2, 1991). See also pp. 92–3 fn. 68, 139.

[68] W. S. Churchill, *The Second World War. Volume 4: The Hinge of Fate* (Houghton Mifflin, Boston, 1950) pp. 498–9.

the expanding urban population.[69] The other insists that collectivization made a 'negative contribution' to industrial modernization: capital flowed from town to country, not from country to town.

In 1974, reviewing a seminal work published by the Soviet historian Aleksandr Barsov a few years previously,[70] Millar launched an attack on the 'standard model' – the idea that rural exactions financed industrialization.[71] In the first instance, price inflation in kolkhoz markets allowed peasants to shift some of the fiscal burdens placed on them to town dwellers. Secondly, households used cash earned in kolkhoz markets to buy consumer products, thus depriving urban workers. Thirdly, rising grain procurements were a function of declining livestock holdings, not of increased production – in the 1930s people rather than cattle ate grain. Finally, and most importantly, although the state obtained kolkhoz produce 'on the cheap', and though investment in sovkhozy and MTSs failed to compensate for peasant destruction of agricultural stock, substantial transfers of machinery to sovkhozy and MTSs represented a capital flow from town to country which partially offset the procurement 'squeeze' on kolkhozy. In short, argues Millar, villagers received rather than surrendered resources, hence agriculture's contribution to industrialization was extremely modest and mass collectivization 'an unmitigated economic policy disaster'. The 'revisionist' case was refined in 1988. According to Holland Hunter low procurement prices offered by the government in 1928 served only to inhibit grain production and marketings – there was, therefore, no real 'surplus' available in the villages. And since collectivization reduced output to below the 1928 level absolute deficits followed, thereby cutting sharply into both rural and urban consumption.[72]

Modified variants of the standard model have not been without

---

[69] Despite Stalin's 'excessive excesses', concluded Nove in 1964, the decision to industrialize quickly had 'radical consequences... In 1928 any practicable Bolshevik programme would have been harsh and unpopular'. A. Nove, *Economic Rationality and Soviet Politics, or was Stalin Really Necessary?* (Praeger, New York, 1964) pp. 26–32. For a similar view see A. Erlich, *The Soviet Industrialization Debate 1924–1928* (Harvard University Press, 1960) pp. 119–21.

[70] A. A. Barsov, *Balans stoimostnykh obmenov mezhdu gorodom i derevney* (Moscow, 1969).

[71] J. R. Millar, 'Mass collectivization and the contribution of Soviet agriculture to the first five-year plan', *Slavic Review* (4, 1974). See also id., 'Soviet rapid development and the agricultural surplus hypothesis', *Soviet Studies* (1, 1970); J. R. Millar & C. A. Guntzel, 'The economics and politics of collectivization reconsidered', *Explorations in Economic History* (1, 1970). Other 'revisionists' who take issue with the 'standard model' include Karcz, in Millar, *Rural Community*; Z. M. Fallenbuchl, 'Collectivization and economic development', *Canadian Journal of Economics & Political Science* (1, 1967).

[72] H. Hunter, 'Soviet agriculture with and without collectivization', *Slavic Review* (2, 1988).

defenders. Michael Ellman suggests that although falls in agricultural output were a serious setback, and even though gross agricultural supply did not increase, the terms of trade were turned against the countryside. Collectivized agriculture thus played an essential rôle during the first piatiletka, providing food, labour and foreign currency, and becoming a 'residual sector which absorbed the shocks of bad harvests'.[73] Similarly, Wheatcroft, Davies and Cooper agree that much of the Barsov–Millar interpretation is plausible: 'the view that the economic system of the 1930s was primarily a mechanism for exploiting an agrarian "surplus" in order to provide resources for industry is certainly an over-simplification'. They also agree that policy options were available – industry would have continued to expand if the régime had adjusted agricultural prices and persevered with the NEP, but on the other hand they insist that industrial growth rates would have been significantly lower than those actually achieved in the 1930s.[74]

Evaluations

Russian imperatives

All historians agree that the Soviet economy was backward in comparison with the West and most accept that the state's obsession with economic development and national defence had some basis in fact. The Bolsheviks were not the first rulers of Russia to be haunted by fear of the consequences of industrial weakness, nor were they the first to decide that something would have to be done to peasants if modernization was to have any prospect of success. One reason why Alexander II emancipated the serfs in 1861 was because the country lost the Crimean War. Thirty years later Sergei Witte launched an industrialization programme predicated on fiscal policies which, in some districts at least, probably inflicted hardship on the village.[75] His conscious aim was to improve the Empire's chances of surviving as a great power. Stolypin tried to break up the mir for much the same reason; revolution and defeat at the hands of the Japanese in

---

[73] M. Ellman, 'Did the agricultural surplus provide the resources for the increase in investment in the USSR during the first five-year plan?', *The Economic Journal* (4, 1975).

[74] S. G. Wheatcroft, et al., 'Soviet industrialization reconsidered: some preliminary conclusions about economic development 1926–1941', *Economic History Review* (2, 1986).

[75] Witte (1849–1915) was Minister of Finances from 1892 to 1903. The fiscal assumptions underlying the late nineteenth-century industrialization programme bore more than a passing resemblance to Preobrazhenskii's theory of primitive accumulation: 'we ourselves might not eat', remarked Witte's predecessor, 'but we shall export grain'.

1905 convinced him that the root cause of internal disarray and imperial decline was economic backwardness, and in particular agricultural backwardness.[76]

All Russian governments were aware of the intimate connection between agrarian reform, domestic tranquillity, economic strength and military prestige, and no Russian government – least of all the Bolshevik government – dared run the risk of neglecting the country's defences. International tensions did not abate when the foreign armies finally evacuated the borderlands in 1920, and viewed from Moscow there was no reason to expect that peace would last for long: the rise of fascism and the spectacular development of Japan presaged new conflicts, while conservative régimes everywhere made no secret of their hatred of the Soviet Union.

The leadership's fear that hostilities were imminent in the late 1920s may have been misplaced, but they could not afford to disregard the possibility of war. They may have exaggerated the necessity for rapid industrialization, but they were right to see economic advancement as the key to military power. They may have misunderstood the nature and functioning of the peasant world, but their conviction that agricultural progress was the *sine qua non* of industrial modernization was correct. The decision to collectivize must be seen in the context of all these factors, but it is not enough to ascribe causation to war scares or the lessons of history. There were choices to be made about to how to carry forward the reform process. It is here that ideology played a rôle.

Ideologies and realities

Like the tsarist empire the Soviet Union was an 'undergoverned society'. The state perceived its subjects through a cloud of unknowing. In consequence it was always easy for élites to project their own fantasies on to the blank screen of the peasantry. Nineteenth-century Slavophiles gloried in the innate conservatism and wisdom of the 'simple country folk'. Their opponents, the Westernizers, characterized them as the 'dark people'; hostile, intractable, ignorant and uncouth. In the early twentieth century pan-Slavists appealed to the inborn religiosity shared by all Orthodox communicants, Stolypin hoped to charm a bourgeoisie from the endless expanses of rural Russia and Socialist Revolutionaries anticipated a New Jerusalem built on the enduring foundations of the village – in their opinion the mir was an egalitarian institution and its denizens born socialists.

The muzhik was all things to all men, and the new régime was no

---

[76] After 1906 Stolypin fostered the growth of independent peasant households in the belief that prosperous muzhiki would be politically conservative.

better informed and no less shackled by preconceptions than its predecessors. The October Revolution could not have succeeded without peasant support, but Lenin's 'democratic alliance of the proletariat and the poor peasantry', reborn as the smychka after the 'retreat' of 1921, was never intended to be permanent. To Bolshevik leaders peasants were a dangerous anachronism. Rescued from the idiocy of rural life, benighted villagers would eventually be transmogrified into enlightened citizens of a secular, rational community, and a modern agricultural system based on collective farms would sweep away the medieval incoherence of the mir. Lenin's last notes on co-operation were concerned only with the measures necessary to bring this about. He insisted that coercion should be avoided, but he did not deviate from his belief that sooner or later the age-old social and economic foundations of the countryside were to be dug up and cast aside.

It was also axiomatic that peasants could be divided into categories – kulaks, seredniaki and bedniaki – which were embryonic social classes. If left alone most kulaks and some seredniaki would become capitalist farmers, and some seredniaki and most bedniaki would lose their land and decline into wage slavery, economic prisoners of the 'rural bourgeoisie'. Peasants, however, did not necessarily share these perceptions. When Maurice Hindus returned to his native village from Los Angeles in the summer of 1929 he immediately found himself embroiled in discussions over past and future: 'There was a time, my dear,' began Lukian, an old muzhik remembered from childhood,

'when we were just neighbours in this village. We quarrelled, we fooled, sometimes we cheated one another. But we were neighbours. Now we are bedniaki, seredniaki, kulaks. I am a seredniak, Boris here is a bedniak, and Nisko is a kulak, and we are supposed to have a class war – pull each other's hair and tickle each other on the toes, eh? One against the other, you understand? What the devil!' And he shrugged his shoulders as though to emphasize his bewilderment at the fresh social cleavage.[77]

The obvious difficulty of identifying these groups (Lewin maintains that the terms 'kulak', 'rural capitalism', and 'rural capitalists' had no commonly agreed content, before or after the Revolution), and the conviction of some non-party specialists that the political economy of

---

[77] Hindus, *Red Bread*, p. 32.

the village was quite otherwise,[78] did nothing to shake Lenin's faith. The same is true of the party's Left and Right wings. Bukharin was less afraid of kulaks than Preobrazhenskii, but both agreed that there were kulaks to fear. Their prognoses were based on the a priori assumption that class antagonisms were fermenting in the village, and that it was the state's duty to ensure socialism's victory: what the contending factions disagreed about was tactics – how much time it would take to refashion the countryside and which methods to use. Indeed, these were minor perturbations on the surface structures of theory in comparison with the deep-seated ideological predilections which united all Bolshevik intellectuals; a preference for 'large-scale' solutions, an instinctive aversion to all things 'backward' and rural, and an emphasis on 'will' which effortlessly fused with the long-standing Russian political tradition of revolution 'from above'.[79]

Stalin and the grain crisis

This was the background to the grain crisis of 1927/28. The fixation with the 'kulak danger', as Millar and others have suggested, may well have been just one more fantasy, but it was a very powerful one, and it was voiced in a context peculiar to the late 1920s. If the régime was always determined – somehow or other – to overcome the village, this depended on at least a modicum of unity within the ruling élite. By the second half of the decade a consensus was emerging; due in part to Stalin's changes of mind and the defeat of his rivals, in part to the party's changing composition and in part to the growing impatience with the NEP displayed by middle- and lower-ranking activists, young party members and ordinary workers. The catalyst was Stalin's recourse to coercion. Arguments over the grain problem have never been fully resolved and will probably always remain contentious. There is insufficient quantitative evidence to permit any firm conclusions about gross production or the exact relationship

---

[78] M. Lewin, 'Who was the Soviet kulak?', *Soviet Studies* (2, 1966). Aleksandr Chaianov (1888–193?), who worked in the People's Commissariat of Agriculture in the 1920s, expressed misgivings about the efficacy of categorizing farmers as kulaks, seredniaki and bedniaki. In his view the life cycle of the peasant household was such that as the years passed each family was likely to find itself impoverished, relatively well off, or somewhere between these two extremes. Statistical photographs which purported to identify a kulak 'class' were therefore illusory. There were no permanent classes emerging in the village, only phases in the life cycle of a given household. No one in the Politburo or the central committee took his views seriously. See D. Atkinson, *The End of the Russian Land Commune 1905–1930* (Stanford University Press, 1983); A. V. Chaianov, *The Theory of Peasant Economy* (trans. D. Thorner, et al., Irwin, Homewood, 1966); S. G. Solomon, *The Soviet Agrarian Debate: A Controversy in Social Science 1923–1929* (Westview, Boulder, 1977).
[79] For an intriguing discussion of some of these factors see R. Pethybridge, *The Social Prelude to Stalinism* (Macmillan, London, 1974).

between output and marketings, but it hardly matters: for many peasants the seizures and levies were indistinguishable from the horrors of War Communism.[80] The NEP collapsed as farmers withdrew from the market, an event which, in the leadership's mind, served to confirm what were self-evident truths – there was not enough grain; 'kulaks' menaced the régime; bedniaki and seredniaki were favourably disposed towards collectives; working-class support was assured; socialized agriculture would solve all problems.

These truths were refracted through the person of the General Secretary. Stalin stumbled into a bloody civil war with the peasants, but he stumbled along a path which the party, increasingly reflecting his own ideological proclivities, was already inclined to take. In this sense alone collectivization – or something very like it – was, as Stalinist historians believed, Russia's destiny.[81]

The view from below

There is no doubt that Stalin sought, or at the very least connived at, the physical annihilation of 'kulaks' in 1929–30, though he may have expressed fleeting hesitations later on.[82] Things are less clear when we turn to other aspects of the policy. Although collectivization could not have occurred without his full assent this does not mean that he, or any other Kremlin-based leader, endorsed everything done in the provinces. Historians now have strong grounds for believing that the régime was barely in control of its 'transmission belts' – far from the Kremlin one muzhik brandished a chit excusing him from socialization: 'this is not Moscow', announced his interlocutor as he tore it up. And for all their enthusiasm the brigades loosed upon the countryside early in 1930 did not know what they were supposed to do. Little guidance was provided by the centre and Stalin's

---

[80] In summer 1918 the People's Commissariat for Supply established 'committees of the poor'. Staffed by local activists and supported by workers' detachments they seized food stocks supposedly concealed by 'rich' peasants. Those who refused to surrender grain were exiled or imprisoned and their property confiscated. In 1920 'sowing committees' were set up in the provinces and some party leaders advocated the militarization of agricultural labour. See O. Figes, *Peasant Russia, Civil War: The Volga Countryside in Revolution 1917–1921* (Oxford University Press, 1989); L. T. Lih, *Bread and Authority in Russia 1914–1921* (University of California Press, 1990).

[81] James Hughes's recently published 'microhistorical' study of the Urals puts forward a similar interpretation. 'The intellectual revolution in Stalin's outlook towards NEP', writes Hughes, 'was accelerated by his experiences of distinct Siberian conditions... by the end of January 1928 he had crossed the Rubicon and was inexorably determined to implement his revolutionary agrarian programme'. J. Hughes, *Stalin, Siberia and the Crisis of the New Economic Policy* (Cambridge University Press, 1991) p. 210.

[82] A secret circular of 8 May 1933 signed by Molotov and Stalin and sent to all party, judicial and OGPU organizations told unauthorized bodies to stop arresting peasants and instructed the appropriate authorities to free half the 800,000 people currently in prison.

attention was riveted on grain procurements and de-kulakization. Lewin and Davies have shown that the government never took collective farms seriously as an immediate and large-scale prospect in the heyday of the NEP. TOZy and arteli were starved of resources and planners began to think through the organizational implications of a socialization programme only at the last minute.[83]

Moreover, there was little reason to imagine that any villager – rich or poor – would take kindly to life in the collectives. 'Ignorant beasts we may be', wailed one muzhik to Hindus,

> We are not learned; we are not wise. But a little self-respect we have, and we like the feeling of independence. Today we feel like working, and we work; to-morrow we feel like lying down, and we lie down; the next day we feel like going to town, and we go to town. We do as we please. But in the kolkhoz, brother, it is do-as-you-are-told, like a horse – go this way and that, and don't dare turn off the road or you'll get it hard, a stroke or two of the whip on bare flesh... We'll just wither up on the socialist farm, like grass torn out by the roots.[84]

In consequence collectivization proceeded in a jerky, haphazard manner, much influenced by the accidents of place and personality. Force was undoubtedly the main recourse but there was some 'negotiation' between brigaders and putative kolkhozniki: 'it was unlikely that many peasants would await the workers with bread and salt on the village square', surmises Viola, but if a twenty-five thousander overcame their resentments he might, after they had examined his hands to make sure he was accustomed to manual labour, enter into some sort of useful relationship with the village.[85]

All this affected Stalin and the Stalinists, sometimes frightening them into hesitation and retreat and sometimes persuading them that the policy was working; dizziness afflicted the leaders too, not just the local activists. *Quo vadis?* should have been inscribed over the portals of the central committee's rooms in November 1929.

The impact of collectivization
Thus far the debate is informed by a relative lack of acrimony. Matters are otherwise when we turn to Stalin's rôle and the broad impact of collectivization. Perhaps Stalin did not foresee the chaos which attended the 'great change'. It is also just possible to conceive that he did not fully recognize the probable outcome of his actions –

---

[83] Davies, *Industrialization 1*, pp. 109–12; Lewin, *Soviet Studies* (2, 1965).
[84] Hindus, *Red Bread*, p. 34.
[85] Viola, *Best Sons*, pp. 155–9.

mass starvation. Historians can never be sure on either count. But it is clear that the March 1930 retreat was temporary. In the months following the publication of the 2 March *Pravda* article he was determined to press ahead, and Conquest's researches point inexorably to the conclusion that by 1932 the General Secretary willingly exploited the 'food weapon' in what was now perceived as the final battle with the peasantry.

The real difficulties facing historians are located elsewhere, however, in the quarrel over population shortfalls and the deaths attributable to famine and de-kulakization. On the one hand estimates vary so widely that there is more than a suspicion of covert bias, on the other controversy has too often been overlaid by the worst kind of overt special pleading – for or against Stalin, for or against the Soviet experiment. The peasant's fate has become a stick with which each side tries to beat the other, and the contending factions are at liberty to trade blows with venomous abandon because no protagonist has access to anything like a full range of primary sources.

No one would challenge the assertion that collectivization was a tremendous national tragedy, or that the policy replicated many features of serfdom, but even though GARF's doors and the party's files are now being thrown open to researchers, an agreed figure on the death toll is unlikely to emerge: it is doubtful if anyone was keeping systematic records.[86] Moreover, until very recently only one important party source, the Smolensk Archive, has been available to Western historians. Some use has been made of documents relating to collectivization, but Smolensk province might have been untypical.[87] As more local archives open up, the best way forward would seem to be through the gradual accretion of studies of particular regions or social groups. Though historians are still largely ignorant of the details the Soviet countryside's political, social and economic geography was not uniform, and consequently the experience of parts of the Ukraine, the North Caucasus, Kazakhstan or the Volga might not have been replicated everywhere. Local and social histo-

---

[86] In January 1937 a national census was ordered but the results were suppressed in September. The first post-collectivization census to be published was carried out in January 1939, but it is so distant from the previous one (1926) that all previous attempts to measure population shortfalls have been speculative. In any case the 1926 census enumerators missed out some important districts and the 1939 census was heavily censored. As we have already noted (p. 3, fn. 6) both the 1937 and 1939 censuses are now available.

[87] See D. Brower, 'Collectivized agriculture in Smolensk: the party, the peasantry, and the crisis of 1932', *Russian Review* (2, 1977); M. Fainsod, *Smolensk Under Soviet Rule* (Macmillan, London, 1958) chs. 12–15; R. T. Manning, 'Peasants and the party: rural administration in the Soviet countryside on the eve of World War II', in J. W. Strong, ed., *Essays on Revolutionary Culture and Stalinism: Selected Papers from the Third World Congress for Soviet and East European Studies* (Slavica, Columbus, 1990).

ries would not 'explain away' collectivization, but they would help researchers to appreciate, in a given district or population cohort, exactly what happened and how. A better understanding of provincial, ethnic and republican social dynamics would also enable historians to correlate central policy gyrations with peripheral realities – to discover if and where the draconian laws of 1931–2 were actually applied, for example.[88]

If new perspectives are generated in this way, the fact remains that collectivization was revolution on a massive scale; social, political, cultural and economic revolution. The entire country was transformed. Millions died and millions more changed their way of life irrevocably. It is not surprising, therefore, that disagreements abound. So vast was the scope of the collectivization drive, so devastating were the repercussions, so complex were the socio-economic configurations of the populations affected and so multifarious are the ideological propensities of academics that historians will never be able to sink their differences.

Much the same is true of arguments over socialized agriculture's contribution to industrialization. In the first place, all parties to the debate are hamstrung by the unreliability of Soviet statistics. Secondly, historians and economists frequently talk past rather than to each other, and the latter too often underrate the significance of non-measurable variables – the scale of the foreign threat, the importance of ideology and the part played by meditations on Russia's past. These cannot be left out of the equation – indeed, they fundamentally shaped Bolshevik perceptions of what constituted economic reality. Wheatcroft, Davies and Cooper's conclusion that the NEP could have returned respectable, if unspectacular, rates of industrial growth into the 1930s is well argued and accords with the available evidence. But this is to describe a land which the party (or, at least, one section of it) never intended to inhabit. That collectivization did not correspond to the dictates of Western economic theory is neither here nor there. Bolsheviks wanted to change the world, not to manage it. 'Counter-factual models' – attempts to construct alternative futures by extrapolating trends from a given period – have occasionally been advanced to conjure other worlds or delineate the follies of the past (including the supposed folly of collectivization), but modelling is beset by a host of methodological and philosophical difficulties and mathematical forecasts leave historians mired in the realm of speculation. Viola, for example, dismisses Hunter's attempts to project the NEP forward into the 1930s as un-historical conjecture about 'what might have been' if agriculture had been placed under an 'economic bell jar', and concludes that 'Soviet agriculture without collec-

[88] See p. 50. For a pointer in this direction see L. Viola, 'The campaign to eliminate the Kulak as a class, winter 1929–1930: a re-evaluation of the legislation', *Slavic Review* (3, 1986).

tivization is tantamount to Soviet agriculture without Soviet power'.[89]

The *longue durée*

In the final analysis, therefore, each researcher still has to make what amounts to a subjective judgement on the 'necessity' for collectivization, and we should end by returning to the fundamental questions posed by historians: why was collectivization launched at all and how should it be characterized?

Industrialization – in any country and under any political or social system – involves more or less rapid urbanization and the growth of populations no longer able to feed themselves. For two centuries modernization has entailed the death agony of the peasantry and of traditional societies everywhere. Farming methods, and the social arrangements clustered around them, which permitted successive generations of rural inhabitants to wrest a living from the niggardliness of nature have been, and are being, ruthlessly destroyed by governments or the workings of *laissez-faire* economic systems: for governments, food surpluses mean political, social and economic aggrandizement; for capitalists, they mean higher profits. Katia's story could be told many times over in nineteenth-century North America, Ireland and Scotland – or in present-day Latin America, Africa and Asia. Only the details would change: the realities of dispossession and suffering would remain the same. Set in the frame of world history since the turn of the eighteenth century, Stalin's agrarian revolution is noteworthy only for the scale and speed of its implementation, and the compression of the misery involved into an extraordinarily short time-span.

We should also bear in mind that ours has been a very violent century. Theodore von Laue has argued vigorously that Stalin's actions must be seen in the context of the assorted barbarities of European and American imperialism and the immense slaughter of the Great War.[90] The Victorian confidence, shared unconsciously by élites of most political persuasions, that modernization was a benign, progressive and relatively peaceful process disappeared for good in the blood-soaked trenches of Flanders and the killing fields of Tannenberg. By 1929 the practice of exterminating whole populations in the pursuit of this or that social or political goal (albeit in wartime) was unexceptional, a commonplace of discourse and action throughout the world. Collectivization belongs not only to a Bolshevik or Russian tradition. It is part and parcel of the experience of Western civilization.

[89] L. Viola, 'Back on the economic front of collectivization *or* Soviet agriculture without Soviet power', *Slavic Review* (2, 1988).
[90] T. H. von Laue, 'Stalin in focus', *Slavic Review* (3, 1983).

Suggestions for further reading

R. Conquest, *The Harvest of Sorrow: Soviet Collectivization and the Terror–Famine* (Hutchinson, London, 1986). An overtly anti-Stalinist account built on the premiss that all the horrors of collectivization, de-kulakization and famine were consciously sought by the Soviet régime.

R. W. Davies, *The Industrialization of Soviet Russia 1: The Socialist Offensive; The Collectivization of Soviet Agriculture 1929–1930* (Macmillan, London, 1980); id., *The Industrialization of Soviet Russia 2: The Soviet Collective Farm 1929–1930* (Macmillan, London, 1981). The classic study of the collectivization drive which is likely to remain the standard against which all others are judged. Volume 1 actually starts in 1917 and Davies's narrative is helpfully broken down into short, manageable sections.

M. Lewin, *The Making of the Soviet System: Essays on the Social History of Inter-War Russia* (Methuen, London, 1985). Includes all Lewin's journal articles cited in the footnotes to this chapter, and much else besides which is useful.

id. *Russian Peasants and Soviet Power: A Study of Collectivization* (trans. I. Nove & J. Biggart, George Allen & Unwin, London, 1968). Particularly good on Bolshevik perceptions of the 'accursed problem' (the 'peasant question').

J. R. Millar, *The Soviet Economic Experiment* (ed. S. J. Linz, University of Illinois Press, 1990). Includes the 1976 Millar–Nove debate on collectivization and several other journal articles relating to controversies over the grain problem, the immediate background to collectivization and the contribution of socialized agriculture to industrialization.

L. Viola, *The Best Sons of the Fatherland: Workers in the Vanguard of Collectivization* (Oxford University Press, 1987). An excellent monograph on the twenty-five thousanders viewed from the perspective of a social historian.

Z. A. Medvedev, *Soviet Agriculture* (Norton, New York, 1987). A readable account by an eminent émigré historian (the brother of Roy Medvedev) which covers the entire period 1900 to 1985.

3 INDUSTRIALIZATION

*Subjection of Nature's forces to man, machinery... railways,
electric telegraphs... whole populations conjured out of the
ground – what earlier century had even a presentiment that such
productive forces slumbered in the lap of social labour?*
                                    Karl Marx & Friedrich Engels, 1848.

Narrative

The industrialization debate

By the mid-1920s industry had recovered from the worst of the Civil
War and for the first time Bolsheviks were in a position to ponder
the régime's long-term economic future. In August 1924
Preobrazhenskii published *The Fundamental Law of Socialist
Accumulation*. Tackling the problem of modernization in the context
of the USSR's international isolation and the obvious dearth of
domestic resources – human and material – he urged the government
to buy cheap grain from villagers and sell dear food to housewives.
The resultant monetary surplus would be 'pumped over' to fund
heavy industry's growth: sacrificing peasant and working-class consumption to investment would be the price of overcoming Russia's
backwardness.[1] These sentiments were echoed by Trotsky. Ever
since 1920 the War Commissar had been championing planned
industrial development, and by 1923 he had come round to the view
that the countryside would have to shoulder most of the cost.

Preobrazhenskii's article marked the beginning of the 'industrialization debate', a controversy which was to shake the party for the
next four years. Lev Shanin, an employee of the State Bank where
fiscal conservatism held sway, argued forcefully against the Left's
strategy, asserting that the NEP's market tendencies should be
allowed free reign and foreign trade expanded. *Laissez-faire* policies
would be a more effective way of financing industrialization than
high taxes. His superior agreed: 'if we really want to catch up with
the tempo and scale of foreign industry', proclaimed Sokol'nikov,

---

[1] See pp. 55–6.

Commissar for Finance, the country could proceed 'only by stimulating agricultural exports'.[2]

Initially, Bukharin stood somewhere between these two extremes. On the one hand he vilified primitive socialist accumulation as a 'Trotskyist deviation' and appealed for a symbiosis between agriculture and industry. The terms of trade should be turned in the peasant's favour since this would entice farmers on to the domestic market and encourage exports. As more food became available labour productivity would rise, helping industry in the short term, whilst in the medium term grain exports would pay for imported capital equipment. In the meantime the smychka should be maintained, even if this meant 'growing into socialism' at a 'snails-pace'. On the other hand he rejected the notion of too great a reliance on Western capitalism. The government's long-term aim should be to devise an autarkic socialist economy. In April 1925, however, Bukharin moved closer to Shanin's position. Speaking in Moscow he envisaged a buoyant rural sector exhibiting demand on light industry, the profits of which, in due course, could be diverted to investment in heavy industry.

> If the peasant wants to put up a iron roof tomorrow he will be denounced and that will be the end of him. If the peasant buys a machine he does it 'so that the communists may not see.' The technical improvement of agriculture is enveloped in a kind of conspiracy... Our policy... should develop in the direction of removing, and in part abolishing many restrictions which put the brake on the growth of the well-to-do and kulak farm.[3]

'To all peasants', announced Bukharin, 'we say "enrich yourselves"' – a provocative phrase which he was soon forced to withdraw.[4]

---

[2] Cited A. Erlich, *The Soviet Industrialization Debate 1924–1928* (Harvard University Press, 1960) p. 28. See also S. Oppenheim, 'Between Right and Left: G. Ia. Sokol'nikov and the development of the Soviet state 1921–1929', *Slavonic & East European Review* (4, 1989). Other fine works on the industrialization debate include R. Day, *Leon Trotsky and the Politics of Economic Isolation* (Cambridge University Press, 1973); N. Jasny, *Soviet Economists of the Twenties: Names to be Remembered* (Cambridge University Press, 1972); M. Lewin, *Political Undercurrents in Soviet Economic Debates from Bukharin to the Modern Reformers* (Princeton University Press, 1974).

[3] Cited J. F. Hough & M. Fainsod, *How the Soviet Union is Governed* (Harvard University Press, 1979) p. 138.

[4] Nove points out that Bukharin was echoing the phrase *enrichissez-vous* used in the 1840s by François Guizot (1787–1874), chief minister in the last days of Louis Phillipe's 'bourgeois' government. A. Nove, *An Economic History of the USSR* (Allen Lane, London, 1969) p. 123. Bolshevik intellectuals steeped in Marx's interpretation of French history could hardly be expected to react favourably.

Indeed, passions were aroused, not by the details of fiscal techniques, but by anxieties over the 'class forces' generated by the NEP, the social consequences of the alternatives on offer and, more generally, by differing visions of the future. Convinced that an incipient rural bourgeoisie – the kulaks – posed a genuine threat, the Left believed that manipulating prices in agriculture's favour would only hasten class differentiation, pauperize workers and consign industrialization to the remote future. Pumping over would obviate both dangers and release the forces slumbering in the lap of socialist Russia. Speaking to Komsomolites in 1926, Trotsky deployed imagery guaranteed to stir the blood of even the most jaundiced youngster:

> Recently we opened the power station of Shatura, one of our best industrial installations, established on a turf bog. From Moscow to Shatura is only a little over a hundred kilometres. A stone's throw, it would seem; and yet what a difference in conditions! Moscow is the capital of the Communist International. You travel a few score kilometres and – there is wilderness, snow, and fir, and frozen mud, and wild beasts. Blacklog cabin villages, drowsy under the snow. From the train one's eye catches the wolf's footprint in the snow... extreme contradictions; supreme achievements of technology and generalizing thought and primordial Siberian wilderness.[5]

The Right, on the other hand, believed that Lenin's worker–peasant alliance – in effect conciliation of the countryside – was the only way forward. Bukharin cautioned against a 'proletarian dictatorship which is in a state of war with the peasantry', and, like Trotsky tried to enthuse the Komsomol. Never, he declared,

> not in the epoch of Oriental despotisms, nor in the period of the so-called classical world, nor in the Middle Ages, nor under the capitalist régime – never was there such an example where the ruling class posed as its fundamental task the overcoming and destruction of the difference between the predatory city and the village on which it preys – between the city, which reaps all the benefits of culture, and the village, which is sacrificed to ignorance.[6]

Stalin equivocated. He condemned the Left's prescriptions and, in

[5] Cited I. Deutscher, *The Prophet Unarmed. Trotsky: 1921–1929* (Oxford University Press, 1959) p. 211.
[6] Cited S. F. Cohen, *Bukharin and the Bolshevik Revolution: A Political Biography 1888–1938* (Wildwood House, London, 1971) p. 171.

private, disassociated himself from Bukharin's speech. In June 1925 he told students at the Sverdlov Communist University that internal policies should be based on the assumption that the Soviet Union would remain the world's only socialist régime for at least twenty years. Five months later he referred to the need for 'Leninist hardness' to secure a revolutionary transition from the NEP to a socialist economy but eschewed any overt criticism of the smychka. In contrast Kamenev and Zinoviev, now aligned with Trotsky, openly attacked Bukharin's formulation and asserted that the Bukharin–Stalin view of the NEP menaced the dictatorship of the proletariat. Delegates to the fourteenth party congress in December 1925 (the 'industrialization congress') expressed support for economic modernization and voted down Kamenev's and Zinoviev's objections. Stalin's ambivalence continued into the new year. *Concerning Questions of Leninism*, published in February 1926, elaborated the concept of socialism in one country, and while he endorsed resolutions in favour of 'catching up with' and 'surpassing' the West at the fifteenth party conference in October–November, like everyone else he insisted that this could only be done through improving the standard of living of the entire population, urban and rural.

The planning agencies

While the debate raged, several organizations were busy with the task of mapping out industry's future. The 1919 party congress had already committed Bolsheviks to the principle of a 'general plan'. With this in mind Goelro was established in February 1920.[7] In the fullness of time darkness would be banished from every hamlet and cheap energy made available to industry. A second agency, Gosplan, emerged the following year and published its first annual economic plan in August 1925. Gosplan's 'control figures', intended as predictors of future economic performance, marked an important step on the road to full-scale planning. By 1926 the Commission's activities had expanded to include preparatory work on the general plan, a 'perspective' five-year plan and annual 'operational' plans. Alternative schemes drafted by Vesenkha (nominally responsible for the overall supervision of the economy) led to more arguments. 'Geneticists' in the planning apparatus believed that programmes should be limited by economic realities. 'Teleologists', on the other hand, viewed plans as goals to be achieved. They favoured setting

---

[7] The driving force behind Goelro was the engineer Gleb Krzhizhanovskii (1872–1959), an old friend of Lenin's. While still a student he helped found the Union for the Struggle of the Liberation of the Working Class, the forerunner of the RSDRP. From 1921 to 1930 he directed the work of Gosplan. Later he became vice-president of the Soviet Academy of Sciences.

high targets to overcome the 'objective conditions' revealed by Gosplan's figures.[8]

The birth of the first piatiletka

If caution, support for the NEP and a dread of provoking the peasantry characterized the geneticists (who tended to be non-party specialists) the teleologists (drawn for the most part from the party) were far less circumspect.[9] For them rapid industrialization was possible if pursued with energy and enthusiasm. They manifested a scarcely veiled impatience with the NEP and glossed over the difficulties with the smychka which would inevitably result from rushing ahead.

By 1927 four factors had shifted party opinion decisively in favour of rapid industrialization, with a pronounced bias towards group A industry. In the first place, manufacturing had more or less recovered to pre-1914 levels. Since there was little more idle capacity to bring on stream further advance was thought to be impossible without building new plants. The 'period of restoration' was over: party activists looked forward to the beginning of 'socialist construction'. Secondly, the Left's defeat allowed the Stalinists to adopt – admittedly in a crude form – Preobrazhenskii's and Trotsky's so-called 'super-industrialist' policies without fear of political reprisals from the United Opposition. Thirdly, Britain's decision to break off diplomatic relations with the Soviet Union in May 1927 combined with deteriorating relations with France and Poland, suspicions of Japan and the failure of the Chinese communists to persuade most Soviet leaders that invasion was highly probable in the near future. Finally, the party's apparently successful management of agriculture (prior to the Ural–Siberian method of winter–spring 1928/29) convinced many that accelerated industrialization was feasible.[10] As if to symbolize the new mood, the decoration 'Hero of Labour' was introduced in July to reward higher productivity and better labour discipline. The following month Sovnarkom ordered sharp cuts in administrative costs to help finance industrial expansion.

Though when the fifteenth party congress met in December 1927 everyone spoke of acting within the framework of the NEP (obtaining peasant products voluntarily by economic means), Stalin abandoned his previous reservations. After warning delegates of an impending imperialist attack he insisted that more attention should

---

[8]   See E. H. Carr, *The Russian Revolution from Lenin to Stalin 1917–1929* (Macmillan, London, 1979) ch. 11; Nove, *Economic History*, ch. 5.
[9]   This is how things turned out in the end, although initially both schools of thought included party members and non-party specialists.
[10]   For the war scare and the Ural–Siberian method see pp. 39, 41, 42.

be paid to economic independence and heavy industry. Indeed, so potent had the vision of industrialization become that seven of the congress's twenty-nine sessions were devoted to examining rival draft five-year plans drawn up by Vesenkha and Gosplan, but despite the excitement nothing emerged besides general 'directives' devoid of any statistical content. Nevertheless, some spectacular projects were already underway. Investment earmarked for new enterprises doubled in the economic year 1926/27 and a start was made on three giant schemes; the Volga–Don canal, the Dneprostroi hydroelectric complex in the Ukraine and the Turksib railway line which was to link Turkestan's cotton fields to Siberia's grain and timber regions.

Whilst industrial recovery, the defeat of the Left, the war scare and the ostensible solution of the grain crisis encouraged Stalin to think in terms of a radical abandonment of the NEP, the new orientation alarmed those still committed to the old policy: Tomskii feared that all-out industrialization would lower workers' living standards and extinguish the last vestiges of trades union autonomy; Sokol'nikov was shocked by the fiscal profligacy advocated by teleologists.[11] These two were joined by Rykov and – more significantly – Bukharin. The quarrels between Stalin and Bukharin at the July 1928 central committee plenum, and the views articulated in the latter's 'Notes of an economist' two months later, were not just about agriculture:[12] the General Secretary's erstwhile ally was equally horrified by the increasingly overblown targets in successive Gosplan and Vesenkha drafts. Meanwhile Stalin threw his weight behind the teleologists. At the November 1928 central committee plenum he described Peter the Great's industrialization drive as 'an attempt to leap out of the framework of backwardness' and insisted on the need to catch up with and surpass the advanced capitalist countries encircling the USSR. The plenum approved Vesenkha's call for a massive twenty-five per cent increase in capital investment for industry for 1928/29. The following month Kuibyshev, the current head of Vesenkha and one of the rising Stalinists, rammed home the message: there was no alternative to the speedy development of heavy industry.

Bureaucratic rivalry between Vesenkha and Gosplan, crisis in agriculture and violent conflict within the party élite were fundamental to the shaping of the first plan: competing agencies vied with each

---

[11] In April 1928 the state budget was effectively subordinated to the plan. See R. W. Davies, *The Development of the Soviet Budgetary System* (Cambridge University Press, 1958) ch. 5.

[12] See pp. 16, 41–2.

other by touting ever more ambitious proposals,[13] the early months of collectivization stirred memories of Civil War heroics, party leaders enamoured of high targets and 'Bolshevik tempos' accused their opponents of lacking faith in the Soviet people or betraying socialism. The upshot of all this was that by the end of 1928 planning was no longer about rational economic calculation. The piatiletka had become a symbol of revolution rekindled. Now dominated by Stalin's supporters, the Politburo continually pressed for the upward revision of targets. Following the spring 1928 'Shakhty Affair', when fifty-five engineers from the Donbass mines were convicted of 'sabotage' and collusion with 'international capital', many 'bourgeois specialists' (white-collar workers deemed hostile to the party line) were arrested or dismissed. Shortly afterwards the central committee ordered the mobilization of 1,000 communists to study engineering, thereby signalling the start of a major drive for workers' technical education. Gosplan's geneticists (along with many other faint-hearts) were purged,[14] and in April 1929 two joint Vesenkha–Gosplan drafts – the 'basic variant' and the more ambitious 'optimum variant' – were submitted to the sixteenth party conference for approval.

What was revealed to delegates should have amazed even the most sanguine Left-wing super-industrialist. The 1,700 pages of the optimum variant 'Five-Year Plan for National Economic Construction', recommended to the conference by the Politburo, envisaged the doubling of Soviet industry's fixed capital stock between 1928/29 and 1932–3. On the basis of the electrification of the entire economy pig iron output was to rise from 3.3 to ten million tons per year, coal from 35.4 to seventy-five million tons and iron ore from 5.7 to nineteen million tons. Light industry would expand by seventy per cent, national income by 103 per cent, agricultural production by fifty-five per cent and labour productivity by 110 per cent. Within five years production costs were to fall by thirty-five per cent and the retail price of industrial goods by twenty-three per cent. The annual rate of investment, set at a staggering 21.4 per cent for 1928/29, would reach 23.8 per cent in 1932–3.

The first piatiletka in action

The publication of these wildly optimistic figures and the apparent breakthroughs of the 1928/29 economic year loosed a torrent of ever more grandiose schemes and prognoses. Targets were raised again

---

[13] For details of the various drafts see E. H. Carr & R. W. Davies, *Foundations of a Planned Economy 1926–1929* (Vol. 1, part 2, Macmillan, London, 1969) ch. 37; R. W. Davies, *The Industrialization of Soviet Russia 3: The Soviet Economy in Turmoil 1929–30* (Macmillan, London, 1989) ch. 6.

[14] The purge struck down those who had 'solidarized' with kulaks – 'Right deviationists' – as well as 'wreckers'. See pp. 109–10, 110 fn. 8.

and again in industry after industry and dubious reports of 'overfulfilment' flooded into Moscow. Exhortations to 'fulfil the five-year
plan in four years' (a slogan endorsed by the General Secretary in
June 1930) deluged the press.[15] 'Bacchanalian planning', as Naum
Jasny calls it,[16] received a further stimulus as collectivization took
hold.[17] As the demands grew the vision of a country transformed
assumed millenarial proportions. Society would be wholly recast.
Workers would labour out of enthusiasm and not for base gain.
Material incentives would wither away. Hectic campaigns for 'socialist emulation' swept the land, changes to the working week followed
one another in bewildering succession, and in June 1929 the central
committee decreed the immediate acceleration of graduate training
in technical subjects. Further resolutions in September 1929, con-
firming the worst fears of the now powerless Tomskii, stated that the
main task of social insurance was to promote higher labour productivity and that one-man management should be imposed in every
enterprise. A few months previously the lineaments of the Gulag
forced labour system began to emerge. Sovnarkom instructed the
OGPU to make all places of detention self-supporting and to establish timber camps in the country's remote regions; their first duty was
to earn foreign exchange, not to rehabilitate the inmates.[18] Harking
back to the heady days of War Communism some activists thought
that money would disappear and a socialist economy be constructed
in no more than a year or two.[19] When the sixteenth party congress
assembled in June 1930 Sergei Ordzhonikidze,[20] soon to be appoint-

[15] More succinctly 'five in four'. Posters appeared announcing that '2 + 2 = 5'. Stalin
went still further seven months later: in February 1931 he intimated that the first
piatiletka's basics might be fulfilled in three years.

[16] N. Jasny, *Soviet Industrialization 1928–1952* (University of Chicago Press, 1981) pp.
73–80.

[17] Davies has shown how collectivization prompted a fourfold increase in the target
for tractors by 1932–3, and according to Tatjana Kirstein between 1929 and 1930 the
anticipated capacity of the Magnitogorsk Metallurgical complex was raised from
650,000 to 2,500,000 tons, in part to make the complex comparable to the steelworks in
Gary, Indiana. Davies, *Industrialization 3,* p. 192; T. Kirstein, 'The Ural–Kuznetsk
Combine: a case-study in Soviet investment decision-making', in R. W. Davies, ed.,
Soviet Investment for Planned Industrialization 1929–1937: Policy and Practice
(Berkeley Slavic Specialties, Berkeley, 1984).

[18] By autumn 1929 about 64,000 prisoners had been transferred from prisons to timber
camps. Despite Sovnarkom's instruction talk about rehabilitating inmates through
'honest labour' continued.

[19] Krzhizhanovskii envisaged a planned economy governed by a 'red book' which
detailed labour policy, a 'blue book' concerned with energy inputs, and a 'yellow
book' (to be produced only 'insofar as monetary language is retained') which
described the plan in fiscal terms. Details of this and other visions of a moneyless
economy can be found in Davies, *Industrialization 3,* pp. 173–8.

[20] Born in 1893 'Sergo' joined the RSDRP in 1903, became active in the Georgian
underground and befriended Stalin. Elected to the central committee in 1912 he
played a prominent rôle in the Revolution and the Civil War.

ed head of Vesenkha, spoke in glowing terms of the drive to autarky. Stalin affirmed that the 'socialist offensive' was rushing forward on all fronts and that industrial modernization was inseparable from the total renovation of the educational system; a vast new proletarian 'technical intelligentsia' would soon displace bourgeois specialists. Declaring an end to the period of 'growing into socialism' he sanctioned resolutions urging all communists and Komsomolites to engage in 'shock work' and socialist emulation.

When the first piatiletka was declared complete in December 1932 no major targets had been reached, but there were some dramatic advances. In these four or five years the Soviet economy was fundamentally transformed. In the Urals, the Kuzbass, the Volga district and the Ukraine hundreds of mining, engineering and metallurgical enterprises were in the making. New factories materialized in the empty lands of non-Russian republics scarcely touched by the modern world. More than half the machine tools on stream in the USSR by 1932 were fabricated or installed after 1928. Gigantic schemes like the Magnitogorsk combine (part of the Ural–Kuznetsk iron and steel complex) were built from scratch, the Turksib railway line opened in 1930 and the first of the Dneprostroi's new turbines began to turn in 1932.[21]

The crisis of 1932–3
Despite these triumphs, two years were to pass before the second plan was officially confirmed. Extravagant claims of overfulfilment in sector after sector belied the realities of chaos and confusion. Breakneck industrialization caused enormous social strains and vast economic dislocations, so much so that in 1932–3 the entire experiment seemed on the verge of collapse. Costs were running far in excess of Gosplan's predictions and sudden bottlenecks appeared everywhere. The railways were quite unable to deal with the loads they were expected to carry. As numbers employed in industry, construction and the bureaucracy mushroomed cities and towns burgeoned at an astounding rate, expanding on average by about 50,000 inhabitants a week between 1928/29 and 1932.

The resultant pressure on housing, transport and social services was colossal and the demand for consumer goods far beyond capacity. Indeed, production targets for textiles and many other group B industries were progressively downgraded throughout the first

[21] For a brief summary of the first piatiletka's achievements see R. Munting, *The Economic Development of the USSR* (Croom Helm, London, 1982) ch. 4. For a thorough analysis see E. Zaleski, *Planning for Economic Growth in the Soviet Union 1918–1932* (trans. M. MacAndrew & G. W. Nutter, University of North Carolina Press, 1971) ch. 6, and the older but still useful M. Dobb, *Soviet Economic Development Since 1917* (6th ed., Routledge & Kegan Paul, London, 1966) ch. 10.

piatiletka. As rationing gripped the lives of millions, black and grey markets flourished in every town and production site. Workers scampered from job to job in search of better conditions and managers tried to hang on to skilled labour by offering higher wages and all manner of official and unofficial perks;[22] the latter due in part to Stalin's disavowal of egalitarianism in June 1931 – in order to counter 'flitting' and absenteeism wage scales were to be restructured, differentials widened, bonuses introduced and piece rates imposed across industry. Inflation soared, fuelled by over-investment, the government's introduction of sales taxes, the uncontrolled printing of money and desperate food shortages caused by all-out collectivization and famine.[23]

Drafting the second piatiletka

The 'storming' mentality drove all before it as drafts for a second piatiletka took shape. In May 1931 Kuibyshev, now chairman of Gosplan, defined the strategic goal of the coming years as the elaboration of a fully socialist economic system. Between 1933 and 1937 agriculture would be completely mechanized, further huge investments poured into group A industries and even larger sums disbursed to the consumer goods sector. The revolution in education and training foreshadowed in the first plan would be speeded up, eliminating differences between town and countryside and physical and mental labour. Gosplan was to submit detailed proposals to the government by autumn 1932, but as a result of the crisis investment levels and production targets were slashed in 1933, and not until the following year did the economy begin to stabilize.

When the seventeenth party congress met in January 1934 and ratified what turned out to be a third draft of the second piatiletka (even though the plan was supposed to have been operational since January 1933), Kuibyshev's ambitious schemes were forgotten. Money was to remain. The mirage of a fully socialist economy faded away,[24] to be replaced by sober calls to improve living standards,

[22] According to Nove coal miners changed their jobs three times on average in 1930. Nove, *Economic History*, pp. 198–9.
[23] The international depression which followed the 1929 Wall Street Crash also affected matters. World-wide prices for raw materials slumped. Since the Soviet Union exported raw and semi-finished goods in order to buy foreign machinery the terms of trade turned against the planners. The dimensions of the crisis are detailed in R. W. Davies, 'The Soviet economic crisis of 1932: the crisis in the towns' (unpublished paper, Soviet Industrialization Project Seminar, Centre for Russian & East European Studies, University of Birmingham, 1985); S. G. Wheatcroft, 'The Soviet economic crisis of 1932: the crisis in agriculture' (unpublished paper, Soviet Industrialization Project Seminar, Centre for Russian & East European Studies, University of Birmingham, 1985).
[24] See R. W. Davies, 'The socialist market: a debate in Soviet industry 1932–33', *Slavic Review* (2, 1984).

revitalize transport, consolidate the gains of the first plan and teach the newly recruited labour force to 'master technique' – to handle recently installed machinery more efficiently. Bourgeois specialists, hounded by disgruntled workers and party activists alike, were to be treated with respect and consideration.[25] Though the USSR had been transformed into an industrial country, reported Stalin, there were many defects, due for the most part to managerial neglect: labour productivity was too low; the output of metals and consumer goods below expectation and the quality of finished goods poor.

'Three good years'

The 1932–3 crisis quickly gave way to what became known as the 'three good years' of 1934–6. By January 1937 the planners and their political masters could look back on the previous thirty-six months with some satisfaction. Machine making and metalworking flourished, rendering the country virtually self-sufficient in these sectors, and the policy of relocating industry away from strategically vulnerable western regions continued apace.[26] Many projects started under the first plan – the metallurgical enterprises of Tula, Zaporozh'e and Lipetsk, the Ural–Kuznetsk complex and the Azovstal' combine on the Black Sea, for instance – finally came on stream and began to deliver returns on investment. As against the 1,500 enterprises opened during the first piatiletka 4,500 became operational during the second.[27] Labour productivity rose and labour norms (the amount each worker was expected to do in a set period of time) were substantially increased, due largely to the promotion of the 'Stakhanovite movement'.[28] Ruthless attempts to sort out the mess on the railways met with some success. The 'three good years' also owed something to developments in agriculture. By the middle of the decade the worst excesses of collectivization were over and the bony hand of famine had withdrawn from the countryside; though food remained scarce peasant markets were legalized in 1932–3 and rationing abolished in 1935.[29]

[25] The party had started to distance itself from spets-baiting in mid-1931. See pp. 96, 211 fn. 69.
[26] Drafts of the second piatiletka earmarked one quarter of capital investment to Asiatic Russia.
[27] Munting estimates that by 1937 about eighty per cent of the Soviet Union's industrial products were fabricated in new enterprises. Munting, *Development*, p. 94. Soviet sources habitually listed industrial units as enterprises – one blast furnace equalled one 'enterprise', for instance. Nevertheless, more enterprises came on stream during the second piatiletka.
[28] In August 1935 Aleksei Stakhanov, a Donbass miner, overfulfilled his quota by 1,400 per cent. 'Stakhanovism' deluged factories and building sites. In December 1935 the central committee ordered norms to be raised to levels set by 'Stakhanovite cadres'.
[29] For a thorough analysis of the 'three good years' see Jasny, *Industrialization*, chs. 6–7.

1937 and the third piatiletka

Notwithstanding some impressive achievements and the ritual obei-
sances to overfulfilment, the second plan failed in several important
respects. After 'three good years' 1937 ushered in a period of drift
and stagnation. In the first place, significant distortions appeared as
the Politburo, worried by international events, abruptly redirected
large sums to the defence industries. Secondly, a hard winter in
1937–8 caused drastic fuel shortages, precipitating, on the one hand,
severe difficulties in many factories, and on the other renewed crisis
on the railways; train journeys were cancelled and enterprises
starved of the materials necessary to meet their targets. Thirdly, consumer goods investment was once more sacrificed to the insatiable
appetites of group A industry. Finally, Stalin's speech at the infa-
mous 1937 'February–March plenum',[30] averring to widespread
wrecking and sabotage which, in his view, was hampering economic
development, coupled with the massive purge unleashed by Nikolai
Ezhov,[31] head of the NKVD, soon combined to reap a grim harvest
of key personnel. The myriad lines of communication between individuals, factories, government and party institutions which kept
industry running atrophied as thousands upon thousands of managers, engineers and functionaries were shot or vanished into the
maw of the Gulag.

Ezhov's purge and the lowering prospect of war combined to influence the framing of the third plan, scheduled to run from January
1938 to the end of 1942. Preparatory work began in February 1936
and the final draft was to be submitted to the government by the
middle of 1937. Within a year, however, the planning process was in
chaos because the bulk of Gosplan's specialists had fallen victim to
the NKVD. A talented young economist, Nikolai Voznesenskii,
became head of Gosplan in January 1938 and set about rebuilding
the shattered morale of the Commission's remaining staff.[32] When in
March 1939 the eighteenth party congress formally adopted
Voznesenskii's proposals, Molotov, delivering the main report,

---

[30] See pp. 116–17.
[31] Born in 1894, Ezhov joined the party in 1917 and became a political commissar during the Civil War. During the NEP he held several party posts and one job in the state
apparatus.
[32] Kuibyshev died, perhaps from natural causes, in January 1935. Following his death
and prior to Voznesenskii's appointment Gosplan heads succeeded each other with
dizzying rapidity. Most were shot or sent to the Gulag. Voznesenskii joined the party
in 1919 and trained as an economist. For a biographical sketch see M. Harrison, 'N. A.
Voznesensky (1 December 1903 – 30 September 1950): a Soviet commander of the
economic front', *Warwick Economic Research Papers 242* (University of Warwick,
1983). For an insider's view of Gosplan in the late 1930s see J. Miller, 'Soviet planners
in 1936–37', in J. Degras & A. Nove, eds., *Soviet Planning: Essays in Honour of Naum
Jasny* (Blackwell, Oxford, 1964).

stressed the importance of the further rapid development of heavy industry in general and the defence sector in particular. Spectacular increases in production were envisaged. Gross industrial output was to rise by ninety-two per cent. On the other hand 'gigantomania' – the planners' and politicians' penchant for ambitious projects – was roundly condemned and much was made of the continued pressing need to master technique, raise labour productivity and defer to the professional competence of engineers and technicians. Elsewhere Molotov declared that the first and second plans had, in the main, laid the foundations for a socialist society: the next five years would complete the transition to socialism and witness the dawn of the communist epoch.

Like much else in Europe these schemes were to go awry. The third piatiletka ran for only three and a half years. When Hitler's armies invaded Russia in the early hours of 22 June 1941 all economic activity was subordinated to military exigencies.

Interpretations

NEP versus piatiletka

'The control figures', announced Krzhizhanovskii in October 1929,

> have the object of mobilizing fifty per cent of the national income in the current year for financing the economy. Such a goal can be posed only when a war is taking place. In the name of this war... a war with the highest goals, it is necessary to require an improved quality of labour, and tension of the will.[33]

What persuaded the leadership to start this war? Most researchers agree that economic considerations played a crucial rôle.

As with collectivization, Stalinist historians aver that the Politburo, led by the General Secretary, acted on rational grounds derived from the doctrines of scientific socialism in order to resolve the dilemmas voiced by the party's Left and Right wings, and that once underway both industry and agriculture profited from the first plan.[34] Similarly, many Westerners agree (though not for Stalinist reasons) that the NEP had run its course. First there was the problem of under-capacity. Since 'restoration' – bringing back on stream factories lying idle since the Civil War – was virtually complete by

---

[33] Cited Davies, *Industrialization 3*, pp. 183–4.
[34] Of the numerous Stalinist economic histories see, for example, P. I. Khromov, *Ekonomicheskoe razvitie Rossii v XIX–XX vv* (Moscow, 1950). For the ultra-orthodox Stalinist line see the central committee's *History of the Communist Party of the Soviet Union (bolsheviks): Short Course* (Moscow, 1939).

1925/26, further expansion required massive structural changes.[35] The ambitious investment programmes canvassed after 1926 (Dneprostroi, the Turksib line) made sense and necessitated a major extension of the state's rôle. Secondly, fiscal policies placed the régime in a quandary. As the scissors crisis demonstrated the smychka could not be maintained without low retail prices – if they rose farmers would refuse to market food. But as the NEP unfolded, urban and rural incomes rose faster than output, a factor which should have prompted price increases. Instead, terrified of a second scissors, the Politburo kept prices down. This in turn created 'goods famines' which in turn precipitated the denouement. Rather than facing rising prices farmers had to contend with growing shortages: the upshot was that peasants withdrew from the market. Finally, anxious to preserve industrial investment, the state cut grain procurement prices in 1926/27, thus causing peasants to reduce marketings and concentrate on livestock production. Matters had reached an impasse. The country could modernize only by shattering the NEP's parameters. Persevering with a mixed economy was therefore not an option,[36] and until the 1960s a Stalinist version of Preobrazhenskii's primitive socialist accumulation was thought by the majority of the Anglo-American scholarly community – Alec Nove in Glasgow and Naum Jasny in Washington, for instance – to have operated during and after 1928.[37]

Scholars disinclined to accept this straightforward 'stagnation or growth' interpretation fall into a number of categories. Some conclude that growth rates after 1928 were roughly comparable to those achieved under the tsars in the last twenty years of the nineteenth century and, by implication, cast doubt on the whole endeavour.[38] Others concentrate their fire on socialized agriculture: the idea that collectivization squeezed fiscal surpluses out of the peasantry, remarked Zbigniew Fallenbuchl in 1967, 'may well be one of those myths which are often repeated but which explode when they are more carefully checked'.[39] The following year Barsov concluded that

---

[35] Most scholars accept that 1913 output levels were reached somewhere between 1925 and 1927. See R. W. Davies, ed., *From Tsarism to New Economic Policy: Continuity and Change in the Economy of the USSR* (Macmillan, London, 1990).
[36] For aspects of this interpretation see A. Baykov, *The Development of the Soviet Economic System: An Essay in the Experience of Planning in the USSR* (Cambridge University Press, 1946); Dobb, *Soviet Economic Development*; A. Gerschenkron, *Economic Backwardness in Historical Perspective* (Harvard University Press, 1962); Nove, *Economic History*.
[37] Jasny, *Industrialization,* pp. 195–8; Nove, *Economic History,* pp. 209–11.
[38] See, for example, G. W. Nutter, *Growth of Industrial Production in the Soviet Union* (Princeton University Press, 1962). Nutter also thinks that increased production and productivity during the third plan was due largely to Soviet acquisition of the Baltic states and parts of Poland and Bessarabia in 1939–40.
[39] Z. M. Fallenbuchl, 'Collectivization and economic development', *Canadian Journal of Economics & Political Science* (1, 1967).

(for the first plan at least) capital flowed from industry to agriculture – not *vice versa* – and that both urban and rural living standards were reduced to finance capital accumulation.[40] As we have seen, Barsov's work sparked off a debate amongst Western economic historians – Ellman, Millar and Nove in particular – over whether or not rural consumption was sacrificed to industrial advance.[41] A third group thinks that persevering with the NEP was economically feasible but would have given only modest returns on investment into the 1930s.[42] Finally, some commentators object to the first piatiletka on philosophical as well as economic grounds. Peter Rutland, for example, characterizes Soviet planning as 'embedded utopianism', a monstrous offspring of the insidious ideology of rationalism and the dangerous belief in human perfectibility.[43] There, for the moment, the controversy rests: most historians now accept that since the macroeconomic relationship between industry and agriculture is far from clear, the first plan cannot simply be 'deduced' from the NEP in economic terms.

Social and political causes

If researchers are divided over economic matters the same is true of writing on other aspects of causation. Until the 1970s the paradigm of 'revolution from above' dominated the literature. Social causes and processes were discounted. By and large historians – Western, émigré and Soviet – focused their attention on five issues: Stalin's rise, the foreign threat, the industrialization debate, the defeat of the party's Left and Right wings and the changing composition of the Politburo and central committee. The consensus was that by the late 1920s a nascent Stalinist party-state was strong enough to launch industrialization on its own initiative.[44]

In recent years many have been keen to modify this interpretation, characterizing the array of political and economic changes and

[40] A. A. Barsov, 'Sel'skoe khoziaistvo i istochniki sotsialisticheskogo nakopleniia v gody pervoi piatiletke', *Istoriia SSSR* (3, 1968). Barsov developed his ideas in *Balans stoimostnykh obmenov mezhdu gorodom i derevnei* (Moscow, 1969); id., 'NEP i vyravnivanie ekonomicheskikh otnoshenii mezhdu gorodom i derevnei', in M. P. Kim, ed., *Novaia ekonomicheskaia politika: voprosy teorii i istorii* (Moscow, 1974).
[41] See pp. 61–3. See also J. R. Millar, 'A reply to Alec Nove', *Soviet Studies* (1, 1971); A. Nove, 'The agricultural surplus hypothesis: a comment', *Soviet Studies* (3, 1971); id., 'A reply to a reply', *Soviet Studies* (2, 1972).
[42] See Davies, *Tsarism to NEP*. See also the conclusions to S. G. Wheatcroft, et al., 'Soviet industrialization reconsidered: some preliminary conclusions about economic development 1926–1941', *Economic History Review* (2, 1986).
[43] P. Rutland, *The Myth of the Plan* (Open Court, La Salle, Illinois, 1985) ch. 3. For a similar hostile view of Soviet planning see M. Dohan, 'The economic origins of Soviet autarky 1927/28–1934', *Slavic Review* (4, 1976).
[44] With the notable exception of Carr, *Russian Revolution*, and Carr & Davies, *Foundations 1–2*, most of the works cited in this chapter published before the mid-1970s follow this line.

dilemmas as necessary, but not sufficient causal factors. Lewin and Roger Pethybridge, for instance, suggest that the low cultural level of the population helped shape the first piatiletka's social and economic agenda.[45] More recently, Merridale's account of Moscow's party organization details a brief 'intersection between the Stalinist élite and a vocal part of the factory workforce' – enthusiasts for socialist transformation – in the summer of 1928. Similarly Chase concludes that the mid-1920s were a 'psychological turning point' for workers; expectations rose as large-scale projects were started: 'gradually, the simple desire for a job, any job, gave way in the mild prosperity of these years to the demand for a right to a job'.[46] In addition Fitzpatrick's extensive researches into education and social mobility (discussed in chapter 6) unravel the complex relationships between central prognoses and mass aspirations on the eve of the Great Breakthrough.

Plan fulfilment

Further difficulties arise over the measurement of plan fulfilment. The official index of industrial production registered an increase of 852 per cent between 1928 and 1940, but few analysts outside the USSR were content to take this claim at face value: in 1962, for example, the American academic Warren Nutter listed eight different output indices, all calculated from different bases and all showing substantially lower figures.[47] Analogous problems arise when historians look at particular industries or sectors. A 1972 Soviet handbook asserted that between 1928 and 1940 oil production increased from 11.6 to 31.3 million tons, coal from 35.5 to 165.9 million tons, steel from 4.3 to 18.3 million tons and electricity generation from five billion to 48.3 billion kilowatt-hours, and that group B industries expanded much more slowly: the output of cotton cloth rose from 2,700 million to only 4,000 million square metres.[48] Most Western researchers – Abram Bergson, Maurice Dobb, Paul Gregory and Robert Stuart, Naum Jasny, Alec Nove, Eugène Zaleski – ring their own changes on these figures,[49] but despite many caveats all agree

[45] M. Lewin, 'Society, state and ideology during the first five-year plan', in S. Fitzpatrick, ed., *Cultural Revolution in Russia 1928–1931* (Indiana University Press, 1978); R. Pethybridge, *The Social Prelude to Stalinism* (Macmillan, London, 1974).

[46] C. Merridale, *Moscow Politics and the Rise of Stalin: The Communist Party in the Capital 1925–1932* (Macmillan, London, 1990) p. 218; W. J. Chase, *Workers, Society and the Soviet State: Labor and Life in Moscow 1918–1929* (University of Illinois Press, 1987) pp. 297–8.

[47] Nutter, *Industrial Production*, pp. 157–60.

[48] *Narodnoe khoziaistvo SSSR 1922–72 gg* (Moscow, 1972) pp. 136–41.

[49] The relevant texts are A. Bergson, *The Real National Income of Soviet Russia Since 1928* (Harvard University Press, 1961); Dobb, *Development*; P. R. Gregory & R. C. Stuart, *Soviet Economic Structure and Performance* (Harper & Row, New York, 1974); Jasny, *Industrialization*; Nove, *Economic History*; Zaleski, *1918–1932*; id., *Stalinist Planning for Economic Growth 1933–1952* (University of North Carolina Press, 1980).

that group A industries expanded enormously throughout the course of the three five-year plans and that group B performed far less well. Similarly most authorities accept that economic activity was subject to sharp discontinuities: explosive growth between 1928/29 and 1931, crisis and near collapse in 1932–3, 'three good years' between 1934 and 1936, stagnation, rearmament and distortion in and after 1937.[50]

According to several historians, specifically 'Stalinist' features undermined what should have been the positive aspects of consciously directed economic development. In 1973 Hunter argued that the first piatiletka was internally inconsistent and incoherent, while Davies's recently published magisterial survey of the period 1929–30 comments that undoubted successes were marred by 'major imperfections and defects'.[51] In Zaleski's view, Stalin's decision to ignore specialist advice resulted in the economy loosing 'all linkage' with the plan by 1931. He also surmises that the main purpose of interwar planning was to promote a myth of balanced rational economic development in order to induce the population to accept the deprivations and sufferings attendant upon rapid modernization, and highlights a series of factors which he believes distorted economic forecasts beyond all recognition: inconsistencies between sectors and ill-considered readjustments emanating from Moscow, incompetence and high staff turnover in Gosplan, the chaotic overlap between central and local planning agencies and the confusions and delays resulting from centre–periphery horse-trading. Zaleski considers that while the planning system helped the régime to control the economy, it also allowed managers to protect themselves from preposterous demands – by using personal influence to get extra investment for their factories, for instance, or by deliberately underestimating enterprise capacity and taking on more unskilled labour to meet unexpected contingencies (this last being an important cause of over-shooting employment and cost parameters and underfulfilling productivity targets).[52]

Living standards
What of the gains and losses for workers? No one disputes that the plans ended the misery of long-term unemployment, which dogged the lives of thousands in the 1920s, but many have noted that inflation, the agony of collectivization and the failures of group B industries should be added to the equation. In the main historians accept

---

[50] For an excellent summary of the discontinuities in economic development before 1941 see R. W. Davies, 'Economic and social policy in the USSR 1917–1941', in P. Mathias & S. Pollard, eds., *The Cambridge Economic History of Europe* (Vol. 8, Cambridge University Press, 1989).
[51] H. Hunter, 'The overambitious first Soviet five-year plan', *Slavic Review* (2, 1973); Davies, *Industrialization 3*, p. 486.
[52] Zaleski, *1918–1932*, p. 150, chs. 6–7; id., *1933–1952*, ch. 19. Much the same line is taken in Jasny, *Industrialization*, and Nutter, *Industrial Production*.

that breakneck industrialization drastically lowered workers' living standards, though Davies injects a note of caution by pointing out that the tremendous social flux of the 1930s – and the political control of statistics – makes it very difficult to generalize about the fate of entire social groups.[53]

The secular trends have been neatly summarized by John Barber.[54] In the first place food shortages after 1928 and rising prices after 1932 hit workers hard. To some extent rationing cushioned the blow (compared with low grade clerical personnel and villagers, proletarians were well off), but in Leningrad meat, milk and fruit consumption declined by two-thirds between 1928 and 1933. Similar figures obtained in Moscow, where up to ten officially designated 'vegetarian days' punctuated each month. Far from metropolitan centres things could be much worse: during the 1932–3 winter, recalled the American engineer John Scott, Magnitogorsk's riggers 'got no meat, no butter, and almost no sugar. They received only bread and a little cereal grain'.[55] On the other hand enterprises sometimes registered 'dead souls' (fictitious workers) on the pay-roll and distributed their ration cards to the factory's hands; equally the better-paid could shop at kolkhoz markets, while managers anxious to keep skilled operatives on site often disbursed extra rations. Subsequently, although more food became available after 1935, workers still consumed less meat and dairy products than ten years previously. In any event queues and shortages reappeared in 1939–40 and rationing in 1941.

Secondly, meteoric urbanization compounded an already desperate housing situation; much stock was destroyed between 1914 and 1920 and little repair carried out during the NEP. Each Soviet citizen had on average 5.88 square metres of living space in 1928, a figure well below the 8.25 'sanitary norm' but higher than most workers' allocations – many had only a couple of square metres to call their own. As another American, Andrew Smith, discovered, by 1932 even in Moscow thousands lived in overcrowded factory barracks:

[53] Davies, *Cambridge Economic History,* p. 1040. An exception is A. Vyas, *Consumption in a Socialist Economy: The Soviet Industrialization Experience 1929–37* (People's Publishing House, New Delhi, 1978). Vyas does not deny, for instance, that real wages fell, but he challenges the 'liberal Western view which ignores the social costs of perpetual backwardness'.

[54] J. D. Barber, 'The standard of living of Soviet industrial workers 1928–1941', in C. Bettelheim, ed., *L'industrialisation de l'URSS dans les années trente. Actes de la Table Ronde organisée par le Centre d'Études des Modes d'Industrialisation de l'EHESS (10 et 11 décembre 1981)* (Éditions de l'École des Hautes Études en Sciences Sociales, Paris, 1982).

[55] J. Scott, *Behind the Urals: An American Worker in Russia's City of Steel* (Indiana University Press, 1973) p. 78.

Kuznetsov lived with about 550 others, men and women, in a wooden structure about 800 feet long and fifteen feet wide. The room contained approximately 500 narrow beds, covered with mattresses filled with straw or dried leaves. There were no pillows, or blankets... Some of the residents had no beds and slept on the floor or in wooden boxes. In some cases beds were used by one shift during the day and by others at night. There were no screens or walls to give any privacy... There were no closets or wardrobes, because each one owned only the clothing on his back.[56]

The 'three good years' did nothing to improve matters; indeed, housing conditions seem to have deteriorated as the decade wore on.

Finally, rising prices cancelled out pay increases. Industrial workers' real wages rose steadily in the mid-1920s, declined precipitously throughout the first piatiletka and recovered somewhat between 1934 and 1936 – though not to the 1928 level.[57] Thereafter, as resources were switched to heavy industry (particularly defence), real incomes almost certainly fell back. 'Social wages' (educational and health provision) may have indirectly raised living standards, but since the value of other disbursements (pension and welfare payments) fell sharply in real terms during the 1930s, the social wage *in toto* did little to offset price inflation.[58] Hardship was mitigated by two factors, however; the ending of mass unemployment and the enormous growth of the labour force.[59] The first directly benefited the jobless, the second helped working-class families by drawing women into industry, thus increasing disposable income.[60] Simultaneously many peasants became workers and thus achieved urban standards of consumption.

In general, concludes Barber, living standards fell continuously between 1928 and 1933, stabilized in 1934, rose throughout the 'three good years' and fell back after 1936, but at no point did they recover

[56] A. Smith, *I Was a Soviet Worker* (Robert Hale, London, 1937) p. 43.

[57] In Moscow they may have been as low as fifty-three per cent of the 1928 level in 1932 and probably reached only two-thirds of the 1928 level by 1937.

[58] According to Jasny real wages did not regain their 1928 level until 1958, while Gregory and Stuart note that in 1937 consumer goods prices in state and co-operative stores were seven times higher than in 1928 and the average price of farm products over five times greater. Jasny, *Industrialization*, p. 9; Gregory & Stuart, *Structure & Performance*, pp. 85–6.

[59] The number of unemployed fell from 1,298,000 in August 1929 to 240,000 in November 1930. For a full treatment see R. W. Davies, 'The ending of mass unemployment in the USSR', in D. Lane, ed., *Labour and Employment in the USSR* (Wheatsheaf, Brighton, 1986).

[60] In Moscow, for example, the numbers employed per family rose from 1.37 in 1929 to 1.67 in 1937. Simultaneously family size declined: consequently the ratio of dependants to wage earners – 2.26 in 1927 – stood at only 1.59 in 1935.

to the late NEP levels. The reasons for this were several: forced collectivization, uncontrolled urbanization, wastage, industry's failure to lower costs and increase productivity, and the slump in world trade which followed the Wall Street Crash. The prime cause, however, was the absolute priority given to capital investment over consumption.

Forced labour

For one group in Soviet society there is universal agreement that life became incomparably harder: de-kulakized peasants and others forced to toil alongside free workers or in the NKVD's sprawling empire of prison camps. Gulag inmates were frequently put to big projects – typically canal construction – requiring the utilization of vast hordes of unskilled labourers.[61] If disagreements abound on the numbers incarcerated and the rate of attrition (Wheatcroft draws a sharp distinction between Gulag captives and those working under duress as exiles and Conquest's figures on the death toll have been the subject of vitriolic debate),[62] nobody challenges the view that millions died and millions more were permanently broken in body and spirit.

In 1947, Dallin and Nicolaevsky thought that by late 1928 the camp population stood at 30,000, rising to two million within thirty-six months. The increase was due partly to the criminalization of labour discipline offences in 1931, but more importantly to collectivization deportations and the widespread arrests of 'wreckers', 'saboteurs' and 'former people' (priests, bourgeois specialists, sometime members of banned political parties or those from non-proletarian backgrounds) triggered by the Shakhty Affair and the régime's

---

[61] The two most famous examples are the Moscow–Volga and Baltic–White Sea canals, the latter lending its name to a popular brand of Soviet papirosy (Russian-style cigarettes) – 'Belomorkanal'.

[62] For arguments over the death toll see R. Conquest, 'Excess deaths and camp numbers: a comment', *Soviet Studies* (5, 1991); id., *The Great Terror: Stalin's Purges of the Thirties* (Macmillan, London, 1968); id., *Kolyma: The Arctic Death Camps* (Oxford University Press, 1979); A. Nove, 'How many victims in the 1930s?', *Soviet Studies* (2, 1990); id., 'How many victims in the 1930s–II?', *Soviet Studies* (4, 1990); S. Rosefielde, 'An assessment of the sources and uses of GULag forced labour 1929–1956', *Soviet Studies* (1, 1981); id., 'Incriminating evidence: excess deaths and forced labour under Stalin: a final reply to critics', *Soviet Studies* (2, 1987); S. G. Wheatcroft, 'On assessing the size of forced concentration camp labour in the Soviet Union 1929–1956', *Soviet Studies* (2, 1981); id., 'Towards a thorough analysis of forced labour statistics', *Soviet Studies* (2, 1983); id., 'New demographic evidence on excess collectivization deaths', *Slavic Review* (3, 1985); id., 'More light on the scale of repression and excess mortality in the Soviet Union in the 1930s', *Soviet Studies* (2, 1990). See also pp. 60–1, 135–7.

determination to rush headlong into socialism.[63] Following a lull coinciding with the 'three good years' the numbers soared again. As Ezhov's police scoured the country for 'enemies', and ever more draconian labour laws were imposed on workers, multitudes disappeared from all walks of life. According to Conquest's 'highly conservative' calculations published in 1968 about eight million were in the Gulag by the end of 1938.[64] Another author surmised a total of nearly seven million on the eve of the German invasion, or about eight per cent of the entire labour force.[65]

Subsequent research has cast doubt on these figures. In 1981, Wheatcroft suggested a maximum of four to five million Gulag inmates by 1939,[66] an assessment, observed Roger Munting, which excluded an unknown number of Poles, Lithuanians, Estonians and Latvians deported to the interior following the seizure of the Baltic states and Eastern Poland in 1939–40.[67] Currently, Wheatcroft's 1981 estimates are being revised downwards. On the basis of a careful study of glasnost' and post-Soviet materials, Wheatcroft and Davies list just over 2.6 million detainees in 1937 (in camps, colonies, prisons and labour settlements) and just under three million two years later.[68] Given a census count of between 167.3 and 168.9 million this means that in 1939 the NKVD managed around 1.8 per cent of the total population.

Society in turmoil

In recent years a cohort of 'revisionist' social historians has pushed research beyond attempts to generalize the impact of industrializa-

---

[63] D. J. Dallin & B. I. Nicolaevsky, *Forced Labour in Soviet Russia* (Yale University Press, 1947) p. 54. 'Counter-revolutionaries' were 'unmasked' in the gold mines and the food processing industry in 1930. The following year defendants in the 'Industrial Party' trial – for the most part Vesenkha or Gosplan white-collar workers – were arraigned for collusion with anti-Soviet émigrés. Between 2,000 and 7,000 specialists are thought to have been removed from their posts following the Shakhty Affair. After 1933 the pace slackened. Although nine specialists were convicted in the Kemerovo Mine Complex sabotage trial in November 1936 (see pp. 115–16, 130), the prosecution was more interested in establishing links with Piatakov and an alleged plot to kill Molotov.

[64] Conquest, *Great Terror*, p. 709.

[65] S. Swianiewicz, *Forced Labour and Economic Development: An Enquiry into the Experience of Soviet Industrialization* (Oxford University Press, 1965) p. 39.

[66] Wheatcroft, *Soviet Studies* (2, 1981) p. 286. See also id., *Soviet Studies* (2, 1983).

[67] Munting, *Development*, p. 173. See also below pp. 159–60.

[68] From 1934 all camps, colonies, settlements and prisons were subordinated to the Gulag. Wheatcroft & Davies point out that these figures exclude an unknown number of people 'sent into exile without confinement in a camp or settlement' and 'an unknown but large number of former prisoners and exiles of various kinds who had been freed from their places of confinement but were excluded by a note in their internal passport from living in certain cities'. R. W. Davies, et al., *The Economic Transformation of the Soviet Union 1913–1945* (forthcoming) ch. 4 pp. 27–8. MS kindly supplied by R. W. Davies. See also pp. 135–7.

tion on living standards and wrenched the debate on social change away from a fascination with what has sometimes been called 'gulagology'. All, in one way or another, emphasize a series of inter-related factors: urbanization, social mobility and the rise of a new technical intelligentsia, the influence of the new labour force on industry and society and shop-floor mediations between operatives and those charged with carrying out the plans.

The first piatiletka's authors envisaged that employment in state enterprises would rise from 11.4 million in 1927/28 to 15.8 million in 1932–3. In fact totals shot up to 22.8 million – 6.4 million in industry alone instead of the anticipated 3.9 million. Many new workers were peasants fleeing collectivization and famine, but rapid industrializa-tion also provided opportunities for urban dwellers: unemployed cadre proletarians found their skills in demand and women flooded into the factories by the thousand. Rates of increase were much slow-er during the second and third plans: numbers in state enterprises reached 26.7 million in 1937 (7.9 million of them industrial workers) and 31.2 million in 1940 (8.3 million industrial workers). Overall the urban population rose by some thirty million between 1926 and 1939; on average towns and cities accommodated 200,000 extra people every month (but because some 'rural settlements' were re-classified as 'urban' these calculations should be treated with caution).

Labour and social historians have pointed out that the tumult of collectivization and the voracious demand for labour unloosed by the first plan had immediate and profound consequences.[69] In Lewin's phrase frantic industrialization generated a 'quicksand' society.[70] Overcrowding, dirt and squalor, and the psychological and physical disorders arising from them, became daily facts of life as successive waves of newcomers overwhelmed towns and construction sites. As millions of dispossessed and disorientated villagers fled the country-side in search of a better life urban centres underwent a sea change. The sudden 'ruralization of the cities' (perhaps 18.5 million rural peasants left their villages between 1926 and 1939) resulted in mas-sive labour turnover and prodigious overcrowding. Factories and mines, towns and cities, inundated by surging tides of humanity, lost all cohesion. Ruralization also engendered the precipitous collapse of cultured behaviour, unleashing a Hobbesian war of all against all in the scramble to survive and supplying 'a propitious hunting

---

[69] See, for example, V. Andrle, *Workers in Stalin's Russia: Industrialization and Social Change in a Planned Economy* (Harvester/Wheatsheaf, Hemel Hempstead, 1988); H. Kuromiya, *Stalin's Industrial Revolution: Politics and Workers 1928–1932* (Cambridge University Press, 1988); A. D. Rassweiler, *The Generation of Power: The History of Dneprostroi* (Oxford University Press, 1988).

[70] See Lewin, in Fitzpatrick, *Cultural Revolution*; id., *The Making of the Soviet System. Essays in the Social History of Inter-War Russia* (Methuen, London, 1985) p. 221.

ground for the ruthless, the primitive, the blackmailer, the hooligan, and the informer'. Society's middling ranks were drawn into the maelstrom, preferring to quit their posts and move on rather than face the inevitable and dire consequences of failure, real or imagined.[71] In the words of the despairing Ordzhonikidze Russia seemed to have become one huge 'nomadic Gypsy camp'.

The party, engineers and workers

If the first piatiletka was revolution rekindled, aver the revisionists, this was not just a matter of geographical mobility, building new factories, eliminating unemployment, or even allowing women greater room for independence. The quicksand society provided scope for rapid social advancement:[72] 'it is not the lack of construction materials that constitutes the essential constraint', reported Kuibyshev in July 1930, 'but the shortage of trained and educated personnel'.[73] He estimated that in order to meet industry's demands 435,000 engineers and technicians were needed. Since only 119,000 were available in 1928 many workers became vydvizhentsy and found jobs as foremen, supervisors or specialists. Others attended likbez and rabfak courses before going on to university or college. 'My parents and brothers were joyful at the turn of events, remembered Viktor Kravchenko after he was selected for technical training,

> Mother, in particular, had never reconciled herself to my remaining a foreman like her husband. In her heart she was worried because the revolution had interrupted my education... Even my father seemed thoroughly happy... 'My son will be an engineer', I heard him say to his cronies one evening around the family samovar. There was pride in his tone.[74]

But the central committee's decision in July 1928 to conjure a technical intelligentsia from the working class was intended, not only to meet the current demands, but also to foster the growth of new political cadres – loyal, qualified proletarians responsive to Moscow's orders. Reared in the traditions of the tsars' élite technical institu-

[71] Lewin, *Making*, pp. 220–1.

[72] See S. Fitzpatrick, 'Cultural revolution as class war', in id., *Cultural Revolution*; id., 'Cultural revolution in Russia 1928–1932', *Journal of Contemporary History* (1, 1974); id., *Education and Social Mobility in the Soviet Union 1921–1934* (Cambridge University Press, 1979); id., 'The Russian Revolution and social mobility: a re-examination of the question of social support for the Soviet régime in the 1920s and 1930s', *Politics & Society* (2, 1984); id., 'Stalin and the making of a new élite 1928–1939', *Slavic Review* (3, 1979).

[73] Cited Zaleski, *1918–1932*, p. 120.

[74] V. Kravchenko, *I Chose Freedom: The Personal and Political Life of a Soviet Official* (Robert Hale, London, 1947) p. 58.

tions most of the old bourgeois specialists fled the country in the early 1920s. The few who remained were politically suspect; sympathetic to Bukharin and the geneticists or hostile to all manifestations of socialism – Nick Lampert points out that only 2.1 per cent of Soviet engineers were party members in 1927.[75] During the NEP workers and rank-and-file Bolsheviks looked askance at these 'former people' – more often than not the specialists and technicians ordering them about were the same individuals patrolling the shop floor before 1917 – and contrasted their poverty with the material privileges bestowed on the qualified and cultured by harassed factory bosses desperate to secure the services of competent personnel.

Though the quality of education and training declined during the first plan thousands benefited from the régime's decision to throw open the doors of universities and technical colleges to proletarians, but as the symptoms of economic crisis multiplied pressure for change grew. In June 1931 Stalin called for the 'maximum care of those specialists, engineers and technicians of the old school who are definitely turning to the side of the working class'. A secret central committee circular found in the Smolensk Archive and cited by Kendall Bailes ordered managers to enhance their authority and improve their working conditions.[76] Social historians have detected further signs of disquiet within the élite. Lunacharskii resigned as Commissar for Narkompros in March 1929 (in protest, according to Fitzpatrick and Roy Medvedev, against the new emphasis on vocational training, the transfer of some institutes to Vesenkha and widespread purging of students by social origin),[77] and in August 1931 the central committee criticized schools for failing to equip pupils for higher and technical education. By the mid-1930s proletarian and plebeian aspirations no longer attracted the régime's unqualified support.[78]

Social revolution was paralleled by tumult on the shop floor. After 1928 white-collar employees (bourgeois or proletarian) were subjected to a wave of spets-baiting. Mass mobilization under the banner of socialist construction elicited a ready response from many workers (young communists in particular) committed to the régime's goals. But shop-floor attempts to revolutionize patterns of work and authority at the bench 'from below' – production communes, shock brigades, Komsomol 'light cavalry detachments' – met with opposi-

[75] N. Lampert, *The Technical Intelligentsia and the Soviet State. A Study of Soviet Managers and Technicians 1928–1935* (Macmillan, London, 1979) table 12 p. 71.
[76] K. E. Bailes, *Technology and Society under Lenin and Stalin. Origins of the Soviet Technical Intelligentsia 1917–1941* (Princeton University Press, 1978) p. 55.
[77] See p. 191; R. A. Medvedev, *On Stalin and Stalinism* (trans. E. de Kadt, Oxford University Press, 1979) p. 105; Fitzpatrick, *Cultural Revolution*, pp. 15–16.
[78] See chapter 6.

tion or incredulity from engineers. Operatives, local officials and party leaders were quick to interpret such professional scepticism as 'wrecking' or 'sabotage'. 'Old' workers – those whose careers stretched back to the NEP or pre-1917 years – resented the erosion of the Revolution's hard-won gains caused, on the one hand, by the influx of raw peasants indifferent to working-class traditions, and on the other by the peremptory style of the bosses who ruled the factory following the imposition of one-man management. Oppressed and chivied by managers compelled to meet impossible targets, they seized the opportunity to take out their frustrations on specialists. Spets-baiting and trials like the Shakhty Affair were thus part and parcel of the coincidence of working-class aspirations and central prognoses. Though policies were initiated from above they were often greeted with approval in the shops and canteens.[79]

Mobilization overtook the factories once more in the second half of the decade. Following the retreat occasioned by the 1932–3 economic crisis and the stabilization of the 'three good years', Moscow encouraged Stakhanovism in order to rescue the industrialization drive from bureaucratic ossification. Bonuses and gifts were showered on the favoured few. Ordinary workers responded with violence, sabotage or demands to be classified as Stakhanovites, but the attempt to resurrect the mood of grass-roots enthusiasm associated with the first piatiletka soon broke down under the hammer blows of Ezhov's purge – in Lewis Siegelbaum's words 'the politics of productivity took second place to other considerations' – and by 1939 the emphasis on the record breaking overfulfilment of norms had been quietly dropped.[80] Barber adds that even though the movement fell well short of its objective in raising productivity, it may have elevated the status of some workers whilst simultaneously reanimating the Bolshevik spirit of mass participation and proletarian creativity.[81]

But vydvizhenie and Stakhanovism were only one side of the coin. Forced industrialization was accompanied by the systematic destruction of trade union influence and the elaboration of a tranche of regulations which restricted workers' rights.[82] A few weeks after viola-

[79] See Bailes, *Technology*, pp. 60–1, 119; H. Kuromiya, '*Edinonachalie* and the Soviet industrial manager 1928–1937', *Soviet Studies* (2, 1984); id., *Stalin's Industrial Revolution*; Lampert, *Technical Intelligentsia*. See also L. H. Siegelbaum, 'Production collectives and communes and the "imperatives" of Soviet industrialization 1929–31', *Slavic Review* (1, 1986).
[80] L. H. Siegelbaum, *Stakhanovism and the Politics of Productivity in the USSR 1935–1941* (Cambridge University Press, 1988) pp. 281–2.
[81] J. D. Barber, 'Stakhanovism reassessed' (unpublished paper, Soviet Industrialization Project Seminar, Centre for Russian & East European Studies, University of Birmingham, 1986).
[82] The process began in the late 1920s. See M. Dewar, *Labour Policy in the USSR 1917–28* (Royal Institute of International Affairs, London, 1956); J. B. Sorenson, *The Life and Death of Soviet Trade Unionism 1917–28* (Atherton Press, New York, 1969).

tions of labour discipline were criminalized, 'staff offices' were set up to organize labour supply for industry. After November 1932 one day's absenteeism could lead to instant dismissal. Internal passports followed in December and a 1938 decree introduced 'work books'. These were entrusted to managerial care, further restricting geographical mobility. Between 1938 and 1940 the working week lengthened, the notice period rose from one week to one month, penalties for poor timekeeping increased, social benefits were reduced, and absenteeism or quitting without permission became criminal offences. Measures like these eventually bore fruit. Despite the eruption of Stakhanovism, as the decade wore on institutions, enterprises and the position of workers inside the factory began to stabilize. The rate of labour turnover, in particular, fell markedly.[83]

Restrictions on freedom of movement, endless reorganizations and campaigns, successive waves of in-migration, continual purging, the abrogation of egalitarian wage policies and the plethora of unofficial bonuses and perks induced by retreat, Stakhanovism and stabilization – all this, in Don Filtzer's view, resulted in the atomization of the industrial labour force and led workers to develop novel methods of defence. By 1940 a specifically 'Stalinist' form of production relations had become embedded in the factory. Workers pursued their grievances individually, not collectively, quarrelling with local management over norms, task fulfilment and the rate for the job. Managers accepted a large degree of slack in the labour force for the sake of industrial peace and connived in fabricating success stories to keep Moscow happy.[84]

Evaluations

Ideology and history
Classical Marxism was predicated on several assumptions. In the first place capitalism would raise productive capacity to levels which would allow socialism, and later communism, to be built on the basis of material plenty. Secondly, revolution would be international: capitalist countries were pre-ordained to converge towards a moment of simultaneous collapse. Having fulfilled their historical mission bourgeois régimes would give way to the New Jerusalem. Liberated from the scourge of want, emancipated from the distractions and follies of

[83] 1930s labour policy is summarized in J. D. Barber, 'The development of Soviet employment and labour policy 1930–41', in Lane, *Labour & Employment*; R. Conquest, *Industrial Workers in the USSR* (The Bodley Head, London, 1967).
[84] D. Filtzer, *Soviet Workers and Stalinist Industrialization: The Formation of Modern Soviet Production Relations* (Pluto Press, London, 1986). See also L. H. Siegelbaum, 'Soviet norm determination in theory and practice 1917–1941', *Soviet Studies* (1, 1984).

nationalism and religion, mankind, led by the proletariat – 'the class that holds the future in its hands' – would pass 'from the realm of necessity into the realm of freedom'. Wrested from the enfeebled grasp of a dying oligarchy the means of production would be dedicated to the common weal. The meek would at last inherit the earth.

The Bolsheviks were destined to inherit no such happy world. Excepting a few tantalizing moments following the collapse of the German and Austro-Hungarian Empires at the end of the Great War there was no international socialist revolution. Capitalism, though grievously wounded, managed to survive, and as the European tumults subsided and the Soviet leaders looked homeward to their isolated Republic a sombre prospect unfolded before their gaze.

The Tsarist Empire was by no means an insignificant player on the world stage, but it was hardly a fully developed industrial power. At the very best old Russia was still in transition, passing, in Marxist terminology, from the feudal to the bourgeois mode of production. Though by 1914 the physiognomy of metropolitan centres like St Petersburg displayed many economic and social features characteristic of advanced capitalism, by and large the country exhibited a countenance of intense localism, rural poverty and economic backwardness. Towns and factories were few and far between, connected by tenuous railway lines, roads of uncertain provenance and rivers more often than not frozen solid for half the year.

Even in conditions of peace this was no antechamber to the socialist paradise, but the wars and revolutions which raged across the land between 1914 and 1921 had cataclysmic effects on this meagre legacy. Mines and factories stood silent and open to the winds.[85] The railways were in ruins. Trade was reduced to primeval barter. The industrial bourgeoisie, never a significant group, vanished from the scene, along with most managers and technicians. Workers virtually ceased to exist as a class: many were promoted to posts in the burgeoning party-state apparatus (and were thus no longer proletarians) or perished on the battlefields of the Civil War. Many more died of hunger or disease or fled to their native villages.[86] 'It was as if', remarks Lewin, 'most of the fruits of the social and economic development Russia experienced since 1861 were wiped out and its culture, spiritual and political, had reverted to some earlier primitive stage difficult to define or date.'[87] Much would have to be rebuilt before Soviet

---

[85] In 1920 industrial output stood at one fifth of the 1913 level, coal production at one tenth and metal production at one fortieth.
[86] Of the 2.6 million workers employed in 1917 only 1.2 million remained in 1920. By 1921 Moscow had lost half its population, Petrograd two-thirds. The remaining inhabitants kept themselves alive by chopping up and burning their furniture.
[87] Lewin, *Making*, p. 296.

Russia could even begin to contemplate the transition to socialism – whatever that might mean in the absence of international revolution.

Notwithstanding this appalling scenario, industrialization remained central to the Bolshevik's world view. Indeed, given their attachment to Marxism it could not be otherwise. And while there can be no doubt that the NEP succeeded in undoing the bulk of the material damage suffered by industry as a result of war and revolution – by the mid-1920s the industrial workforce had more or less been reconstituted and a high percentage of technocrats were back at work – Russia in the second half of the 1920s was still a poor and underdeveloped country. Somehow or other the economic prerequisites for socialism, which were supposed to have matured in the womb of the *ancien régime*, would have to be constructed by the conscious activity of the workers' republic.

This was very much part of the native political tradition. State sponsored industrialization drives had a long history. Peter the Great founded factories, mines and shipyards in the Urals, the Volga district and St Petersburg and the first plans to harness the waters of the Dnepr were drawn up under Catherine the Great. In the 1840s Nicholas I instructed his government to report on the pros and cons of railway construction. Fifty years later Alexander III's Minister of Finances presided over an industrialization drive which, in several respects, anticipated Stalin's headlong rush towards modernization. In the last days of the Duma Monarchy, Russian capitalists called on the government to draft a seven-year plan for the economic exploitation of Siberia. Finally, the NEP itself was not a *laissez-faire* economy. The state controlled industry's 'commanding heights' – large-scale enterprises – and could strongly influence the economy via its monopoly of banking, credit and international trade. In Davies's phrase the NEP represented planning 'through and not against the market'.[88]

The dilemmas of industrialization

In 1962 the veteran economic historian Alexander Gerschenkron claimed that without fundamental change in the late 1920s the prospects for further economic advance would have been poor,[89] but the NEP did not collapse of its own accord. The crises of the NEP were partly of the régime's own making. If arguments over the transition to a socialist economy – the industrialization debate – were sit-

---

[88] Davies holds that the government established 'effective machinery' for planning within the parameters of a 'mixed market economy'. Central economic agencies provided credit and exercised financial control over wholesale prices, tariffs and wages, and direct, or 'physical' controls over imports and the iron and steel industries. Davies, *Cambridge Economic History*, pp. 1015–16.

[89] Gerschenkron, *Economic Backwardness*, pp. 143–5.

uated in a matrix of bleak economic facts, the manner in which the government handled and the population experienced these facts is also pertinent.

Given the complex four-way relationship between workers, peasants, the intra-party struggle and fiscal policy, the decision to allocate large sums to capital investment in 1926/27 was almost bound to lead to trouble. Similarly the prognoses of both the Left and the Right pointed towards impoverishment and instability. If the peasant's tax burden rose housewives would pay more for food. Conversely, if the muzhik was given his head the countryside would dictate terms to the city; downward pressure on wages was the inevitable corollary of the low retail prices necessary to lure farmers on to the market. Both prospects were unpalatable. The first would erode the party's support in the towns and estrange the peasantry, the second would alienate the régime's natural supporters, the industrial working class. Manœuvring between the Scylla of higher prices and the Charybdis of lower wages, Stalin's response was to keep down retail prices and keep up wages whilst exerting ever more pressure on the peasantry. In an economy of scarcity this inevitably led to inflation, 'goods famines' and the rapid growth of speculative private trade. Cheap scarce commodities were snapped up by nepmeny and sold on at market prices. The harsher line taken towards speculators in 1926 (the wave of arrests under article 107 of the Criminal Code) removed the symptom but not the cause,[90] and the situation was exacerbated by further price cuts in 1927.

The net effect of all this was twofold. Firstly, the hatred of the NEP felt by rank-and-file activists and workers crystallized into a mood of renewed revolutionary militancy. Secondly, intolerable strains were placed on the smychka. In the scramble for consumer goods those living near the factories did best, a fact which deprived peasants of access to industry's products and helped to precipitate the grain crisis whilst simultaneously threatening investment programmes. Vesenkha's reaction was to tighten price controls and extend 'physical controls' (central direction of allocation and distribution) rather than leave matters to the market. To many Soviet citizens the delicate threads which linked town and village seemed to be unravelling before their eyes. Inside the party, on the other hand, the supposed advantages of central direction and planning were contrasted with the apparent failures of fiscal manipulation and market forces.

The view that the first piatiletka was simply a 'revolution from above', imposed by Stalin on a recalcitrant population without support from the lower party echelons and some sections of the urban

[90] See pp. 39, 41.

masses, cannot therefore be seriously entertained. The first plan was certainly not launched in response to pressure from below, but popular discontents and the prevailing ambience – exasperation with the NEP, impatience with backwardness and the widespread tendency to equate trade and markets with speculation – did play a part in bolstering the confidence of those in the élite anxious to embark on the road of socialist transformation, and it did make the Right's policies seem increasingly unattractive to many inside and outside the party.

But the decision to abandon the NEP was not taken solely – or perhaps even primarily – for strictly economic reasons: as for collectivization Bolsheviks of many hues wanted to transform the world, not to replicate it. Further industrialization would not only usher in an epoch of plenty and raise the cultural and material level of the masses, it would also underpin the party's vanguard rôle by creating a large working class, demonstrate socialism's superiority and strengthen the socialist camp in the international arena. All this pointed ineluctably towards concentration on group A industries. Only when the infrastructure of a modern economy was firmly in place could workers, secure behind the ramparts of a strong socialist republic, begin to enjoy the fruits of industrial civilization.

Would the NEP have collapsed if the government had behaved differently? Was the threat of an imperialist war real or illusory? We can never know the answers to these questions. We can never be sure whether or not Stalin and his allies were pushed into rapid industrialization by internal and external pressures or opted for the Great Breakthrough with open eyes. At the very least, however, the first piatiletka was implicit in the NEP and grew out of the manifold social, political and economic conundrums of the late 1920s as articulated by the leadership. Moreover planning (or at least state directed economic activity), though refracted through the ideological registers of emergent Stalinism, was a traditional Russian response to the dilemmas of modernization, a development strategy bound up with the problems of industrializing the far-flung lands of European and Asiatic Russia.

The nature of planning

Many Western economic historians of the older generation fail to take sufficient account of both the *longue durée* and the social and political context of the late 1920s,[91] but they are right to insist that the planned economy was, in crucial respects, planless. This is not a matter of disagreements between geneticists and teleologists in the planning agencies; the three five-year plans required elements of

---

[91] Of the texts cited in this chapter see, for example, Gregory & Stuart, *Structure & Performance*, ch. 2; Jasny, *Industrialization*, ch. 1.

both, a recognition of objective constraints and a determination to overcome those constraints. It has more to do with Jasny's concept of 'Bacchanalian planning'.

As the first plan took hold military metaphors abounded. 'There are no fortresses the Bolsheviks cannot storm', declared Stalin to the sixteenth party congress. Industries became 'fronts' (the 'metal front', the 'engineering front'). Cadres and resources were mobilized, commanders appointed and dismissed, offensives launched, advances detailed, victories celebrated and retreats punished. In the mad rush to make good the 'lag' behind the West, the language of revolution rekindled thrust aside tried and tested indicators of economic performance resulting, not only in bottlenecks, crises and distortions, but also in the *ad hoc* elaboration of administrative techniques designed to overcome them. Physical controls displaced economic calculation, though the latter was partially restored in 1931. Vesenkha was abolished in January the following year and its functions divided between the big economic commissariats. As the decade progressed, these assumed more and more responsibility for resource allocation and plan fulfilment, mushrooming within a few short years into vast overlapping bureaucratic empires, each ruled by an autocratic boss.

The 'command–administrative system' was in the making. Since all manner of resources were in short supply, the boss's main tasks were firstly to ensure that he secured the means necessary to meet targets; secondly, to convince Stalin and his colleagues that these targets had actually been met; and thirdly to protect his commissariat's pet projects from the depredations of rival bureaucracies. The same imperatives echoed down the chain of command. Regional agencies fought amongst themselves, vied with each other for Moscow's favour and tried to bury their mistakes under a welter of paperwork. Enterprise directors grabbed resources as best they could, inflated their successes and disguised their failures. The centre, frustrated by all manner of lies and obfuscation, responded with ever more violent purges which – until the relative stabilization of 1939 – wracked the system from top to bottom.[92] It is small wonder, as Jerry Hough and Merle Fainsod pointed out in 1979, that Soviet statistical series for the 1930s vary so wildly and are so contradictory, and that despite the labours of many economic historians the measurement of plan performance will never become an exact science.[93]

But if economic activity was never, in any meaningful sense, planned, Stalinist controls and the command–administrative system were reasonably well adapted to pushing forward the development of heavy industry. Commissariat industrialization, however wasteful

[92] See pp. 121–3.
[93] Hough & Fainsod, *How the Soviet Union is Governed*, p. 153.

and chaotic, ensured that most of the régime's strategic goals received top priority. Equally, appeals to Soviet or Russian patriotism induced many to accept the burdens occasioned by the concentration on group A industries,[94] while purging, terror, and the all-pervasive atmosphere of permanent emergency prevented the emergence of overt manifestations of organized popular discontent which might threaten the party's monopoly of power or undermine the industrialization drive.

Social history

The shift of Western scholarly attention away from the description and measurement of plan fulfilment and towards investigation of industrialization's social dimensions started in the mid-1970s and gathered pace in the 1980s. It shows no signs of abating. The reasons for this are several.

In the first place, most early accounts of Stalin's industrialization drive were situated squarely in the context of the Cold War. The world-wide 'communist threat' had to be countered on the historical as well as the ideological and political fronts. American academics in particular took little care to disguise their dislike of the USSR. Much ink was dedicated to detailing the follies and disasters of planning and unflattering comparisons were made with the United States. On the other side of the divide some historians were anxious to highlight planning's positive aspects. Several of the older generation who went through the searing experience of the 1930s depression and recalled Russia's contribution to the defeat of fascism were inclined to contrast the Soviet achievement with the failures of *laissez-faire* economics and the political compromises of Western capitalism. On the whole social historians are of a younger vintage; less conditioned by the politics of the thirties, forties and fifties, and (perhaps) more likely to be aware of their own ideological predilections. In the second place, *détente* – the lifting of East–West tensions in the late 1960s and early 1970s – played a part in reorientating scholarly interests. It is not so much that new primary sources became available to researchers; although the problems of access to materials eased when perestroika and glasnost' took hold much of the best work currently available was written before the late 1980s. It is rather a matter of the increasing frequency of contacts with Russia. Researchers were able to spend more time pouring over the newspapers and journals of the 1930s housed in Moscow and Leningrad, with occasional forays into TsGAOR. Finally, and perhaps most importantly, the 'new cohort', as Fitzpatrick calls it,[95] has been profoundly influenced by

---

[94] For a discussion of these cultural and ideological factors see chapter 6.
[95] S. Fitzpatrick, 'New perspectives on Stalinism', *Russian Review* (4, 1986) p. 389.

and has benefited from a revolution in the history profession. From the mid-1960s onwards social history experienced a renaissance in America and Western Europe. 'History with the politics left out' became, in fields as diverse as early-medieval France and twentieth-century China, 'history from below'. In their accounts of the large-scale transformation of the Soviet Union, younger researchers have been more willing than most of their older colleagues to utilize the insights of sociology, social psychology or anthropology in the search for linkages between high politics, macro-economics and the experiences of broad layers of the population.

There is no doubt that social history has enriched our understanding of the industrialization drive enormously. Several fine monographs detail the impact of peasant migration, conflicts between new and old workers, relationships between enterprise bosses, workers and central and local élites or the experiences of the technical intelligentsia. A new historical landscape has unfolded, and the process of discovery is likely to accelerate in the post-Soviet world. But the basic question remains: did the industrialization drive improve the life of the Soviet people?

A few days after arriving at Moscow's Elektrozavod in 1933, Smith noticed two 'blonde buxom village girls' working in the factory's technical department:

> They never had to live in the barracks and pay in advance as the others did. They lived in an apartment house on the Matroskaya Tishina... They were always well-dressed, well-rouged and well-perfumed in strange contrast to the evident poverty of their fellow-women workers.[96]

During the same year Scott recorded his impressions of a Magnitogorsk apparatchik:

> Schevchenko was a great activist among the technical personnel. He was called an engineer by his subordinates. Actually... his technical knowledge was limited, and his written Russian contained many mistakes. His present job was sectional assistant director of construction. He was responsible to the director and to the party for the fulfilment of construction plans.[97]

Between 1928 and 1941 many young girls destined for a life of domestic service under the old régime – or even the NEP – found themselves working in a large new factory's planning office with

---

[96] Smith, *Soviet Worker*, p. 103.
[97] Scott, *Behind the Urals*, p. 24.

apartments and salaries to match, and many a semi-literate was furnished with a desk in some organization or another. Equally, many a peasant escaped the horrors of collectivization by finding a job in industry or building. For the masses socialist construction meant social and geographical mobility on an unprecedented scale.

These are the images of revisionist social history, but there is another side to all this. As Tomskii feared, 'face to production' turned trade unions into little more than state agencies. The parents of the girls in the planning department might well be slaving in the Gulag. They themselves might perish in Ezhov's 'Great Purge'. As he fiddled the books and fretted over Moscow's latest demands, the party stalwart sitting in his provincial office might recall the egalitarian dreams of the Revolution and Civil War. And the peasant might fare no better away from his native village. Early one morning in January 1933, Scott sat down to brew tea with his comrades. Outside it was minus thirty-five degrees centigrade. A young worker burst into the shop:

> 'Boy, it's cold!' he said, addressing everybody in the room. 'I don't think we should start work up on top today. One of the riveters froze to death up there last night...' 'Yeah?' said everybody at once. 'Who was it?' But nobody knew who it was. It was just one of the thousands of peasants and young workers who had come to Magnitogorsk for a bread card, or because things were tough in the newly collectivized villages, or fired with enthusiasm for socialist construction.[98]

Forced industrialization gave birth to a world of extremes. Somehow or other the two sides of the coin have to be kept in mind.

Suggestions for further reading

K. E. Bailes, *Technology and Society under Lenin and Stalin. Origins of the Soviet Technical Intelligentsia 1917–1941* (Princeton University Press, 1978). An excellent study. Discusses the régime's attitude towards specialists and the rôle of technicians and engineers in socialist construction.

R. W. Davies, 'Economic and social policy in the USSR 1917–1941', in P. Mathias & S. Pollard, eds., *The Cambridge Economic History of Europe* (Vol. 8, Cambridge University Press, 1989). A concise and informative summary by the West's foremost economic historian of Soviet Russia.

---

[98] Scott, *Behind the Urals*, p. 14.

A. Erlich, *The Soviet Industrialization Debate 1924–1928* (Harvard University Press, 1960). The best monograph on the high politics of disputes within the party over industrialization, planning and the fate of the NEP.

D. Filtzer, *Soviet Workers and Stalinist Industrialization: The Formation of Modern Soviet Production Relations* (Pluto Press, London, 1986). A fine study of Stalinist labour policy and the social history of the Soviet working class in the 1930s. Written from a Trotskyist standpoint.

H. Kuromiya, *Stalin's Industrial Revolution: Politics and Workers 1928–1932* (Cambridge University Press, 1988). Links the high politics of the first piatiletka to the shop-floor experiences and perceptions of 'new' and 'old' workers.

A. D. Rassweiler, *The Generation of Power: The History of Dneprostroi* (Oxford University Press, 1988). Examines one of the most significant construction projects of the first piatiletka from its pre-revolutionary origins to the post-Second World War years. Particularly useful for labour policy and centre–periphery tensions.

L. H. Siegelbaum, *Stakhanovism and the Politics of Productivity in the USSR 1935–1941* (Cambridge University Press, 1988). A fine social history of Stakhanovism which locates the movement within the everyday realities of Stalinist politics, planning and industrialization.

4 PURGES AND POLITICS

> *Where did this wolf-tribe appear from... Does it really stem from our own roots? Our own blood?*
> *It is our own.*
>
> Aleksandr Solzhenitsyn, 1973.

Narrative

Stalin under attack

If Stalin was *primus inter pares* by 1929 it was by no means clear that he would survive for long. At the sixteenth party congress in June 1930 several speakers dwelt on the necessity for unrelenting struggle against 'opportunists'; proponents of moderate growth stigmatized by the General Secretary as 'agents of our class enemies'. One orator revealed the existence of Lower Volga cadres nursing views similar to Bukharin's: shouts from the floor showed that many regarded this as tantamount to calling for a *coup d'état*. Nevertheless, delegates re-elected Rykov, Tomskii, Uglanov and Stalin's erstwhile duumvirate partner to the central committee.

But it was not just the Right's broken generals and scattered foot-soldiers who posed a threat, however small. Given breakneck indus-trialization and chaos in the villages, some Stalinists, too, harboured doubts about their leader's fitness for office. In the Politburo per-haps only Kaganovich and Molotov supported Stalin unreservedly; Kalinin and Voroshilov had sympathized with Bukharin while Kosior, the Ukraine's party boss, demurred at blaming collectiviza-tion excesses on local apparatchiki. The remaining four – Kirov, Kuibyshev, Ordzhonikidze and Rudzutak – may have expressed mis-givings about terrorizing unruly Bolsheviks.[1] Whatever the truth of the matter dissenters were still at large elsewhere. In December, Syrtsov and three others lost their central committee seats for orga-nizing a 'left–right bloc' against the vozhd'.[2] More signs of unrest

---

[1] See L. Schapiro, *The Communist Party of the Soviet Union* (2nd ed., Eyre & Spottiswoode, London, 1970) p. 397.

[2] All four had supported Stalin against the Right but were alarmed by collectivization excesses. Syrtsov favoured a partial return to market polices, pooh-poohed the Stalingrad Tractor Plant as an empty gesture and dismissed industrial statistics as 'eye-wash'. Davies found no evidence of a 'bloc' and surmised that they were selected as scapegoats to warn other waverers. See R. W. Davies, 'The Syrtsov–Lominadze Affair', *Soviet Studies* (1, 1981).

appeared as famine gripped the Ukraine. In the autumn of 1932 Riutin circulated a 200 page document calling for lower capital investment, an end to forced collectivization, the rehabilitation of oppositionists, including Trotsky, and Stalin's dismissal: 'Stalin and his clique are destroying the communist cause', fumed Riutin, 'and the leadership of Stalin must be finished as quickly as possible'.[3] He was expelled from the central committee in September, along with Kamenev, Zinoviev and seventeen others. The following January the central control commission charged Ivan Smirnov with forming an 'anti-party group' which sought to replace Stalin.[4]

Dissatisfaction resurfaced at the 1934 party congress, the first to be held since the economic crisis.[5] Early in the proceedings several senior provincial delegates asked Kirov to take over as General Secretary. When he refused congress abolished the title: by implication the other secretaries (Kaganovich, Kirov and Andrei Zhdanov – elected straight after the congress) were now Stalin's equals.[6] Recent disclosures suggest that discontent reappeared on the congress's final day. When auditors opened ballot boxes containing voting papers for the new central committee, Piatakov emerged as a full member; Bukharin, Rykov and Tomskii as candidates. Stalin doubtless sanctioned these choices – none of the four gave the slightest hint of opposition during the debates – but 300 delegates had crossed out Stalin's name. Kirov, on the other hand, polled all but three of the 1,225 votes cast. Kaganovich quickly hushed up the affair.[7]

The localities under attack
Notwithstanding Kosior's scepticism, the sixteenth party congress pinned responsibility for failures in industry and agriculture on the localities. Resolutions on Rabkrin and the central control commis-

---

[3] Riutin had previously been a secretary of the right-wing Moscow party committee. His first name is given variously as Mikhail or Martimian.

[4] Smirnov (b.1881), a Syrtsov associate and a Bolshevik since 1903, held several important party posts after 1917. He was expelled for 'double-dealing' in 1934 and shot two years later.

[5] see pp. 81–2.

[6] Thereafter Stalin was referred to merely as 'the Secretary' in all official party and state documents. The change of title may have been Stalin's own idea, perhaps to take the edge off criticism. Zhdanov (b. 1896) joined the party in 1930.

[7] See R. A. Medvedev, *Let History Judge: The Origins and Consequences of Stalinism* (trans. C. Taylor, Knopf, New York, 1971). The election story is detailed in *Moscow News* (27 November 1988); D. Volkogonov, *Stalin: Triumph & Tragedy* (trans. H. Shukman, Weidenfeld & Nicolson, London, 1991). Interviewed on British television (Thames TV, *Stalin*, 20 March 1990) Ol'ga Shatunovskaia, then a young woman working in the central party apparatus, asserted that on Stalin's instructions Kaganovich surreptitiously removed and burnt all but three of the offending ballot papers. Stalin thus appeared to be no less popular than Kirov. Not all historians accept the veracity of these accounts. See N. Mikhailov and V. Naumov, 'Skol'ko delegatov XVII S''ezda partii golosovalo protiv Stalina?', *Izvestiia TSK FPSS* (7, 1989).

sion noted that a recent chistka (1928–30) had removed 'tens of thousands' of unreliable and 'hostile' rank-and-file communists:[8] henceforth both organizations should concentrate on fighting 'bureaucratism' and ensuring local compliance with central directives. Purging would extend to all branches of management, administration and the economy. Moscow ordered a second chistka in December 1932, this time accompanied by a recruitment freeze. A hierarchy of special 'purge commissions' answerable to Rudzutak rooted out 'passive elements' in general (those who failed to attend meetings, etc.) and three groups of enemies in particular:

> *Double-Dealers...* trying to undermine the party's policy under cover of a false oath of 'allegiance'... *Open and Secret Violators* of party and state iron discipline who do not carry out... decisions, but discredit and cast *doubt* upon the decisions... by calling them 'unrealistic' and 'unrealizable'; *Turncoats*, who have allied themselves with bourgeois elements... and who do not combat kulak elements, grafters, idlers, and robbers of communal property.[9]

Stalin lambasted provincial cadres once more at the 1934 congress of victors. After extolling socialist construction he maintained that 'nine-tenths' of all defects were due to the absence of appropriate mechanisms for checking the implementation of Moscow's decisions. Sunk in 'bureaucratism', regional satraps disavowed 'self-criticism' and brushed aside local grievances. Two other luminaries spoke along similar lines: Rudzutak asserted that half the membership did not even bother to read *Pravda* and Kirov claimed that most problems could be solved by improving political education.[10] What was needed, continued Stalin, was a Soviet control commission answerable to Sovnarkom. Moreover, now that the danger of a schism had passed, the old central control commission should be reborn as a party control commission directly subordinate to the central committee. Congress duly abolished Rabkrin, transferred its powers to the Soviet control commission and appointed Kaganovich to head the

---

[8] The chistka, lasting from November 1928 until May 1930, focused on self-criticism, lax discipline and bureaucratic obfuscation. Membership decreased by about eleven per cent although some 37,000 were readmitted on appeal. Simultaneously several thousand apparatchiki were sacked.

[9] Cited A. Avtorkhanov, *Stalin and the Soviet Communist Party: A Study in the Technology of Power* (Atlantic Books, London, 1959) p. 203.

[10] Indeed, Stalin and Kirov, supported by Zhdanov, may have been united in emphasizing cadres' 'political work' at the expense of direct involvement in economic management. See J. Arch Getty, *Origins of the Great Purges: The Soviet Communist Party Reconsidered 1933–1938* (Cambridge University Press, 1985) pp. 94–5, and below p. 130.

new party control commission with Ezhov as his deputy. In addition, recruitment policy eased but admission rules were tightened – aspirants now required more testimonials from existing members. Finally, congress revealed the existence of a 'special' central committee section headed by Aleksandr Poskrebyshev, Stalin's private secretary.[11]

By 1935 around twenty per cent of party members had lost their cards,[12] but one by-product of the chistka was the discovery that local files were in a mess; about eight per cent of those on the books could not be traced or had quit. Consequently, in May 1935 the party control commission ordered local secretaries to conduct a proverka ('verification' of party documents) under Ezhov's supervision. Matters did not go well: although four-fifths of members had been examined and just over nine per cent expelled, reported Ezhov in December, the regions put up strong resistance. In some districts verifications had to be repeated two or three times and the process had taken six instead of the anticipated two or three months. Moscow then sanctioned an obmen ('exchange of party documents') for spring 1936: dog-eared cards were to be replaced and borderline proverka cases reviewed, but once again secretaries defied Moscow – blocking proverka appeals and expelling rank-and-file Bolsheviks as they pleased.[13]

The Kirov Affair

Unlike the 1933–5 chistka (probably aimed at those who resisted policies which lead to famine),[14] the proverka and the obmen affected mainly the lower apparatchiki; Bolshevik administrators and managers. But while Stalin berated his opponents and Ezhov struggled to discipline the provinces, dramatic events unfolded in Leningrad.

---

[11] Congress also announced the existence of a whole series of 'special sections' in the party, stretching downs to the localities. Reputedly in close contact with the secret police, Poskrebyshev (1891–1966) was elected to the central committee in 1939.

[12] In addition more apparatchiki were sacked. Between 1930 and 1934 the central control commission examined 611 senior Bolsheviks charged with 'counter-revolutionary activities' and expelled three-quarters of them. Between 1931 and 1933 various purge commissions in the thirteen largest regional organizations (encompassing sixty-five per cent of all members) dealt with 40,000 cases of 'political deviation' and expelled 15,414 members. Pavel Postyshev removed 4,000 'nationalists' from the Ukraine's apparatus. Belarus was also hard hit. See T. Szamuely, 'The elimination of opposition between the sixteenth and seventeenth congresses of the CPSU', *Soviet Studies* (3, 1966). Postyshev was born of working-class parents in 1888, joined the party in 1904, took part in the Revolution and fought in the Civil War.

[13] In some districts the obmen continued until November. Proverka appeals dragged on fitfully for the rest of the decade.

[14] Getty, however, contends that the chistka was directed at rank-and-file 'passives' and 'apolitical' Bolsheviks. See p. 132.

These increased tension and soon pushed purging in a new and lethal direction.[15]

At four o'clock in the afternoon of 1 December 1934, the young communist Leonid Nikolaev walked into the Smol'nyi building, the local party headquarters, and shot Kirov in the back. The following day a special decree on terrorist offences gave the recently reorganized NKVD wide-ranging powers of trial and execution.[16] Within a few weeks thirteen members of a supposed 'Leningrad centre' (including Nikolaev) and at least ninety-eight others scattered across the country had been shot for preparing 'terrorist acts against officials of the Soviet régime'. When the central committee circulated a letter instructing local organizations to hunt down 'Trotskyists' and 'Zinovievites' thousands more were arrested – including, of course, Kamenev and Zinoviev. 'I am guilty of nothing, nothing, nothing before the party, before the central committee and before you personally,' pleaded Zinoviev to Stalin,

> I swear to you by everything that is sacred to a Bolshevik. I swear to you on Lenin's memory. I cannot even imagine what could have aroused suspicion against me. I beg you to believe my word of honour. I am shaken to the depths of my soul.[17]

These entreaties were to no avail. In January 1935 Kamenev, Zinoviev and seventeen other adherents of an alleged 'Moscow centre' were tried in camera on charges of 'moral and political responsibility' for Kirov's assassination. Like the others Kamenev accepted 'moral responsibility' but declined to offer a full confession – 'I must be blind,' he remarked laconically, 'I have reached the age of fifty but have never seen this "centre" of which it appears I have been a member'. Although Andrei Vyshinskii,[18] the prosecuting attorney, produced no direct evidence of guilt all were convicted. 'Spontaneous' meetings in factories and offices demanded the 'supreme penalty' (shooting), but the delinquents escaped with long prison terms – five years for Kamenev, ten for Zinoviev and between five and ten for the rest. A few days later twelve high-ranking Leningrad NKVD operatives were tried and imprisoned. Mass

---

[15] Prior to his stewardship of the proverka Ezhov helped organize the 1933–5 chistka. Party membership fell by about 300,000 in 1935 and 200,000 in 1936.

[16] The NKVD absorbed the OGPU in July 1934 and soon mushroomed into a vast bureaucratic empire, controlling the Gulag, border and internal troops, the civil police, intelligence and security, registry offices, fire and forest guards, hydrotechnical and railway construction, roads, archives and population transfers.

[17] Cited Volkogonov, *Stalin*, p. 277.

[18] Vyshinskii (1883–1954) joined the RSDRP in 1902 and supported the Mensheviks. He became a Bolshevik in 1920, a law professor soon afterwards and public prosecutor in 1935.

arrests of the city's 'bourgeois elements' quickly followed.[19] In March, Moscow ordered Soviet libraries to remove all books by Kamenev, Trotsky and Zinoviev (Lunacharskii, Preobrazhenskii and Shliapnikov were added to the list later on), and in the summer the Society of Old Bolsheviks and the Society of Former Political Prisoners were disbanded.[20] In a move which doubtless aided Vyshinskii in later trials an *ad hoc* committee comprising Georgii Malenkov, Matvei Shkiriatov and Ezhov (the party control commission's chief since February) seized their archives.[21] Simultaneously plans were afoot to reorganize the Komsomol with a view to removing more 'enemies'.

The Stalin constitution

Despite these threatening developments the Kirov Affair seemed to have fizzled out by the middle of 1935: only one central committee member fell from grace; Avel' Enukidze, expelled in June for 'personal and political dissoluteness' on the basis of evidence supplied by Lavrentii Beriia,[22] a fellow Georgian working in Transcaucasia. Other harbingers of moderation soon followed. In February 1935, in the midst of the 'three good years',[23] Molotov announced a major constitutional review directed towards the 'further democratization of the electoral system': de-kulakization, collectivization, industrialization and nationalization of the means of production required new arrangements which would reflect society's advance to socialism.

Proposals drawn up by Stalin, Radek and Bukharin (the latter did most of the work) were published in June 1936 and submitted to popular debate. Six months later an extraordinary Soviet congress ratified the 'Stalin constitution'. Equality between races and sexes, the right to work, leisure, welfare benefits, education, housing, priva-

---

[19] These included former tsarist aristocrats, officials and industrialists. Estimates of the number rounded up range from 1,000 to 40,000.

[20] The Society of Old Bolsheviks, founded in 1921, had been allowed some latitude in criticising the party line. Founded in 1918, the Society of Former Political Prisoners included amongst its members other socialists active before the Revolution as well as veteran Bolsheviks.

[21] Malenkov (1902–1988) joined the party in 1920 and became a central committee secretary in 1939. Shkiriatov (1883–1954) joined the party in 1906. After 1917 he worked in the central party apparatus. Like Malenkov, he was elected to the central committee in 1939.

[22] Enukidze (1877–1937) was active in the Transcaucasian underground before 1917. The reasons for his disgrace are unclear. Some historians believe that he annoyed Stalin by publishing a memoir which downgraded the latter's rôle in the local revolutionary movement, others that he was a victim of Beriia's ambition or that he fell foul of the 1933–5 chistka's drive against graft. Beriia (1899–1953) joined the party in 1919. During the 1920s he worked in the Transcaucasian OGPU and became first secretary of the region's party committee in 1934.

[23] See p. 83.

cy and limited personal property were all enshrined in the document. Freedom of speech, publication and assembly, and of religious belief and anti-religious propaganda, were also guaranteed. Finally, since, according to Stalin, socialist construction had all but removed class antagonisms characteristic of the NEP – leaving only proletarians, peasants and the Soviet intelligentsia working together in harmony – direct elections to soviets at all levels and the re-enfranchisement of priests and former Whites had at last become feasible. But because Bolshevism represented all interests other parties remained illegal and the right to nominate candidates for election to soviets belonged to 'public organizations and societies of the working people' – i.e. the party, defined as the 'leading core' of all proletarian bodies.

The first show trials

Political calm did not last for long, however. As Bukharin laboured over the constitution, allegations that Zinoviev and Kamenev had actually organized Kirov's murder surfaced in a secret central committee circular – 'On the Terrorist Activities of the Trotskyite–Zinovievite Counter-Revolutionary Bloc' – dated 29 July 1936 and probably written by Ezhov. 'Now when it has been proved', ran the conclusion,

> that the Trotskyite–Zinovievite monsters unite in the struggle against the Soviet state all the most hostile and accursed enemies of the toilers of our country – the spies, provocateurs, diversionists, White Guardists, kulaks, etc... the inalienable quality of every Bolshevik under present conditions should be the ability to recognize an enemy of the party, no matter how well he may be masked.[24]

The first great 'show trial' opened a month later in Moscow's October Hall, the trade union building and the venue for all subsequent trials of Lenin's old associates. Sixteen defendants, including Kamenev, Zinoviev and the Smirnov and Syrtsov 'groups', expelled from the central committee a few years previously, were also accused of plotting to kill Stalin, Kaganovich, Kosior, Ordzhonikidze, Postyshev, Voroshilov and Zhdanov, and of forming an 'opposition bloc' with Trotsky in 1932. Fourteen confessed. 'Yes, I often told untruths', admitted Zinoviev to Vyshinskii,

> I started doing that from the moment I began fighting the Bolshevik party. In so far as Smirnov took the road of fighting the party, he too is telling untruths. But it seems, the difference

---

[24] Cited M. Fainsod, *Smolensk Under Soviet Rule* (Macmillan, London, 1958) p. 233.

between him and myself is that I have decided firmly and irrevocably to tell at this last moment the truth, whereas he, it seems, has adopted a different decision.[25]

All were shot on 24 August. According to police gossip Zinoviev became hysterical when the executioner arrived: the officer panicked and killed him in a nearby cell. Kamenev's body was repeatedly kicked by the NKVD lieutenant who delivered the *coup de grâce*. Forty-three other high-ranking Bolsheviks disappeared without trial.

Confessions extracted from Kamenev and Zinoviev by NKVD interrogators implied that Bukharin, Rykov and Tomskii had sympathized with their actions. On 22 August these three, along with Piatakov, Radek and Uglanov, fell under suspicion. Tomskii immediately committed suicide; Radek was arrested a month later. The NKVD then abandoned the matter, but on 25 September Stalin and Zhdanov (Kirov's successor in Leningrad) telegraphed the Politburo from their holiday retreat in the Caucasus criticizing Genrikh Iagoda,[26] the NKVD's commissar, for laxity:

> We consider it absolutely necessary and urgent that Comrade Ezhov be appointed to the post of People's Commissar for Internal Affairs. Iagoda has clearly shown himself incapable of exposing the Trotskyite–Zinovievite bloc. The OGPU is lagging four years behind schedule for this task. This has been noted by all the party workers and by the majority of representatives of the NKVD.[27]

The following day Ezhov replaced Iagoda as NKVD chief. The cryptic phrase 'four years behind' was probably a reference to early 1930s factions and platforms opposed to Stalin – especially Riutin's.[28]

A second show trial – this time of the 'Anti-Soviet Trotskyist Centre' – followed in January 1937. Various counts of terrorism, sabotage, wrecking, opposition to industrialization and collectivization, plotting the assassination of party leaders, espionage and treasonable contacts with Trotsky, Japan and Germany were levelled against the principle defendants: Piatakov (Ordzhonikidze's deputy at the Commissariat for Heavy Industry),[29] Radek, Sokol'nikov, Nikolai

---

[25] Cited R. Conquest, *The Great Terror: A Reassessment* (Hutchinson, London, 1990) p. 96.
[26] Iagoda (b.1891) joined the party in 1907. After the Civil War he worked in the Cheka, GPU and OGPU. He was appointed head of the newly enlarged NKVD in July 1934.
[27] Cited Avtorkhanov, *Stalin*, p. 217. Throughout the 1930s the NKVD's secret police section continued to be called the OGPU in everyday speech.
[28] See p. 109.
[29] Ordzhonikidze became Commissar for Heavy Industry in 1932 when Vesenkha was split into three economic commissariats – heavy industry, light industry and timber.

Muralov and Leonid Serebriakov.[30] After prolonged subjection to the NKVD's 'conveyor' system – deprivation of sleep, beatings and continual questioning – confession once again formed the basis of Vyshinskii's case. Despite his superior's intervention Piatakov was amongst the thirteen sentenced to death: rumour has it that Ordzhonikidze then telephoned Ezhov and called him a 'filthy lick-spittle'. A few days later he had a long and angry talk with Stalin, pleading for an end to the terror. Stalin upbraided him for weakness. The following day Ordzhonikidze died, allegedly of heart failure.[31] Radek escaped the executioner's bullet, only to be murdered by a fellow Gulag inmate in 1938.

The February–March plenum

A week after Ordzhonikidze's death the central committee met. Until recently very little was known about the 1937 'February–March plenum': delegates assembled for eleven instead of the customary three to five days – implying considerable debate – but few speeches were published in full.[32] After Zhdanov demanded more local accountability delegates approved resolutions in favour of secret ballots and the rank-and-file's right to recall, criticize and purge their elected leaders. Stressing the point that the new constitution 'meant much greater glasnost" he drew the moral for the party: 'repressive organs are as much needed today as they were in the Civil War', he declared, but on the other hand 'practice must become consistently democratic, enabling all party organs to be electoral'. Molotov claimed that widespread wrecking threatened industrial advance and encouraged workers to extend criticism beyond the party. Stalin also took up the theme of wrecking, blaming provincial satraps for lack of vigilance: pressures from above and below were essential to curb these evils, and to check the spread of local patronage networks. Moreover, cadres should get out of economic management and offer guidance to soviets, kolkhozy and commissariats instead.

These speeches reflected current preoccupations – chistki, economic management, the constitution – but the plenum did more than

---

[30] Muralov (1877–1937), previously close to Trotsky, was one of the chief organizers of the 1917 Moscow uprising and a high-ranking Red Army commander during the 1920s. Serebriakov (1890–1937) joined the party in 1905 and became a central committee secretary in 1919. He was expelled from the secretariat in 1927 for Trotskyism.

[31] In his 'secret speech' to the 1956 twentieth party congress Khrushchev asserted that Ordzhonikidze committed suicide. Conquest also believes that he chose or was forced to kill himself. See Conquest *Terror: Reassessment*, pp. 167–73; N. S. Khrushchev, *Khrushchev Remembers* (trans. S. Talbott, Book Club, London, 1971) pp. 83–5.

[32] According to Khrushchev it was here that 'many members actually questioned the rightness of the established course regarding mass repressions under the pretext of combating "double-dealing"'. Details of the plenum are now being published in Russia. See *Voprosy istorii* (2–9, 1992).

consider 'organizational matters': Stalin's main report ('On the Inadequacies of Party Work and Measures for Liquidating the Trotskyite and other Double-Dealers') repeated the claim that Trotskyism menaced socialism, asserted that spies roamed the country and reiterated the doctrine of 'sharpening class struggle' – an ideological justification for mass purging:

> The further we move forward, the more success we have, the more embittered will the remnants of the destroyed exploiter classes become, the sooner they will resort to extreme forms of struggle, the more they will blacken the Soviet state, the more they will seize on the most desperate means...[33]

In the same vein, Molotov's long harangue against wreckers painted a lurid picture of spies and saboteurs at large in the State Bank and the commissariats of light and heavy industry, food production, forestry, agriculture and communications. Ezhov, now styled 'General Commissar for State Security',[34] drew the necessary conclusions. After repeating Stalin's assertion that the NKVD was 'four years behind' (maybe it was then that Iagoda turned on his tormentors and snarled that he could have arrested the lot of them six months earlier) he accused Bukharin of concealing knowledge of Trotsky's treasonable activities. Bukharin struggled hopelessly against the encroaching darkness:[35] 'I'm not Zinoviev or Kamenev and I won't lie about myself!' he shouted. 'If you won't confess', barked Mikoian, 'you're just proving that you're a fascist hireling'.[36] A special sub-committee decided that both he and Rykov were traitors. They were expelled from the party on the spot and dragged to the Lubianka, the central NKVD prison just off Red Square.

On 13 March, nine days after the plenum dispersed, *Pravda* denounced Bukharin, Rykov and Tomskii (posthumously) for criminal links with Trotskyists. Five days later Ezhov stated that Iagoda had been a tsarist police informer.

---

[33] Cited Volkogonov, *Stalin*, p. 284. The doctrine of sharpening class struggle (the closer the approach to socialism, the more intense the struggle), appears to have been forming in Stalin's mind since the late 1920s. At the 1934 party congress he announced that a 'classless, socialist society' was within sight but that the goal could be reached only 'by means of strengthening the organs of the dictatorship of the proletariat, by means of expanding the class struggle'.

[34] The new post was created specially for Ezhov. *Pravda* announced the appointment on 28 January.

[35] At first Bukharin went on hunger strike, but he abjectly cancelled his move during the plenum.

[36] For these outbursts see Conquest, *Terror: Reassessment*, p. 176; Volkogonov, *Stalin*, p. 286.

The Great Purge Trial

The third and last great show trial took place almost exactly a year later, early in March 1938. Bukharin, Iagoda, Rykov and the veteran Bolsheviks Krestinskii and Khristian Rakovskii appeared in the dock alongside fifteen others.[37] As in previous trials the charges were nothing if not comprehensive: wrecking; undermining the Red Army; plotting the USSR's dismemberment, the overthrow of socialism and the restoration of capitalism; conspiracy with Rightists, Trotskyists, Zinovievites, Mensheviks, Socialist Revolutionaries and bourgeois nationalists; espionage on behalf of Japan, Britain, Poland and Germany; the assassination of Kirov, Kuibyshev and Viacheslav Menzhinskii,[38] and the murder of Maxim Gorky and his son.[39] Bukharin was also accused of attempting to seize power in 1918 and plotting to kill Lenin and Stalin; Iagoda of endeavouring to poison Ezhov.

Bukharin pleaded not guilty to the counts of espionage and assassination. Krestinskii pleaded not guilty to all charges on the trial's first day but changed his mind on the second – no doubt after a night with his NKVD interrogators. All the others confessed in full. After venting his spleen in his closing diatribe (Bukharin – 'the acme of monstrous hypocrisy, perfidy, jesuitry and inhuman villainy'; Iagoda – 'surrounded, as with flies, with German, Japanese and Polish spies'; Rykov – 'a semi-Trotskyite... turned deserter') Vyshinskii pointed towards the broad, sunlit uplands:

> Time will pass. The graves of the hateful traitors will grow over with weeds and thistle... But over us, over our happy country, our sun will shine with its luminous rays as bright and joyous as before. Over the road cleared of the last scum and filth of the past, we, our people, with our beloved leader and teacher, the great Stalin, at our head, will march as before onwards and onwards, towards Communism![40]

[37] Rakovskii (b.1873) joined the party in 1917 and was expelled ten years later for Trotskyism. Before then he was the Ukraine's prime minister and Soviet ambassador to France.

[38] Menzhinskii (1874–1934) was educated in St Petersburg where he was well known in literary circles. He joined the party in 1902. In 1926 he became head of the OGPU, a post which he held until his death.

[39] Gorky, real name Aleksei Peshkov, was born in 1868 and spent his youth wandering across Russia. He published a series of popular stories, took part in the 1905 Revolution, befriended Lenin and helped the Bolsheviks financially. After living in America and Europe he returned to Russia in 1917, emigrated twice and returned for good in 1936. He died on 18 June 1936; poisoned, perhaps, on Stalin's orders. According to Gorky's widow their son died of natural causes.

[40] R. C. Tucker & S. F. Cohen, eds., *The Great Purge Trial* (Grosset & Dunlap, New York, 1965) p. 586. This is a translation of the verbatim report of the trial.

A few hours after the court returned guilty verdicts all were shot except Rakovskii and two others.[41] According to one contemporary 'Bukharin and Rykov died with curses against Stalin on their lips. And they died standing up – not grovelling on the cellar floor and weeping for mercy like Zinoviev and Kamenev'.[42]

The Ezhovshchina

The climax of the storm of accusations, expulsions, trials, convictions, incarcerations and executions – known to Russians as the 'Ezhovshchina' – has no clear chronological boundaries. Some historians view the July 1936 letter ('On the Terrorist Activities of the Trotskyite–Zinovievite Counter-Revolutionary Bloc') as the beginning of the process; others point to the second Kamenev–Zinoviev trial, the Stalin–Zhdanov telegram urging Ezhov's promotion or the 1937 February–March plenum as the real turning point. Most agree, however, that the Ezhovshchina peaked in the second half of 1937 and faded away late in 1938.

Although the practice of staging show trials ceased after Bukharin's demise many other luminaries vanished in 1937–8. Rudzutak was under arrest by May 1937. Bauman, head of the central committee's scientific department since his disgrace in 1930,[43] fell with many of his staff in October. Enukidze and seven others confessed to bourgeois nationalism, espionage and terrorism in December. All were shot. With the exception of Zhdanov Leningrad's entire central committee disappeared in the twelve months after May 1937. In 1937–8 all members of the Ukraine's Politburo, Secretariat and Orgburo were arrested, along with virtually all commissars and provincial secretaries.[44] Similar offensives against 'nationalists' swept most other republics: five of Armenia's highest ranking party officials disappeared, six vanished in Turkestan, seven in Georgia, ten in Uzbekistan, eleven in Azerbaidzhan, twelve in the RSFSR, thirteen in Kirgizia, fifteen in Tadzhikistan, nineteen in Belarus and twenty-three in Kazakhstan.

The Great Purge also engulfed the military. Several officers associated with Iona Iakir, commander of the Kiev military district, were implicated in Kamenev's and Zinoviev's second trial. Vitovt Putna

[41] Rakovskii was sentenced to twenty years, the other two to twenty-five and fifteen years. All three were shot in 1941.
[42] V. Kravchenko, *I Chose Freedom: The Personal and Political Life of a Soviet Official* (Robert Hale, London, 1947) p. 283. Kravchenko got this story (third or fourth hand) from a friend who knew some of Ezhov's associates.
[43] See pp. 44–5.
[44] Postyshev, charged with 'violations of party democracy', was relieved of his responsibilities in 1937 and arrested early in 1938. After a short period of 'direct rule' from Moscow Khrushchev took over as the Ukraine's first party secretary.

(previously military attaché in London) and Vitali Primakov (deputy commander of Leningrad's military district) were in prison by October 1936. Both were named in the 1937 'Anti-Soviet Trotskyist Centre' proceedings. Muralov, a co-defendant at the trial, had been arrested in April 1936. In May 1937, Marshal Nikolai Tukhachevskii and Ian Gamarnik (head of the army's political administration) lost their posts of Deputy Commissars for Defence.[45] Tukhachevskii was simultaneously dismissed as Chief of General Staff. Avgust Kork, director of the crack Frunze Military Academy, and Al'bert Lapin, the Far Eastern Army's Chief of Staff, were arrested the same month. The following month charges of 'Trotskyism', breaches of 'military duty and oath of allegiance', treason to the Red Army and 'the peoples of the USSR' were laid against Tukhachevskii, Iakir, Ieronim Uborevich (commander of the Belarusian military district), Robert Eideman (head of civil defence), Kork, Putna, Boris Fel'dman (the army's chief of administration) and Primakov.[46] All were dead by mid-June. Gamarnik, similarly arraigned, avoided execution by committing suicide. By December 1938 three of the Soviet Union's five marshals had gone, virtually all commanders, eight or ten of the most senior naval officers, about two-thirds of the corps commanders, some sixty per cent of the 200 or so divisional commanders and about half the 400 brigade commanders. Air force personnel, cadres in mechanized units and military intelligence suffered disproportionately, as did political commissars and Spanish Civil War veterans.

But the Ezhovshchina spread far beyond the officer corps and the party élite. An avalanche of monstrous charges, nightmarish allegations, incredible scenarios and random arrests overwhelmed swaths of the population while terrified, vindictive or simple-minded apparatchiki flung denunciations at all and sundry. 'The task of our organization', wrote one Smolensk party official,

is in every way to develop and increase Bolshevik vigilance, decisively and daringly to expose and unmask people who have had some connection with Trotskyism in the past. It is not important whether the connection is direct or indirect.[47]

[45] Tukhachevskii, born in 1893 into the minor nobility, was an NCO in the tsar's army. He joined the party in 1918 and distinguished himself in the Civil War. Far more cultured than most other officers (he was a talented amateur violinist and instrument maker) he was also one of the Red Army's most brilliant and innovative commanders, rising to the rank of Marshal at the age of only forty-two. He took little care to disguise his contempt for Stalin.
[46] Later reports claimed that on Trotsky's instructions they planned to assassinate government and party leaders. For full details see Conquest, *Terror: Reassessment*, ch. 7; J. Erickson, *The Soviet High Command: A Military–Political History 1918–1941* (Macmillan, London, 1962) part 5.
[47] Cited Fainsod, *Smolensk*, p. 235.

The Belarusian Academy of Sciences turned out to be a 'centre for the espionage work of enemies of the people'. Japanese intelligence, claimed the NKVD, recruited Ukrainian Byzantinists via contacts with other historians lecturing in the Soviet Far East. Excoriated as 'a serpent's nest of traitors' scheming 'to diminish the population of the Soviet Union', all the statisticians on the staff of the 1937 census board were shot. Boris Numerov, a distinguished scientist working at Leningrad's world-famous Pul'kovo Observatory, supposedly organized a 'counter-revolutionary astronomers' group' which engaged in wrecking, espionage and terror. The unfortunate compiler of a Russian–Upper Mari dictionary was denounced as a 'bourgeois nationalist' for omitting the words 'de-kulakization', 'opportunism' and 'kolkhoznik' from the book's final draft, a 'counter-revolutionary' for failing to include entries on Lenin, Marx, Molotov, Stalin and Voroshilov, and an 'enemy' for inserting a few revolutionary terms 'in order to mask his wrecking activities'.

Spouses, sons, daughters, cousins, in-laws, friends and acquaintances – almost anyone connected with the accused – were arrested, charged, put through the 'meat grinder' (the conveyor system) and convicted. Frantic to meet their quotas lest they themselves be 'unmasked' as wreckers, NKVD operatives pounced on the innocent and elaborated an ever expanding network of 'Trotskyite centres', 'Japanese hirelings', 'White Guardists' and 'fascist spies'. Apparatchiki, doctors, dentists, lecturers, music teachers, writers, film directors and theatre managers – anyone with any kind of filing system or tally of names who could provide lists of 'accomplices' – were particularly at risk. Hundreds of thousands, perhaps millions, died in the Gulag or ended their days with a bullet in the back of the head, their bodies flung into hastily dug mass graves.

The eighteenth party congress

Stalin intimated that matters were out of control by criticizing the persecution of industrial cadres in October 1937. The tide began to turn when the January 1938 central committee plenum launched a new recruitment drive, condemned the 'heartless and bureaucratic attitude' of 'careerists' responsible for false accusations and 'criminal' expulsions, and praised NKVD officers who reversed unjust decisions. Ezhov became Commissar for Water Transport just before Bukharin's trial (a clear warning – Iagoda became Commissar for Communications immediately after his removal from the NKVD) and lost control of the secret police in December.[48] Beriia took over as General Commissar for State Security.

[48] Rumours concerning Ezhov's fate swept Moscow – that he had gone mad and was incarcerated in a lunatic asylum or that he had been handed over to a mob somewhere and strung up in the streets with a placard round his neck reading 'I am shit'. In fact he was shot in 1939.

When the eighteenth party congress met in March 1939 Stalin, after reporting that the 1933–5 chistka, the proverka and the obmen had liquidated spies, wreckers, assassins and followers of Bukharin, Trotsky, and Zinoviev, etc., reviewed the gains and the losses:

> It cannot be said that the cleansings were not accompanied by grave mistakes. There were, unfortunately, more mistakes than might have been expected. Undoubtedly, we shall have no further need to resort to the method of mass cleansings. Nevertheless, the cleansings of 1933–1936 were unavoidable and their results, on the whole, were beneficial.[49]

Zhdanov went further, claiming that in future expulsions 'must be reduced to a minimum', that mass purging contradicted party statutes, and that chistki, the proverka and the obmen had allowed scope for persecution 'under the flag of "vigilance"'. But no one condemned the Ezhovshchina. And no one mentioned the fate of non-communists swept into the whirlwind. Indeed, according to Zhdanov 'by far the most important work' of hunting down 'enemies' occurred after 1936.

The spring of liberalism

The January 1938 plenum and the deliberations of the eighteenth party congress signalled the end of Ezhov's 'Great Purge'. By early 1939 random arrest and torture had virtually stopped. Several thousand camp inmates were released and many more rehabilitated (given back their party cards or, if rehabilitated posthumously, the documents were returned to the next of kin). In the provinces wholesale shootings ceased; those awaiting execution suddenly found their cases under review and a few thousand bemused convicts were whisked from the Gulag to special acquittal hearings.

But Beriia's 'spring of liberalism' (the disavowal of mass arrests) and Zhdanov's attempt to limit purging did not mean the end of arbitrariness. Several high-ranking army officers and central committee members were shot after 1938, often without even the flimsy formalities of trial and confession. And when some local party organizations expressed unease over continuing NKVD lawlessness, Moscow dispatched a secret telegram to clarify matters:

> the use of physical force by the NKVD as from 1937 on was authorized by the central committee. The central committee considers that methods of physical coercion must continue to be applied in exceptional cases to well-known and inveterate enemies of the people.[50]

[49] Cited Getty, *Origins*, p. 191.
[50] Cited Avtorkhanov, *Stalin*, p. 228. The telegram was dated 20 January 1939.

Most of these 'inveterates' seem to have been Ezhov's creatures. Beriia shot NKVD operatives for 'violations of socialist legality' and re-staffed the commissariat with his own henchmen. Only on the eve of the Russo-German war were the police once more unleashed against ordinary citizens on a massive scale.[51]

Interpretations

The Soviet view

Because in Stalin's time Soviet scholars were obliged to describe all aspects of policy as inevitable, correct and beneficial, historians asserted that the purges cleared the country of spies, traitors, wreckers and saboteurs, while the show trials exposed the heinous crimes of sworn enemies lurking within the party.[52] Little changed until the twentieth party congress in 1956. 'Oppositionists' (Bukharin, Kamenev, Rykov, Trotsky, Zinoviev and their allies) remained 'enemies', but Khrushchev pilloried Stalin for ignoring 'Leninist norms' – maliciously branding central committee members deviationists and illegally repressing numerous honest communists and Soviet apparatchiki.[53] Brezhnev's appointment as General Secretary in 1964 signalled the end of the 'thaw'. Anxious to defend socialism's achievements, some in the Politburo wished to stop de-stalinization. Others were determined to continue – or at least uphold – Khrushchev's work. In the end the whole issue was so contentious that the leadership shelved all debate. Only with Gorbachev's appointment in 1985 did the problem of Stalinism resurface, but this time criticism was not limited to outraged disavowals of repression inside the party-state apparatus, nor was it confined to the intelligentsia. As glasnost' took hold, thousands of letters, commentaries and memoirs flooded the press. Encouraged by central committee radicals, historians, novelists, journalists and film-makers portrayed the 1930s in the most horrific terms. Many followed the 'totalitarian' line, holding Stalin or the party directly responsible for all the misfortunes which befell the Soviet people, including the purges.[54]

[51] See pp. 159–60.
[52] For the classic Stalinist interpretation see the central committee's *History of the Communist Party of the Soviet Union (bolsheviks): Short Course* (Moscow, 1939).
[53] See T. H. Rigby, ed., *The Stalin Dictatorship: Khrushchev's 'Secret' Speech' and other Documents* (Sydney University Press, 1968). Khrushchev launched an even more scathing attack on Stalin at the twenty-second party congress in 1961. That year Stalin's body was removed from the Lenin Mausoleum.
[54] See R. W. Davies, *Soviet History in the Gorbachev Revolution* (Macmillan, London, 1989); W. Laqueur, *Stalin: The Glasnost Revelations* (Unwin Hyman, London, 1990). In 1989, for example, *Moscow News* reported that R. Conquest's *The Great Terror: Stalin's Purges of the Thirties* (Macmillan, London, 1968) had 'come by unofficial channels to the Soviet Union, and quickly circulated amongst the intelligentsia, and was valued by them as one of the most significant of foreign researches into Soviet history'. The book was serialized by the Leningrad journal *Neva* in 1989-90.

Totalitarianism

The publication of Solzhenitsyn's three-volume *Gulag Archipelago* in the 1970s lent powerful support to the view that the purges were the necessary and logical corollary of Bolshevism.[55] Like virtually all earlier Western and émigré writers, Solzhenitsyn traced a direct causal link between Leninism and the whole paraphernalia of mass repression.[56] In the first place, Lenin's debt to nineteenth-century Russian nihilism prefigured a terroristic polity. Secondly, the organizational innovations of the second RSDRP congress in 1903, when Lenin insisted on a vanguard rôle for social democrats, goading workers towards revolution at the behest of a self-appointed élite, pointed towards brutal despotism. Trotsky's sharp denunciation of his future ally in 1904 was only too prescient:

> Lenin's methods lead to this: the party organization at first substitutes itself for the party as a whole; then the central committee substitutes itself for the organization; and finally a single 'dictator' substitutes himself for the central committee.[57]

Thirdly, the Civil War witnessed the construction of an all-embracing police machine used indiscriminately against opponents, within or outside Bolshevism. Finally, Lenin's notion of democratic centralism, embedded in the party's rule book in 1919, coupled with the ban on factions, pushed through the tenth party congress two years later,[58]

---

[55] A. Solzhenitsyn, *The Gulag Archipelago 1918–1956* (Vols. 1–3, trans. T. P. Whitney & H. T. Willets, Fontana/Collins, London, 1973–8). Volume one deals with origins of the purges and the experience of arrest and interrogation, volume two with camp life, volume three with resistance and the winding down of the Gulag system after Stalin's death.

[56] The number of books on the purges which basically follow the totalitarian line is vast. Of the Western and émigré literature see, for example, H. Arendt, *The Origins of Totalitarianism* (2nd ed., Harcourt Brace, New York, 1966); J. Armstrong, *The Politics of Totalitarianism: The Communist Party of the Soviet Union from 1934 to the Present* (Random House, New York, 1961); Avtorkhanov, *Stalin*; Z. K. Brzezinski, *Ideology and Power in Soviet Politics* (Praeger, New York, 1962); id., *The Permanent Purge: Politics in Soviet Totalitarianism* (Harvard University Press, 1956); H. Carrère d'Encausse, *A History of the Soviet Union 1917–1953. Volume 2. Stalin: Order Through Terror* (trans. V. Ionescu, Longman, London, 1981); A. Dallin & G. W. Breslauer, *Political Terror in Communist Systems* (Stanford University Press, 1970); M. Fainsod, *How Russia is Ruled* (Harvard University Press, 1953); C. J. Friedrich & Z. K. Brzezinski, *Totalitarian Dictatorship and Autocracy* (Harvard University Press, 1956); B. I. Nicolaevsky, *Power and the Soviet Elite: 'The Letter of an Old Bolshevik' and Other Essays* (ed. J. D. Zagoria, Praeger, New York, 1965); A. Orlov, *The Secret History of Stalin's Crimes* (Random House, New York, 1953); Schapiro, *Communist Party*.

[57] Cited I. Deutscher, *The Prophet Armed. Trotsky: 1879–1921* (Oxford University Press, 1954) p. 90.

[58] See pp. 10, 24–5.

gave Stalin the organizational means to impose mass terror. The abrogation of intra-party democracy and the tendency for congress, the central committee and the central control commission to become creatures of the Politburo were all in place long before Stalin's victory over 'left oppositionists' and 'right deviationists'.

Many writers also stress the importance of the tsarist political heritage. The second volume of Tucker's Stalin trilogy, for example, claims that by the nineteenth century Russia was ruled through an autocratic, centralized, bureaucratic system (Tucker draws parallels between Stalin, Ivan the Terrible and Peter the Great) which eased the General Secretary's elaboration of a repressive and despotic régime.[59] Some also believe that Stalin was clinically insane.[60]

By far the most important element of the totalitarian explanation, however, is to be found by reference to the deep structures of Bolshevik ideology. Marxism–Leninism's pretensions to 'scientific' knowledge of history's 'laws' rendered the party infallible, an institution qualitatively different from and superior to all other political manifestations; past, present and future. And since Bolshevism's leaders embodied 'truth' they were not only always right against the constituency they purported to represent – the proletariat – but always right against everyone else, wherever and whoever they might be. Such a conception could brook no contradiction – indeed, in the face of truth loyal opposition was untenable. Moreover, the habit of theoretical extrapolation (a given opinion pointing 'objectively' towards a predetermined rather than to a hypothetical end) abolished the distinction between principled dissent, the betrayal of socialism and counter-revolution. The upshot of all this was that only 'double-dealers', 'traitors' and 'class enemies' questioned the 'general line'.

For Solzhenitsyn and Conquest, the most influential contemporary spokesmen for this school, Stalin really was, in the slogan of the 1930s, 'the Lenin of today', but one far more brutal, unscrupulous and cunning than the dead leader. Driven on by morbid suspicion, lust for power and a monstrous ideology he consciously planned and directed the entire purge process. He sanctioned Kirov's murder to rid himself of Politburo 'moderates' opposed to harsh measures against Syrtsov, Riutin and Smirnov. The 2 December 1934 decree

---

[59] R. C. Tucker, *Stalin in Power: The Revolution from Above 1928–1941* (Norton, New York, 1990).
[60] For speculations on Stalin's mental condition see R. C. Tucker, *Stalin as Revolutionary 1879–1929: A Study in History and Personality* (Chatto & Windus, London, 1974) ch. 12; Conquest, *Great Terror*, ch. 3 (this is the first edition of id., *Terror: Reassessment*). Stories of Stalin's insanity stem from an examination carried out by the famous neuropathologist Vladimir Bekhterev in December 1927. He reportedly told his colleagues that Stalin suffered from paranoia.

on terrorist offences was part of the scheme since it unshackled the
secret police and opened the door to the show trials.[61] The letter of
July 1936 on the Trotskyite–Zinovievite Bloc and the Stalin–
Zhdanov telegram of September marked two further calculated steps
in the dictator's bloody progress. The mysterious reference to the
security forces' four years dilatoriness in unmasking enemies was a
direct reference to the 'Riutin Platform', an unambiguous signal that
opponents who had previously escaped death would now be dealt
with. Thereafter the way ahead was clear: totally dependant on the
paranoid autocrat, droves of brutal subordinates and apparatchiki
made fantastic accusations against all and sundry; only to find themselves taking their turn in the NKVD's prisons, the dock and the exe-
cutioners' cellars.

If the purges grew out of the logic of Bolshevism, runs the argument, the Ezhovshchina grew out of the logic of purging. The
swelling chorus of hysterical denunciation meant that by 1937–8 the
entire population – atomized, terrorized and able to survive only by
conspiring in the general madness – trembled under the NKVD's
heel. State functionaries who showed any scruples, like the security
officers and provincial prosecutors who, according to Conquest,
struggled to carry out their orders with some semblance of legality,
were ruthlessly consigned to oblivion. By a kind of political geometry
the police could even deduce the crime from the victim's social background or present position – 'What was your job?' asked one inter-
rogator in the early 1930s. 'A planner', answered the prisoner. 'Write
me a statement that explains "planning at the factory and how its is
carried out,"' continued the officer, 'after that I'll tell you why
you've been arrested.' Only when the police, party and state
machines had been rendered totally supine, only when the tyrant's
paranoia had been temporarily assuaged, and only when it seemed
that terror threatened to unravel the very fabric of society and the
economy was Stalin minded to call a halt. True to form he then sanctioned another massive 'turnover of cadres'. But though Ezhov and
his vicious satraps fell victim to Beriia and his henchmen, the lineaments of the totalitarian polity remained unchanged.[62]

Marxist variants
Variations on the totalitarian theme have been played by several
Marxist scholars, most famously by Stalin's exiled arch-enemy.

[61] Conquest believes that other early murders were directly related to Kirov's death:
Stalin killed Gorky, for example, because he offered to defend Kamenev and Zinoviev
at their second trial.
[62] For classic totalitarian explanations see Conquest, *Great Terror*, chs. 2–5; id., *Inside
Stalin's Secret Police: NKVD Politics 1936–39* (Macmillan, London, 1985);
Solzhenitsyn, *Gulag 1*, part 1.

Indeed, Trotsky's theories anticipated most Western writings on the subject. According to Trotsky totalitarianism arose in the context of domestic backwardness and the international situation after the Great War; it did not emerge from Marxist–Leninist ideology or the party form. If the bureaucrats – personified by Stalin – owed their ascendancy to the belated European revolution and the Russian pro-letariat's numerical weakness and cultural poverty, material depriva-tion caused the bureaucratic state to metamorphose into a police state. 'The basis of bureaucratic rule', observed Trotsky in 1936,

> is the poverty of society in objects of consumption... When there are enough goods in a store, the purchasers can come whenever they want to. When there are few goods, the pur-chasers are compelled to stand in line. When the lines are very long, it is necessary to appoint a policeman to keep order. Such is the starting point of the power of the Soviet bureaucracy.[63]

Just as Thermidorian reaction accounted for the General Secretary's rise so police hegemony presaged 'Bonapartism'. Initially Trotsky thought that a Red Army general would seize power and roll back the Revolution. By 1935, however, he had come to identify Stalin with Napoleon, but a Stalin constrained by a 'degenerated' workers' state, one where collectivization and nationalization (necessary but not sufficient conditions for socialism) still obtained. And just as police rule gave birth to despotism, so despotism, locked in the matrix of nationalization, spawned totalitarianism. Operating through the command–administrative system and the NKVD Stalin was forced to expand his own power in order to control the régime:

> '*L'État, c'est moi*' is almost a liberal formula by comparison with... Stalin's totalitarian régime. Louis XIV identified himself only with the State. The Popes of Rome identified themselves with both the State and the Church... The totalitarian state goes far beyond Caesaro-Papism, for it has encompassed the entire economy of the country as well. Stalin can justly say, unlike the Sun King, '*La Société, c'est moi*'.[64]

But because material scarcity remained, and since neither the

---

[63] Cited B. Knei-Paz, *The Social and Political Thought of Leon Trotsky* (Oxford University Press, 1978) p. 382. For Thermidor and Trotsky's explanation of Stalin's rise to power see pp. 30–1.

[64] L. Trotsky, *Stalin: An Appraisal of the Man and his Influence* (trans. C. Malamuth, Hollis & Carter, London, 1947) p. 421. Trotsky's mature analysis of Stalinism can be found in *The Revolution Betrayed: What is the Soviet Union and Where is it Going?* (trans. M. Eastman, Harcourt & Brace, New York, 1937), written in Norway in 1936.

bureaucracy nor the police could solve the country's social and economic problems in an egalitarian fashion, socialism – the USSR's legitimating ideology – stood in opposition to the state form. Scapegoats had to be found to explain the contradiction. 'Forced to hide the reality, to deceive the masses', argued Trotsky, Stalin resorted to a 'frame-up system' (the show trials), and a medieval witch-hunt for 'enemies of the people' caricatured as 'Trotskyists' (real or imaginary adherents of Stalinism's most implacable adversary). Purging and terror, however, did more than act as lightning conductors for mass discontent. By abolishing the distinction between public and private life they disorganized incipient social groupings which might menace Stalin's dictatorship. Moreover, terror included a psychological dimension: since Stalin and the bureaucrats were alienated from society, paranoia and distrust pervaded the government. Stalin feared rivals in the apparatus, the apparatchiki feared Stalin, but each needed the other because both feared the masses. Terror, purging and paranoia thus became permanent and necessary adjuncts of state power in the USSR.

Isaac Deutscher, Trotsky's biographer and a sometime supporter of the Fourth International,[65] followed a similar line. Deutscher agreed that parallels with French history were useful and that Stalin functioned in a milieu of social and economic backwardness. He also characterized terror as 'rational', speculating that the General Secretary launched a pre-emptive strike against Old Bolsheviks, apparatchiki and the high command to counter the threat of a *coup d'état* should war break out. Stalin, contends Deutscher, was probably thinking of 1917: government disunity and the army's political unreliability were major factors in tsarism's collapse. By staffing the party-state with inexperienced cadres and officers completely dependant on himself he may have been attempting to strengthen the régime.[66] Deutscher's interpretation differs from Trotsky's in one important respect, however. Though boundlessly cruel and probably insane, Stalin played a positive historical rôle because he was a great 'modernizer', dragging the USSR into the twentieth century. He 'perpetrated cruelties excusable in earlier centuries but unforgivable in this', but on the other hand

Russia had been belated in her historical development. In England serfdom had disappeared by the end of the fourteenth century. Stalin's parents were still serfs. By the standards of

---

[65] Deutscher, born in Cracow in 1907, was expelled from the Polish communist party in 1932. He emigrated to England in 1939. Though he broke with the Fourth International (Trotsky's rival to the Komintern) in 1938, he remained sympathetic to Trotskyism down to his death in 1967.
[66] I. Deutscher, *Stalin: A Political Biography* (2nd ed., Penguin, 1972) pp. 375–81.

British history, the fourteenth and twentieth centuries have, in a
sense, met... in Stalin. The historian cannot be seriously surprised if he finds in him some traits usually associated with
tyrants of earlier centuries.[67]

Like Trotsky and Deutscher, the Soviet dissident Roy Medvedev
represented Stalinism as distinct from Leninism (ironically,
Medvedev fell foul of the censors for espousing a Marxist–Leninist
interpretation).[68] He also pointed to social and economic factors
inherited from the *ancien régime* which shaped the politics of the
1930s. But Medvedev's analysis is not deterministic. He lays far
greater stress on personality than other Marxist historians: 'what...
were the basic motives of Stalin's crimes?', he asked with reference
to the Ezhovshchina.

The first and most important was Stalin's *measureless ambition*.
This incessant though carefully hidden lust for power appeared
in Stalin much earlier than 1937. Even though he had great
power, it was not enough – he wanted absolute power and
unlimited submission to his will.[69]

Stalin murdered Kirov, not because of some original sin woven into
the body of Bolshevism but because provincial delegates to the 1934
party congress, alarmed by increasing terror and the murderous
chaos of collectivization, begged Kirov to take over as General
Secretary and return the party to Leninist norms. Thereafter, drawing on materials made public by Khrushchev, Medvedev elaborates a
picture of unfettered evil: free of all restraints, a mentally unbal-
anced despot surrounded himself with criminal thugs in the pursuit
of total power. Ezhov, for example, sent Stalin around 400 lists
throughout 1937–8 naming 44,000 party, government, military and
cultural figures whose execution required the General Secretary's
personal approval – the merest tip of the iceberg but conclusive
proof of Stalin's overall responsibility for and active participation in
the terror.

Revisionism
All totalitarian interpretations share in common the conviction that
the General Secretary was central to the political processes of the

[67] Deutscher, *Stalin*, p. 340. For other British based Trotskyist analyses of Stalinism
see R. H. McNeal, 'Trotskyist interpretations of Stalinism', in R. C. Tucker, ed.,
Stalinism: Essays in Historical Interpretation (Norton, New York, 1977).
[68] Medvedev was born in 1925. His father, a distinguished Marxist philosopher, perished in the Ezhovshchina. His *magna opera* are *Let History Judge* and *On Stalin and
Stalinism* (trans E. de Kadt, Oxford University Press, 1979).
[69] Medvedev, *Let History Judge*, pp. 324–5.

1930s. Without his personality – and (whatever its antecedents) personal dictatorship – chistki, the show trials and the Ezhovshchina can be neither understood nor explained. Recently, however, the totalitarian school has come under systematic attack. Western 'revisionist' historians (influenced, perhaps, by quarrels between 'intentionalist' and 'structuralist' scholars working on Nazi Germany) regard Stalin as an insufficient, and in some cases extraneous causal factor.[70] The revisionist case can be considered under five headings: 'Stalin, Kirov and Ezhov', 'social pressures', 'structuralism', 'Ezhov unleashed' and 'the Stalinist polity'.

Stalin, Kirov and Ezhov

Something of a bombshell was dropped when John Arch Getty's *Origins of the Great Purges* appeared in 1985. Though agreeing that the show trials could not have occurred without Stalin's overt consent, Getty is unconvinced that he organized Kirov's murder and sceptical of claims that Kirov headed a moderate grouping at the 1934 party congress; although there were quarrels amongst the élite there was no Kirov–Stalin polarization. As for the 2 December 1934 decree on terrorist offences, this was no more than a panic response to the murder of an important party figure. After a spasm of bloodletting which ensnared a rag-bag of unfortunates in the Leningrad and Moscow 'centre' trials, the decree quickly fell into desuetude.

Getty also takes issue with traditional views of the July 1936 Trotskyite–Zinovievite Bloc letter and the September Stalin–Zhdanov telegram. Citing evidence from Harvard University's Trotsky Archive (the 'exile papers' made available to scholars only in 1980) he claims that in the early 1930s middle-ranking party officials did approach Trotsky with a proposal to form an opposition bloc, that the contacts almost certainly became known to the OGPU, and that a Trotsky–Zinoviev alliance was in the making in 1932.[71] The curious reference in the Stalin–Zhdanov telegram to the police being 'four years behind' in unmasking enemies therefore had some basis in fact. Moreover, Ezhov's elevation had nothing to do with a plot to smash the party. A series of explosions which rocked Siberia's Kemerovo Mine Complex two days before may have caused Stalin to doubt Iagoda's competence: Ezhov's known penchant for ferreting

---

[70] For a brief review of German debate see G. Eley, 'History with the politics left out – again?', *Russian Review* (4, 1986). Eley identifies two approaches to Nazism: 'intentionalists' give pride of place to politics and ideology – especially to Hitler's rôle. For 'structuralists', on the other hand, social, economic and institutional factors were more important in shaping the régime.
[71] See J. Arch Getty, 'Trotsky in exile: the founding of the Fourth International', *Soviet Studies* (1, 1986); P. Broué, 'Trotsky et le bloc des oppositions de 1932', *Cahiers Léon Trotsky* (5, 1980).

out enemies looked a better bet in the face of what might have been sabotage.

Social pressures

In much the same spirit, revisionists are disinclined to characterize Stalin as the demiurge of history when they turn to the purges, focusing their attention instead on the stresses and strains of the moment and the complexities of politics and policy-making. Long ago, the old revolutionary Victor Serge considered that the charges levelled against bourgeois specialists in the late 1920s and early 1930s arose from the régime's hunt for scapegoats to explain away the failures of the Great Breakthrough.[72] Several contemporary historians have followed this neo-Trotskyist line, arguing that the Shakhty Affair – an early, if mild instance of purging – was seized on by Stalin to discredit Bukharin and destroy the technical intelligentsia's *esprit de corps*.[73]

Others descry popular processes at work. Young party radicals saw the first years of collectivization and industrialization as one aspect of a wider 'cultural revolution': as they loudly traduced religion and 'bourgeois' figures so workers, inspired by visions of a new world but bewildered by the appalling realities of daily life, took out their frustrations on the old engineers. Spets-baiting and the hounding of bourgeois elements were thus both an effect and a cause of the general assault on the intelligentsia: if the Shakhty Affair gave proletarians and militants licence to criticize 'the bosses', these voices from below encouraged élites to victimize specialists and party satraps in an attempt to appease plebeian anger.[74] Terror, therefore, had roots in Soviet society, not just in Stalin: as the decade progressed workers and iconoclasts utilized purging to settle old scores or address contemporary grievances.

Structuralism

Unlike totalitarians 'structuralists' – those who concentrate on institutional instead of ideological, personal or social factors – are at pains to disaggregate 'the purges', drawing clear distinctions between

---

[72] V. Serge, *Memoirs of a Revolutionary 1901–1941* (trans. P. Sedgwick, Oxford University Press, 1963) p. 248. The book was first published in 1951.
[73] See K. E. Bailes, *Technology and Society under Lenin and Stalin: Origins of the Soviet Technical Intelligentsia 1917–1941* (Princeton University Press, 1978) p. 71; S. F. Cohen, *Bukharin and the Bolshevik Revolution: A Political Biography 1888–1938* (Wildwood House, London, 1971) pp. 281–3; H. Kuromiya, *Stalin's Industrial Revolution: Politics and Workers 1928–1932* (Cambridge University Press, 1988) ch. 1; N. Lampert, *The Technical Intelligentsia and the Soviet State: A Study of Soviet Managers and Technicians 1928–1935* (Macmillan, London, 1979) pp. 39–41. For the Shakhty Affair see p. 79.
[74] For these matters – 'cultural revolution' and popular responses to early Stalinism – see chapter 6.

show trials, chistki and the Ezhovshchina. Rather than planned, coherent policies they see the latter two as by-products; on the one hand of conflicting élite perceptions of the party's rôle in a period of unparalleled socio-economic turmoil, on the other of tensions between centre and periphery.[75]

To structuralists the 1928–30 chistka was no political witch-hunt. Few lost their cards for 'violations of party discipline'; most were expelled for 'passivity', 'criminal offences' and 'defects in personal conduct'.[76] Thereafter, in the scramble for allies as collectivization and industrialization took off, indiscriminate admissions occurred at local level. Some 1.4 million new members flooded in between 1931 and 1933, grossly inflating the 'passive element' and threatening to reduce the party to an amorphous mass of political troglodytes, Stalinist hangers-on and careerists. The second chistka (1933–5) was therefore very much a re-run of the first, but the centre – a purge commission headed by Rudzutak with the assistance of Ezhov, Kaganovich and Kirov – was now determined to impose its will on a recalcitrant periphery. As it became evident that regional party bosses were only too successful in safeguarding local interests and shielding their 'own people', so for the next three and half years Moscow found itself embroiled in a struggle to discipline the provinces.

Ezhov's proverka and the obmen, therefore, were continuations of earlier 'house-cleaning' policies. The new feature was Moscow's attempt to mobilize rank-and-file communists against enemies – stigmatized as 'Trotskyists' but in reality local party bosses. Stalin followed up his congress of victors attack on insouciant regional élites with the 1935 slogan 'cadres decide everything'. This direct appeal to local activists signalled the opening of another front in the struggle against the entrenched power of provincial barons: an order in the summer of 1936 to speed up proverka appeals and an autumn instruction on unfair expulsions are interpreted as Zhdanov's attempt to prevent local satraps ridding themselves of honest – if politically illiterate – members who asked too many awkward questions. Anti-bureaucrat drives and calls for the democratic 'verification' of officials raged across the country, but there was no consensus on the best way forward: on the one hand Zhdanov wished to re-educate 'defective' cadres; on the other Ezhov and Molotov favoured

---

[75] Most notably Getty, *Origins*; G. T. Rittersporn, *Stalinist Simplifications and Soviet Complications: Social Tensions and Political Conflicts in the USSR 1933–1953* (Harwood, Chur, 1991); id., 'The state against itself: social tensions and political conflict in the USSR 1936–38', *Telos* (41, 1979). For a recent attempt to put the show trials in perspective see M. Reiman, 'Political show trials of the Stalinist era', *Telos* (54, 1982–83).
[76] See Getty, *Origins*, table 2.1 p. 56, table 2.2 p. 47.

mass purging. Stalin equivocated before eventually coming down on Ezhov's side at the February–March plenum.[77]

Ezhov unleashed

For structuralists, the conjunction of Zhdanov's drive for criticism and democracy, attempts by radicals (Molotov and Ezhov) to liquidate saboteurs and wreckers and tensions in Moscow over the obduracy of local organizations combined to produce a unique event. Competing élite perceptions and prescriptions, grass-roots pressures, centre–periphery tensions and political in-fighting over democratization and re-education – out of this mishmash grew the Ezhovshchina.

Previous chistki were limited to Bolsheviks (with occasional sidesweeps at specialists and state employees) and tried to exclude undesirables via the party's own machinery. The 'Great Purge', on the other hand, run by Ezhov's 'militant' NKVD, was generalized throughout society's upper echelons; overwhelming the party, the military, the administration, specialists, managers and the intelligentsia. Finally, though tacitly authorized by Stalin, the Ezhovshchina quickly ballooned out of control: local 'families' and bureaucratic empire builders hijacked the process to remove rivals, protect friends and extend their own powers. The finishing touch was added by spy mania, fostered by the régime as the menace from Germany and Japan grew apace, thus adding an extra dimension to the concept of 'the enemy within'.

The Stalinist polity

Apart from disagreeing with totalitarian theorists over purging, revisionists offer several alternative descriptions of the Stalinist polity. For the sake of convenience these can be classified as 'tyrannical', 'pluralistic' and 'centre–periphery'.

Before and after Stalin, averred Harry Rigby in 1977,[78] the USSR was run by innumerable bureaucracies, a 'mono-organizational' system which reflected the revolutionary intelligentsia's world view, itself a reflection of tsarism (autocracy, the primacy of state over society and the tradition of 'revolution from above'). One-man rule arose in the context of Lenin's death, a factor which ruptured the post-1917 collective or 'oligarchical' style of government. Contenders for power used extreme methods to achieve victory in the intra-party struggle and, no less importantly, to achieve unity. During the 1930s, therefore, terror and one-man rule overlaid the mono-organizational system; a 'Stalinist phase' characterized by the aggressive assertion of

---

[77] Getty takes the plenum to be a serious attempt at party democratization in the spirit of the new constitution. See Getty, *Origins*, chs. 4–6; id., 'Party and purge in Smolensk 1933–38', *Slavic Review* (1, 1983).

[78] T. H. Rigby, 'Stalinism and the mono-organizational society', in Tucker, *Stalinism.*

a single truth, the destruction of over-mighty barons, the atomization of human relations and the use of plebiscites (via the 1936 constitution) as simulacra of democracy. By 1937 a classical tyranny had emerged, a polity which met Aristotle's three requirements: the tyrant's subjects had no will of their own, no trust in each other and no scope for initiative. But Stalin's tyranny differed from those of the classical world: on the one hand, state control of mass communications greatly extended its range; on the other the system was short-lived – as Stalin aged and the problems confronting the régime multiplied the mono-organizational element came once again to the fore.

In contrast, pluralistic accounts stress the importance of conflict at the apex of the party-state machine. Several historians suggest that 'Stalinism' was vague enough to accommodate variant readings of the 'general line' and flexible enough to allow heads of large bureaucracies considerable latitude.[79] Elsewhere Robert McNeal detected 'a half-conscious striving for something like a *rechtsstaat* [law-bound state] in the party' between 1934 and 1939.[80] Cautiously supported by Zhdanov, apparatchiki tried to evade the Ezhovshchina's fury by contrasting 'legality' (the party's statutes) with arbitrariness. Despite Zhdanov's coded appeals to due process (glasnost', the new constitution) Ezhov defeated this 'soft line' at the February–March plenum, but the January 1938 plenum saw attempts to turn the phrase 'enemies of the people' against NKVD militants, and by the following year (the eighteenth party congress) Zhdanov was able to push through new party statutes which outlawed mass purging.

Centre–periphery interpretations shift the focus towards friction between Moscow and the provinces as the key factor in shaping the Stalinist polity.[81] In the regions powerful satraps – usually incompetent Civil War veterans – functioned as the loci of government. Given dire shortages of cadres these 'mini-Stalins' improvised: they ignored the law and elaborated patronage networks ('families') in order to to get things done, and to protect themselves from the Kremlin's impossible demands. Stalin and the Politburo were half

---

[79] See for example, S. Fitzpatrick, 'Ordzhonikidze's takeover of Vesenkha: a case study in Soviet bureaucratic politics', *Soviet Studies* (2, 1985); J. Harris, 'The origins of the conflict between Malenkov and Zhdanov: 1939–41', *Slavic Review* (2, 1976); E. A. Rees, 'The purge on the Soviet railways 1937', *SIPS 34* (Discussion Paper, Centre for Russian & East European Studies, University of Birmingham, 1992). All show how powerful Stalinists responded to policy initiatives in their own way or used them to advance their own interests.

[80] R. H. McNeal, 'The decisions of the CPSU and the Great Purge', *Soviet Studies* (2, 1971).

[81] See Getty, *Origins*; id., *Slavic Review* (1, 1983); G. T. Rittersporn, 'The 1930s and the *longue durée* of Soviet history', *Telos* (53, 1982); id., *Stalinist Simplifications*; id., *Telos* (41, 1979).

aware of the problem but unable to articulate appropriate solutions – popular anger over inefficiency and corruption could not be dealt with by publicly defaming military heroes since this would undermine one of the régime's most potent legitimating myths. Instead, bungling was explained in terms of organizational defects. When chistki failed to solve problems the discourse of 'the enemy within' gained ground: 'subversives' 'masked' themselves as loyalists whilst engaging in 'sabotage'. But the struggle against 'wrecking' compelled local bosses to inflate disorder and arbitrariness – and to extend their patronage networks – thus reproducing factors which prompted the 'discovery' of 'enemies' in the first place. The 'central political event of the 1930s', contends Gábor Rittersporn, was a series of unsuccessful attempts to eliminate malpractice without threatening the party's political monopoly. By 1938, however, the entire system was in chaos. The retreat from mass purging represented the only solution: the apparatus ('real Stalinism') had 'defeated' Stalin.[82]

The victims

If there is no consensus on the origins, significance and processes of purging, disagreements over the numbers affected are, if anything, even more pronounced. Few dispute the devastating effect on the party élite;[83] rather, argument focuses on the global impact. In 1959, Abdurakhman Avtorkhanov believed that Ezhov 'considerably overfulfilled' his 'plan' to liquidate five million people.[84] Nine years later the Soviet dissident Andrei Sakharov asserted that the NKVD rounded up 1.2 million communists during the Ezhovshchina and shot 600,000; the rest died in prison, adding to the ten or fifteen mil-

---

[82] G. T. Rittersporn, 'Soviet politics in the 1930s: rehabilitating society', *Studies in Comparative Communism* (2, 1986); id., 'Staline en 1938: apogee du verbe et defaite politique', *Libre* (6, 1979).
[83] When the eighteenth party congress met in 1939, 1,108 of the 1,966 delegates to the 1934 congress had been arrested. Of the 858 still free a mere fifty-nine attended the new congress – less than two per cent. Only sixteen out of seventy-one members of the old central committee and eight out of sixty-eight candidates remained at liberty. Ninety-eight had been shot. Total party membership fell by 850,000 (thirty-six per cent) between 1934 and 1939, or about 1.5 million between 1929 and 1939. In addition around 3,000 police officers and about ninety per cent of provincial prosecutors may have perished in 1937.
[84] Avtorkhanov, *Stalin*, p. 223. Other early estimates include six million Ezhovshchina arrests and between 3.5 and fifteen million Gulag inmates by 1941. See D. J. Dallin & B. I. Nicolaevsky, *Forced Labour in Soviet Russia* (Yale University Press, 1947) pp. 54, 86; N. Jasny, 'Labor and output in Soviet concentration camps', *Journal of Political Economy* (5, 1951).

lion camp deaths between 1936 and 1939.[85] Conquest projected seven million arrests in 1937–8, one million executions, two million camp deaths and a Gulag population of about 9.5 million by January 1939. Medvedev produced similar 'high' figures for the Iagoda–Ezhov years: one million exiled after Kirov's murder, seventeen to eighteen million 'repressed' by 1937 (of whom at least ten million died) and a further five to seven million Ezhovshchina arrests (including a million or so communists and another million ex-members expelled in the 1928–30 and 1933–5 chistki). Of these most were sent to labour camps but about a million apparatchiki were shot.[86] In March 1992, a Russian Federation security ministry official claimed eighteen million 'repressions' and seven million executions for the ten year period 1935–45, but these figures contradict evidence from KGB archives made public in 1990 – 789,096 shot for 'counter-revolutionary crimes' between 1930 and 1953. Moreover, the KGB's 'low' Gulag head counts are taken seriously by the most recent Western scholarly survey: 1934 – 510,307 in camps; 1935 – 965,742; 1936 – 1,296,494; 1937 – 1,196,369; 1938 – 1,881,570, falling to 1,672,438 in 1939 and 1,659,992 in 1940.[87]

Controversy subsides when researchers turn to the victims' sociopolitical profiles. Chistki, the proverka and the obmen – aimed at 'corrupt', 'passive' and 'bureaucratic' elements – were more or less confined to communists but became entangled with assaults on 'enemies' in the early 1930s and 'spies', 'Trotskyites', 'Zinovievites' and 'fascist hirelings' by the mid-1930s. In contrast, most historians depict the Ezhovshchina as affecting (in the main) town dwellers, the edu-

[85] A. Sakharov, *Progress, Coexistence and Intellectual Freedom* (Andre Deutsch, London, 1968) p. 55. For acrimonious exchanges over Sakharov's figures see S. Rosefielde, 'An assessment of the sources and uses of GULag forced labour 1929-1956', *Soviet Studies* (1, 1981); id., 'Incriminating evidence: excess deaths and forced labour under Stalin: a final reply to critics', *Soviet Studies* (2, 1987); S. G. Wheatcroft, 'On assessing the size of forced concentration camp labour in the Soviet Union 1929–1956', *Soviet Studies* (2, 1981); id., 'Towards a thorough analysis of forced labour statistics', *Soviet Studies* (2, 1983).

[86] R. Conquest, 'Excess deaths and camp numbers: a comment', *Soviet Studies* (5, 1991); id., *Great Terror*, appendix A; R. A. Medvedev, *Moscow News* (27 November 1988).

[87] These figures were published by A. N. Dugin, 'Gulag: Otkryvaia arkhivy', *Na boevom postu* (27 December 1989); id., 'Stalinizm: legendy i fakty', *Slovo* (7, 1990). They are discussed in E. Bacon, 'Glasnost' and the Gulag: new information on Soviet forced labour around World War II', *Soviet Studies* (6, 1992). See also *Radio Free Europe/Radio Liberty Research Report* (18, 1992). Earlier 'low' estimates include Ezhovshchina deaths in the tens or hundreds of thousands and party expulsions at less than 200,000. See J. F. Hough & M. Fainsod, *How the Soviet Union is Governed* (Harvard University Press, 1979) p. 177; G. Kennan, *Soviet Foreign Policy 1917–1941* (Nostrand, Princeton, 1960) p. 89; T. H. Rigby, *Communist Party Membership in the USSR 1917–1967* (Princeton University Press, 1968) pp. 178, 209–12; A. L. Unger, 'Stalin's renewal of the leading stratum: a note on the Great Purge', *Soviet Studies* (3, 1969).

cated and the middle ranks and above of Soviet society. But the Great Purge did not just pulverize the regional nomenklatura, the military, the managerial élite and the intelligentsia: priests were frequently accused of fascist sympathies and complicity in sabotage while the Foreign Affairs commissariat and the Komintern were ferociously purged.[88] Finally, even though the Ezhovshchina engulfed many individual workers and kolkhozniki, only one segment of the proletariat – railway workers – seems to have been a particular target of the NKVD.[89]

Evaluations

Past and present

The purges and politics of the 1930s lie at the heart of scholarly concerns over Stalinism. They have always aroused violent passions. Émigrés, disappointed revolutionaries and innocents whose lives and families were destroyed took up their pens to set the record straight and recount their experiences.[90] Glasnost' and the Soviet Union's collapse loosed a tidal wave of recrimination, but often there is little which is qualitatively new in revelations couched primarily – and understandably – in terms of anger, guilt and outrage. This was national catharsis; a debate on the past overlaid with a strong propensity to blame Stalin, Lenin or the party for a mountain of crimes, and one entangled with vehement altercations over the future. In themselves most disclosures – the discovery of another mass grave, a camp inmate's anguished memoirs, the confessions of a superannuated NKVD operative – may help fill out 'blank spaces' in Russia's history, but they cannot generate new insights. It is not sur-

[88] See T. Uldricks, 'The impact of the great purges on the People's Commissariat of Foreign Affairs', *Slavic Review* (2, 1977).

[89] In August 1937 Kaganovich demanded the arrest of incompetent transport officials because the railways 'wrecked' industrialization by failing to respond to the demands placed on them. This triggered a widespread purge which soon engulfed workers returning from the far east when the USSR sold the Chinese Railway Company to Manchukuo, a Japanese puppet state. They were accused of spying for Tokyo. See Rees, *SIPS 34*. For Manchukuo see pp. 151–2.

[90] See, for example, A. Barmine, *One Who Survived: The Life Story of a Russian Under the Soviets* (Putman, New York, 1945); F. Beck & W. Godin, *Russian Purge and the Extraction of Confession* (trans. E. Mosbacher & D. Porter, Hurst & Blackett, London, 1951); I. Erenburg, *Memoirs: 1921–1941* (trans. T. Shebunina, World, Cleveland, 1964); E. Ginzburg, *Journey Into the Whirlwind* (trans. P. Stevenson & M. Hayward, Harcourt & Brace, New York, 1967); A. V. Gorbatov, *Years off My Life: The Memoirs of a General of the Soviet Army A. V. Gorbatov* (Constable, London, 1964); E. Hoffer, *The True Believer* (Harper, New York, 1951); N. Mandelstam, *Hope Against Hope* (trans. M. Hayward, Harvill Press, London, 1971); id., *Hope Abandoned* (trans. M. Hayward, Harvill Press, London, 1974); Nicolaevsky, *Power & the Soviet Elite*; Orlov, *Secret History*; G. Tokaev, *Betrayal of an Ideal* (Indiana University Press, 1954); A. Weissberg, *The Accused* (Simon & Schuster, New York, 1952).

prising that the most anti-Stalinist texts published in the West decades ago should have been in vogue, nor that participants in the debate (many of whom suffered at the hands of the censor or worse) should vilify their late persecutors. But historians should beware of the tendency to defame the entire Soviet experience: moral outrage is not history and researchers should not appear for the prosecution – or the defence.

Counting terror

The first problem in assessing human costs concerns chronology and terminology. How should 'the purges' and 'the terror' be defined and what are their parameters?[91] The second problem is that casualty estimates are clearly incompatible. Even on the basis of a single chronology (1934–9 – from Kirov's murder to Beriia's spring of liberalism), and assuming terror and purging to be coterminous, readers are faced with variant high and low assessments.[92] It might be objected that this gruesome calculus of human suffering is beside the point – by any reckoning many thousands died or lost their freedom and the lives of millions more were wrecked. But it is incumbent on historians to try to be accurate. Moreover, some attempt should be made to sort out the figures, if only to check the wilder excesses of the pro- and anti-Soviet lobbies.

Matters can at least be clarified by imposing sensible definitions. Chistki, show trials and the Ezhovshchina are best disaggregated. Show trials present no difficulties – in terms of total deaths they are insignificant. Chistki ran from 1928 to 1936 (1928–30, 1933–5, the proverka, the obmen), the Ezhovshchina from the February–March plenum to Ezhov's fall (1937–8). Following this schema party expulsions peaked before the Ezhovshchina (1.5 million in 1929–36, around 200,000 in 1937–8). *Prima facie* the best available primary source (the glasnost' KGB materials) suggests a 'low' Gulag camp population – rising steadily from 1934 to 1938 but staying below two million. Numbers declined in 1939–40. On the other hand not all

---

[91] Some historians date 'the purges' from 1929. Others start from Iagoda's appointment (July 1934), Kirov's murder (December 1934), the first show trial (August 1936), or Ezhov's elevation (September 1936). Some subsume chistki, the proverka and the obmen in 'the terror'. Others subsume 'the terror' in the Ezhovshchina but give differing chronologies (see p. 119). Finally, some consider that 'the terror' covers the entire Iagoda–Ezhov–Beriia period (1934–53), or even the entire Stalin period (c.1929–53).

[92] Arrests – seven million 1937–8 (high), party expulsions at less than 200,000 1937–8 (low); deaths – twenty million plus 1936–9 (high), somewhere in the tens of thousands for the Ezhovshchina (low); Gulag population – fifteen million c.1939 (high), just over half a million in 1934 and nearly 1.7 million by 1939 (low). There is also the problem of 'repression', a term which might mean arrest, incarceration, death, dismissal from one's job or expulsion from the party.

forced labour came under Gulag auspices.[93] Though it is virtually impossible to separate out 'terror' deaths from de-kulakization and famine mortalities, execution rates seem to be closer to 'low' estimates:[94] Wheatcroft and Davies surmise that between 1927 and 1938 excess deaths may have amounted to ten million – 8.5 million in 1927–36 and around one to 1.5 million in 1937–8. Of the ten million, most died in the 1933 famine.[95]

These rough and ready calculations chime with political rhythms; a rising Gulag population after Kirov's murder interrupted by Beriia's spring of liberalism; a rising execution level reducing after 1938 for the same reason. Finally, since the Ezhovshchina impacted mainly on educated urban society and the nomenklatura (intellectuals, middle- and upper-ranking apparatchiki, the officer corps), the climax of terror necessarily looms large in the historian's mind. In contrast to 'repressed' rank-and-file Bolsheviks, Ezhov's victims left strong traces in the historical record; memoirs, published family reminiscences, accounts by émigré acquaintances, etc. Moreover, as one Western specialist notes, these traces have profoundly influenced memory and perception: 'You are interviewing an elderly woman, now in her eighties,' writes Mary McAuley by way of illustration,

> about life at the time of the Great Purge, and you have already established that she lived in a communal apartment, in which ten families shared a kitchen and a bathroom. Should you ask the seemingly straightforward question 'how many people did you know who were arrested in 1937?', the response would probably be one of wide-eyed amazement, 'Haven't you read Solzhenitsyn?' Don't you know that *everyone* was arrested?' If you continue with: 'But were any members of your family arrested?', there may well be a pause... 'Well, no, not in my family, but everybody else was.' Then you ask: 'How many people were arrested in the communal apartment you lived in?' There's a very long pause, followed by 'Well, hm, I don't really remember, but yes, yes there was one, Ivanov, who lived at the room down at the end, yes, now I remember.' From here you might move on to ask about the office she worked in, and gradu-

---

[93] One contemporary Russian based group argues that the 1990 KGB figures list only Gulag inmates and exclude those flung into other camps run by various economic commissariats – timber, heavy industry, etc. For this debate see Bacon, *Soviet Studies* (6, 1992); A. Nove, 'How many victims in the 1930s?' *Soviet Studies* (2, 1990) id., 'How many victims in the 1930s–II?', *Soviet Studies* (4, 1990); *Radio Free Europe/Radio Liberty Research Report* (18, 1992); *Report on the USSR* (32, 1990; 36, 1990).
[94] See pp. 60–1, 92–3.
[95] R. W. Davies, et al., *The Economic Transformation of the Soviet Union 1913–1945* (forthcoming) ch. 4, p. 36. MS kindly supplied by R. W. Davies.

ally build up a picture of her environment, but this is still a long way from being able to disentangle her views of today from those of the time.[96]

But none of this explains why terror and purging occurred in the first place.

Early Bolshevism

Marx's espousal of scientific socialism gave Russian social democrats tremendous self-confidence in their fight against tsarism and rival revolutionary groups. But self-confidence bred intolerance: from his earliest days in the RSDRP Lenin exhibited a fetish for ideological purity and the 'correct line'; the debris of bitter quarrels and the wreckage of expelled factions litter early Bolshevism's history. On the other hand Lenin was hardly consistent and it is by no means the case that he always got his way. The correct line was always changing, giving rise to the rapid shifts, violent splits and short-lived alliances characteristic of the incestuous, hothouse world of the émigré revolutionary. After 1917, the avalanche of crises afflicting the Soviet régime served only to magnify these fissile tendencies. Leninists were now confronted with a plethora of enemies. Hard choices set former comrades at each others throats, while the lack of any agreed agenda for socialism and the ideological brawls simultaneously convulsing other socialist groups created a welter of new opportunities for dispute. Vociferous factions – Democratic Centralists, Left Communists, the Workers' Opposition, the Military Opposition – tested party loyalty to the limit and beyond.[97] In addition, as Bolsheviks set about constructing the proletarian dictatorship, all manner and conditions of people joined their ranks: careerists; 'former people' with something to hide; anti-Bolshevik socialists, muzzled by the one-party state, who hoped to carry their politics into the heart of government and well-intentioned workers with only the most sketchy knowledge of Marxism. It is understandable that leaders should be obsessed with the membership's quality and ideological make-up and that they paid great attention to expelling undesirables.

What gave purging a special urgency was the Civil and Imperialist War and the introduction of the NEP. By 1919, the invasion of the former Empire's territory by the armies of fourteen hostile states, coupled with the depredations of various native White and 'Green' movements,[98] imperiled the Revolution's survival. The central committee, a few years previously little more than a peripatetic debating

---

[96] M. McAuley, *Soviet Politics 1917–1991* (Oxford University Press, 1992) pp. 56–7.
[97] See pp. 9–11.
[98] Green (peasant) armies fought against both the Reds and the Whites.

society squabbling in the cafés of Western Europe, underwent profound changes. In the drive for victory everything was sacrificed to
the exigencies of the moment, and the first victim was dissent. The
Civil War was won, in part, by silencing the raucous cacophony of
pre-1917 Bolshevism. In securing the Soviet Republic much was lost:
many dreams evaporated and many socialists fell by the wayside.
The first great post-revolutionary chistka (the 1919 're-registration')
expelled ten to fifteen per cent of the membership. Once the battlefields fell silent new dangers appeared. Lenin's NEP deeply affront-
ed many communists' ideological sensibilities. Bolshevism very
nearly tore itself asunder: in the ensuing purge of 1921 one-quarter
of the membership lost their cards.[99] No 1930s chistka resulted in
such a high expulsion rate.

Theorizing terror

Totalitarian theorists like Conquest are keen to locate the precondi-
tions for Stalin's purges in the fabric of Bolshevism, but this was not
the only possible future bequeathed by Marx and Lenin. Conversely,
while Trotsky, Deutscher and Medvedev insist that Stalinism differed from Leninism, sharp distinctions cannot easily be drawn.
Purging was woven in the fabric of a changing body: there were
many Lenins, many Leninisms and many Bolshevisms, but only one
– marked by exclusivity, fear of disunity and the resolute search for
enemies – was being nurtured by the crushing brutalities and narrow-
ing options of the immediate post-revolutionary years.[100] In fact,
once the country settled down to the edgy prosperity of the NEP,
chistki withered on the vine: an uneasy stillness descended on the
rank-and-file – if not on the élite.[101]

In one form or another, therefore, purging pre-dated Stalin's
ascendancy. Only when the 'second revolution' unfolded, with all its
attendant panics and confusions, did the practice re-surface as a
major policy instrument. The 1928–30 and 1933–5 chistki, the proverka and the obmen should, as revisionists assert, be seen in this light.
Frantic to gain control over its intractable local organs, terrified lest
Bolshevism should finally disintegrate, the leadership fell back on
the customary expedient. It is also plausible that millenarial calls for
'cultural revolution', trumpeted abroad by young radicals in the
heady days of the Great Breakthrough, fused with a genuine desire
on the part of some in the Kremlin to widen the space for mass participation. Evidence suggesting that leaders were inclined to trust
'honest proletarians' and disinclined to heed dolorous calls for cau-

[99] Rigby, *Membership*, ch. 1.
[100] For a discussion of this point see M. Lewin, *The Making of the Soviet System:
Essays in the Social History of Inter-War Russia* (Methuen, London, 1985) part 3.
[101] Expulsions ran at three to four per cent per annum in 1924–6.

tion emanating from the old engineers (or that the régime attacked the technical intelligentsia in order to deflect working-class anger away from itself) is equally compelling.[102] Moreover, the tensions accompanying collectivization and the first piatiletka loosed a babble of discordant tongues at the centre – Syrtsov, Riutin and Smirnov. But the expulsion of these 'groups' and the simultaneous ejection of defeated luminaries like Kamenev and Zinoviev did not result in their immediate imprisonment or execution. This was a continuation of the intra-party struggle; not necessarily the ante-chamber to a new and bloody continent of Stalinist purges.

All protagonists are right to focus on Kirov's death for, whatever the facts, only afterwards was the NKVD unleashed against the party. If many totalitarians were too eager – in a fit of Cold War animosity – to convict Stalin of Kirov's murder, Getty's notion that Kirov posed no significant threat looks like succumbing to the attrition of the times: the congress of victors ballot box scandal does not prove that Stalin murdered Kirov, but since there is now a strong case for concluding that the General Secretary had much to gain from Kirov's demise, Getty's position is seriously undermined.[103] If Stalin was responsible, however, historians are still not at liberty to represent the affair as one component of a master plan comprising chistki, the proverka, the obmen, the show trials, the destruction of the high command and the Ezhovshchina: all these could have had quite different and differing causes. Indeed, the scandal sheds rather more light on other matters: it endorses the revisionist view that the party was far from being a mere tool of the leadership and lends weight to the idea that intra-élite conflicts continued well into the 1930s, and may have played a part in shaping later purges.

In his review of Getty's book, R. W. Davies maintained that disclosures made in the context of Khrushchev's de-stalinization campaign confirmed many of the more extravagant rumours circulating in the 1930s.[104] Notwithstanding Davies's caution, and bearing in mind that Khrushchev had his own political axe to grind (and much to hide besides; the 'butcher of the Ukraine' was no anti-Stalinist in the 1930s), one of revisionism's most significant contributions is in the area of source criticism. Getty alerts us to the fact that previous purge studies have too often ignored primary sources and relied upon unverified 'corridor gossip', enticing the unwary towards 'grand

---

[102] See pp. 96–7, 208–9, 211–12.
[103] For recent assessments of the Kirov Affair see R. Conquest, *Stalin and the Kirov Murder* (Hutchinson, London, 1989); *Report on the USSR* (22 February 1991).
[104] *The Times Higher Education Supplement* (27 September 1985).

analytical generalizations' which are little more than 'history-by-anecdote'.[105]

This brings us to a major problem with revisionist methodology. Strictures against the uncritical use of 'secondary' rumour and gossip as historical sources are well made: the difficulty is that primary sources can be handled uncritically too. It is hard to think of more biased and censored sources for the 1930s than *Pravda* or the published accounts of various party congresses, conferences and central committee plenums. In a world dominated by 'court politics' – one where telephone calls, table-talk and unminuted Politburo conversations formed the basis of policy making – primary (i.e. official) materials should be treated with circumspection, and rumour should not be rejected out of hand.[106]

The culture of terror

Totalitarian 'secondary source' depictions of the psychology of terror and the growth of a police state are credible.[107] Conquest's view that by August 1937 the secret police, forced to meet quotas, were so overwhelmed with prisoners that they resorted to torture in order to extract quick confessions, makes sense.[108] There is too much corroborating evidence for this to be dismissed as idle tittle-tattle. Moreover, Solzhenitsyn's vivid cameos of lives wasted and broken, or Viktor Kravchenko's graphic memories of his first purge, cannot simply be put aside as idiosyncratic experiences telling us nothing about the origins of purging:[109] they may appear to reveal little about causes but they speak volumes about the brutal process at work. And once such processes became normative they in turn became causes, part and parcel of terror. In the Soviet film *Defence Counsel Sedov* the hero, a courageous young lawyer, is given the job of defending three kolkhozniki accused of sabotage. After securing an interview with a Deputy Commissar for Justice and overcoming numerous obstacles Sedov discovers that frightened incompetents (local apparatchiki) fabricated the charges to cover up their mismanagement of a

---

[105] Getty is particularly scathing of the *Letter of an Old Bolshevik*, a text which profoundly influenced many earlier interpretations. The *Letter* was once thought to be a report of conversations between Nicolaevsky and Bukharin when the latter visited Paris in 1936, but as Getty shows it is a 'spurious source', no more than a record of 'Nicolaevsky's collection of contradictory and unattributed rumours floating around Europe in the 1930s'. Getty, *Origins*, pp. 5, 215.

[106] For sharp critiques of revisionist methodology see N. E. Rosenfeldt, 'Problems of evidence: one-sided selectivity in source material', *Slavic Review* (1, 1983); R. C. Tucker, 'Problems of interpretation', *Slavic Review* (1, 1983).

[107] For a meditation on the rôle of terror in Stalinist 'state building' see A. W. Gouldner, 'Stalinism: a study of internal colonialism', *Telos* (34, 1977–78).

[108] Conquest, *Great Terror*, p. 307.

[109] See Solzhenitsyn, *Gulag 2*; Kravchenko, *I Chose Freedom*, ch. 10.

kolkhoz. The defendants are duly acquitted. The climax of the film comes when at a conference of Soviet lawyers the Deputy Commissar praises Sedov fulsomely for upholding the principles of 'socialist legality'. Sedov's embarrassment turns to horror as he hears that he has been appointed head of a purge commission charged with the task of hunting down the *real* 'counter-revolutionaries'; provincial bosses responsible for 'sabotaging Soviet agriculture' and levelling 'false accusations against the Soviet people'. Everyone in the hall applauds vigorously, including the freed kolkhozniki.[110]

Small fictions illuminate large realities, and it is with such images in mind that we should approach the wider problem of the Stalinist polity.

The Old Bolsheviks
The Soviet régime had always been desperately insecure. Except for a brief moment in 1917, and perhaps in the Civil War, the Bolsheviks could never be sure of a popular mandate. The frail peace of the NEP was accompanied by an ingrained belief that matters were balanced on a knife edge, that the slightest mishap could precipitate mass unrest, blow the party apart and instantly reverse the fortunes of Socialist Revolutionaries, Mensheviks – or even of straightforward reactionaries – all of which would bring the whole rickety enterprise crashing to the ground. Anxiety increased once the risky adventures of collectivization and forced industrialization commenced. Frightened leaders espied monstrous legions of counter-revolutionaries emerging from every nook and cranny, and not all enemies were imaginary. Foreign states remained hostile. The Civil War had not been forgotten. Émigrés in a dozen European capitals conspired against the régime. Peasants rose against the government. Nationalist sentiment had not suddenly been extinguished by a decade of Soviet power. Bourgeois specialists (few of them Bolsheviks and most trained under the tsars) harboured scarcely veiled doubts about current policies, whilst inside the Kremlin rumour, gossip, plot and counter-plot swept through the central committee.

By 1934, Zinoviev and Kamenev were politically bankrupt. There is no evidence that they had any significant following in the central committee or the party at large. Bukharin, Rykov, Tomskii and other former Right Oppositionists were thoroughly marginalized. Trotsky could be discounted: despite the occasional smuggled letter he was of no significance. But in the frenzied atmosphere of the times they all appeared to pose an enormous threat, an alternative to the fragile unity coalescing around Stalin. Their utter ruin seemed necessary if the régime was to be saved and its policies secured, and their trials

---

[110] *Defence Counsel Sedov* was released during the glasnost' years.

are examples of an emerging Stalinist polity which foreshadowed the Ezhovshchina.[111]

The accusations levelled against Old Bolsheviks were frequently based on the half-remembered political battles of a bygone era. Bukharin, for example, did briefly contemplate carrying on the government without Lenin at the height of the Brest-Litovsk quarrel in 1918. He was also a champion of the party's Left Communists. The faction had close contacts with the Left Socialist Revolutionaries who rose against the régime in summer 1918, and the Bolsheviks claimed that one of their members shot Lenin through the neck. But this does not mean that Bukharin ever intended to assassinate Lenin.[112] This was a fabrication; like the other charges a nightmare distortion extracted by torture, isolation and dire threats against the relatives of the accused. If there was any organized opposition to the régime historians should probably look to the Red Army. There may have been talk of a *coup d'état* amongst the officers. It is more likely, however, that German Intelligence tried to stoke the fires of suspicion raging across Russia in order to weaken the Soviet military. Cordial and routine contacts between the General Staff and high-ranking Wehrmacht officers, coupled with Tukhachevskii's foreign trips, would have provided the necessary element of verisimilitude. Forged documents of German origin implicating the high command in treasonable activities were passed to the NKVD and may have reached Stalin by the spring of 1937.[113]

The Caliban state

Seen through the eyes of committed Stalinists, therefore – ordinary folk too – the show trials might well have seemed convincing. 'How can it be', agonized General Gorbatov after Tukhachevskii's death,

> that men who took such a part in routing foreign interventionists and internal reactionaries... have suddenly become enemies of the people?' Finally, after mulling over a host of possible explanations, I accepted the answer most common in those days... 'Obviously,' many people said at the time... 'they fell

---

[111] Further harbingers are not difficult to find. Stalin's reference to the dangers of nationalist deviation in the Ukraine in his speech to the 1934 party congress, for example, doubtless intensified the search for 'bourgeois nationalists' in other republics, weaving another strand into the complex tapestry of purging.

[112] This was not the first time that Bukharin's rôle in 1918 had been dragged up. See pp. 17–18. In August 1918 Fania (or Dora) Kaplan tried to assassinate Lenin. She was probably an anarchist rather than a Left SR.

[113] See Deutscher, *Stalin*, p. 379; Erickson, *Soviet High Command*, pp. 433–6. Since the 1920s the German and Soviet armies had been co-operating in violation of the Versailles treaty.

into the nets of foreign intelligence organizations while abroad...'[114]

Kravchenko suggested that most citizens took a different view of the Old Bolsheviks' demise: 'the population at large... were pretty indifferent to what seemed to them a family quarrel among their new masters'.[115] As for the Ezhovshchina, fear of terror does not seem to have been widely felt outside society's upper echelons: workers shrugged their shoulders or applauded attacks on bosses and intellectuals.[116] Indeed, Ezhov's purge sometimes elicited a robust plebeian response. When Magnitogorsk's chief engineer vanished,

> chaos reigned in the plant. A foreman would come to work in the morning and say to his men, 'Now today we must do this and that.' The workers would sneer at him and say: 'Go on. You're a wrecker yourself. Tomorrow they'll come and arrest you. All you engineers and technicians are wreckers.'[117]

Evidence like this has sometimes tempted revisionists to claim that working-class approbation for purging, coupled with action from below (the 'verification' of officials at mass meetings), constituted a form of democracy. But even if, as Rittersporn avers, the régime was 'truly popular' (able to respond to proletarian frustrations by lashing out at unpopular groups or demonizing 'former people'),[118] it was not democratic. 'To see "action from below" as *per se* democratic is just fantasy', argued Conquest in reply to revisionist speculations:

> It is true that (for example), although the temperature was −27°C, a crowd of 200,000 turned out in Moscow to demand the carrying out of the death sentences on Piatakov and his fellow accused. And the government acceded to their wishes: a model of successful mass pressure from below![119]

Nevertheless, as the search for unity drove élites hither and thither, 'democratic fantasy' (criticism, verification, the constitution, hints of party democratization, Ezhov's radicalism) did produce a kind of

---

[114] Gorbatov, *Years off My Life*, p. 103. Gorbatov was sentenced to fifteen years imprisonment in June 1937. He was released in spring 1941 and participated in the invasion of Germany.

[115] Kravchenko, *I Chose Freedom*, p. 216.

[116] See R. W. Thurston, 'Fear and belief in the USSR's "Great Terror": response to arrest 1935–1939', *Slavic Review* (2, 1986).

[117] J. Scott, *Behind the Urals: An American Worker in Russia's City of Steel* (Indiana University Press, 1973) p. 194.

[118] Rittersporn, *Studies in Comparative Communism* (2, 1986).

[119] R. Conquest, 'Revisionizing Stalin's Russia', *Russian Review* (4, 1987).

populist régime; one characterized, not by democracy but by plebisc-itary demagogy: a tyrannical polity involving chaos, mistrust and paranoia which provided lethal safety valves for the appeasement of plebeian anger.

Antecedents and parallels

Trotsky's analysis was not so wide of the mark:

> Napoleon... concentrated the fruits of the regime born out the the revolution in the hands of the new bourgeois aristocracy. Stalin guards the conquests of the October Revolution not only against the feudal–bourgeois counter-revolution but also against the claims of the toilers, their impatience and their dissatisfac-tion... Leaning for support on the topmost layer of the new social hierarchy against the lowest – sometimes *vice versa* – Stalin has attained the complete concentration of power in his own hands. What else should this regime be called if not Soviet Bonapartism?[120]

But Trotsky did not have to ransack French history to make his point. Domestic parallels and antecedents abound. Nineteenth-cen-tury tsars also ruled through fear ('close to the tsar, close to death', ran the old saying) while confusion and intrigue riddled the entire political process. Over-mighty barons rose and fell, successive rulers struggled to master the bureaucracy and struck out against 'enemies'. Alexander I, for instance, toyed with constitutional reform but ended up by imposing one-man management in the bureaucracy and sacri-ficing his favourites. Some historians maintain that Nicholas I too suffered from paranoia: like Stalin he elaborated 'secret' chancel-leries; like Stalin he relied on a spy network operating through a 'super-ministry' which resembled the NKVD – the 'Third Section'. Alexander III switched the emphasis to the Ministry of Finances; under Witte this became, for a while, a commissariat of moderniza-tion which dominated everything and brooked no opposition. Nicholas II looked to the MVD to maintain his supremacy – Stolypin scapegoated Jews as 'enemies' and utilized terror against the masses. As in other areas (agriculture, industry, cultural policy) Stalin's Russia differed quantitatively, not qualitatively, from the *ancien régime* – in the scale and degree of arbitrariness.

Stalin's rôle

Somehow or other historians have to get to grips with the problem of Stalin's precise rôle in the Soviet polity. Obviously he could not con-

---

[120] Cited Knei-Paz, *Social & Political Thought*, p. 403.

trol everything – an absurd proposition given the country's size, the upheavals of the Great Breakthrough and the manifest weakness of the party-state machine. Though Poskrebyshev's 'special section' functioned as his personal chancellery (tapping the telephone lines of all the important party leaders) he probably could not even control everything happening in the central committee, still less the commissariats. But he could control what happened to the Old Bolsheviks. It is inconceivable that the show trials occurred without his active consent. As for the military purge, despite the possibility of Nazi intrigue it seems that no German documents were submitted in evidence at Tukhachevskii's trial: Deutscher's notion that Stalin destroyed the officers lest they turn against the régime therefore remains the most plausible explanation.[121]

But if this was a Stalinist party it was not necessarily Stalin's party. It was not all his doing. He sometimes permitted and sometimes encouraged others in the élite to follow the road that led to mass purging. It is also likely that he did not always know where he was going or what his associates were up to.[122] Rittersporn goes so far as to suggest that Stalin ratified Ezhov's purge against the Politburo's wishes,[123] but it is hard to believe that allies and subordinates could have flaunted his will so openly. And even if the Ezhovshchina was a unique event, arising from the confluence of a number of disparate factors, it was Stalin who tipped the balance in Ezhov's favour. Whatever the motivation for his appointment as NKVD head, Ezhov was a known advocate of radical mass purging; it is difficult to imagine that a politician as astute as the General Secretary did not envisage at least some of what was to follow, if only because the power of the secret police had been growing steadily.[124]

---

[121] The Main Military Soviet and the Main Naval Soviet, both created in 1938, brought the armed forces under Politburo control. Political commissars, abolished in 1934, were reinstated in May 1937.

[122] One Westerner working in Gosplan was convinced that apparatchiki 'made the Stalin of the 1930s as much as he made them'. J. Miller, 'Soviet planners in 1936–37', in J. Degras & A. Nove, eds, *Soviet Planning: Essays in Honour of Naum Jasny* (Blackwell, Oxford, 1964) p. 119.

[123] Rittersporn, *Libre* (6, 1979).

[124] In March 1933 the OGPU was empowered to carry out executions. The NKVD could detain without trial and send victims to labour camps. The December 1934 decree on terrorist acts laid out the following parameters: a ten-day limit on investigations; one day between accusation and trial; no legal representation of the accused; no presence of the accused; no appeals for clemency; death sentence to be carried out within one day of conviction. It may have been little used but it established an alarming precedent. A further decree of June 1934 declared that relatives of convicted traitors were liable to imprisonment or deportation. The following April children over twelve became liable to all penalties, including shooting. The new law was probably a response to the pressing problem of delinquent orphans (see p. 198), but taken together with the 1934 decrees it certainly made it easier for the police to extract confessions from 'counter-revolutionaries' with families to consider.

We should conclude by recalling that Stalin functioned in a socio-economic environment teetering on the brink of disaster and in a country in which, since the late nineteenth century, social, economic and political stability were virtually unknown. 'Men make their own history,' wrote Marx, 'but not in circumstances of their own choosing.' If we reverse this quotation ('history makes men, but not in circumstances of their own choosing') we can appreciate that before the Revolution a specific historical context doubtless made the man and his associates, that one variant of Leninism to some extent made the man and his associates, and that after 1917 an extraordinarily harsh environment certainly made the man and his associates. But, since history is about people, personality (however problematic) cannot be extracted from the equation. Stalin gave a special twist to the solutions offered up to current problems – or at least accelerated their development – one of which was terror and the physical annihilation of opponents, real or imagined. 'Until 1936', contends Davies,

> Stalin as supreme political leader was working under the restraints of his colleagues, liable to be criticized in the Politburo and perhaps occasionally voted against. After 1937, he still took advice from all and sundry, but he could ignore it. He had raised himself roughly to the position occupied by Alexander III or Nicholas I in relation to their advisers. But he lacked their unchallenged, God-given authority, and maintained his status by acquiring some of the characteristics of Ivan Grozny, and by permitting and encouraging witch-hunts worthy of the Inquisition.[125]

Future research will probably reinforce the view that 'the purges' should be disaggregated; that their origins were complex; that the centre comprised only one set of actors; that local satraps, NKVD operatives and workers manipulated and distorted purges for their own ends, and that the entire process was – in the widest sense – a social event. Now that Russian archives are opening up we shall probably also discover more about central committee platforms, Politburo factions and the dimensions of local and national resistance. But none of this will solve the difficulty of the exact relationship between Stalin, the Stalinists, the apparatus and society, nor will it provide definitive answers to the intractable problem of the individual's rôle in history. In the court politics and the immense chaos of the 1930s not everything was written down.

[125] *THES* (27 September 1985).

Suggestions for further reading

J. Arch Getty, *Origins of the Great Purges: The Soviet Communist Party Reconsidered 1933–1938* (Cambridge University Press, 1985). The seminal revisionist text; essential reading for purging in the 1930s.

H. Carrère d'Encausse, *A History of the Soviet Union 1917–1953. Volume 2. Stalin: Order Through Terror* (trans. V. Ionescu, Longman, London, 1981). A concise survey of the main features of Stalinism from a totalitarian perspective.

R. Conquest, *The Great Terror: A Reassessment* (Hutchinson, London, 1990). Update of *The Great Terror: Stalin's Purges of the Thirties* (Macmillan, London, 1968). Classic totalitarian texts which emphasize Stalin's rôle in politics and purging.

R. A. Medvedev, *Let History Judge: The Origins and Consequences of Stalinism* (trans. C. Taylor, Knopf, New York, 1971). The most impressive work on Stalinism to emerge from the Soviet Union before glasnost'.

G. T. Rittersporn, *Stalinist Simplifications and Soviet Complications: Social Tensions and Political Conflicts in the USSR 1933–1953* (Harwood, Chur, 1991). A revisionist monograph which tries to de–personalize and reconceptualize Stalinism.

L. Trotsky, *The Revolution Betrayed: What is the Soviet Union and Where is it Going?* (5th ed., trans. M. Eastman, Pathfinder Press, New York, 1973). Reprint of the major Trotskyist analysis. Includes a useful introduction.

D. Volkogonov, *Stalin: Triumph & Tragedy* (trans. H. Shukman, Weidenfeld & Nicolson, London, 1991). An interesting and powerful glasnost' study which draws heavily on previously unpublished archival sources.

5 WAR AND LATE STALINISM

I know how much the German people loves its Führer. I should therefore like to drink his health.

Stalin, 24 August 1939.

Narrative

The background to war

The Great Depression, engulfing most of the world within a few months of the collapse of the New York stock exchange in October 1929, affected Germany more than any other European country. As unemployment and inflation soared the Weimar Republic crumbled under the Nazi onslaught, but these developments were greeted with relative equanimity in Moscow. According to the Komintern the NSPD would soon fail: the theory of 'social fascism' portrayed Hitler as the creature of big business and predicted that only left-wing reformism could thwart the long awaited German socialist revolution. In anticipation of the Führer's imminent demise, local communists were told to ignore the Nazis and concentrate their fire on the social democrats. Nevertheless, in 1932 the Soviet Union insured against disaster by signing non-aggression treaties with Poland and the three Baltic states – countries separating Germany from the USSR – followed by a two-year pact with France, Europe's most formidable military power.[1] Hitler's triumph forced a change of policy. The Soviet Union joined the League of Nations in 1934 and pushed hard for 'collective security' – inter-state action to counter fascist expansionism. The following year the Komintern instructed communists everywhere to form 'popular fronts' with other parties to stem the fascist tide while the Franco-Russian pact was converted into a fully-fledged military alliance and extended to include Czechoslovakia.

Despite these European alarms, until the late 1930s the main threat seemed to come from Asia. When Japan occupied Manchuria and set up the puppet state of Manchukuo in 1932, Moscow feared a Sino-Japanese agreement which would divert the aggressor westwards to Mongolia, a Russian satrapy since 1921. Four years later the Berlin–Tokyo 'Anti-Komintern Pact' confirmed suspicions that a

---

[1] A similar arrangement was negotiated with Italy in 1933. These treaties were modelled on the five-year Soviet–Lithuanian non-aggression pact of September 1926.

new anti-Bolshevik crusade was in the making.[2] Stalin responded by restoring diplomatic relations with Nanjing, delivering arms to the Kuomintang and concluding an alliance with Chiang Kai-shek. Japan's assault on China in 1937 triggered Soviet forays into Manchuria and led to the crushing defeat of Manchukuo forces by the Red Army in summer 1939.[3]

The border wars
Fighting in Asia marked the start of a series of border conflicts which prefaced the Russo-German war. On 17 September 1939, two days after the Manchukuo armistice, the second border war began when Russia invaded eastern Poland.

The origins of the Polish campaign lay in the reorientation of Soviet policy after the Munich débâcle. As Hitler's ambitions multiplied – remilitarization of the Rhineland preceded the *Anschluss* and Czechoslovakia's dismemberment at the 1938 Munich conference – Stalin's anxieties increased, but efforts to help Prague via the Franco-Russian alliance proved abortive; the Red Army could do nothing without crossing Poland's frontiers, something Warsaw would not accept.[4] Speaking at the eighteenth party congress in March 1939 the General Secretary now characterized Western appeasement as a capitalist ploy to drive Hitler eastwards. Meanwhile, as desultory talks with Britain and France on military co-operation foundered over the issue of Polish neutrality, Molotov, Maxim Litvinov's successor at the Foreign Commissariat,[5] echoed Stalin's concerns and made plain his country's determination to stay out of European quarrels.

On 23 August 1939, as the Anglo-French negotiators wound up their business, Molotov and Ribbentrop (Germany's foreign minister) initialled a treaty committing both sides to neutrality in the event of general European war, but the Nazi–Soviet pact contained other provisions kept from public scrutiny. Secret protocols allocated Lithuania and western Poland to Germany, while Russia's domain included eastern Poland, Estonia, Finland, Bessarabia (the north-eastern section of Romania bordering the Ukraine) and Latvia.

---

[2] The pact, signed in November 1936, committed each party to counter the Komintern's activities and to co-operate in other ways against the Soviet Union. Italy joined a year later.
[3] For details of the Manchukuo war see I. Nish, *Japanese Foreign Policy 1869–1942: Kasumigaseki to Miyakezaka* (Routledge & Kegan Paul, London, 1977).
[4] Only in Spain, where civil war broke out in July 1936, was the Red Army able to offer some resistance to fascism, though Stalin's commitment fell far short of unconditional support for the Spanish Republic.
[5] Litvinov (1876–1951) was Foreign Commissar from July 1930 to May 1939. He may have been sacked because he was Jewish and a firm supporter of collective security, factors which might have complicated Russo-German rapprochement.

Hitler's violation of Poland on 1 September and the Wehrmacht's meteoric advance forced Stalin's hand. Soviet forces entered Silesia and captured 200,000 Polish troops before hostilities ceased late in September.[6] Britain and France, who declared war on Germany on 3 September, did nothing.

Within two months Stalin found himself embroiled in a third conflict. Pressure on Helsinki – Moscow wanted to 'rectify' frontiers and lease islands in order to protect Leningrad and Murmansk – prompted a Soviet offensive on 30 November. Sheer weight of numbers compelled the Finns to negotiate, but worries that Britain might assist his beleaguered enemy obliged Stalin to conclude a lenient peace. Though to Russia's advantage, the March 1940 treaty was purchased at considerable cost. The General Secretary's unprovoked aggression isolated the USSR and seriously damaged its military prestige; between 175,000 and 200,000 Russians died in the 'Winter War' as against Finnish losses of 23,000,[7] figures which persuaded foreign observers – not least Hitler – that Soviet forces had been irreparably disabled by the Ezhovshchina.

The fourth border war, or rather a series of manœuvres arising from the Nazi–Soviet pact, involved no military embarrassments. Under duress Estonia, Latvia and Lithuania signed agreements in 1939 allowing Red Army troops on to their soil.[8] Allegations that Lithuanians had kidnapped Russian soldiers led to annexation in June 1940, simultaneously Romania lost Bessarabia and northern Bukovina. The following month the three Baltic states were transformed into Soviet republics and Romania's territory divided between the Ukraine and the newly created Moldavian SSR.

The Great Fatherland War

Russia's poor showing in Finland contrasted sharply with Germany's spectacular run of victories. 'Blitzkrieg' (lightning war) secured Denmark, Norway, the Low Countries and France in 1940 and the elimination of Greece and Yugoslavia in 1941. Britain alone still opposed the Third Reich, but Hitler deemed Churchill's position hopeless and confidently expected London to sue for peace. There seemed no reason to postpone the assault on Russia, in preparation

---

[6]   Of these at least 14,700 were incarcerated in Soviet labour camps. Only forty-eight survived. At Katyn forest in 1943 the Germans unearthed the bodies of over 4,000 Polish soldiers executed by the NKVD. The fate of the other prisoners remains a mystery.

[7]   Stalinist sources put the Red Army's losses at 48,000 killed. The treaty resulted in the surrender of 16,000 square miles of Finnish territory and the creation of the Karelo-Finnish SSR. For details of the Russo-Finnish war see V. Tanner, *The Winter War: Finland Against Russia 1939–1940* (Stanford University Press, 1957).

[8]   Lithuania was transferred to the Soviet sphere of influence after Poland's destruction.

since December 1940. After five and a half weeks delay, caused by deployments in the Balkans, the Germans crossed the Soviet border at dawn on Sunday 22 June 1941.

'Operation Barbarossa', a military leviathan comprising 2,800 tanks, 4,950 aircraft, 47,260 artillery pieces and 5.5 million Axis troops, overwhelmed the defenders and rolled forward at breathtaking speed.[9] Paralysis seized Moscow and the general staff. Stalin's refusal to believe that Hitler had abrogated the Nazi–Soviet pact resulted in the Defence Commissariat telling front-line units to eschew military action. By August, having previously annexed the Baltic republics, enemy forces were deep into Belarus and the Ukraine. Fighting spread to the Donbass in October, Leningrad was besieged, Kiev captured and Moscow threatened. Wehrmacht officers on the hills around the city could glimpse the golden towers of the Kremlin glinting in the winter sunlight, but Marshal Zhukov's makeshift fortifications,[10] combined with growing civilian resistance, bad weather and supply difficulties (the Axis front ran for 1,500 kilometres from north to south and 600 kilometres from east to west) conspired to halt the tanks, allowing Zhukov to mount a brief counter-attack in December which drove the Nazis 200 kilometres back from the capital, the first reverse ever suffered by the Wehrmacht. This was little enough when set against the catastrophes of summer and autumn. Russia's situation was parlous indeed. Enfeebled by the deaths of at least 1.5 million soldiers and the capture of twice that number, the military was further weakened by enormous equipment losses. Only America's declaration of war against Germany in December relieved the gloom, holding out the prospect of substantial aid over and above that already offered by Roosevelt.[11]

1942 opened with Stalin's order for a general offensive, but the initiative soon slipped from his grasp. Frustrated by mounting casualties and the failure of 'Operation Typhoon' (the Moscow campaign), Hitler took personal command of the army and launched another colossal Blitzkrieg, this time southwards towards the Caucasus. Most of the Ukraine and all of Crimea fell into German hands. Only in September, after wild scenes of panic, did the Russian line stabilize at Stalingrad. Neither side would give up the city, but the Wehrmacht, now ranged on a front stretching for nearly 2,000 kilo-

---

[9] Soviet figures were higher in some categories but much equipment was obsolete. Bulgaria, Finland, Hungary, Italy and Romania participated in the attack, along with SS volunteers recruited from Western Europe.

[10] Georgii Zhukov (1896–1974) joined the party in 1919, survived the Ezhovshchina and became a central committee candidate in 1941.

[11] In July 1941 American negotiators arrived in Moscow to discuss the extension of 'lend-lease', the means by which the USA supplied war materials to Britain.

metres from Berlin to Mozdok (the furthest point of advance south-eastwards) and another 2,000 kilometres from Finland to near the Turkish border, was perilously exposed. Months of bitter fighting ended with the surrender of 90,000 Germans and the death of a further 800,000 in the ruins of the city – Russia lost 1.1 million.

Confronting the most powerful army ever assembled in Europe, by their own efforts the Soviet people had inflicted a defeat on the Third Reich from which it would never recover. Stalin first described the Russo-German conflict as the 'Great Fatherland War' in July 1943 – a deliberate reference to the 'Great Patriotic War' against Napoleon – but the struggle had already been globalized. The 'Grand Alliance' with Britain and America ensured Russia's survival. Nevertheless, excepting massive bombing raids on Berlin and the Ruhr, the 1942 North African campaign and the Anglo-American invasion of Italy in September 1943, the Red Army fought on alone. Only when the long anticipated 'second front' opened (the June 1944 Normandy landings) did Hitler transfer substantial ground forces from the east.

At enormous cost Russia gradually pushed westwards throughout 1943. There was only one threatening moment. Hitler's last throw came in July, a ten day offensive around Kursk designed to encircle Soviet armies in the Ukraine. Instead the Germans found themselves encircled, sustaining even more casualties than at Stalingrad. By December two-thirds of the territory lost since 1941 had been recovered and 200,000 Axis soldiers trapped in the Crimean peninsular. The following year witnessed a rash of successes known as Stalin's 'ten great victories': the relief of Leningrad in January; the incursion into Romania early in spring; the liberation of Crimea in May; the defeat of Finland and the re-conquest of Belarus in June; followed by the invasion of Poland, Bulgaria, Estonia and Latvia, the seizure of Belgrade and the expulsion of Axis troops from Finland and northern Norway. Victory came in 1945. Early in January the Red Army entered Germany, linking up with American soldiers on the River Elbe in April while other units captured Budapest and Vienna. Zhukov's assault on the capital precipitated Hitler's suicide on 30 April and the surrender of Nazi forces in the east on 9 May, Soviet troops having breached Berlin's defences and raised the hammer and sickle over the Reichstag a week previously.

The Red Army's campaigns ended where they started, in Manchuria. On 6 August 1945 Truman,[12] anxious to defeat Japan before Stalin could open hostilities against Tokyo and lay claim to far eastern territory,[13] dropped the atomic bomb on Hiroshima.

[12] Roosevelt died on 12 April 1945.
[13] The Grand Alliance deadline for a Soviet declaration of war against Japan was 8 August. Japan sued for peace on 19 August.

Russia immediately declared war, thus guaranteeing the USSR a say in the post-war settlement of Asia.

The fruits of peace

As the Russians surveyed the devastation around them the price extracted by the invader slowly became apparent. Globally the Second World War took the lives of between fifty and sixty million people. Of these nearly half – perhaps twenty-eight million – were Soviet citizens.[14] Between fifteen and nineteen million were civilians, victims of hostage shooting, slave labour, starvation, cross-fire and bombing. The Germans captured just over 5.75 million Red Army personnel: as many as 4.7 million may have died from hunger, execution, cold, illness and forced labour. According to estimates published in 1990, overall nearly nine million soldiers lost their lives.[15] Nor was this the end of the story. Enormous quantities of pre-war capital stock had vanished – 679 billion rubles worth. 'The German-fascist invaders', notes one 1987 Soviet history,

> completely or partially destroyed and burnt 1,710 towns and settlements and more than 70,000 villages and hamlets; burnt and destroyed more than six million buildings and rendered homeless about twenty-five million people; destroyed 31,580 industrial enterprises... 65,000 kilometres of railway lines and 4,100 stations, 36,000 post and telegraph installations, telephone exchanges and other communications enterprises; destroyed and looted tens of thousands of kolkhozy and sovkhozy, slaughtered, seized or drove back to Germany seven million horses, seventeen million cattle and oxen, twenty million pigs, twenty-seven million sheep and goats. In addition they destroyed and looted 40,000 hospitals and other medical establishments, 84,000 schools, colleges, universities and research institutes and 43,000 public libraries.[16]

But a special place in the litany of suffering should be reserved for Leningrad.

'Let no-one forget; let nothing be forgotten', wrote the Leningrad

---

[14] Since there were no published censuses between 1939 and 1959 it is impossible to be sure of the true number. The estimate of twenty-eight million occurs in L. Riabovskii, 'Dvatsat' millionov ili bol'she?', *Politicheskoe obozrenie* (10, 1989). V. I. Kozlov, 'O liudskikh poteriakh Sovetskogo Soiuza v Velikoi Otechestvennoi voiny 1941–1945 godov', *Istoriia SSSR* (2, 1989) suggests a figure of forty million, but this is probably too high.
[15] M. A. Moiseev, 'Tsena pobedy', *Voenno-istoricheskii zhurnal* (3, 1990).
[16] Cited J. D. Barber & M. Harrison, *The Soviet Home Front 1941–1945: A Social and Economic History of the USSR in World War II* (Longman, London, 1991) p. 42.

poet Ol'ga Berggol'ts on the mass grave at Piskarevskii.[17] No one knows exactly how many perished during the siege. About 800,000 Leningraders starved during the terrible winter of 1941–2, a figure which exceeds total deaths – civilian and military – sustained by Britain, the British Empire and dominions and the USA in all theatres of war between 1939 and 1945. 'Death stalked Leningrad at winter's end', wrote Harrison Salisbury,

> The city was filled with corpses. They lay by the thousands on the streets, in the ice, in the snowdrifts, in the courtyards and cellars of the great apartment houses... One March night a sanitary brigade drove up to the courtyard 'morgue' at the Hermitage and carted off forty-six bodies... There were corpses in the gardens of the Anichkov Palace... on the Fontanka and in the vaults of the Aleksandrinskii Theatre. There were twenty-four bodies in the Nikol'skii Cathedral, awaiting delivery to a cemetery – one in a coffin, twenty-three wrapped in sheets and rags. Bodies piled up in the hospitals. In many institutions the doctors and nursing personnel were too ill or weak to care for patients.[18]

In the mornings, mothers dragged their children's bodies along Nevskii Prospekt in little sledges to the nearest morgue, or simply abandoned them somewhere. 'To take someone who has died to the cemetery,' recalled one man, 'is an affair so laborious that it exhausts the last vestiges of strength in the survivors, and the living, fulfilling their duty to the dead, are brought to the brink of death themselves.' There was no heating, no public transport and no water supply. No one could wash. Typhus and scurvy afflicted the weakened denizens. Almost no pets remained. They had all been eaten to supplement iron rations; in November a meagre 250 grams of bread per day for workers, 125 grams for other categories – 'blockade bread', 'black, sticky, like putty, sodden, with an admixture of wood pulp and sawdust', recalled one survivor. Crazed with hunger, some resorted to cannibalism.[19] But Leningrad did not surrender.

The Cold War

Against these staggering losses the Generalissimo, as he was now styled, could point to the tremendous expansion of Soviet influence.

[17] Berggol'ts (1910–75) was born in St Petersburg and graduated from Leningrad University in 1930. Her poem on the defence of Leningrad graces the stone wall of the Piskarevskii cemetery, located to the north of the city, which contains the remains of those who died during the siege.

[18] H. Salisbury, *The Siege of Leningrad* (Secker & Warburg, London, 1969) p. 506.

[19] For food supply in Leningrad see W. Moskoff, *The Bread of Affliction: The Food Supply in the USSR During World War II* (Cambridge University Press, 1990) ch. 10.

Having retaken Finnish and Baltic territories lost in 1941 the military also exercised absolute sway over Hungary, Romania, Bulgaria, Czechoslovakia and Poland – the latter's borders were eventually moved westwards – and partial control over Germany, Austria, Yugoslavia, Albania, China and Japan. But on the other hand Stalin had to contend with the awesome power of America, temporarily the sole possessor of the atomic bomb and the only belligerent to emerge from the war richer rather than poorer.

Moscow's fear of America's nuclear monopoly – neither Britain nor the USA was prepared to share the secrets of the 'Manhattan Project' with their erstwhile ally – fused with arguments over the future of Hitler's shattered empire. Under these pressures the Grand Alliance quickly fell apart. While Churchill fulminated against the 'iron curtain' and America's president articulated the 'Truman doctrine', Stalin institutionalized communist hegemony in Soviet occupied Germany.[20] The Socialist Unity Party, cobbled together from fragments of pre-war left-wing organizations, came into being in April 1946, but the West refused the party permission to canvass outside the Russian sector, a circumstance which, in combination with other quarrels, led to the 'Berlin blockade' of 1948 and the formal division of Germany in May 1949.

The pattern was repeated elsewhere. Except in Yugoslavia, by the end of the decade political parties run from Moscow controlled Eastern Europe. The United States countered by pouring money into Western Europe (the Marshall Plan of June 1947) and forging a new anti-communist alliance (NATO, the North Atlantic Treaty Organization founded in March 1949). 'Cold war' had displaced real war, unthinkable on a grand scale once Russia had its own atomic weapon in 1949. Only one last flare-up occurred before Stalin's death. Following Japan's collapse Korea was split into two; the North, recognized by the Soviet Union in 1948, the South by the USA a year later. With Stalin's blessing North Korean troops crossed the line dividing the two states in June 1950. United Nations forces led by America checked the incursion, invaded the North, and almost reached the Sino-Soviet border before they were repulsed by soldiers of the newly established Chinese People's Republic. Stalin refused to commit Soviet troops, and since neither side could defeat the other truce negotiations dragged on into the post-Stalin era.

The nationalities

In numerical terms, of all the Soviet peoples who fell under Nazi rule

[20] Churchill first used the phrase in his 'Fulton speech' of March 1946. Twelve months later, alarmed by temporary communist successes in the Greek civil war and aware that Britain could no longer afford to police the eastern Mediterranean, Truman promised aid to any and all willing to oppose revolutionary socialism.

the Slavs suffered most, but proportionally the Jews endured far more. Five million lived in the USSR in 1941, the vast majority in the old tsarist 'Pale of Settlement' sprawling across Belarus, the Ukraine and the RSFSR's western regions – districts held longest by Germany.[21] By 1945 over 2.5 million had vanished. Herded by the SS into cattle trucks, those who survived long journeys through frozen landscapes were incinerated in the camp ovens or worked to death by the Reich Ministry for Occupied Eastern Territories, Hitler's colonial administration. Slavs, of course, were *Untermenschen* (subhumans), and Jews not human at all, but Nazi scholars subtly delineated the other subject nations one from the other: Georgians (regarded as pure Aryans) enjoyed somewhat better treatment than Estonians, Latvians and Lithuanians (considered 'Germanizable'), but Armenians (virtually indistinguishable from Jews due to their alleged penchant for trade and urban life) experienced the full force of Hitler's wrath. All other eastern peoples were lumped together as 'mongols' – *Untermenschen* like the Slavs.

Though dismissive of National Socialism's racial taxonomies Stalinist ideology had its own discriminatory categories. Moscow's border wars added over twenty-two million people to the USSR's population, mostly non-Russians. All were suspected of harbouring treasonable sentiments. Claims that Soviet Asians had spied for Japan prompted the large-scale resettlement of Koreans and Chinese during the 1937–9 Manchurian campaign.[22] Much the same fate awaited other suspect groups and inhabitants of the newly annexed European territories. By the autumn of 1940 nearly 1.2 million people had been deported from western Belarus and the western Ukraine,[23] while in November 1940, five months after Stalin's henchmen arrived in the Baltic capitals,[24] Lithuania's new government listed 700,000 individuals (nearly one quarter of the population) deemed hostile to socialism, the bureaucratic basis for the mass

---

[21] Soviet Jews were allocated a 'national homeland' in May 1934, the remote Birobidzhan Autonomous Region of the Far Eastern Region, but settler population never exceeded 50,000.

[22] Most ended their days in Uzbekistan. Soviet Chinese and Koreans were allowed considerable cultural autonomy up to 1937. See W. Kolarz, *The Peoples of the Soviet Far East* (Archon Books, New York, 1969).

[23] By summer 1941 four expulsions (February, April and June 1940 and June 1941) had dispatched somewhere between 440,000 and 1.25 million Poles deep into the interior, though there is certainly considerable numerical overlap with the Ukrainian and Belarusian deportations. For estimates of the numbers involved see J. T. Gross, 'A note on the nature of Soviet totalitarianism', *Soviet Studies* (3, 1982); V. S. Parsadanova, 'Deportatsiia naselenii iz zapadnoe Ukrainy i zapadnoe Belorusii v 1939–41 gg', *Novaia i noveishaia istoriia* (2, 1989).

[24] Vyshinskii was appointed Soviet plenipotentiary in Latvia, Zhdanov controlled Estonia and Dekanozov (a deputy Commissar for Foreign Affairs) ran the Lithuanian government.

incarceration which swept the region a few days before Operation Barbarossa.[25]

Hitler's invasion provoked a further wave of arrests. Soviet Germans in Leningrad and other cities, as well as 400,000 residents of the Volga–German Autonomous Republic (immediately abolished) disappeared into the interior in August, but the most violent phase of Stalin's attack on the nationalities occurred as the Red Army pushed westwards. Entire peoples accused of collaboration – the Balkars, Chechens, Ingushes and Karachais (Islamic Caucasian mountain tribes), the Meskhetians (southern Georgians), Soviet Greeks, Crimean Tartars and the steppe Kalmyks – were rounded up and exiled between October 1943 and June 1944.[26] More deportations accompanied post-war collectivization. 100,000 Baltic 'kulaks' were banished to Siberia and Kazakhstan in 1949, along with numerous Estonians, Latvians, Lithuanians, Ukrainians and Cossacks charged with aiding the enemy. Overall, according to recent Russian publications, nearly 3.3 million were exiled or resettled between 1941 and 1948, plus another 215,242 who arrived later.[27]

The final act was played out in the context of the Zhdanovshchina and the foundation of Israel.[28] Determined to eradicate cultural pluralism and terrified lest some of its citizens look abroad for their salvation, the régime turned on the country's remaining Jews – now branded 'zionists' and 'rootless cosmopolitans' – and alleged that Jewish doctors were planning a *coup d'état*.[29]

The economy

Between 1941 and 1953, war and its problems dominated all economic activity. At first chaos threatened. By November 1941, a third of industry was lost or in jeopardy,[30] in part due to the régime's determination to cripple the Wehrmacht; on 29 June Sovnarkom and the central committee ordered local soviets and the military to sabotage everything Hitler might use – the 'scorched earth' policy which

[25] On the night of 14–15 June 1941 nearly 134,000 Balts were entrained for Siberia and Central Asia.
[26] Of the 1.5 million detainees about 500,000 may have perished before they reached the Gulag. For the details see R. Conquest, *The Nation Killers: The Soviet Deportation of Nationalities* (Macmillan, London, 1970); A. M. Nekrich, *The Punished Peoples: The Deportation and Tragic Fate of Soviet Minorities at the End of the Second World War* (Norton, New York, 1978).
[27] See N. F. Bugai, 'K voprosy o deportatsii narodov SSSR v 30–40–kh godakh', *Istoriia SSSR* (6, 1989); id., '40-e gody: "avtonomiiu nemtsev Povolzh'ia likvidirovat'...', *Istoriia SSSR* (2, 1991). See also 'Iz spravka Otdela spetsposelenii MVD SSSR po rabote sredi spetsposelentsev', *Istoriia SSSR* (1, 1992).
[28] For the Zhdanovshchina see pp. 177–8, 204–6 and chapter 6.
[29] See pp. 166, 205–6.
[30] In the four months after June the country lost forty-one per cent of its rail network, sixty per cent aluminium plant and sixty-three per cent of coal, iron and steel capacity.

destroyed so much built at such cost during the 1930s. But simultaneously vulnerable enterprises began to move themselves away from the front. 'Among the mountains and the pine forests', reported *Pravda*'s correspondent in September 1942,

> winter had already come when Sverdlovsk received Comrade Stalin's order to erect two buildings for the plant evacuated from the south. The trains packed with people and machinery were on their way. The factory had to start production in its new home – and it had to do so in no more than a fortnight!... It was then that the people of the Urals came to this spot with shovels, bars and pick-axes: students, typists, accountants, shop assistants, housewives, artists, teachers. The earth was like stone, frozen hard by our fierce Siberian frost. Axes and pick-axes could not break the stony soil. In the light of arc-lamps people hacked at the earth all night. They blew up the stones and the frozen earth, and they laid the foundations... Their feet and hands were swollen with frostbite, but they did not leave work. Over the charts and blueprints, laid out on packing cases, the blizzard was raging. Hundreds of trucks kept rolling up with building materials... On the twelfth day, into the new buildings with their glass roofs, the machinery, covered with hoar-frost, began to arrive. Braziers were kept alight to unfreeze the machines.[31]

Production started two days later. Stories like this could be repeated a thousandfold: from November 1941 to April 1942 1,523 key enterprises were dismantled, carried eastwards in a million railway trucks (mainly to Western Siberia, Central Asia and the Ural and Volga regions), and reassembled in wooden sheds or put to work under the frozen skies, one of the most stupendous and successful of such operations ever witnessed. Huge investment inputs complemented this astonishing logistical feat. During the war the government authorized the construction of 3,500 new large-scale factories and the conversion of numerous civilian industries to military production. Slowly the tide began to turn. Munitions output doubled in 1942 and peaked in 1944, providing the generals with equipment far superior in quality and quantity to anything the Axis forces could muster when the Red Army finally entered Germany.

Allied aid, mostly from America, supplemented the products of Stalin's 'fortresses of the rear', totalling ten billion dollars worth by 1944 and including four million tons of food, but this did not even begin to offset nutritional shortfalls. Feeding the Red Army, workers

---

[31] Cited A. Werth, *Russia at War 1941–1945* (Barrie & Rockliff, London, 1964) p. 219.

in vital industries and the Soviet people at large (in that order) was carried out against the background of the loss of forty per cent of Russia's grainlands by late 1941. Yields fell dramatically in 1942–3, reaching only half the 1940 level, and agriculture was further weakened as each belligerent seized draft animals and conscripted the rural population.

By the time peace came, twenty-five per cent of pre-war capital stock had been destroyed – in the occupied areas the figure rose to sixty-six per cent. Post-war reconstruction would therefore be a daunting task. Stalin responded by announcing long-term strategic goals for the next fifteen years and launching the fourth piatiletka in March 1946. Several factors boosted reconstruction: better use of capacity reduced to chaos by the Ezhovshchina, equipment sequestrations from the occupied territories, reparations from the defeated Axis powers and the ruthless exploitation of enemy prisoners. At first civilian needs received priority – 2.5 million people living in underground hovels were rehoused within nine months of Germany's surrender, for example – but as East–West tensions increased so did the bias towards capital construction and defence. Targets for group B industries had not been met when the piatiletka ended. By contrast, after a faltering start heavy industry forged ahead, so much so that in 1950 group A overshot its sector plan by twenty-eight per cent.[32]

In the countryside wartime emergencies induced some relaxation. Private plots supplying free markets grew at the expense of the socialized sector and zven'ia (teams of about ten workers roughly equivalent in size to the peasant's extended family) became the basic labour unit in kolkhozy, but these changes were quickly reversed. In October 1946, a 'Special Council on Kolkhoz Affairs' set about resocializing fourteen million acres of 'illegal' plotland. Meanwhile collectivization was imposed in the Soviet Union's new territories (a process complete by 1950), plans were announced for a massive forestation programme (a scheme which expired with Stalin), zven'ia gave way to larger 'brigades', MTS payments rose sharply and farm sizes increased.[33] But despite the commotion there was scant improvement. Grim realities belied Malenkov's optimistic prognosis for agriculture at the nineteenth party congress in October 1952; drought afflicted the country's grainlands in 1946, the 1952 harvest was below that of 1940 and by the following year livestock numbers had still not reached 1928 levels.

---

[32] The fifth piatiletka, scheduled to run from 1951 to 1955, was not formally adopted until October 1952. Little changed in the remaining months of Stalin's life: group A still received priority.

[33] By 1952 payments to MTSs had risen by twenty per cent in comparison with 1940 while between 1950 and 1952 the total number of kolkhozy fell from 252,000 to 97,000.

The party-state

In May 1940, shortly after Stalin criticized the army's lamentable performance in Finland,[34] Semen Timoshenko succeeded Voroshilov as Defence Commissar.[35] Thereafter new training programmes were hastily improvised and a few officers released from the Gulag. Little else changed.[36] In flagrant disregard of lessons gleaned from the border wars, regulations stressing the primacy of offensive action, drawn up on the eve of the Ezhovshchina, remained the basis of all strategic thinking. Front-line units were thus badly prepared for the shock of June 1941 and the army leadership hopelessly disorientated. Although invasion triggered mass mobilization and some voluntary enlistment, only in July did a new high command emerge – 'Stavka', chaired by Stalin and responsible for military planning throughout the conflict.

Civilian government responded more rapidly. The NKVD functioned as normal – supplying forced labour and hunting down spies and traitors (real or imaginary) – and took on new tasks as the war progressed; directing evacuations and deportations, managing secret industrial enterprises and liaising with partisan detachments. Some organizational changes were made to Beriia's police apparatus in 1943,[37] but the main innovation occurred at the centre of the party-state machine just eight days after Hitler's attack. GOKO, founded on 30 June, assumed absolute power over the country for the next four years. Like Stavka, GOKO was headed by Stalin; unlike Stavka it was not a military body. Three of the four other members (Beriia, Malenkov and Molotov) were civilians, only Voroshilov represented the armed forces.[38] Two years later the General Secretary wound up the Komintern, a sop to Churchill and Roosevelt which temporarily loosened Moscow's hold over foreign communist parties, but the travails of war also prompted changes within the USSR, leading eventually to the derogation of central control and the weakening of GOKO's grip on the party-state machine.

[34] In April Stalin addressed a session of the Supreme Military Council discussing shortcomings revealed by the Finnish campaign.

[35] Timoshenko (1895–1970) joined the party in 1919, fought in the Civil War and became commander of the Kiev military district. He was elected to the central committee in 1939.

[36] Saluting reappeared in May 1940, 'assistant commissars' replaced political commissars in August (previously abolished in 1934 they were reinstated in 1937), a harsh new military code followed in October and the reorganization of the high command in December.

[37] A new commissariat (NKGB) controlled the secret police, the remnants of the NKVD continued to run the Gulag.

[38] Kaganovich, Mikoian and Voznesenskii were added in 1942 and Voroshilov removed in 1944.

The first group to gain some independence were the officers. Flattered by Stalin's 1942 decision to abolish political commissars and resurrect much of the paraphernalia of the old imperial army – epaulettes, dress swords and segregated messes – as victory beckoned the people hailed the officer corps, and in particular the high command, as the nation's deliverer. In addition, by 1945 marshals and generals disbursed enormous patronage in their own right. As well as consuming vast quantities of the country's industrial output they exercised suzerainty over huge tracts of Europe (from Berlin to the liberated eastern territories) and controlled the lives of nearly sixteen per cent of the working population – the 11.6 million Soviet citizens then in uniform.

Next came the enterprise directors and the provincial apparatchiki – 'commanders of the industrial front' far from the Kremlin who suddenly found their powers augmented by wartime exigencies – and the plethora of local élites which grappled with the manifold problems of supply and organization.[39] All were given substantial leeway. Managers sought out labour and raw materials on their own initiative, local soviets administered food rations as best they could,[40] while in Leningrad, cut off from Moscow for twenty-seven months, regional committees ran things with relatively little central interference. In the same way partisan units, operating deep behind enemy lines and comprising about 250,000 guerrillas at their peak, were of necessity granted considerable latitude.

Finally, the Church also benefited. Total war required the population's total commitment, a fact which caused the régime to modify its anti-religious stance: services were permitted and priests enjoyed more freedom. In 1943 – an extraordinary event – Stalin even went so far as to receive the head of the Orthodox community in the Kremlin. 'Metropolitan Sergei', recalled one observer,

> put the case for a large number of seminaries, as the Church lacked priests. At this point Stalin suddenly broke his silence. 'Why haven't you got any personnel? Where have they got to?' he asked, taking his pipe from his mouth and staring intently at the company... Sergei was not discountenanced... 'We lack personnel for several reasons, one of which is that we train a man to be a priest, but he becomes a Marshal of the Soviet Union.' A satisfied grin moved the dictator's mouth. He said, 'Yes, yes, I was a seminarist. I even heard about you.'... At the end of the

---

[39] About 350,000 party members were sent to the rear during the war, mostly to areas where industrial enterprises had been relocated. Many were economic specialists and industrial managers.

[40] Civilian rationing was officially introduced by Sovnarkom in July 1941, but the centrally run system soon broke down. See Moskoff, *Bread of Affliction*, chs. 5, 7.

conversation the ancient and ailing metropolitan was exhausted... Stalin took him by the arm with great care like a real sub-
deacon, led him down the stairs and bade him farewell in the
following words: 'My Lord, that is as much as I can do for you at
the present time!'[41]

The party, on the other hand, declined in importance. Though
numbers rose from around 3.9 million in 1941 to 5.6 million in 1945,
turnover was equally spectacular, a by-product of mass slaughter,
mass mobilization, the general derangement of the Stalinist polity
and the new emphasis on nationalism; 'Soviet patriotism' replaced
ideological fervour and political work fell into desuetude.[42] In the
military, where saturation reached very high levels,[43] the party's right
to select cadres was severely curtailed in 1943. Instead, membership
became a privilege distributed by front-line commanders as the army
rolled westwards, a reward for courage under fire rather than fidelity
to Bolshevism. Recruitment policy was tightened in 1944, a harbinger of the general move away from wartime innovations which gathered pace over the next few years. As the military shrank – numbers
fell to three million in 1947 – political commissars reappeared in all
units. Nikolai Bulganin, a 'political general' close to Stalin, took over
as Defence Minister in 1947.[44] Zhukov, head of the Allied Control
Commission in Berlin, lost his central committee seat in 1946 and
was abruptly dispatched to the Odessa military district, moving to
the even more obscure Urals region two years later. Most of the high
command shared a similar fate.[45]

Analogous changes took place in the party-state machine, though
in a rather more complex fashion. Immediately after Japan's collapse
GOKO's functions were split between the Politburo and the
Orgburo, but six years later the nineteenth party congress abolished
both institutions, setting up instead a central committee 'Presidium'

[41] Cited R. A. Medvedev, *All Stalin's Men* (trans. H. Shukman, Blackwell, Oxford,
1983) pp. 95–6.
[42] See chapter 6.
[43] By 1945 twenty-five per cent of military personnel held a party card. In the population at large 'party saturation' reached only three per cent.
[44] Bulganin (1895–1975) joined the party in 1917. During the 1920s he worked in
Vesenkha, moving to posts in the government in the 1930s and to the military administration in the following decade. In 1944 he replaced Voroshilov in GOKO. People's
Commissariats were renamed ministries in April 1946. Sovnarkom thus became the
Council of Ministers.
[45] The downgrading of the high command was associated with a thoroughgoing
reform of the military. The Red Army was renamed the Soviet Army in February
1946. Following Stavka's abolition control of defence policy passed to the Council of
Ministers.

headed by Stalin.[46] Meanwhile, economic ministries were demilitarized and refashioned during and after 1945, the NKVD's reorganization confirmed in 1946,[47] Soviet preponderance in foreign communist parties re-established via the foundation of the Kominform in the autumn of 1947, and party control over the bureaucracy energetically reimposed by Malenkov, the central committee secretary in charge of cadre promotion.

Although, as in the 1930s, party cadres were subjected to systematic purging between 1945 and 1953,[48] only on three occasions did mass terror, or the threat of mass terror, reappear. 'Party renewal' – the attempt to reassert ideological hegemony in state and society – may have been spearheaded by Zhdanov; Stalin's heir apparent, Malenkov's chief rival and a Secretariat functionary closely associated with Voznesenskii, a central committee member since 1939 elected to the Politburo in 1947. Zhdanov spent most of the war isolated in Leningrad running the Defence Council (the city's government throughout the nine hundred day blockade), returning to the capital only in late 1944. Voznesenskii's links with Zhdanov went back ten years. From 1935 to 1937 he was director of the city's planning apparatus. In August 1948, having virtually lost control of his party offices a month previously, Zhdanov suddenly died. Immediately afterwards the MGB set about purging Leningrad's wartime leadership. By July 1949, all members of the city and regional party committees had been executed for treason. Sacked in March 1949, Voznesenskii was placed under house arrest and shot in 1950.

Two more imbroglios followed the 'Leningrad Affair'. In November 1951 Stalin alleged that Georgian Mingrelian tribesmen were about to secede from the USSR. Many apparatchiki and many more ordinary citizens lost their lives in the ensuing bloodbath. Finally, in January 1953 *Pravda* announced that nine physicians, seven of them Jewish, had killed a number of Soviet leaders, including Zhdanov, and conspired to wipe out the rest. They were also accused of wrecking, sabotage and spying for the USA, but unlike the 'Mingrelian Case' the 'Doctors' Plot' never developed into a full-scale purge; all the charges were dropped when Stalin died two months later.

[46] The Presidium consisted of twenty-five full and eleven candidate members. Unlike the Politburo it included large numbers of leaders working in the Soviet apparatus, but an inner core, comprising members of the old Politburo, seems to have functioned as the real locus of the party-state.
[47] The MGB (Ministry of State Security) and MVD (Ministry of Internal Affairs), both founded in 1946.
[48] According to one source about 100,000 communists were expelled per annum between 1945 and 1953. Total party membership thus grew very slowly, standing at only twenty per cent above the 1945 level by 1953. T. H. Rigby, *Communist Party Membership in the USSR 1917–1967* (Princeton University Press, 1968) p. 281.

Interpretations

Barbarossa: before and after

Virtually all historians agree on two things: firstly, that the Komintern's activities accelerated the Weimar Republic's demise; secondly, that Stalin completely misjudged the Third Reich – Nazi diplomacy was not always anti-Soviet but National Socialist ideology was consistently anti-communist.[49] Foreign policy specialists have also drawn attention to the equivocations of the bourgeois democracies and the vengeful disposition of authoritarian régimes, fascist and neo-fascist. In their belief that Hitler's appetites could be gratified solely at Eastern Europe's expense, Western leaders were no less myopic than the General Secretary, while the right, which saw Nazism as the chief bulwark against communism, positively welcomed the prospect of Germany's *Drang nach Osten*. Anglo-French prevarications after Munich thus practically forced Stalin into Hitler's arms, but viewed from Moscow the Nazi–Soviet treaty seemed well timed: skilful (if cynical) diplomacy appeared to have deflected the aggressor westwards.[50]

There is less consensus on the problem of territorial aggrandizement. One interpretation characterizes the Red Army's pre-1941 border campaigns as imperialistic, indistinguishable from Germany's drive for European dominion and Japan's pursuit of Asian hegemony: the non-aggression pact's secret protocols facilitated Russian control of Eastern Europe, but in misreading Hitler's intentions Stalin plunged his burgeoning empire into a savage conflict. Another attributes a mixture of isolationist and revolutionary motives to the régime: the government tried to secure national frontiers in the hope that Bolshevism's long-standing enemies – Britain, France, Germany and Japan – would at least leave the country alone, or, having consumed each other in a second world war, would rekindle the fires of international socialism.[51]

[49] Though tensions rose after Hitler came to power trade between the two countries continued unabated until the invasion.

[50] The pioneering work on Soviet foreign policy in the 1930s is M. Beloff, *The Foreign Policy of Soviet Russia* (Vols. 1–2, Oxford University Press, 1947). More recent treatments include E. H. Carr, *The Twilight of the Comintern 1930–1935* (Macmillan, London, 1982); J. Haslam, *Soviet Foreign Policy 1930–33: The Impact of the Great Depression* (Macmillan, London, 1983); id., *The Soviet Union and the Struggle for Collective Security in Europe 1933–39* (Macmillan, London, 1984); S. M. Miner, *Between Stalin and Churchill: The Soviet Union, Great Britain, and the Origins of the Grand Alliance* (University of North Carolina Press, 1988). For a useful overview see I. Deutscher, *Stalin: A Political Biography* (2nd ed., Penguin, 1972) chs. 10–11.

[51] See V. Mástny, *Russia's Road to the Cold War: Diplomacy, Warfare and the Politics of Communism 1941–1944* (Columbia University Press, 1979); R. A. Medvedev, *Let History Judge: The Origins and Consequences of Stalinism* (trans. C. Taylor, Knopf, New York, 1971) ch. 12; A. Read, *The Deadly Embrace: Hitler, Stalin and the Nazi–Soviet Pact 1939–1941* (Joseph, London, 1986).

Similar divisions inform post-1944 foreign policy analysis. Specialists who perceive augmented Russian power in Eastern and Central Europe as a step towards global domination are challenged by those who consider Stalin's conduct reactive. For the first group, Western action belatedly halted Soviet expansionism: NATO and the Marshall Plan bridled Stalin in Europe; United Nations intervention in Korea frustrated his Asian schemes; the Truman doctrine essayed the containment of communism world-wide. For the second, the institutionalization of Soviet power in the occupied territories was primarily defensive. Exhausted by war, confronted by nascent American imperialism, Russia forged a cordon sanitaire from the ruins of the Axis empires, the Rubicon which the capitalist warmongers crossed at their peril.[52]

Defeat and victory

The defeat inflicted on the Red Army by the Axis in 1941 beggars description: far more calamitous than the Napoleonic invasion, far more terrible even than the disasters of 1914–17. Four years later that defeat had been turned into a victory of stunning proportions. In comparison Alexander I's destruction of the *Grande Armée* in 1812 pales into insignificance.

Until recently these images have coloured all studies of the Great Fatherland War. They have also prompted researchers to tackle a series of fundamental problems: why was Hitler's initial Blitzkrieg so devastating, how did the country survive, and, having weathered the storm, what enabled the régime to overcome the Third Reich? Since the mid–1940s historians have furnished answers to these questions by reference to established analytical categories; military, political and economic. Each contains two interpretative viewpoints, 'negative' and 'positive'. The first emphasizes Soviet incompetence (particularly in 1941) and Germany's military and political failures. The second highlights the USSR's tenacity and responsiveness in the context of total war.

The negative view

By May 1941 socialism was in mortal danger. Due in no small measure to Moscow's largesse (the Wehrmacht benefited from Soviet deliveries of food and raw materials) the capitalist powers had failed

---

[52] For this discussion see, in addition to the works cited on the previous page, W. E. Griffith, ed., *The Soviet Empire: Expansion and Détente* (Lexington Books, Lexington, 1976); T. T. Hammond, ed., *The Anatomy of Communist Takeovers* (Yale University Press, 1975); G. Kennan, *Russia and the West Under Lenin and Stalin* (Hutchinson, London, 1961); M. McCauley, ed., *Communist Power in Europe 1944–1949* (Macmillan, London, 1977); W. O. McCagg, *Stalin Embattled 1943–1948* (Wayne State University Press, 1978); A. B. Ulam, *Expansion and Coexistence: Soviet Foreign Policy 1917–1973* (2nd ed., Holt, Rinehart & Winston, New York, 1974).

to exhaust each other and Germany bestrode western, central and eastern Europe.[53] The Russo-German conflict was therefore the result of a colossal blunder – Stalin's trust in Hitler. In Medvedev's phrase 'one-man rule combined with the one man's limitations' to produce disaster.[54] Moreover, having discounted the likelihood of hostilities and persistently courted Hitler,[55] the trauma of invasion seems to have provoked Stalin's complete collapse. Historians now have access to his appointments diary: he was inactive for a couple of days at the end of June and broadcast to the nation only on 3 July. 'Molotov said that Stalin was in such a state of prostration', reported Mikoian,

> that he wasn't interested in anything, he'd lost all initiative and was in a bad way. Voznesenskii, appalled to hear this, said, 'You go on ahead, Viacheslav, and we'll be behind you.' The idea was that, if Stalin was going to continue to behave in this way, then Molotov ought to lead us and we would follow him... We got to Stalin's dacha. We found him in an armchair in the small dining room. He looked up and said, 'What have you come for?' He had the strangest look on his face, and the question itself was pretty strange too. After all, he should have called us in. On our behalf Molotov said power had to be concentrated in order to ensure rapid decision-making and somehow to get the country back on its feet, and Stalin should head the new authority. Stalin made no objection and said, 'Fine.'[56]

Later he compounded his errors by toying with the idea of a separate peace – first in 1941 and again in 1943 – thus strengthening German resolve while sowing doubts in Western minds.[57]

[53] See Deutscher, *Stalin*, ch. 11; Medvedev, *Let History Judge*, ch. 12; D. Volkogonov, *Stalin: Triumph & Tragedy* (trans. H. Shukman, Weidenfeld & Nicolson, London, 1991) ch. 7.
[54] Medvedev, *Let History Judge*, p. 454.
[55] In November 1940 Molotov visited Berlin to discuss Soviet adherence to the 'tripartite pact', the Axis alliance between Germany, Italy and Japan. A British air raid interrupted Hitler's boast that the European war was virtually over, prompting a few caustic remarks from Molotov as everyone scurried to the nearest shelter. In the end negotiations foundered on Japanese objections.
[56] Cited Volkogonov, *Stalin*, p. 411.
[57] In October 1941 Stalin reportedly offered Hitler Moldavia, the Baltic Republics and huge swaths of Belarus and the Ukraine. Allied prevarications over the second front prompted hints of a second offer in 1943; according to a British intelligence officer Molotov made a 200 mile journey into German occupied territory in June to discuss terms with the Nazis. See H. Koch, 'The spectre of a separate peace in the East', *Journal of Contemporary History* (3, 1975); McCagg, *Stalin Embattled*, ch. 8; V. Mástny, 'Stalin and the prospects of a separate peace in World War II', *American Historical Review* (5, 1972); Volkogonov, *Stalin*, pp. 412–3; W. Stevenson, *A Man Called Intrepid: The Secret War* (Macmillan, London, 1976) p. 381.

To these political mistakes were added military follies, long known
to Western scholars but detailed with increasing boldness inside
Russia under glasnost'.[58] Stalin's penchant for offensive deployments
and his faith in Hitler impeded the Red Army's post-1940 reorganization and eased Germany's advance. He then executed a string of
front-line generals, weakening still further a command structure
already ravaged by the Ezhovshchina, while continuing to squander
resources in futile manœuvres.[59] As a result panic swept the defence-
less capital in mid-October and the régime trembled on the edge of
collapse. 'It was said that a *coup d'état* had occurred in the Kremlin',
recalled Viktor Kravchenko,

> that Stalin was under arrest, that the Germans were already in
> Fili on the edge of the city... Crowds surged from street to
> street, then back again in sudden waves of panic. Already riot-
> ing and looting had begun. Stores and warehouses were being
> emptied by frenzied mobs. The impression spread that there was
> no more government; that millions of Muscovites had been
> abandoned to their fate without food, fuel or weapons. Order
> was collapsing.[60]

Deliverance came, not from the Red Army, but from Axis miscalcu-
lations and the fortuitous intervention of natural forces. In Hitler's
view once Blitzkrieg had undermined Soviet morale the Russian
state would disintegrate, not in a matter of years, as was the case in
the Great War, but within weeks. This would be achieved by annex-

---

[58] The classic Western studies of the Russo-German war are J. Erickson, *Stalin's War
with Germany: The Road to Stalingrad* (Weidenfeld & Nicolson, London, 1975); id.,
Stalin's War with Germany: The Road to Berlin (Weidenfeld & Nicolson, London,
1983). Two official Soviet histories of the conflict exist, *Istoriia Velikoi Otechestvennoi
voiny Sovetskogo Soiuza 1941–1945 gg* (Vols. 1–6, Moscow, 1961–5) and *Istoriia
Vtoroi Mirovoi voiny 1939–1945 gg* (Vols. 1–12, Moscow, 1973–82). Both mirrored
current political thinking: the first was a product of Khrushchev's thaw, the second
reflected the ideological predilections of the Brezhnev era. A third history was in
preparation when the USSR collapsed. For surveys of glasnost' writing on the Great
Fatherland War see R. W. Davies, *Soviet History in the Gorbachev Revolution*
(Macmillan, London, 1989) ch. 8; W. Laqueur, *Stalin: The Glasnost Revelations*
(Unwin Hyman, London, 1990) ch. 11.
[59] Deficiencies revealed by the Finnish campaign had not been remedied by June 1941
and arrangements for the protection of the newly incorporated European territories
were incomplete. See M. Garder, *Histoire de l'Armée Soviétique* (Librairie Plon, Paris,
1959) ch. 9; A. M. Nekrich, *1941 22 iiunia* (Moscow, 1965); N. Pavlenko, 'Na pervom
etape voiny: zametki voennogo istorika', *Kommunist* (9, 1988); V. Petrov, *June 22
1941: Soviet Historians and the German Invasion* (University of South Carolina Press,
1968).
[60] V. Kravchenko, *I Chose Freedom: The Personal and Political Life of a Soviet
Official* (Robert Hale, London, 1947) pp. 375–6; For another vivid description of the
'Moscow panic' see Werth, *Russia at War*, ch. 10.

ing non-Russian territories and seizing the capital. The military aspect of these plans began to go awry almost immediately. Short of supplies, completely unprepared for the autumn rains and winter frosts (troops hastily moved from the Balkans were still in Mediterranean gear), the Wehrmacht ground to a halt outside Moscow, allowing the Red Army to recover, launch a counter-offensive and start the long haul to Berlin. Thereafter, though Stalin continually obstructed the high command and interfered in matters beyond his competence,[61] the Soviet economy began to out-produce Germany, a portent of victory underwritten by generous allied aid and guaranteed by Hitler's refusal to place the Third Reich on a full war footing until 1944.[62]

The political aspect, German hopes of support from disaffected national minorities, was at first rather more successful. Pre-war policies – mass collectivization and mass terror – evinced mass discontents, resentments accentuated by the country's multinational character and amplified by recent territorial acquisitions. In consequence numerous Soviets welcomed the invaders as liberators: Baltic irregulars rose against the Red Army in the first days of the war, pro-German demonstrations swept L'vov, and for the next three years tens of thousands of Ukrainians, Belarusians, Georgians and Balts co-operated openly with the Wehrmacht, Gestapo and SS. Vlasov's 'Russian Liberation Army', recruited from anti-Soviet deserters and Russian prisoners of war, added to Moscow's distress.[63] One source estimates that as many as two million Soviet citizens may have donned German uniforms,[64] but in the end Nazi ideology proved self-defeating. Vlasov's battalions were never permitted scope for independent action; rivalry between the Wehrmacht, the SS and the

[61] For Stalin's military incompetence and his failure to heed professional advice see Volkogonov, *Stalin*, ch. 9. For allied aid see the figures in Barber & Harrison, *Soviet Home Front*, table 12 p. 221 and the discussion in M. Harrison, *Soviet Planning in Peace and War 1938–1945* (Cambridge University Press, 1985) appendix 3. A detailed treatment can be found in G. C. Herring, *Aid to Russia 1941–1946: Strategy, Diplomacy, the Origins of the Cold War* (Columbia University Press, 1973); R. H. Jones, *The Roads to Russia: United States Lend-Lease to the Soviet Union* (University of Oklahoma Press, 1969); L. Martel, *Lend-Lease Loans and the Coming of the Cold War: A Study of the Implementation of Foreign Policy* (Westview Press, Boulder, 1979).
[62] See Harrison, *Soviet Planning*; S. R. Lieberman, 'Crisis management in the USSR: the wartime system of administration and control', in S. J. Linz, ed., *The Impact of World War II on the Soviet Union* (Rowman & Allanheld, Totowa, 1985); N. A. Voznesenskii, *War Economy of the USSR in the Period of the Patriotic War* (Moscow, 1948).
[63] The Russian Liberation Army is discussed in C. Andreyev, *Vlasov and the Russian Liberation Movement: Soviet Reality and Émigré Theories* (Cambridge University Press, 1987).
[64] G. Fischer, *Soviet Opposition to Stalin* (Harvard University Press, 1952) p. 45.

Reich Ministry for Occupied Eastern Territories frustrated the development of native anti-Soviet movements while Nazi barbarities turned putative allies into deadly enemies.[65]

The positive view

If June 1941 revealed Stalinism's limitations – rigidity, paralysis and confusion in the face of the unexpected – subsequent events demonstrated the system's vigour and flexibility. 'Superior force' and 'defence in depth' quickly became Stavka's guiding principles. Their effectiveness was demonstrated in 1943: the Kursk counter-attack was launched only after huge static deployments had absorbed and dissipated the initial German assault. Thereafter Soviet commanders proceeded on a step by step basis, massing resources, overwhelming the enemy and pausing to consolidate before resuming their advance.[66] Moreover, by 1943 the Wehrmacht had to contend, not only with powerful conventional forces, but also with a strong guerilla movement supported by the local population. Partisan units in contact with the NKVD frequently timed their raids to coincide with Stavka's offensives.[67]

Leningrad's survival and military successes raised Soviet morale, as did the régime's toleration of religion and assiduous cultivation of Soviet patriotism.[68] 'The Stalingrad epic', wrote the the novelist and playwright Vasilii Grossman,

> is a page written with fire and blood, and stamped with the staunchness of our troops, the courage of our workers, their unbounded patriotism... Sanguinary battles are once more being waged in the very same place where Red troops had defended Tsaritsyn. Once more the names of the villages and hamlets associated with Tsaritsyn's defence are being enumerated in the war bulletins. The troops are marching past the old trenches, long overgrown with grass, that have been described by historians of the Civil War; and no small number of veterans

[65] For Nazi policy towards the nationalities see A. R. Alexiev, *Soviet Nationalities in German Wartime Strategy 1941–1945* (Rand Corporation, R-2772-NA, August 1982); id., 'Soviet nationalities under attack: The World War II experience', in S. E. Wimbush, ed., *Soviet Nationalities in Strategic Perspective* (Croom Helm, London, 1985); A. Dallin, *German Rule in Russia 1941–1945: A Study of Occupation Policies* (2nd ed., Macmillan, London, 1981); T. J. Schulte, *The German Army and Nazi Policies in Occupied Russia* (Berg, Oxford, 1989).
[66] See Erickson, *Road to Stalingrad*, book 2; id., *Road to Berlin*, ch. 3.
[67] See J. Armstrong, ed., *Soviet Partisans in World War II* (University of Wisconsin Press, 1964).
[68] For Russian Orthodoxy see W. C. Fletcher, 'The Soviet Bible Belt: World War II's effects on religion', Linz, *Impact of World War II*.

of Red Tsaritsyn's defence – workers, party members, fishermen and peasants – are volunteering for the defence of Red Stalingrad.[69]

But patriotism was not just induced by propaganda. Arriving in the city soon after an air raid, Grossman jotted down the details of one engagement involving a few of the defenders, Lieutenant Skakun and his comrades:

> Cut off from its regiment... this ack-ack battery fought alone... repulsing enemy attacks from the air and ground. Earth and air, fire and smoke, the iron clangour of exploding bombs, the wailing of shells and clatter of machine-gun bursts fused in one chaos. There were girls in his battery... they fought side by side with their fellow gunners. Every time the ack-acks fell silent the Regimental Commander thought, 'They're done for, done for!' And each time the distinct, even volley of ack-ack guns came to his ears again. This terrible battle lasted for twenty-four hours. Only in the evening of the next day did the four men who were left... and the wounded commander get to the regiment. They said that during the fighting the girls had never once gone off to the shelter...[70]

Stalinist vignettes like this are not exaggerations. Extraordinary heroism was a commonplace of everyday life – something shared by party members, Komsomolites, workers, kolkhozniki, partisans and front-line soldiers; men and women of all nationalities united by hatred of the invader and inspired by memories of Revolution and Civil War, and by pride in the achievements of socialist construction.

The 'positive' factor most frequently discussed by historians, however, is the command–administrative system's resilience in the face of what seemed to be certain defeat. Enormous territorial losses, unfavourable weather and declining manpower seriously reduced agricultural production, but despite these problems collectivized farming, augmented by private markets, supplied enough food to keep military personnel and the millions of workers who serviced the burgeoning wartime economy from absolute starvation.[71] On the

---

[69] V. Grossman, *The Years of War 1941–1945* (Moscow, 1946) pp. 187–8. Grossman (1905–64) graduated in physics and mathematics from Moscow University before turning to literature.

[70] Grossman, *Years of War*, p. 187.

[71] Nearly six million able-bodied men left the countryside between 1941 and 1945, a fall of about sixty per cent. See Barber & Harrison, *Soviet Home Front*, pp. 187–8; A. Nove, 'Soviet peasantry in World War II', in Linz, *Impact of World War II*. The best monograph on wartime agriculture currently available in Russian is Iu. V. Arutiunian, *Sovetskoi krest'ianstvo v gody Velikoi Otechestvennoi voiny* (Moscow, 1970).

industrial front the concentration on group A enterprises, increasing defence production and the construction of new factories in and behind the Urals – distinguishing features of the three pre-war plans as well as the period 1941–5 – furnished the Red Army with the means to wear down the enemy.[72] In 1940 the country had at its disposal 10,565 aircraft, 2,794 tanks (an eighty per cent increase on the 1937 figure), 15,300 artillery pieces and nearly 1.5 million rifles and carbines. Though much was destroyed in June 1941, by following a policy of 'rearmament in depth' before the invasion (investment, not only in weapon stocks, but also in basic industries and civilian engineering) the USSR was able to recover rapidly from Operation Barbarossa's initial devastating impact.[73]

If the material bed-rock for Russia's victory was laid down in the 1930s, runs the argument, so was the organizational base. Central direction of agriculture and command–administrative industrialization – the latter strengthened by Voznesenskii's post-Ezhovshchina rationalization of Gosplan – provided GOKO with a rough and ready means of economic management.[74] But the elaboration of a war economy did not proceed smoothly. Soviet economic mobilization was partly improvised and partly planned. The switch from civilian to military production and the relocation of vital industries to the east which occurred immediately after June 1941 was largely *ad hoc*.[75] Only in late 1942 did GOKO abandon emergency measures in favour of a more formal system of planning and control, and only by 1943 had the crisis induced by invasion been fully overcome.[76] Nevertheless, the command–administrative system functioned astonishingly well: between 1941 and 1945 ten million people were evacu-

---

[72] See chapter 3 and J. M. Cooper, 'Defence production and the Soviet economy 1929–1941', *SIPS 3* (Discussion Paper, Centre for Russian & East European Studies, University of Birmingham, 1976).

[73] See Harrison, *Soviet Planning*, table 2 p. 8, ch. 2 part 1.

[74] In July 1940 the working week was increased and the production of sub-standard goods criminalized – managers and engineers in the affected enterprises were liable to prison sentences of between five and eight years. Both measures were intended to boost military output. Three months later a 'state labour reserve' was organized to mobilize boys for vocational courses and the direction of labour imposed on skilled workers and specialists. For Voznesenskii's tenure as head of Gosplan see Harrison, *Soviet Planning*, ch. 1.

[75] GOKO's main achievement in the early days of the war was to disperse the commissariats to the interior. Despite the 'Moscow panic' virtually the entire party-state apparatus was safely evacuated in mid-October, mostly to Kazan', Kuibyshev and Sverdlovsk. Most organizations returned to the capital in summer 1943.

[76] See Barber & Harrison, *Soviet Home Front*, chs. 7, 11; Harrison, *Soviet Planning*, chs. 2, 4; S. R. Lieberman, 'The evacuation of industry in the Soviet Union during World War II', *Soviet Studies* (1, 1983); id., in Linz, *Impact of World War II*; M. S. Zinich, 'Iz istorii stakostroeniia i tiazhelogo mashinostroeniia v pervyi period Velikoi Otechestvennoi voiny', *Istoriia SSSR* (6, 1971).

ated to the east, vast new industrial conurbations arose in the Urals, Siberia and Central Asia, by 1944 total production was four per cent higher than in 1940, and by the following year the country had more operating railway lines than at any time in its history. The war years witnessed the greatest triumphs of Soviet planning

1945–53

In comparison with the topics discussed elsewhere in this book the period 1945–53 has attracted relatively little scholarly interest. Moreover, Western, Soviet and post-Soviet writing has concentrated almost exclusively on high politics and Stalin's rôle within the party-state machine.

One interpretation holds that Germany's defeat rendered the General Secretary's position impregnable. Others might be allowed some limited scope for action – Beriia in the secret police, Khrushchev, Malenkov and Zhdanov in the central committee secretariat – but the deportation of potentially troublesome national minorities, Nazi atrocities, the upsurge of Soviet nationalism and the mobilization of the population around patriotic motifs signalled the apotheosis of the vozhd', the supreme leader whose word was law. Sovereignty over the police, the government and the party, maintained Roger Pethybridge, allowed Stalin

> to penetrate into any sector of Soviet life, enforce all his designs, and prevent the rise of likely rivals for power. The victorious course of the war merely served to shore up his unassailable position and enabled him to reassert his control over national life with great rapidity after 1945.[77]

Most histories published in the first three post-war decades take much the same line.[78] Competition between Malenkov and Zhdanov probably occasioned the latter's fall in 1948; Beriia almost certainly deployed the security apparatus against his enemies; Bulganin, Khrushchev, Mikoian and Molotov manipulated their own bureaucratic bailiwicks in the struggle for influence. But none of this

[77] R. Pethybridge, *A History of Postwar Russia* (Allen & Unwin, London, 1966) p. 49.
[78] In addition to the biographies cited in chapter 1 see J. Armstrong, *The Politics of Totalitarianism: The Communist Party of the Soviet Union from 1934 to the Present* (Random House, New York, 1961); R. Bauer, et al., *How the Soviet System Works* (Harvard University Press, 1956); Z. K. Brzezinski, ed., *The Soviet Bloc* (Harvard University Press, 1960); R. Conquest, *Power and Policy in the USSR* (Macmillan, London, 1961); H. S. Dinerstein, *War and the Soviet Union* (Stevens, London, 1959); C. J. Friedrich & Z. K. Brzezinski, *Totalitarian Dictatorship and Autocracy* (Oxford University Press, 1956); L. Schapiro, *The Communist Party of the Soviet Union* (2nd ed., Eyre & Spottiswoode, London, 1970); id., *Totalitarianism* (Pall Mall, London, 1972).

touched the Generalissimo. The Leningrad Affair – instigated by Stalin or prosecuted with his approval – sealed the fate of Zhdanov's supporters. Two years later Beriia's star began to wane. Like many of his closest aides the police chief hailed from Mingrelian Georgia; the Mingrelian Case was therefore Stalin's shot across the bows of an over-mighty Soviet baron.[79] According to Khrushchev several luminaries, notably Mikoian and Molotov, were in grave personal danger in the last months of Stalin's life.[80] And since many of the ruling clique were of Jewish origin there is general consensus that the Doctors' Plot foreshadowed renewed bloodletting within the upper leadership.[81]

Whilst agreeing that the struggle against Hitler raised Stalin's prestige to new heights and – more significantly – legitimized the Soviet system in the people's eyes, a second interpretation argues that acute political imbalances began to appear after 1945. Leaders who clambered to prominence in the 1930s found themselves menaced by new élites thrown up by the war. Aleksei Kuznetsov's promotion, from Leningrad's Defence Council to the central committee department in charge of checking the security forces, threatened Beriia,[82] for example, while Voznesenskii's appointment as deputy chairman of the Council of Ministers, and his elevation to the Politburo in 1947 alarmed established figures like Kaganovich, Molotov and Voroshilov. Voznesenskii also angered Stalin by publishing a popular treatise on economics.[83] In consequence the pre-war oligarchy seized on the Leningrad Affair as a means to cut the new cohort down to size while Stalin utilized anti-semitism (widespread in Russian society), the cult of personality and his reputation for doctrinal infallibility to keep rivals at bay.[84]

---

[79] See Conquest, *Power & Policy*, ch. 7; J. Ducoli, 'The Georgian purges (1951–53)', *Caucasian Review* (6, 1958) and for a recent treatment V. F. Nekrasov, *Beriia: konets kar'ery* (Moscow, 1991).

[80] N. S. Khrushchev, *Khrushchev Remembers* (trans. S. Talbott, Book Club, London, 1971) pp. 308–10.

[81] For a glasnost' account of the Doctors' Plot see Ia. L. Rapoport, *Na rubezhe dvukh epokh. Delo vrachei 1953 g* (Moscow, 1988).

[82] Kuznetsov (1905–50) was of a younger vintage than the other Stalinists. He joined the party when he was twenty. After working in the Komsomol he moved to the Leningrad party organization in the 1930s. Like many others he was elected to the central committee in 1939.

[83] Voznesenskii's *War Economy of the USSR*.

[84] For an elaboration of this interpretation see Medvedev, *Let History Judge*, ch. 13. See also R. Conquest, *Stalin: Breaker of Nations* (Weidenfeld & Nicolson, London, 1991) ch. 14. Apart from the interest aroused by Voznesenskii's monograph, the 1951 decision to commission a new textbook on economics seems to have excited behind the scenes discussions amongst economists – until, that is, Stalin foreclosed debate by publishing his *Economic Problems of Socialism* on the eve of the nineteenth party congress. See J. F. Hough & M. Fainsod, *How the Soviet Union is Governed* (Harvard University Press, 1979) p. 185.

The idea that the General Secretary was only one actor – albeit the most important – in a complex political drama is supported by researchers who focus their attention on policy debates. Walter McCagg portrays Stalin as an embattled despot facing powerful interest groups outside the party (the high command, industrial managers and local soviet apparatchiki – the chief beneficiaries of wartime exigencies) and political challenges from within (Marxist ideologues ambitious to cast Eastern Europe and post-war Russia in a new political mould).[85] Others have adduced further instances of tension and disagreement, this time at the apex of the party-state machine. During interminable dinners at Stalin's dacha – usually attended by Beriia, Malenkov, Khrushchev, and to a lesser extent Molotov – views were exchanged with relative freedom on a wide range of issues, economic problems in particular,[86] but the most striking example of the confusions and hesitations which may have disturbed the apparently uniform façade of late Stalinism has been unearthed by students of ideology.

In a major speech, delivered at Moscow's Bolshoi Theatre in February 1946, the General Secretary asserted that monopoly capitalism was the root cause of the recent European war and that Russia's victory over Germany was due to the superiority of the USSR's social and political system, a pronouncement usually interpreted as the prelude to Zhdanov's party renewal campaign. Since capitalism remained so did the threat of hostilities; the Soviet Union was therefore obliged to look, not only to its military, but also to its ideological defences. According to Werner Hahn, however, Zhdanov was an incipient 'moderate' who lost out to 'extremists' within the ruling clique. Like many others he imagined that wartime relaxation at home and détente with the West would continue. His aims were modest: on the one hand to curtail Malenkov's power, on the other to confine ideological renewal to the party. But by 1947 the tide was turning against him. Deteriorating international relations, destabilizing competition within the élite, and (following the decision to switch resources from civilian to defence needs) the fear that economic austerity might provoke large-scale social unrest, persuaded Stalin to reduce the population's contacts with foreigners and stimulate the most primitive form of cultural nationalism. Thereafter Zhdanov's

[85] McCagg, *Stalin Embattled*, parts 2–3.
[86] See T. Dunmore, *The Stalinist Command Economy: The Soviet State Apparatus and Economic Policy 1945–53* (Macmillan, London, 1980). See also Conquest, *Power & Policy*, ch. 1; S. Bialer, ed., *Stalin and His Generals: Soviet Military Memoirs of World War II* (Pegasus, New York, 1969); R. C. Tucker, *The Soviet Political Mind* (Praeger, New York, 1963) pp. 27–35. The image of policy-making as personal and unofficial is suggested by M. Djilas, *Conversations With Stalin* (Harcourt, New York, 1962) pp. 76–7; Khrushchev, *Khrushchev Remembers*, p. 311. Molotov seems to have fallen out of favour during Stalin's last years.

enemies hijacked his campaign and unleashed a sweeping 'Zhdanovshchina' which had little to do with Zhdanov and actually peaked after his death.[87]

Social history

If research into the high politics of late Stalinism is still in its infancy, the same is even more true of social history. Several authors have outlined the impact of the Second World War on Soviet society but as yet there is little substantive debate on these matters.

In the first place, the conflict impinged directly on virtually every family. Not only did the enormous size of the military and the staggering level of casualties leave psychological and physical scars which even today have still not healed, family structures began to change. A rash of weddings in summer 1941 (couples marrying before they were parted) was followed by a steep decline in both marriages and births as young men left for the front, and a corresponding rise in divorces and unofficial liaisons. In Siberia, for example, marriages fell from 4.7 per thousand head of population in 1941 to 2.3 in 1943, while in Moscow over the same period births fell from 22.2 to 8.5 per thousand. Later, in 1944 and 1948, the régime responded by tightening divorce laws, granting generous allowances to large families, financially penalizing couples with less than three children and introducing civil awards – 'heroine-mother' and 'motherhood glory' – for particularly fecund women.

Secondly, the geographical distribution of population changed significantly. Untold numbers who fled of their own accord added to the millions evacuated eastwards. Many never returned to ruined homes and deserted families. Thirdly, the peasant's life became incomparably harder: not all kolkhozniki benefited from the zveno system, MTSs were denuded of tractors and lorries, and since there were no reserved occupations in farming the burdens of physical work fell heavily on spinsters, wives and daughters – by 1945 eighty per cent of collective farm workers were women. Finally, the industrial workforce was transformed in a manner no less dramatic than during the first piatiletka: numbers employed in large-scale industry fell from 8.3 to 7.2 million between 1940 and 1945; average length of work experience declined sharply, as did average age and skill profile. On the other hand the level of female participation increased markedly: fifty-one per cent of workers in large-scale industry were women in 1945 as against forty-one per cent in 1940.[88]

[87] W. G. Hahn, *Postwar Soviet Politics: The Fall of Zhdanov and the Defeat of Moderation 1946–53* (Cornell University Press, 1982). A similar interpretation is offered in T. Dunmore, *Soviet Politics 1945–53* (Macmillan, London, 1984); J. F. Hough, 'Debates about the postwar world', in Linz, *Impact of World War II*.
[88] For these social aspects see Arutiunian, *Sovetskoi krest'ianstvo*; Barber & Harrison, *Soviet Home Front*, ch. 6; A. V. Mitrofanova, *Rabochii klass SSSR v gody Velikoi Otechestvennoi voiny* (Moscow, 1984); Nove, in Linz, *Impact of World War II*.

Given the traumatic impact of the anti-fascist struggle on the people at large – huge losses, massive population transfers, the emasculation of the village and the total disruption of family life – Sheila Fitzpatrick hypothesizes that the late 1940s were characterized by a near universal longing for economic and political liberalization, but while there was no repetition of mass purging, release from emergency constraints was delayed until after Stalin's death, due in part to prolonged economic crisis, in part to the régime's growing xenophobia and petrifaction.[89] The abrogation of zven'ia reaffirmed the régime's commitment to socialized agriculture, dashed hopes of fundamental reform, reduced still further the rural standard of living and convinced the enterprising – males in particular – to spurn the village.[90] For workers the picture was equally discouraging. The draconian labour laws of the late 1930s and early 1940s seem to have been ignored during the war, and though money payments rose dramatically, by 1950 inflation had reduced real wages to 1940 levels. In addition, differentials between manual and white-collar workers grew apace,[91] thus fostering the development of an urbanized bureaucratic stratum which, in the absence of a second Ezhovshchina, finally began to assume the features of a distinct caste within Soviet society.

Evaluations

International dilemmas
For Bolshevik intellectuals the October insurrection was both an end and a beginning, the climax of a native movement stretching back to Decembrism and the augury of international socialism. Moreover, without pan-European revolution – or at the very least a successful German rising – Lenin and his associates firmly believed that their régime was destined to suffer the same fate as the Paris Commune: in Churchill's words the allies would 'strangle the infant Bolshevik at birth'. No illusions were shattered, therefore, when the capitalists excluded Moscow from the Versailles peace conference and conjured

---

[89] S. Fitzpatrick, 'Postwar Soviet society: the "return to normalcy" 1945–53', in Linz, *Impact of World War II*.
[90] See R. Conquest, *Agricultural Workers in the USSR* (The Bodley Head, London, 1968); J. F. Karcz, 'From Stalin to Brezhnev: Soviet agricultural policy in historical perspective', in J. R. Millar, ed., *The Soviet Rural Community* (University of Illinois Press, 1971).
[91] See R. Feldmesser, 'Equality and inequality under Khrushchev', *Problems of Communism* (9, 1960); L. J. Kirsch, *Soviet Wages* (Massachusetts Institute of Technology Press, 1972) p. 3; E. V. Koplov, et al., eds., *Sotsial'noe razvitie rabochego klassa SSSR* (Moscow, 1972) p. 143; *Narodnoe khoziaistvo SSSR 1922–1972 gg* (Moscow, 1972) p. 350.

a tranche of jealously independent 'successor states' from the wreck-age of the continental empires, a cordon sanitaire contrived in part to protect bourgeois Europe from the socialist bacillus.[92] Equally no one was surprised when the West supported the Whites in 1918. And no one imagined that the defeat of the imperialists in 1919–20 was complete. Most party leaders assumed that sooner or later European capitalism, abetted by Japanese militarists, Chinese war-lords and American financiers, would try once more to destroy the workers' republic. These perceptions fused with memories of numerous humiliations endured under the *ancien régime* (from the Crimean to the First World War) to form the background to Stalin's foreign poli-cy in the 1930s, and they should not be dismissed as specious or unre-alistic. Russia had a huge and vulnerable land border – a factor which had been of long-standing concern to the country's rulers – and no friends and many enemies. The Kuomintang massacred Shanghai's communists in 1927; Japanese expansionism threatened Mongolia and Siberia; Britain and France could scarcely bring them-selves to recognize the USSR while Finland, Poland and the Baltic states drew their *raison d'être* from a heady brew of chauvinism, anti-communism and Russophobia.

Apart from the USSR only the Weimar Republic, that other pari-ah of the international community, disputed the new European order, a circumstance which drove the two 'revisionist' powers towards an uneasy accommodation during the 1920s.[93] But Soviet interest in Berlin's affairs extended beyond the usual diplomatic niceties. Hope lingered on that one day Germany's proletariat would take up the banner of international revolution, something that by 1929 appeared at last to be more than a pipe dream. Not only did Western economic disarray contrast sharply with events at home – if the Wall Street Crash was proof positive of capitalism's collapse the simultaneous launch of the first piatiletka pointed to socialism's inherent superiority – as the Weimar Republic reeled under the impact of global financial crisis local communists seemed on the brink of power. Few statesmen believed that Hitler would become Chancellor, still less that a Nazi régime could last for more than a few weeks. Viewed in context, therefore, the theory of social fascism

---

[92] France's president, Georges Clemenceau, called the new democratic nationalist Eastern European states *un fil de fer barbelé* – 'a length of barbed wire' protecting Europe from revolutionary socialism. French financiers who had lent millions to the tsarist régime were particularly hostile. See D. Thomson, *Europe Since Napoleon* (2nd ed., Penguin, 1966) ch. 24.

[93] On the one hand Germany hoped to reverse those provisions of the Versailles Treaty which crippled her economy and army, on the other to regain lost territories. Germany was the first country to accept a Soviet ambassador (1922). Trade and mili-tary agreements soon followed. Relationships were formalized by treaty in 1926.

seemed apposite; indeed, in the final analysis the Komintern's policy appeared to be both revolutionary and anti-fascist. Once before in 1918–19 moderate socialists had foiled the revolution.[94] This time there would be no mistake. German communism would remove the root causes of fascism and imperialism forever. On the other hand, to many revolutionaries social fascism made no sense at all. Before Stalin, Marxists had always sharply distinguished moderate social democracy from right-wing reaction, and there were voices in the Komintern – not to mention Trotsky – who advocated a far more discriminatory policy.[95] The German Communist Party's blind sectarianism, instigated from Moscow, assisted Hitler's rise to power.

Thereafter Stalin had to digest several unpalatable facts. While Hitler's success boosted right-wing authoritarianism throughout Europe, the West's commitment to collective security remained lukewarm. By the summer of 1939, given Polish intransigence and the Anglo-French reluctance to treat seriously with Russia, Stalin's options had virtually disappeared. A general European war seemed inevitable, but the Red Army, still engaged in Manchukuo and seriously weakened by the Ezhovshchina, was in no condition to face the Third Reich. The Nazi–Soviet pact was thus a logical response to an appalling international dilemma, a defensive measure assembled in Berlin and Moscow but manufactured in London, Paris and Warsaw.

Defensive thinking also determined Stalin's foreign policy after 1945. Profoundly debilitated by four years of struggle against the most vicious imperialist régime ever to emerge from Europe, Russia was quite unable to risk further conflict. When Germany surrendered Soviet forces stopped fighting, confined their activities to the occupied territories and grudgingly accepted the intrusive presence of West Berlin deep within the socialist sphere of influence. When British soldiers crushed the Greek communists Moscow did nothing, even though a friendly government in Athens would have eased Russia's position in the Black Sea and eastern Mediterranean. When United Nations forces entered North Korea Stalin refused to commit Soviet troops, despite the fact that the régime owed its very existence to the USSR.

Therefore, the protestations of Cold War historians notwithstanding, there is no reason to suspect the existence a Stalinist plot to swallow up Europe. In fact the evidence points in the opposite direc-

---

[94] After the Grand Fleet mutinied at Kiel in the summer of 1918, soviets sprang up all over northern Germany and revolutionary socialists seized power in Bavaria.

[95] See Carr, *Twilight of the Comintern*; I. Deutscher, *The Prophet Outcast. Trotsky: 1929–1940* (Oxford University Press, 1963) ch. 11. As early as March 1930 Trotsky called for joint action between communists and moderate socialists to halt the spread of European fascism: 'the first quality of a truly revolutionary party', he wrote, 'is the ability to face realities'.

tion. Russia's victory over Germany was, to a large extent, Pyrrhic. The USSR's economy was in ruins and Stalin quickly demobilized the bulk of the country's massive army. Moreover, after 1945 a virulently anti-communist *Pax Americana* ruled the world, not a *Pax Sovietica*, and any withdrawal from the occupied territories would have been taken as a clear sign of weakness, an invitation to increase the pressure on the socialist camp. But on the other hand the Soviet presence in Eastern and Central Europe did little to enhance Russia's security. America's burgeoning nuclear arsenal rendered the notion of a territorial cordon sanitaire predicated on large-scale land warfare obsolescent, while Stalin's overt domination of the People's Democracies served only to emphasize Moscow's isolation and exacerbate Cold War tensions.

Stalin's wars

Whether or not Stalin's border wars were exercises in territorial aggrandizement is a moot point. In one sense the Manchukuo campaign, the seizure of eastern Poland, the assault on Finland and the occupation of the three Baltic states were clearly expansionist – and brutally so. But to characterize all four as mere examples of Soviet imperialism is to simplify to the point of distortion.

Japan, not Russia, invaded mainland Asia, and Tokyo's ambitions were a matter of record. Hirohito's soldiers trod many a familiar path when they entered Manchuria in 1931: three times in living memory – during the Civil War, the Russo-Japanese War (1904–5) and the Sino-Japanese War (1894–5) – they had marched into Korea, northern China and eastern Siberia. Here Stalin's conduct was entirely reactive. Not to have engaged the enemy in 1937 would have been to invite incursions into the RSFSR's eastern regions and to have signalled the Soviet Union's helplessness to Europe's watchful foreign ministries. Indeed, Stalin seems to have expected full-scale hostilities to break out in Asia, but once it became clear that bourgeois states were disinclined to curb European fascism, and were only too willing to give Hitler a free hand in the east, the nightmare prospect of a war on two fronts unfolded. No sensible analyst expected Britain to remain at loggerheads with Germany over Poland for long. As in Manchuria, therefore, not to have activated the Nazi–Soviet pact's military clauses would have been to court German aggression. Moreover, Stalin's actions could be characterized as 'defensive': the occupation of eastern Poland and the Baltic states delineated a boundary which the Wehrmacht could not cross without encountering the Red Army. Similarly, given friendly relations between Berlin and Helsinki, Leningrad and Murmansk (the former an important defence industry centre, the latter Russia's only ice-free port north of the Black Sea) appeared dangerously exposed.

Like the other western border wars, the Winter War must be seen against the background of the general failure of collective security; the Manchukuo crisis, Germany's headlong rush towards the mastery of Europe and the miasma of suspicion and insecurity enveloping Moscow. They are classic illustrations of Clausewitz's dictum that war is diplomacy carried on by other means. The Soviet Union inhabited an unforgiving world, and if Stalin's actions were ruthlessly acquisitive, the Western powers' silence over Germany's occupation of the Rhineland,[96] their refusal to check Mussolini in Abyssinia,[97] their betrayal of Czechoslovakia or their policy of non-intervention in Spain were equally self-serving.[98]

But if Stalin's diplomacy was no more and no less cynical than that of any other European leader, his assessment of the German Chancellor was spectacularly misconceived – by 1939 the scales had finally fallen even from Chamberlain's purblind eyes. The invasion of Poland, the Baltic states and Finland failed to enhance Russia's security. Though intensive military preparations were made between 1939 and 1941,[99] after 1940 Stalin seems to have imagined that the Franco-German armies would exhaust each other, that a European conflict would unleash the slumbering forces of international revolution, and that Russia, safe behind the paper ramparts of the Nazi–Soviet pact, would be left alone. There is no doubt that he trusted the Führer and was taken completely by surprise in June 1941. The vision of the Generalissimo as supremely confident in the face of this and subsequent disasters is no longer tenable: the evidence points conclusively, not only to his early loss of nerve,[100] but also to his morbid suspicions of the Western allies and his willingness, as late as 1943, to contemplate a 'second Brest-Litovsk' – the ceding of enormous areas of the USSR to the Third Reich in exchange for a separate peace.

[96] Though in direct contravention of the Versailles Treaty, Britain and France did nothing when Hitler re-militarized the Rhineland in 1936.
[97] The League of Nations' response to Mussolini's invasion of Abyssinia in October 1935 was limited to branding Italy the aggressor and imposing a few trifling economic sanctions, all of which were cancelled in July 1936. In any case oil, iron and steel were excluded from the package.
[98] Cabinet office papers released for publication early in 1991 strongly suggest that Chamberlain's government would like to have supported Franco but was held back by fear of popular outrage. During the Second World War British volunteers who fought on the Republican side were stigmatized as PAFs – 'premature anti-fascists' – and listed as security risks.
[99] See Harrison, *Soviet Planning*, ch. 2 part 1.
[100] According to Khrushchev the central committee convened a plenum in mid-October 1941 but Stalin refused to meet the delegates. See T. H. Rigby, ed., *The Stalin Dictatorship: Khrushchev's 'Secret' Speech' and other Documents* (Sydney University Press, 1968).

The people's war

Most people reading this chapter belong to a generation which has no first-hand experience of total war. And almost no Western European civilians, still less citizens of the United States, have suffered anything resembling Hitler's violation of the east. Even to attempt a description of the horrors endured between 1941 and 1945 seems presumptuous. This was the greatest calamity ever to befall Russia – far worse than the Mongol invasion of the thirteenth century, the collectivization drive or the purges: the bald statistics rehearsed above give some hint of the scope of the tragedy but nothing can convey its intensity.[101]

'Negative' and 'positive' interpretations based primarily on economic, military and political factors will therefore only take researchers so far. They need to be be supplemented by social interpretations. To put it another way the Great Fatherland War should be characterized as a people's war. While the Stalinist régime responded to the ferocious demands imposed on the country – the 'politics of permanent emergency' and the command–administrative system were, in crucial respects, produced respectively by war and the fear of war – Stavka's battle plans and GOKO's orders would have been unavailing without widespread popular determination to destroy fascism.

Much of this had to do with policies emanating from Berlin and Moscow. There is no doubt that Hitler's blunders helped Germany to defeat; the potential of the vast reservoir of Red Army defectors, prisoners and subject nationalities was never fully exploited and Nazi ideology drove millions of waverers into choosing Stalinism as the lesser evil. Equally the re-invigoration of nationalism and Orthodoxy 'from above' by the Soviet régime simultaneously released and stimulated mass support for the struggle against the invader. But the people were not just acted upon by two governments, fascist and communist: the 'positive' factor of spontaneous Soviet patriotism cannot be overestimated. Exactly how this came about still needs to be explored. 'It was the pre-war country which entered the war', recalled one veteran, now a sociologist, in 1987,

> Everything in that country was taken by the people to the front. Their capacity for self-sacrifice, and suspicion of others. Cruelty, and spiritual weakness. Baseness, and naïve romanticism. Officially demonstrated devotion to the leader, and deeply-concealed doubts. The thick-headed rigidity of bureaucrats and people playing safe, and a lively hope that something will turn up. The heavy burden of indignity, and the feeling that the war

[101] See pp. 156–7. For recent work on the initial period of the war see *Soviet Union/Union Soviétique* (1–3, 1991). The entire issue is dedicated to the years 1941–2.

was just. Nothing was left behind, nothing was forgotten. And both soldiers and Marshals had to cope with all this.[102]

Nevertheless, within a few months Soviet patriotism had become more than just an official slogan. Nothing emanating from Stavka or GOKO could have convinced Leningraders to defend their city, or made Lieutenant Skakun's battery keep fighting during that terrible day in Stalingrad,[103] or forced ordinary soldiers to endure the unimaginable horrors of the Kursk battle. 'Examples of extraordinary courage and endurance by the Russians were reported', wrote Alexander Werth,

> for instance of soldiers staying put in their trenches while the heavy German tanks were sweeping across them, and then firing at them from behind. Altogether, it was reckoned that some 6,000 tanks and 4,000 planes were involved in the Battle of Kursk... It was concentrated carnage within a small area more terrible than had yet been seen. When, a few weeks later, I travelled through the fair Ukrainian countryside... I could see how the area... had been turned into a hideous desert, in which every tree and bush had been smashed by shell-fire. Hundreds of burned-out tanks and wrecked planes were still littering the battlefield, and even several miles away from it the air was filled with the stench of thousands of only half-buried Russian and German corpses.[104]

And no amount of NKVD pressure can account for the sense of relief with which Soviet citizens welcomed their advancing army. General Sobennikov recollected that 'there was still some firing going on' when Orel was liberated after the Kursk battle,

> You can imagine the dawn, and the houses around still blazing... but I remember how an old woman stood at the corner of Pushkin Street, and she was making the Sign of the Cross, and tears were rolling down her wrinkled face. And another elderly woman, well-educated judging by her speech, ran towards me and gave me flowers, and threw her arms around my neck, and talked, and talked and talked; through the din I couldn't hear what she was saying, except that it was about her son who was in the Red Army.[105]

[102] Cited Davies, *Soviet History*, p. 105.
[103] Some commentators have interpreted the recent disclosure that about 13,500 soldiers were executed for treason during the Stalingrad battle as evidence of low morale. This is hardly plausible: the figure represents only about 1.2 per cent of the total number of Soviet troops who perished defending the city.
[104] Werth, *Russia at War*, p. 684.
[105] Cited Werth, *Russia at War*, p. 692.

Life in the occupied territories, in partisan units, in the rear and at the front had their own dynamics which affected everyone, fusing the population together in a way which the Revolution and Civil War had never done. Perhaps more significantly, the period 1941–5 profoundly altered the USSR's social structure and transformed what – for want of a better phrase – might be termed the 'national psyche' (or more accurately, given the USSR's multinational character, 'national psyches') for many years to come. Here is the agenda for future historians: because, as we have seen, these matters have scarcely been touched upon by academics,[106] the Great Fatherland War as a social event (rather than a political, military or economic cataclysm) remains largely an undiscovered country.

Late Stalinism

To a considerable extent the themes discussed elsewhere in this book excite controversy precisely because of their uniqueness. In contrast 1945–53 seems featureless, a kind of bleak desert separating two fertile battlegrounds: on the one side Stalin's rise, industrialization, collectivization, the purges and the high drama of the Second World War; on the other the succession struggle, de-stalinization and Khrushchev's thaw. This helps to explain why the domestic history (as opposed to the foreign policy) of the period has been so neglected, but there are other reasons.

Political scientists, the first to colonize this inhospitable landscape, left their imprint on the terrain: systems analysis and the comparative approach (the study of international communism) tended to obscure the specificity of post-war Soviet life. Secondly, the want of reliable sources vitiated original research: only now, after the USSR's collapse, are historians beginning to trawl through the archives. Nevertheless, the comparative approach does not always blur what is distinctive – witness the exploration of nineteenth-century industrialization as a global phenomenon – and lack of information does not usually silence historians; medievalists are hardly blessed with a cornucopia of primary sources, for instance, but this has never stopped them from writing imaginative and challenging histories. The most important reasons for sterility lie elsewhere, in the realm of academic perceptions and the broad sweep of mid-twentieth-century bourgeois ideologies.

---

[106] See pp. 178–9. Most Soviet and post-Soviet writing occurs in the form of journalism, memoirs or novels. See, for example, I. Erenburg, 'Liudi, gody, zhizn'', *Novyi mir* (4-6, 1962; 1–3, 1963); K. Simonov, 'Soldatami ne rozhdaiutsiia', *Znamia* (8–11, 1963; 1–5, 1964); id., *Zhivie i mertvie* (Moscow, 1958). In 1988, Grossman's long suppressed *Zhizn' i sudba* was published in Russia. In Grossman's tale the Great Fatherland War liberates the spirit of human freedom in the Soviet people, in opposition to both Nazism and Stalinism. For a general survey of prose and poetry see D. Brown, 'World War II in Soviet literature', in Linz, *Impact of World War II.*

Russia's military successes and the eruption of socialism on to the world stage evoked an unreasoning Western obsession with the 'Soviet threat'. In response, British and American scholars, often funded by the security forces, produced monographs itemizing the onward march of communism, the dark doings of the Kremlin and Stalin's foreign policy machinations. Out of this grew the first coherent non-Marxist explanatory model of Soviet history – totalitarianism – a model formed in the context of the Cold War and the publication of George Orwell's massively influential novel *Nineteen Eighty-Four*. The problem here is not so much Western totalitarianism's overtly anti-Soviet bias (Trotskyists are no less forgiving of Stalinism, for example, and history feeds on the clash of opinions) but the closure of discourse, the failure to ask questions due to the conviction that there is nothing left to discover: once the lineaments of the party-state and the nomenklatura system had been described and categorized, 'mature' or 'late' Stalinism was packaged as the classic representation of Orwell's nightmare – a world without history, a place where nothing changed and nothing signified outside the paranoid mind of the vozhd'.

In order even to begin to ask new questions historians have been forced to deconstruct totalitarianism, a process pioneered by the British journal *Soviet Studies* in the early 1950s and accelerated by profound shifts in international relations.[107] As East–West rivalry fades away the totalitarian school itself is becoming an object of historical inquiry, and consequently the problems surrounding the impact of the Second World War and the meanings which can be ascribed to late Stalinism are being transformed.

While the structures and predilections of pre-war Stalinism resurfaced after 1945 – party purges, the command–administrative system, the emphasis on group A industry, the reimposition of collective farming – the attempt to reassert control over an economy and society profoundly transformed by the experience of 1941–5 looks more haphazard and less successful than was once thought. Moreover, it now seems that whilst the Russo-German conflict strengthened the régime and legitimized the Generalissimo as a symbol of the will to victory, Stalin's personal power was threatened: the prestige of the Red Army's commanders stood very high in 1945 and new clusters of client–patron relationships emerged during the war – in Leningrad and behind the Urals, for example – about which he probably had scant knowledge and over which he may have exercised limited control.

---

[107] In the first few years of its existence *Soviet Studies* published a range of articles on historiography, periodization, law, fiscal policy, education, agriculture, industry, planning, etc., which eschewed polemical appeals to 'totalitarianism'.

We still know very little about domestic politics between 1945 and 1953, in part due to the 'court' system of government that emerged in the 1930s – policy formed by hints, allusions and unminuted table-talk. Nevertheless, what we do know suggests that the régime was mutating. Stalin himself seems to have tried to reassert his authority in several spheres – over the military (Zhukov's demotion), the party (the Leningrad Affair), the security apparatus (the Mingrelian Case), the upper reaches of the Presidium (the Doctors' Plot) and society at large (the Zhdanovshchina). The success or otherwise of these projects, however, is open to question: 'the picture of Soviet politics that emerges', concludes Hahn, 'is one of constant political manœuvring over personnel and policies in the academic and cultural world, party and government apparatus, and regional and central organs'.[108] In addition the – admittedly impressionistic – evidence offered by Svetlana Alliluyeva suggests that towards the end of his life her father's cronies strove to protect themselves from an increasingly arbitrary despot, and that Stalin could not even govern his own personal staff:

> Everything he needed, his food, his clothing, his dachas and his servants, all were paid for by the government. The secret police had a division that existed specially for this purpose and... a book-keeping department of its own. God only knows how much it cost and where it all went. My father certainly didn't know... From time to time he'd make a stab at auditing the household accounts but nothing ever came of it, of course, because the figures they gave him were faked... All-powerful as he was, he was impotent in the face of the frightful system that had grown up around him like a huge honeycomb and he was helpless either to destroy it or to bring it under control.[109]

This was no self-confident tyrant in charge of a smoothly functioning totalitarian machine, but a sickly old man; unpredictable, dangerous, lied to by terrified subordinates, presiding over a ramshackle bureaucracy and raging, like Lear, against failure and mortality.

Suggestions for further reading

J. D. Barber & M. Harrison, *The Soviet Home Front 1941–1945: A Social and Economic History of the USSR in World War II* (Longman, London, 1991). Neatly summarizes recent research – Soviet, post-Soviet and Western – on key aspects of life during the

[108] Hahn, *Postwar Soviet Politics*, p. 183.
[109] S. Alliluyeva, *Twenty Letters to a Friend* (trans. P. Johnson, Hutchinson, London, 1967) pp. 219–20.

Great Fatherland War as well as offering many valuable insights of its own.

T. Dunmore, *Soviet Politics 1945–53* (Macmillan, London, 1984). Concentrates on changes in government structures and the quarrels amongst the leadership over domestic and foreign policy.

W. G. Hahn, *Postwar Soviet Politics: The Fall of Zhdanov and the Defeat of Moderation 1946–53* (Cornell University Press, 1982). Closely argued work on the manœuvrings amongst the élite which challenges the 'monolithic orthodoxy' view of late Stalinism.

M. Harrison, *Soviet Planning in Peace and War 1938–1945* (Cambridge University Press, 1985). The standard Western monograph on the economic aspects of the Great Fatherland War.

S. J. Linz, ed., *The Impact of World War II on the Soviet Union* (Rowman & Allanheld, Totowa, 1985). Includes useful contributions from Barbara Anderson and Brian Silver (demography), Sheila Fitzpatrick (society), William Fletcher (religion), Jerry Hough (politics), Cynthia Kaplan (the party) and Alec Nove (the peasants).

W. O. McCagg, *Stalin Embattled 1943–1948* (Wayne State University Press, 1978). Discusses the oscillation between 'revolutionary' and 'unrevolutionary' goals at home and abroad and Stalin's battle to regain control of the party-state after the war.

W. Moskoff, *The Bread of Affliction: The Food Supply in the USSR During World War II* (Cambridge University Press, 1990). A fine account of the politics of food, the experience of hunger and the terrible sufferings endured by the Soviet people.

6 CULTURE AND SOCIETY

The revolution is merciless, not only to those who lag behind, but also to those who run ahead.

Nikolai Ustrialov.[1]

Narrative

Education

In December 1927 the fifteenth party congress substantially increased educational spending. As a result, primary and secondary schooling grew massively over the next few years: nearly 7.9 million pupils attended 118,558 schools in 1927/28, figures which rose to 9.7 million and 166,275 respectively by 1933. But despite opposition from Narkompros, expansion was accompanied by the transformation of the entire pedagogical system. Collectivization, the launch of the first piatiletka, campaigns against 'bourgeois elements', the Shakhty Affair and the drive to create a proletarian technical intelligentsia all combined, within a few months of the congress decision, to precipitate a wave of ideological militancy, the like of which had not been seen since the days of the Revolution and Civil War. Andrei Bubnov, a Red Army veteran who replaced Lunacharskii at Narkompros in September 1929,[2] purged his commissariat of 'right deviationists' and vowed to refashion education to meet the demands of socialist construction. Schools were handed over to collective farms or factories, pupils and teachers abandoned formal instruction, learnt through 'productive labour' or found themselves mobilized in the battle to fulfil the plan. Propagandists like Viktor Shulgin advocated 'de-schooling', expelling class enemies (the offspring of kulaks and 'former people'), and looked forward to the 'withering away of the school' altogether.[3]

[1] Ustrialov (b.1890) was a prominent liberal émigré. He returned to Russia in 1935 and perished during the Ezhovshchina three years later.
[2] Born in 1883, Bubnov joined the RSDRP in 1900 and became a political commissar during the Civil War. Lunacharskii died in 1933, on his way to become ambassador to Spain.
[3] Shulgin founded the Institute of Marxist–Leninist Pedagogy – a vehicle for his ideas – in 1928. For a discussion of his theories see G. Lapidus, 'Educational strategies and cultural revolution: the politics of Soviet development', in S. Fitzpatrick, ed., *Cultural Revolution in Russia 1928–1931* (Indiana University Press, 1978).

Universities and polytechnics were no less affected by the raging tide of bellicose radicalism. Placed under Vyshinskii's tutelage and transferred from Narkompros to Vesenkha or the big economic commissariats, most were broken up and remodelled along narrow specialist lines: of the twenty-one universities functioning in 1923/24 only eleven remained in 1932. On the other hand 900 specialist departments and 566 institutes, seventy of which were formed from scratch, sprang into existence between 1927/28 and 1934. Over the same period student numbers rocketed from 168,500 to 458,300; of these thirty and fifty-eight per cent respectively came from the bench, thanks largely to the proliferation of 'likbez points' and rabfaki. As in schools struggle on the 'cultural front' prompted mass expulsions of 'class alien' adolescents and staff purges. Enthusiastic undergraduates (usually Komsomolites straight from rabfaki) and Narkompros trouble-shooters answerable to Bubnov hounded out 'bourgeois' academics.[4] Into their places stepped lecturers fresh from the Institute of Red Professors, an organization headed by the historian Mikhail Pokrovskii dedicated to enforcing Bolshevik hegemony in higher education.[5] Even the Academy of Sciences was sucked into the maelstrom. In 1929 its governing body bowed to the storm by reluctantly accepting a few party nominees. May 1930 saw the imposition of a new charter designed to ease the election of party candidates, purges encompassed Academicians in November and in 1931 several historians were imprisoned.[6]

Conflicting goals, purging, crash programmes and the frequent mobilization of staff and pupils for social and economic tasks reduced schools to chaos; at the sixteenth party congress in June 1930 Bubnov castigated Narkompros's many mistakes and deviations. Shulgin's millenarial theories fell out of favour. The militants were in retreat. In August 1931 the central committee attacked Narkompros for neglecting literacy and failing to impart 'a sufficiency of general knowledge'. Twelve months on, the same body sought to involve parents in restoring discipline and decreed formal teaching

---

[4] In Smolensk, for example, Lapidus recounts that young activists threw out senior administrators and academics in spring 1929, including one linguist charged with 'wrecking' after buying a copy of *The Lay of Prince Igor* (an outstanding work of Old Russian literature) for the University library. Lapidus, in Fitzpatrick, *Cultural Revolution*, p. 91.

[5] The Institute was founded in 1921. Pokrovskii (b.1868) graduated from Moscow University in 1891 and became active in liberal politics before joining the RSDRP's Leninist wing in 1905.

[6] One of the country's oldest educational establishments and its most prestigious research institute, the Academy of Sciences was founded by Peter the Great in 1724. Renamed the All-Union Academy in 1925, its members long claimed institutional autonomy. See D. Joravsky, *The Soviet Academy of Sciences and the Communist Party 1917–32* (Princeton University Press, 1967).

to be the basic pedagogical method for all schools. The following year party leaders deplored the paucity of textbooks, and by 1935 the curriculum had once more been revamped. Arts, mathematics and sciences reappeared, buttressed by compulsory instruction in Marxism–Leninism and the Russian language for all Soviet children. Vocational courses all but disappeared. Instead teachers plodded through prescribed texts and subjected pupils to regular written tests.

The most striking changes occurred in the history syllabus, a portent, not only of pedagogical conservatism, but also of growing Russian nationalism. Pokrovskii's books, works which emphasized Marxist categories, were abandoned in favour of new primers stressing chronology; 'firmly fixing in pupils' minds important events, personalities and dates', as the central committee put it. Later in the decade Ivan the Terrible and Peter the Great received special attention, national heroes whose brutality and cruelty were considered less important than their fabrication of centralized state machines.[7] Analogous changes occurred in higher education: orders promulgated in 1932 reorganized technical training and restored the emphasis on theoretical subjects and examinations – a response to high dropout rates amongst rabfak students. Academic degrees were partially resurrected in 1934 and Russian soon became the *lingua franca* throughout the Soviet Union.[8]

More blows rained down on the militants in the second half of the decade. Selection for universities and polytechnics by social origin disappeared in December 1935 and all restrictions on the entry of students from non-proletarian backgrounds were abrogated by the end of 1936: thereafter only academic and political criteria applied. Simultaneously, the central committee relaxed its hostility towards the Academy of Sciences,[9] raised teachers' salaries and criticized over-specialization, proclaiming that institutes should produce 'cultured cadres' as well as properly trained technicians. The following year Bubnov fell victim to the Ezhovshchina,[10] while in 1938 extra-

---

[7]   Pokrovskii died in 1932. His *Concise Russian History*, *An Outline of the History of Russian Culture* and *Russian History from Ancient Times* were the standard school texts of the 1920s. In May 1934 a central committee decree – 'On the teaching of civic history in the schools of the USSR' – attacked school history for ignoring chronology, neglecting basic facts and over-emphasising abstract ideas. Later on Pokrovskii's portrayals of tsarism were described as too negative. Ivan the Terrible (Ivan IV or Ivan Grozny, 1530–84) was the first Russian ruler to claim the title Tsar (Caesar). Apart from the codification of law and several successful military campaigns his reign was notable for the institution of the Oprichnina, a kind of security police which demolished the power and independence of the old landed aristocracy.

[8]   Narkompros abolished academic degrees in 1918, though the instruction was largely ignored in Moscow University.

[9]   In 1936 the Academy absorbed the Communist Academy, an institution founded in 1918 to study the theory, practice and history of socialism.

[10]   Bubnov was shot in January 1940.

mural departments functioning outside working hours replaced rab-faki. Meanwhile uniforms were imposed on all pupils (including compulsory pig-tails for girls) and with a few exceptions fees of between 300 and 500 rubles per annum introduced for the upper three forms at secondary level in 1940.[11] Apparatchiki therefore had a better chance than workers of getting their children into higher education.

Religion and ethnicity

1928 saw the start of a vigorous anti-religious drive which paralleled the radicalization of education. In the villages, twenty-five thou-sanders smashed up church bells, sent the metal to the piatiletka's new blast furnaces and turned churches into storehouses, clubs or cinemas. OGPU operatives or 'League of Godless' volunteers seized Christian artifacts in industrial settlements;[12] in Shuia, for instance, an old textile town east of Moscow, gun-toting members of Komsomol 'light cavalry brigades' (young zealots aping the modes and manners of the Civil War) burned hundreds of icons in front of angry workers. Decrees promulgated in 1929 restricted worship to 'registered congregations' and outlawed proselytization, regulations which fell particularly onerously on Baptists; evangelicals who, unlike the Orthodox, were committed to spreading God's word. Many thousands were killed or sent to the Gulag. The Ezhovshchina sparked off a second wave of arrests, driving the Church to the mar-gins of society and shattering its cohesion; of 163 Orthodox bishops active in 1930 only twelve remained at liberty nine years later. Convinced that the Soviet régime was the Antichrist incarnate and that the Day of Judgement was at hand, adherents to eschatological sects fled to the impenetrable forests of northern Russia.

Though the espousal of Soviet patriotism during the Great Fatherland War led to the re-establishment of the patriarchate,[13] and despite the formulation of something resembling a Church–State concordat (in 1946 Stalin even encouraged the forcible conversion of Ukrainian Uniate Catholics to Orthodoxy),[14] anti-religious propa-ganda revived in 1944. A Special Council for Church Affairs – jocu-larly known to insiders as 'Narkombog' ('People's Commissariat for

[11] Poor children could compete for state grants to defray these costs.
[12] The League and its satirical journal *Bezbozhnik* (The Godless) were founded in 1925.
[13] Peter the Great abolished the office of patriarch (head of the Church) in 1721. Re-established in August 1917 it disappeared once more in 1925 when Patriarch Tikhon died. Metropolitan Sergei became the new patriarch in 1943 but died the following year. The Church then elected Metropolitan Aleksei of Leningrad.
[14] Much of the Ukraine eventually became Uniate (acknowledging Rome but using the Orthodox liturgy) following incorporation into the Polish–Lithuanian Empire dur-ing and after the fourteenth century.

God') – was organized to keep an eye on Orthodox priests and congregations. Baptists and others, however – Protestants and Catholics from the re-annexed Baltic republics as well as Uniates – continued to suffer the most severe persecution.[15]

Offensives against Slav national feeling coincided with the attack on Christianity. After the Revolution ethnic consciousness increased in Belarus and the Ukraine, fostered by likbez drives in native languages and the 'ruralization of the cities' during the first piatiletka's initial years – many peasants who migrated to the towns spoke only their local tongue. All this changed in the 1930s. One of the state's first actions had been to clarify Bolshevik attitudes towards self-determination; a right, declared Stalin in 1918, which applied only to those representing the proletariat's interests, not to 'bourgeois' régimes like the Rada.[16] This instruction foreshadowed purges of 'national communists' in the early 1930s, the Sovietization of the Baltic republics in 1940, the Russification of education and the growing tendency to conflate Soviet patriotism with Russian nationalism. The Ezhovshchina saw the end of national units in the Red Army and the imposition of Russian as the language of command. At the same time almost all the Ukrainian republic's senior officials were shot and replaced by ethnic Russians.

The same fate befell local communists in Moslem regions, part and parcel of a general assault on religion and nationality in Central Asia, Siberia, the Caucasus and the far east prior to the mass deportations of the Great Fatherland War. In 1929 the anti-religious drive spread to encompass Buddhism, the Armenian and Georgian churches and Islam; by 1942 the 26,279 mosques functioning in 1921 had been reduced to 1,312 and the Islamic Sharia courts abolished. Campaigns reduced the frequency of ritual prayers, fasts and feasts (activities which interrupted industrial work rhythms), and in 1935 Soviet Moslems were forbidden to make the pilgrimage to Mecca.

Taken together with the Russification of local communist parties,

---

[15] Lithuania was largely Roman Catholic whereas most Latvians and Estonians followed the Lutheran confession. Christianity under the Stalin régime is discussed in W. Kolarz, *Religion in the Soviet Union* (Macmillan, London, 1961).

[16] The Rada assumed power in Kiev early in 1917. In November it announced the formation of a Ukrainian People's Republic which it hoped would eventually become part of a democratic Russian federation. Some indication of the extent of support for Ukrainian nationalist parties, and for the Rada's action, can be gleaned from the returns to the All-Russian Constituent Assembly elections of December 1917: just over sixty per cent of all votes were cast for specifically Ukrainian parties, nearly twenty-five per cent for the Russian Socialist Revolutionaries, but only ten per cent for the Bolsheviks. In January 1918 the Rada declared the Ukraine independent, and on 9 February signed a separate peace with the Central Powers. Immediately overthrown by the Bolsheviks, the Rada was briefly resurrected by Germany before being finally disbanded in April 1918.

the imposition of Moscow's plenipotentiaries to oversee economic development, rapid collectivization and the general disturbance of traditional life-styles, these policies triggered revolts amongst the Islamic mountain tribes of the North Caucasus – several Chechen Imams appear to have declared a jihad against Soviet power – and the revival of the Central Asian Basmachi movement.[17] Meanwhile Moscow subjected all the official languages of both areas (except Georgian and Azeri) to a double alphabet reform. The first, in 1929, substituted Latin for Arabic scripts; the second, imposed after 1937, replaced Latin with modified Cyrillic; measures which, in association with industrialization, post-1930 pedagogical reforms and the altered status of women,[18] created urbanized, stalinized élites cut off from their native roots, thus undermining pan-Islamism. In addition, numerous diminutive republics, autonomous regions and districts – often based on tribal units and frequently dividing co-religionists or those speaking the same language – were established in the Caucasus, a factor which exacerbated ancient feuds while deflecting hostility away from Moscow.[19]

Similar changes occurred to the east. By 1936 the great Turkic speaking swath of Central Asia, the area most likely to nurture ultra-montane pan-Turcism, had been fragmented into five republics – Kazakhstan, Kirgizia, Tadzhikistan, Turkestan and Uzbekistan – each with a central committee, security police and Soviet apparatus dominated by Russians. In these remote districts, moreover, the imperatives of modernization strengthened the developing semi-colonial relationship with Moscow. Gosplan USSR ordered Uzbek farms to switch from cereal to cotton production, for example, thus turning the republic into a seller of cash crops for a monopolistic purchaser (Russia's cotton mills), and rejected out of hand alternative plans drawn up by the local Sovnarkom chairman and the republic's party secretary which would have facilitated economic diversity. Both men fell foul of the Ezhovshchina – tried and shot for 'bourgeois nationalism' in 1938.

---

[17] Prior to their deportation in 1944, Chechens lived on the north-eastern slopes of the Caucasus. Basmachi – advocates of Moslem self-determination – started fighting the Bolsheviks in 1918. In 1925 Ibrahim Bek reformed the movement and conducted cross-border raids from Afghanistan until his capture and execution in Tadzhikistan in June 1931. Small-scale raiding continued until 1950. For a full treatment of Islam see A. Benningsen & C. Lemercier-Quelquejay, *Islam in the Soviet Union* (Pall Mall, London, 1967).

[18] See pp. 197–9.

[19] The Abkhazian Autonomous Republic (founded 1931) joined the Adzharian Autonomous Republic (founded 1921) within the Georgian SSR, for example. Nearby was the Kabardin-Balkar Autonomous Republic and the tiny Karachai-Circassian Autonomous Region, and a few miles to the east the Dagestan Autonomous Republic which comprised thirty distinct national groups.

Law

'Sale and purchase is a bourgeois institution', announced the radical jurist Evgenii Pashukanis in 1929,[20] 'socialism does not recognise sales and purchases. It recognizes only direct supply'. Ten years previously the Commissariat for Justice proclaimed crime and litigation to be the result of class conflict, fated to vanish with the passing of the old world; meanwhile courts were to apply 'revolutionary conceptions' of justice to offenders. Pashukanis and his allies, notably Nikolai Krylenko, Petr Stuchka and jurists in the Communist Academy and Pokrovskii's Institute of Red Professors,[21] developed these ideas into a 'commodity-exchange' theory which presaged the 'withering away of law' under socialism. Derived from the institution of private property, the purpose of legislation was to facilitate buying and selling. Since all law – public, criminal and civil – emanated from capitalism, there could be no 'proletarian' or 'socialist' law.[22]

Heartened by the militant disavowal of the NEP and the launch of the first piatiletka, the radicals hoped to replace statutes with basic administrative procedures rooted in the planning mechanism – one supporter at the fifteenth party congress in 1927 thought that once there were enough apparatchiki to 'decide each individual case according to its merits and the interests of the Soviet state' victory on the 'legal front' was assured. Three years later Krylenko's simplified draft criminal code proposed 'measures of class oppression' against potential malefactors as well as convicted felons. Recommended punishments included re-education, expulsion from the community, denial of participation in social organizations and deprivation of political rights – with hard labour added to the gamut of sanctions actually run by Gulag inmates.

This was the first of several radical civil and criminal codes projected over the next few years,[23] but as the millenarial mood of the Great Breakthrough faded away commodity–exchange theory fell from grace. In 1930 and 1931 Pashukanis and his associates were

[20] Pashukanis (1891–c.1938) studied law at St Petersburg University before the Revolution.
[21] Krylenko, like Pashukanis a graduate of St Petersburg University's law faculty, was born in 1885. He took an active part in the 1905 and 1917 Revolutions, and was appointed commander-in-chief of all the armed forces by Lenin in November 1917. During the Civil War he organized 'revolutionary tribunals'. Stuchka (1865–1932), also a graduate of St Petersburg University's law faculty (and a deputy Commissar for Justice in the 1920s), was Pashukanis's teacher, and rather more moderate than his pupil.
[22] According to Pashukanis the state enforced a contractual relationship between offenders and victims – one party to the contract, the criminal, commits an offence for which punishment is meted out equivalent to the damage sustained by the other party, the victim. See E. B. Pashukanis, *Law and Marxism: A General Theory* (ed. C. Arthur, trans. B. Einholm, Ink Links, London, 1978).
[23] Only one was adopted, the 1935 Tadzhik Code which reduced criminal law to a mere 154 articles.

obliged to repudiate de-legalization and to emphasize instead the idea that law served the régime's interests. The ratification of the Stalin constitution in 1936 sealed their fate: socialism required strong and stable criminal mandates to protect state assets and predictable rules governing disputes over residual 'personal' property. In the second half of the decade, the development of civil law and the burgeoning of a vast administrative apparatus tended to stabilize matters. After his success in staging the big show trials Vyshinskii became Procurator General in 1939 and re-defined law as the expression of ruling-class will; in the Soviet instance 'a new, higher type of law' – the will of the proletariat expressed through the party.[24]

Pashukanis and Krylenko disappeared in 1937, but their brief reign – by 1932 the former was director of Moscow's Law Institute and the latter Commissar for Justice RSFSR – fostered an atmosphere of legal nihilism which long persisted.[25] The belief that the law, aided by proletarian hegemony, had mutated into a fully politicized and endlessly flexible means of repressing socialism's opponents, persuaded many judges to ignore the Justice Commissariat's network of 'people's courts' and to transfer cases to 'comrades' courts', peer tribunals first established in the Red Army to deal with minor offenders but now extended to the civilian world. Tribunals were guided by ethical rules arising from emergent socialism and the idea that criminals, as opposed to class enemies, were 'socially friendly'.[26]

Social policy

Comrades' courts frequently assumed responsibility for alimony and child support cases. Legal nihilism and the reaction against it therefore had profound implications for women,[27] but the social upheavals

---

[24] Vyshinskii asserted that courts could convict on the basis of probability or confession.

[25] Though the concept of 'revolutionary justice' held sway in the immediate post-revolutionary years notions of legal nihilism were also propounded. See E. Huskey, 'A framework for the analysis of Soviet law', *Russian Review* (1, 1991); M. McAuley, *Bread and Justice: State and Society in Petrograd 1917–1922* (Oxford University Press, 1991) chs. 4, 18.

[26] Since crime was produced by private property or psychiatric disorder, imputability shifted from the individual to society or medicine. The notion of legal responsibility therefore atrophied. In consequence, criminals were allowed considerable latitude in detention. In the Kraslag district in 1941 (a Siberian Gulag region) thieves knocked gold teeth out of Estonian deportees with pokers, drowned Lithuanians in the latrines for refusing to give up food parcels, plundered those about to be executed and raped girls sentenced as kulaks. The camp authorities did not interfere. There are many other examples.

[27] The evasion of alimony payments and disorderly conduct (domestic violence and drunkenness, for example) usually attracted only modest penalties in comrades' courts.

associated with rapid modernization, coupled with swiftly changing views on sexual behaviour and the rôle of the family, were of equal importance.

After the Revolution the Bolsheviks evolved a liberal civil code. By 1930 the marriageable age stood at eighteen. If the marriage broke down both party's alimony liability ceased after a year. Incest, bigamy, adultery and homosexuality were de-criminalized, abortion and divorce became available on demand. As part of the attack on Islam, polygamy and bride money were banned in Moslem regions, and though hundreds were subsequently raped and killed for outraging tradition, from 1927 onwards many women threw off the veil at mass gatherings held on International Women's Day. Attempts to promote the 'withering away of the family' (according to radicals a 'bourgeois' institution which perpetuated paternalistic concepts of property) were aided by decrees giving women in *de facto* the same rights as those in registered marriages.

The repercussions of these regulations in the context of de-legalization and the tremendous social upheavals contingent upon the Great Breakthrough were dramatic. By 1934, thirty-seven per cent of all marriages in Moscow ended in divorce and the city's birth rate had fallen precipitously; abortions outstripped live births by a factor of 2.7 (154,000 as against 57,000). As families disintegrated the number of strays and orphans soared, a problem aggravated by mass arrests and deportations. In metropolitan districts, in provincial towns and villages and on construction sites thousands starved in back alleys or roamed the streets begging and stealing: Ordzhonikidze's vast 'nomadic Gypsy camp' threatened to overwhelm settled social life. The Kremlin responded by launching a major press campaign in 1934 which trumpeted the virtues of family life and sexual abstinence. Minsk police officers arrested girls for 'immoral appearance' (modern dress) and in many districts kolkhoz chairmen ordered young spinsters to undergo virginity checks. De-feminized images of women – fighters for socialism and heroic shock workers equal to men – gave way to older traditions; registry offices were redecorated, ceremony was restored to weddings and the sale of gold rings, banned during the first piatiletka, once more permitted.[28] Male homosexuality (but not lesbianism) was re-criminalized.[29]

[28] For a discussion of the changing perceptions of women see E. Waters, 'The modernization of Russian motherhood', *Soviet Studies* (1, 1992). Waters shows how the emphasis on crèches and nurseries grew during the 1930s, not only to allow women to participate in socialist construction, but also to encourage them to bear more children.
[29] Pre-revolutionary law on sexual matters was far from clear, but after 1917 homosexuality was generally regarded as a psychiatric disorder. See S. Karlinsky, 'Russia's gay literature and culture: the impact of the October Revolution', in M. B. Duberman, et al., eds., *Hidden From History: Reclaiming the Gay and Lesbian Past* (New American Library, New York, 1972).

Two years later, in April 1936, the tenth Komsomol congress endorsed resolutions advocating greater respect for parental authority and feminine 'honour'. In June, divorce laws were tightened, restrictions placed on abortion and generous social benefits disbursed to large families; measures taken much further after the traumas of the Great Fatherland War. By 1945 abortion was prohibited except where serious health risk could be proved, divorce required expensive court proceedings, and the family as an economic unit strengthened via the restoration of inheritance – a regulation which, since only those born in wedlock could acquire parental belongings, in practice revived the concept of illegitimacy.[30]

Literature, science and the arts

Late in 1929, after much squabbling between rival organizations, the party instructed 'literary forces' to 'consolidate' within RAPP, the Russian Association of Proletarian Writers and the body which dominated literary politics during the first plan. RAPP's task, declared its director, Leopold Averbakh,[31] was to mobilize authors for socialist construction: 'artistic brigades' were formed, eulogies to industrialization, shock work and collectivization hastily penned and well-known figures recruited to the cause. But intolerance and backbiting soon took their toll. Books like *The Struggle for the Promfinplan in the Third Year of the Piatiletka* or *The First Writers' Brigade in the Urals* graced libraries, workers' clubs and likbez points, while talented 'fellow travellers' (sympathetic non-party writers) found themselves pilloried as wreckers or enemies. In consequence, after declaring RAPP's activities inimical to literary progress, the central committee wound up the organization in 1932 and sponsored a revived Union of Writers to include all those broadly in agreement with Soviet policy.

The Union's congress in August 1934 set about determining the parameters of 'socialist realism', a phrase coined two years previously which became the watchword of the Stalin period. Fiodor Gladkov's *Cement* and Mikhail Sholokhov's *The Quiet Don* – both have heroes drawn from the people and shaped by the party – were hailed as models of the new genre, Gorky's *The Mother* as the real

---

[30] For post-war policy towards the family see p. 178. See also K. Geiger, *The Family in Soviet Russia* (Harvard University Press, 1968).
[31] Averbakh (1903–39) worked as a newspaper editor during the 1920s. For RAPP see E. J. Brown, *The Proletarian Episode in Russian Literature 1928–1932* (Columbia University Press, 1953).

archetype.[32] Zhdanov and Radek condemned literary apoliticism as 'bourgeois'. Bukharin, on the other hand, in a speech which cautioned against narrow sectarianism, caught the mood of the times: delegates agreed that socialist realism encompassed all that was best from the past (giant portraits of Cervantes, Gogol, Pushkin, Shakespeare and Tolstoy stared down from the walls), whilst portraying social change as 'progressive' – pointing ineluctably towards mankind's communist future. These sentiments were in line with the General Secretary's views. Writers should become 'engineers of human souls', he remarked to Gorky in 1932, celebrating Russia's glorious history as well as the Stalinist present. Over the rest of the decade stories and films praising soldiers and tsars appeared (Aleksei Tolstoy's three volume novel *Peter the First* and Sergei Eisenstein's film *Aleksandr Nevskii* are typical of the period),[33] along with a mass of lesser popular fictions depicting feats of derring-do during the Civil War, resourceful Komsomol spy-catchers, heroes of labour, edifying accounts of life under socialism, banal scenes of domestic life or trite episodes of romantic love derived from Russian folklore.

Like everything else between 1941 and 1945 literature and the arts were subsumed in the struggle against Hitler. Following Stalin's speech of 7 November 1941 ('let the manly images of our great ancestors – Aleksandr Nevskii, Dmitri Donskoi, Kuzma Minin, Dmitri Pozharskii, Aleksandr Suvorov and Mikhail Kutuzov – inspire you during this war') military leaders and national heroes received even greater prominence than before, Ivan the Terrible in

---

[32] Gorky's *The Mother* was published in 1906. Gladkov (1883–1958), was hailed by foreign critics as the 'Émile Zola of the Russian Revolution'. His *Energy* (written 1930–6) depicts the Dneprostroi in heroic terms in much the same way as *Cement* describes the rebuilding of a factory after the Civil War. The outstanding novelist Sholokhov (1905–84) wrote *The Quiet Don*, an epic tale of the Civil War, in 1926. It was followed by *Virgin Soil Upturned* (1932), a story about collectivization. For socialist realism see C. Vaughan Williams, *Soviet Socialist Realism: Origins and Theory* (Macmillan, London, 1973).

[33] Eisenstein (1898–1948) was the premier Soviet film-maker of his time, best remembered for *October* and *Battleship Potemkin*. *Aleksandr Nevskii* (1938) portrayed the life of the thirteenth-century Russian prince who defeated the Teutonic Knights. Tolstoy (1883–1945), a distant relative of Leo Tolstoy, emigrated after supporting the Whites but returned to Russia in 1923. *Peter the First* was written between 1929 and 1943.

particular,[34] but there was also a tendency to loosen the ideological strait-jacket of socialist realism, creating room for compassionate portrayals of personal suffering, endurance and courage under fire.[35]

The party continued to regard novels and poems as political weapons, however, and the controls elaborated during the 1930s remained in place, exercised through Glavlit and the Union's hold over salaries, publishers, travel permits, housing and medical treatment; a system which served as the model for the other arts. Artists were expected to toe the party line with due regard for the Politburo's sensibilities. Those unable to conform became translators or newspaper correspondents, opted for what Isaak Babel' called the 'genre of silence', perished, like Osip Mandelstam, in the Gulag,[36] or fell out of favour in a blaze of vituperative publicity. Late in 1935, for instance, Stalin walked out of a performance of Dmitri Shostakovich's immensely popular opera *Lady Macbeth of Mtensk*, a politically correct story of murder, adultery and suicide in pre-revolutionary Russia: he was deeply shocked, less by the dissonance of the music than by the lasciviousness of the bedroom scene – where glissandi of trombones underline all too vividly what is happening on stage.[37] Almost immediately, on 27 January 1936, a Committee on Art Affairs directly responsible to Sovnarkom was set up to oversee places of public entertainment. The following day *Pravda*'s 'Confusion instead of music', the first salvo in a barrage against modernism which reached a crescendo in the late 1940s, assailed Shostakovich for 'leftism' and 'bourgeois tendencies', vilified the 'fidgety, screaming, neurotic' score and reviled the entire work as

---

[34] Donskoi (1330–89), Prince of Moscow and later Vladimir, built the stone walls around the Kremlin, but his main achievement was the defeat of the Mongols at Kulikovo Pole in 1380. Minin (d.1616) and Pozharskii (1578–1641) organized the Nizhni Novgorod People's Volunteer Army which freed Moscow from Polish–Lithuanian rule. Suvorov (1730–1800) won spectacular victories against the Turks, Swiss, Italians and French in the late eighteenth century. Kutuzov (1745–1813) was one of Alexander I's chief military commanders in the war against Napoleon. For the 'Ivan cult' see B. Uhlenbruch, 'The annexation of history: Eisenstein and the Ivan Grozny cult of the 1940s', in H. Günther, ed., *The Culture of the Stalin Period* (Macmillan, London, 1990).

[35] See D. Brown, 'World War II in Soviet literature' in S. J. Linz, ed., *The Impact of World War II on the Soviet Union* (Rowman & Allanheld, Totowa, 1985).

[36] Babel' (1894–1941) published his first stories in 1915, became a revolutionary and served in the Red Army during the Civil War. Horrified by his experiences as a collectivization official he was removed for 'rotten liberalism' and arrested in 1939. Mandelstam, born in 1892 and a major poet of the twentieth century, died in a camp near Voronezh sometime during or after 1938.

[37] Shostakovich (1906–75) graduated from the Leningrad Conservatoire in 1925 and composed widely for concert halls, the cinema and the theatre before his disgrace. For music under Stalin see B. Schwarz, *Music and Musical Life in Soviet Russia 1917–70* (Barrie & Jenkins, London, 1972).

'coarse, primitive and vulgar'. There were no further performances under Stalin.

In architecture and town planning, a domain of public art where the party-state was client, patron, and supplier of labour and materials, near absolute control could be imposed without the troublesome intervention of private vision. As in other fields radicals and militants – 'urbanists' ('supercity' enthusiasts who dreamed of eliminating village life), 'disurbanists' (advocates of a 'destationed, anti-family world' in which mobile housing units could be coupled and de-coupled at will) and 'communalists' (supporters of 'socialism in one building' where apartments had no kitchens or dining rooms, only collective arenas for the preparation and ingestion of food) – were pushed aside in the first piatiletka's closing years.[38] They were replaced by exponents of 'Stalinist baroque',[39] the 'wedding cake' style which swept the capital and reached its apogee with the rebuilding of Moscow University after 1945.

Lenin's tomb, refashioned in 1930 – the stone structure was coated with granite, labradorite, marble and porphyry drawn from the four corners of the Soviet Union – became the focus of a massive building programme. Work started in 1931 and peaked three years later, shortly after the seventeenth party congress. By November 1934, recalled one Muscovite, the centre seemed to be one vast construction site: 'walls and corners of buildings collapsed and disappeared like theatre sets', while on the pavements startled passers-by watched familiar vistas crumble into dust. Officially, all the disturbance was designed to ease traffic flow, but since tunnelling for the Moscow metro (a fine example of Stalinist baroque) started in 1935, and given that there were so few vehicles anyway, the real reason for levelling whole districts and widening streets was to make room for what Vladimir Paperny calls 'sacred processions and marching soldiers':[40] 'and *my* aesthetics', thundered Kaganovich, in reply to Lunacharskii's vain protestations over the destruction of ancient churches near the Kremlin, 'demands that the demonstration processions from the six districts of Moscow should all pour into Red Square at the same time'. Arranged by specialists who minutely choreographed every movement and checked banners and slogans, on 1 May and 7 November these displays climaxed in front of the

---

[38] For a vivid account of architectural millenarianism see R. Stites, *Revolutionary Dreams: Utopian Vision and Experimental Life in the Russian Revolution* (Oxford University Press, 1989) part 3.

[39] Also known as 'People's' or 'Mass baroque'. For a portrait of one of the chief Stalinist architects see A. Max Vogt, 'The ultimate palladianist, outliving revolution and the Stalin period: architect Ivan V. Zholtovsky', in Günther, *Culture*.

[40] V. Paperny, 'Moscow in the 1930s and the emergence of a new city', in Günther, *Culture*, p. 231.

Mausoleum, the stage where the General Secretary and his Politburo exhibited themselves to the adoring masses over the mummified corpse of Bolshevism's founder. The dejected Lunacharskii could not help contrasting such mechanical performances with the spontaneity and gaiety of Lenin's time.

As public festivals metamorphosed into stylized exaltations of the vozhd' the dolorous certainties of the 'cult of personality' invaded all other fields of intellectual endeavour. Accolades to 'Lenin's closest friend and disciple' and the 'greatest genius of all time' flooded the country. Vast statues arose;[41] operas, paintings and films magnified Stalin as the Civil War's chief hero; poems extolled his model childhood; novels and folk tales his unique historical rôle. In Marfa Kriukova's *The Tale of Lenin*, for example, Vladimir Il'ich appears as the red sun, Stalin as light and Trotsky as the dark villain. The story ends with the dying red sun sending light out into the world to defeat darkness.[42]

In comparison with the arts, science was somewhat more immune from the encroachments of Stalinist ideology, but after the Shakhty Affair anti-Soviet 'bourgeois elements' were 'discovered' working in almost every laboratory. By the mid-1930s few theories could safely be propounded until they had received the General Secretary's imprimatur – unless the matter impinged directly on defence or socialist construction.[43] The most famous example of direct party interference occurred in plant biology. From 1929 onwards Trofim Lysenko tried to persuade party leaders to adopt his quack 'peasant remedies' for plant breeding.[44] Active discrimination against his opponents – the 'neo-Mendelians' – began in 1932. Elected to the Academy of Agricultural Sciences in 1935, Lysenko became head of the organization and the doyen of 'proletarian science' three years later when Stalin defended his nostrums in *Pravda*. Thereafter many rival institutes were closed and their researchers imprisoned or banned from attending international conferences. In 1940, following the arrest of its director, he took over the élite Institute of Genetics.

---

[41] Even in remote districts. In a village on Siberia's River Enisei where Stalin was exiled a huge marble statue was built next to his hut. In 1961 the statue was tipped into the river. For several years, until the sands covered it, travellers could still see his face staring up from the river bed.
[42] Kriukova (1876–1954) specialized in collecting and publishing epic Russian songs and poems.
[43] The politicians held back from persecuting atomic physicists, for instance. See Z. A. Medvedev, *Soviet Science* (Oxford University Press, 1979) chs. 3–4; L. R. Graham, ed., *Science and the Soviet Social Order* (Harvard University Press, 1990).
[44] Lysenko (1898–1976) graduated from the Poltava School of Horticulture in 1917 and the Institute of Agriculture at Kiev in 1925.

The Zhdanovshchina

Lysenko's power reached its zenith in July 1948. With behind the scenes support from Stalin he finally trounced the neo-Mendelians at a great conclave held in Leningrad 'to consider the situation' in biology. His keynote speech divided science into two 'camps': the 'bourgeois' variety, by cataloguing immutable physical laws, 'disarms practice and orientates man towards resignation'; 'socialist' science, on the other hand – creative and free of 'false objectivism' – heralded the liberation of humanity. Shortly afterwards, in a decree typical of Zhdanov's attempt to assert ideological hegemony in society at large, the central committee declared *ex cathedra* that Lysenko was right and all his opponents were wrong.[45]

Zhdanov had been active in other fields over the previous two years. In 1946 he rounded on Anna Akhmatova and Mikhail Zoshchenko for beguiling the young with 'decadent' and 'vulgar parodies' of Soviet life which contradicted the tenets of socialist realism.[46] On 14 August the party instructed literary journals not to publish any more of their 'ideologically harmful works'. A week later he called Zoshchenko 'the scum of the literary world', full of 'nauseating morality' and 'poisonous hostility' towards the régime. He was particularly stung by the author's *Adventures of a Monkey*: the hero, after escaping from a bombed zoo during the war and sampling Soviet life in a variety of comic encounters, hurries back to his shattered cage where he can breathe freely.

The 'Zhdanov decree' on literature was followed by similar pronouncements on the other arts. Over the next two months theatres were lambasted for staging too many Western plays and cinemas were attacked for showing films which gave a 'distorted picture of the Soviet people'. In June the following year he turned his attention to philosophy, traducing scholars for a 'lamentable absence of Bolshevik criticism and self-criticism' in their meditations upon Western thought.[47] In February 1948 he accused Shostakovich and others of writing 'anti-national' and 'formalist' scores instead of copying the style of classical Russian opera which, according to the

[45] See D. Joravsky, *The Lysenko Affair* (Harvard University Press, 1970); D. Lecourt, *Proletarian Science? The Case of Lysenko* (trans. B. Brewster, New Left Books, London, 1977); Z. A. Medvedev, *The Rise and Fall of T. D. Lysenko* (trans. I. Lerner, Columbia University Press, 1969).

[46] Both were expelled from the Union of Writers. Akhmatova (1889–1966) was a leading pre-revolutionary poet associated with the Acemist movement. She published almost nothing during the Stalin years. Zoshchenko (1895–1958) was a popular and talented satirist. Before becoming a writer he worked as a carpenter, a detective and a professional gambler.

[47] See L. R. Graham, *Science and Philosophy in the Soviet Union* (Allen Lane, London, 1973).

published decree, was 'rich in content and melody', making it 'the finest in the world'. The composers were called in to see Zhdanov at the central committee building, whereupon he is said to have picked out tunes on the piano to illustrate the kind of music required.

Zhdanov's reign as arbiter of the intelligentsia was cut short by his death,[48] but the Zhdanovshchina continued. Literary critics were savaged in January 1949 for finding fault with 'the best plays which depict Soviet patriotism', and in 1950 Stalin himself joined the fray: *Marxism and the Questions of Linguistics* announced that all previous Soviet linguisticians were 'unscientific and anti-Marxist', in particular followers of the 'militant' orientalist Nikolai Marr.[49] These were not the only examples of Stalinist vainglory or vulgar nationalism: xenophobia and ethnic bigotry were there from the start. The Zhdanov decree criticized Akhmatova for writings 'permeated with the spirit of servility' towards foreigners, and no subsequent attack on the intelligentsia was complete without scathing references to 'rootless cosmopolitans'. By the time Stalin died state-sponsored chauvinism had reached extraordinary levels; almost every invention was declared to have originated in Russia, for example – including baseball.

The campaign against 'rootless cosmopolitans' had dire consequences for Soviet Jews. Though all anti-semitic legislation was abrogated in 1917, the internal passport system established in 1932 effectively re-invented racial categories. 'Entry number five' listed nationality, an identity usually drawn from the mother. Jews, therefore, had no means of merging into Soviet society or becoming Russian, nor could they migrate to a national republic – the old tsarist Pale of Settlement had no administrative status and the Birobidzhan Autonomous Region was virtually uninhabitable.[50] Despite the post-1917 diaspora from the Pale, therefore, the idea of a distinct Jewish identity was firmly fixed in the authorities' minds. Official xenophobia, hysteria over subversives and spies, attacks on cosmopolitans – and, after the foundation of Israel, on 'zionists' – soon fused with traditional Slav anti-semitism. Moscow University imposed Jewish quotas and the Jewish Anti-Fascist Committee

---

[48] For Zhdanov's attack on Akhmatova and Zoshchenko and his views on cultural matters in general see A. A. Zhdanov, *On Literature, Music and Philosophy* (Lawrence & Wishart, London, 1950).

[49] Marr (1864–1934) regarded language as part of the Marxian superstructure. He was concerned with the interrelationship of languages and the connections between language, thought, the evolution of material culture and the economy.

[50] Children did not receive their own passports until they were sixteen. At that point, if the parents' nationalities were different, the child could opt for the father's nationality. Thereafter no changes were permitted. This was in contrast to tsarist Russia: to some extent Jews could evade anti-semitism by converting to Orthodoxy. For the Birobidzhan Autonomous Region see p. 159 fn. 21.

(active in rallying international support during the Great Fatherland War) was wound up in 1948. By 1952 the city's Jewish Theatre had been closed and most prominent Yiddish cultural figures arrested. Shortly before Beriia 'unmasked' the Doctors' Plot twenty-six of them were shot.[51]

Interpretations

Totalitarianism revisited

In Stalin's time, wrote Geoffrey Hosking, most Western observers tried to explain the Soviet experience in terms of personal dictatorship. Given the absence of press freedom and legal opposition, and in view of the existence of supposedly similar régimes in Italy and Germany, researches hypothesized a General Secretary who relied upon 'permanent purging' in all spheres of life – political, economic, social and cultural – in order to protect his authority and to combat idleness, inefficiency, corruption and ideological backsliding. Out of this grew the concept of the 'totalitarian state'; a polity possessed of six defining characteristics: central direction of the economy; ubiquitous supervision by the secret police; party-led mobilization of the population; party monopolization of mass communications; adulation of a single leader, and finally the articulation of one official ideology, 'projecting a perfect state of mankind and claiming priority over both the legal order and the individual conscience'.[52]

As was noted previously, totalitarianism arose in response to – or at least in the context of – the Cold War, the period when Western bourgeois democracies proclaimed themselves menaced by Orwell's nightmare in the guise of the Soviet Union.[53] Though never really intended to be theories of culture and society – academics concerned themselves primarily with the political system, high politics and macro-economics – totalitarian hypotheses were influential in other areas. Since Western models (but not Trotsky's analysis) emerged coterminously with the Zhdanovshchina, state control of printed, aural and visual images, the cult of personality and the party's quest for absolute ideological hegemony – apparently self-evident characteristics of late Stalinism – were projected backwards to explain the

---

[51] For the Jewish experience see L. Kochan, *The Jews in Soviet Russia since 1917* (Oxford University Press, 1972); Y. A. Gilboa, *The Black Years of Soviet Jewry 1939–53* (trans Y. Schacter and D. Ben-Abba, Little and Brown, Boston, 1971).

[52] G. Hosking, *A History of the Soviet Union* (Fontana/Collins, London, 1985) p. 205. The phrase 'permanent purge' comes from Z. K. Brzezinski, *The Permanent Purge: Politics in Soviet Totalitarianism* (Harvard University Press, 1956).

[53] See p. 187.

entire configuration of culture and society under Stalin.[54]

The image of society and culture which emerged in the West in the twenty-five years or so after 1945 can be described as follows: all artistic, cultural and scientific endeavour was controlled by Stalin or the party-state; all changes in artistic, scientific and cultural policy occurred at the behest of Stalin or the party-state. By the same token society and social life were at the mercy of Stalin or the party-state. Society was characterized as an inert body acted upon by a leadership cohort actively pursuing Stalinist or communist ideology, not an autonomous or quasi-autonomous series of organizations or interests interacting with the party-state, something both 'massified' and atomized. Massification obliterated pluralism by flooding society with officially approved cultural products; atomization – the use of terror to isolate individuals – blocked the development and articulation of alternative social or cultural visions. Substantive debate between scholars occurred mainly at the 'Kremlinological' and ideological levels – whether or not particular policies were initiated by Stalin, Kaganovich, Zhdanov or some other political leader; whether or not social and cultural policy was specifically 'Stalinist', or developed from a pre-existing tsarist, Leninist or Bolshevist tradition.[55] These perceptions were strengthened by the research base exploited by totalitarian analysts: in the absence of other sources Cold War narratives drew heavily on four types of material: published official decrees, reminiscences of Westerners employed in Russia, impressions gathered by foreign visitors, and finally and most importantly émigré accounts – intelligentsia memoirs in particular.[56]

[54] For particularly influential general studies see Z. K. Brzezinski, *Ideology and Power in Soviet Politics* (Praeger, New York, 1962); R. N. Carew Hunt, *The Theory and Practice of Communism* (Geoffrey Bles, London, 1950); M. Fainsod, *How Russia is Ruled* (Harvard University Press, 1953); B. Moore Jr., *Soviet Politics: The Dilemma of Power* (Harvard University Press, 1950).

[55] See, for instance, F. Barghoorn, 'Stalinism and the Russian cultural heritage', *Problems of Communism* (1, 1953). For a pioneering and influential study, published on the eve of the Stalin period, which tries to situate art and culture in the context of Bolshevik ideology see R. Fülöp-Miller, *The Mind and Face of Bolshevism* (Putman, London, 1927).

[56] Typical examples include M. Gordon, *Workers Before and After Lenin* (Dutton, New York, 1941); H. Griffith, *Seeing Soviet Russia* (John Lane & The Bodley Head, London, 1932); A. P. Pinkevich, *Science and Education in the USSR* (Gollancz, London, 1935); A. Smith, *I Was a Soviet Worker* (Robert Hale, London, 1937); G. B. Struve, *Twenty-Five Years of Soviet Russian Literature* (Routledge, London, 1944); T. Tchernavin, *We, Soviet Women* (trans. N. Alexander, Hamish Hamilton, London, 1935). *Sotsialisticheskii vestnik*, the Menshevik journal published in Berlin between the wars, was also widely used.

Revisionism revisited

'To claim to show that the traditional representation of the "Stalin period" is in many ways quite inaccurate', complained Gábor Rittersporn in 1991,

> is tantamount to issuing a hopeless challenge to the time-honoured patterns of thought which we are used to applying to political realities in the USSR, indeed against the common patterns of speech itself. Even the most radical and headstrong iconoclast can expect little success from such a pointless undertaking.[57]

In fact from the late 1950s onwards, and particularly since the 1970s, there have been numerous challenges to totalitarian theory – even without the benefit of new sources.[58] As Hosking points out the model, in assuming workers, peasants and intellectuals to be passive objects of terror and mobilization, does not explain society as a whole, nor does it examine the rôle played by the ruling stratum – the members of the nomenklatura through whom the vozhd' was obliged to exercise his power.[59]

Totalitarianism's critics differ on many points, but they share in common a 'revisionist' outlook; the belief that Stalin, the Politburo and the leadership in general were not the only, or even the main determinants of change. Instead, revisionists ascribe an important place to those on the lower rungs of the nomenklatura system, to non-party interest groups and to policy recipients – be they workers, peasants, provincial apparatchiki or metropolitan intellectuals. While accepting that policy shifts in law and social matters, education, science and the arts were initiated 'from above', they suggest that the party's dictates may occasionally have been promulgated in response to pressure 'from below', and they insist that Moscow's prescriptions frequently unleashed forces which took the leadership by surprise and made them change direction in order to check ambitious, undis-

---

[57] G. T. Rittersporn, *Stalinist Simplifications and Soviet Complications: Social Tensions and Political Conflicts in the USSR 1933–1953* (Harwood, Chur, 1991) pp. 1–2.
[58] Particularly in the field of labour, economic and political history. See for example the works of J. Arch Getty, V. Andrle, K. E. Bailes, S. F. Cohen, D. Filtzer, S. Fitzpatrick, H. Kuromiya, N. Lampert, C. Merridale, A. D. Rassweiler, L. H. Siegelbaum and L. Viola cited elsewhere in this book, and almost the entire body of work produced by R. W. Davies, Moshe Lewin and E. H. Carr – the latter in particular relied heavily on published official sources.
[59] Hosking, *Soviet Union*, p. 206.

ciplined, wayward or over-enthusiastic subordinates.[60] Hence the abolition of RAPP occurred, at least partially in response to Averbakh's overweening sectarianism. Bubnov's fall was directly related to Narkompros's militant radicalism, while the resurrection of traditional pedagogy in higher education was caused by disquiet over falling standards.[61] Similarly Krylenko's and Pashukanis's demise owed much to the excesses of commodity–exchange theory, the projected abolition of law and the social chaos which accompanied the Great Breakthrough.[62] As for the post-war years they regard the Zhdanovshchina as a struggle to regain control over a culture and society fundamentally transformed by the upheavals of the Great Fatherland War, not as an example of the arbitrary exercise of totalitarian power.[63]

Finally, revisionists are deeply suspicious of the source base exploited by previous researchers, claiming that foreign employees' and travellers' tales are too impressionistic to be of much use, that official statements and decrees did not necessarily affect daily life, and that émigré intelligentsia memoirs – itemizing the concerns of a small minority of the population and invariably anti-communist – have over-determined and grossly distorted Western perceptions of Stalinism and should be treated with the greatest caution.

[60] For the lively and often acrimonious debate on these matters see the articles by J. Arch Getty, D. Brower, W. J. Chase, S. F. Cohen, R. Conquest, G. Eley, S. Fitzpatrick, J. F. Hough, P. Kenez, H. Kuromiya, R. T. Manning, A. Meyer, A. Nove, G. T. Rittersporn, R. C. Tucker and L. Viola, in *Russian Review* (4, 1986 & 4, 1987). See also S. Fitzpatrick, 'The Russian Revolution and social mobility: a re-examination of the question of social support for the Soviet régime in the 1920s and 1930s', *Politics & Society* (2, 1984); H. Reichman, 'Reconsidering "Stalinism"', *Theory and Society* (1, 1988); G. T. Rittersporn, 'Rethinking Stalinism', *Russian History* (4, 1984); id., 'Soviet politics in the 1930s: rehabilitating society', *Studies in Comparative Communism* (2, 1986).
[61] See K. Clark, *The Soviet Novel: History as Ritual* (University of Chicago Press, 1981); id., 'Little heroes and big deeds: literature responds to the first five-year plan'; G. M. Enteen, 'Marxist historians during the cultural revolution: a case study of professional in-fighting'; S. G. Gross, 'Rural scholars and the cultural revolution'; Lapidus, in Fitzpatrick, *Cultural Revolution*.
[62] See D. A. Loeber, 'Bureaucracy in a workers' state: E. B. Pashukanis and the struggle against bureaucratism in the Soviet Union', *Soviet Union/Union Soviétique* (2, 1979); G. T. Rittersporn, 'Soviet officialdom and political evolution. Judiciary apparatus and penal policy in the 1930s', *Theory and Society* (2, 1984); R. Sharlet, 'Pashukanis and the withering away of the law in the USSR, in Fitzpatrick, *Cultural Revolution*; L. Shelley, 'Soviet criminology: its birth and demise 1917–1936', *Slavic Review* (4, 1979); id., 'The 1929 dispute on Soviet criminology', *Soviet Union/Union Soviétique* (2, 1979); P. H. Solomon, 'Soviet penal policy 1917–1934: a reconsideration', *Slavic Review* (2, 1980); id., 'Local political power and Soviet criminal justice 1922–41', *Soviet Studies* (3, 1985).
[63] See T. Dunmore, *Soviet Politics 1945–53* (Macmillan, London, 1984); W. G. Hahn, *Postwar Soviet Politics: The Fall of Zhdanov and the Defeat of Moderation 1946–53* (Cornell University Press, 1982); J. F. Hough, 'Debates about the postwar world', in Linz, *Impact of World War II*.

In each case totalitarian certainties are challenged by texts emphasizing Stalinism's essential ambiguity – hesitation and negotiation on
the part of the leadership, the complexity of lived experience, and
interactions between the masses, the intelligentsia, the Kremlin and
the nomenklatura. Vera Dunham and Sheila Fitzpatrick, for
instance, suggest that the élite's aesthetic predilections were profoundly influenced by pre-revolutionary figures as well as by contemporary poets, novelists, painters and musicians. Equally the tastes of
plebeian *arrivistes* – the ill-educated and culturally insecure beneficiaries of likbez drives and rabfak courses who poured into state and
party offices during the 1930s – created markets for particular kinds
of popular artistic products. The vydvizhentsy's hunger for petty
bourgeois 'chintz and lace curtain' respectability (derided by émigré
intellectuals) was, therefore, no less important than socialist realism
in shaping Stalinist culture and the general tone of Soviet society.[64]

Revolution and retreat

Explicit in totalitarian interpretations is the notion of purposeful
development; the gradual perfection of a new Leviathan – Jack
London's 'iron heel' pressing down on the masses.[65] Implicit in revisionist explanations is the idea that central initiatives were more
often than not hasty reactions to passing exigencies. The first view
sees communist ideology or the party-state as agents of causation;
the second is reluctant to ascribe causation to any one agency and
concentrates on the unplanned, haphazard and problematic nature of
interactions between ideology, society and the political élite.

But a crucial difficulty remains. Towards the end of the first
piatiletka militant radicalism gave way to a new conservative ethos, a
process which accelerated throughout the 1930s and culminated with
the Zhdanovshchina.

In a seminal work published in 1946, Nicholas Timasheff argued
that zigzags in cultural and social policy fell into a well-defined pattern. Following two 'socialist offensives' – the first in 1917–21, the
second associated with collectivization, the first piatiletka and the
initial eschatological drafts of the second plan – a 'Great Retreat'
from revolutionary utopianism took place after 1934. This involved a
'complete abandonment' of the 'communist experiment',[66] or in

[64] V. S. Dunham, *In Stalin's Time: Middleclass Values in Soviet Fiction* (Cambridge
University Press, 1976); S. Fitzpatrick, 'Culture and politics under Stalin: a reap-
praisal', *Slavic Review* (2, 1976).
[65] Bukharin drew on Jack London's *The Iron Heel* (Macmillan, New York, 1908), a
futuristic tale of a totalitarian state, to warn against the dangers posed by Stalin's
accretion of power.
[66] N. S. Timasheff, *The Great Retreat: The Growth and Decline of Communism in
Russia* (Dutton, New York, 1946) pp. 20–1, 354.

Lewin's words 'a set of classical measures of social conservatism, law and order strategies complete with a nationalist revival, and efforts to instil values of discipline, patriotism, conformism, authority and orderly careerism'.[67] As pre-revolutionary cultural, political and military figures were rehabilitated, radical Marxists were purged and their extravagant fantasies ridiculed. Russian nationalism displaced socialist internationalism. Thousands of workers who joined the party during the Great Breakthrough were expelled in the 1933–5 chistka, children of non-proletarian parents flocked into the universities and new party leaders from plebeian backgrounds began to adopt the old intelligentsia's value system. Elsewhere, in the world of work, the Kremlin made its peace with managers and bourgeois specialists. Spets-baiting no longer attracted Stalin's support, trade union pressure for wage egalitarianism was dismissed as a 'petty bourgeois prejudice' and one-man management was fostered throughout industry – 'the earth should tremble when the director walks the factory floor', asserted Kaganovich.

In the immediate post-war years most historians interpreted these developments as the abrupt and complete repudiation of the experiments of the 1920s, the period when Bolshevism finally came to terms with Russia's cultural heritage and the party-state refashioned policy to suit the imperatives of modernization. 'The educational reforms of the early thirties,' wrote Fainsod in 1953, 'with their emphasis on the restoration of discipline, the reinforcement of the authority of the teacher, and the teaching of fundamentals represented a first adjustment of the educational system to the needs of the industrial order',[68] and – it might be added – of the authoritarian polity.

Revisionists, however, posit a different scenario: from the summer of 1928 (the Shakhty Affair) to June 1931 (when Stalin called a halt to attacks on the old technical intelligentsia) a 'cultural revolution' swept Russia,[69] a second socialist offensive – quite distinct from the first – which bore a marked resemblance to events in China during the late 1960s.[70] Though launched from above, avers Fitzpatrick (the Great Breakthrough required a frontal assault on the NEP régime),

---

[67] M. Lewin, 'Society, state and ideology during the first five-year plan', in Fitzpatrick, *Cultural Revolution*, p. 56.

[68] Fainsod, *How Russia is Ruled*, p. 111. For similar interpretations see G. Bereday, et al., eds., *The Changing Soviet School* (Harvard University Press, 1960); A. Inkeles, *Social Change in Soviet Russia* (Harvard University Press, 1968); J. Pennar, et al., *Modernization and Diversity in Soviet Education* (Praeger, New York, 1971).

[69] Speaking to a conference of economists and industrial managers on 23 June 1931 Stalin extended 'every consideration' to bourgeois specialists willing to work loyally alongside the working class.

[70] The period of 'Cultural Revolution' when Mao Tse-tung instigated mass assaults on bureaucrats and party veterans.

cultural revolution had many facets and provided an outlet for tensions maturing in society during the 1920s. On the one hand it encompassed vydvizhenie, a tactic associated with Stalin's drive against the Right Opposition: the party recruited heavily amongst industrial workers, thousands of eager proletarians and communists were drafted into higher education, graduated as 'red' technicians and took over the jobs of bourgeois specialists thrown into the Gulag. On the other it was an 'iconoclastic youth movement' instigated from below which targeted 'reactionary' bureaucrats and 'class enemies'. In universities, schools, research institutes and the professions it was the process by which party fractions and the young seized the initiative from authority figures who had established themselves over the previous decade: students and pupils subjected lecturers and teachers to 're-election' and tried to link their work to 'real life' – the world of socialist construction. Cultural revolution was also the playground for all manner of visionaries, militants and revolutionary theorists, '"hair-brained schemers" whose blueprints for the new society not only attracted disciples among the Communist cultural militants but also in many cases gained solid institutional support'.[71]

Revisionism distinguishes the cultural revolution from Timasheff's first socialist offensive by reference to its overwhelmingly plebeian and egalitarian nature in the context of unprecedented social and economic transformation: hundreds of thousands of men and women of humble parentage assumed positions of responsibility in all areas of Soviet life, even if they did not yet penetrate the upper echelons of the bureaucracy.[72] It also contends that reaction was a more complex phenomenon than Timasheff imagined, 'a retreat from the policies of the first five-year plan period, rather than from the policies followed for the greater part of the 1920s'.[73] Moreover, though the party reined in the militants and turned against egalitarianism after 1931, many initiatives had already run into the sand and many radicals discredited themselves.

But not everything unravelled. In the first place literacy rates shot up. After 1929 the rapid influx of peasants into the industrial labour force drove the proletariat's literacy levels down – thirty-eight per cent of iron and steel workers in western Siberia were illiterate in

---

[71] S. Fitzpatrick, 'Introduction'; id., 'Cultural revolution as class war', in Fitzpatrick, *Cultural Revolution*, pp. 2–7, 11.

[72] See W. J. Chase & J. Arch Getty, 'The Soviet bureaucracy in 1935: a socio-political profile', in J. W. Strong, ed., *Essays on Revolutionary Culture and Stalinism: Selected Papers from the Third World Congress for Soviet and East European Studies* (Slavica, Columbus, 1990); S. Fitzpatrick, *Education and Social Mobility in the Soviet Union 1921–1934* (Cambridge University Press, 1979).

[73] J. F. Hough, 'The cultural revolution and Western understanding of the Soviet system', in Fitzpatrick, *Cultural Revolution*, p. 244.

1932–3, for example, compared with sixteen per cent in 1930. But overall forty million or so individuals attended adult education classes in 1932. And though reading and writing skills remained poor in many industries and areas, by the end of the decade universal primary education and the pullulating likbez campaign had virtually eradicated urban illiteracy. The 1939 census listed ninety-four per cent of town dwellers aged between nine and forty-nine as literate.[74] Secondly, official support for 'family values' did not lead to the complete re-domestization of female rôles, nor was the secularization drive rescinded – Moslem women in particular found greater scope for advancement than ever before. Thirdly, vydvizhentsy continued to staff the mushrooming party-state apparatus: following the Ezhovshchina some were promoted once more, this time to the highest positions. Finally, despite the annulment of positive discrimination in higher education, working-class youngsters still had opportunities for social mobility; through correspondence courses, extra-mural study and the voracious demand for specialist personnel occasioned by successive five-year plans, wartime emergency, postwar reconstruction and the ever growing bureaucracy. The period 1928–31, avow the revisionists, was more than a temporary eruption of iconoclastic millenarianism. It shaped the fabric of Soviet culture and society for the next twenty-five years and beyond.

Evaluations

The problem of culture
'Culture' is one of the most controversial terms within the social sciences. One seminal theorist – Clifford Geertz – describes it as the 'socially established structure of meaning in terms of which people do things'.[75] According to Geertz culture is not a 'level' of social formation but the sum of social formations; something which includes and permeates economics, politics, 'high' culture, 'popular' culture and ideology. Rather than a system of values and beliefs exterior or anterior to the individual or society, culture is the realm of practice which encloses the space for *all* expressions of meaning. In short, it is the totality of experience; the ways in which people deal with life or arrange their perceptions of the world. Moreover, to complicate matters still further, cultures often exist in the plural and stand in relations of domination, subordination, incorporation and resistance.

---

[74] See J. D. Barber, 'Working-class culture and political culture in the 1930s', in Günther, *Culture.*
[75] C. Geertz, *The Interpretations of Culture: Selected Essays by Clifford Geertz* (Basic Books, New York, 1973) p. 12.

Culture, therefore, is one of the most challenging concepts with which academics have to grapple. In consequence, historians of Stalin's Russia are faced with an extraordinarily difficult task. Did cultures exist in the plural, and if so how can they be apprehended by researchers? How did a dominant culture incorporate other subordinate perceptions of the world? What resistance was there to the dominant culture? It is by no means the case that all these questions can be answered. In contrast to the interactions between official ideology and high culture, for example, comparatively little attention has been paid to popular culture.[76] Indeed, a Geertzian or 'anthropological' conception of culture – an attempt to grasp the arranged perceptions of the world characteristic of the various Soviet peoples – has never been essayed by the academic community. Instead attention has focused almost exclusively on state–society linkages. These can be considered under the following headings: 'state and ideology', 'state and society', 'ideology and society', 'massification and atomization', 'tradition and meritocracy' and 'ideology and high culture'.

State and ideology

Contrary to the dicta of Cold War historians Stalinist ideology was never fixed and fast frozen. Throughout the cultural revolution party leaders and militants disputed the nature of socialism and communism and the prerequisites for and future direction of social change. Developments in the early 1930s certainly prefigured a return to older, traditional values and *mores*, but values and *mores* borrowed from a wide range of sources. 'It is sometimes asked whether or not we should slacken the tempo somewhat', reported Stalin to a conference of factory managers in 1931,

> No, comrades... On the contrary, we must quicken it as much as is within our powers and possibilities. This is dictated to us by our obligations to the workers and peasants of the USSR. This is dictated to us by our obligations to the working class of the whole world. To slacken the tempo would mean to lag behind; and those who lag behind are beaten. We do not want to be beaten... One feature of the history of Old Russia was the continual beatings she received due to her backwardness. She was beaten by the Mongol Khans, she was beaten by Turkish Beys, she was beaten by Swedish feudal lords, she was beaten by Polish–Lithuanian Pans, she was beaten by Anglo-French capi-

---

[76] Some work on Stalinist popular culture is now appearing. See, for example, R. Stites, *Russian Popular Culture: Entertainment and Society Since 1900* (Cambridge University Press, 1992) and Stites' bibliography. But since these matters have not yet attracted substantial academic debate they will be left to one side.

talists, she was beaten by Japanese barons. She was beaten by all
– for her backwardness. For military backwardness, for cultural
backwardness, for industrial backwardness, for agricultural
backwardness. She was beaten because to do so was profitable
and and could be done without fear of punishment...
We are fifty or a hundred years behind the advanced countries. We must make good this lag in ten years. Either we do it,
or they crush us.[77]

As the General Secretary revealed so vividly, the trenchant pursuit
of economic modernization fused with Bolshevik élan and meditations upon Russian history, giving birth to an ideological sport incor-
porating elements of idealism, internationalism, Russian
nationalism,[78] Soviet patriotism and *realpolitik*.[79] Leninism and classical Marxism provided some genetic material, but there were clear
hints of earlier and other creations. Intimations of special destiny
echoed sixteenth-century religious dogmas and nineteenth-century
Slavophile precepts.[80] The visible desire to catch up with and surpass
the West paralleled the concerns of successive tsars, from Peter the
Great to Alexander III. Soviet patriotism mirrored Pavel Pestel's
attempts to think through the socio-political consequences of fundamental change within a multinational state, and complemented
Sergei Uvarov's articulation of 'orthodoxy, autocracy and nationality'.[81]
But whatever its parentage this grotesque creature was extraordinarily mutable, changing shape and colour as theory collided with
reality. The mid-1930s were clearly more authoritarian than the late

[77] 'O zadachakh khoziaistvennikov (rech' 4 fevraliia 1931 g)', in I. V. Stalin, *Voprosy
leninizma* (Moscow, 1945) p. 328.
[78] Indeed, attacks on national communists began in the 1920s. Mir-Said Sultangaliev
(1880–1939), a prominent Moslem communist, was purged at the 1923 twelfth party
congress.
[79] Notable by its absence from the list of aggressors was Germany, the nearest thing
Russia had to an ally in 1931.
[80] When the Greek Orthodox Church temporarily accepted Papal authority in 1439
and the Ottomans seized Constantinople fourteen years later, Russian divines argued
that Moscow had become the 'Third Rome', replacing Rome and Constantinople as
the 'City of God'. In the 1840s Slavophiles contrasted the 'collective nature of human
consciousness' in Russia with the West's 'fragmented individualism'. Controversy
between 'Slavophiles' and 'Westernizers' exploded in the 1840s and dragged on fitfully
for the rest of the nineteenth century.
[81] Both men wanted to foster supra-national allegiances which would obliterate ethnic
identities. Pestel' (1793–1826) was a leading Decembrist who espoused the overthrow
of autocracy, the abolition of serfdom and the establishment of an egalitarian and
authoritarian republic. Uvarov (1786–1855) was Nicholas I's Minister of Education
from 1833 to 1849. Orthodoxy, autocracy and nationality, he believed, should be the
guiding principles of educational policy, binding all the Empire's populations to the
régime.

1920s – manifestly so – but Timasheff's 'Great Retreat' did not mark the radicals' final denouement, or even a straightforward relapse into Russian chauvinism overlaid with German- or Italian-style totalitarianism. Shortly afterwards ideology mutated once more. Revolutionary zeal and fidelity to the party-state came to the fore in 1937, but the elaboration of 'socialist legality' in 1939 – espoused by Vyshinskii and endorsed by Stalin at the eighteenth party congress – signalled the end of mass terror and Ezhov's pretensions, even if the régime reserved to itself the right to override its own decrees with impunity. From 1941 to 1945 militarism, anti-fascism and Soviet patriotism emerged as the most important axioms. Thereafter xenophobia, anti-semitism, the cult of personality, party renewal and the aggressive championing of socialist realism dominated the scene.

But continuity was evident in several areas – the party's vanguard rôle and the steady increase in the emphasis on military prowess, for instance. Moreover, hostility towards religion persisted until 1943 and revived, albeit in a muted form, after 1944. Similarly antipathy towards ultramontane ethnic identities never ceased, but here Stalinist policy was ambiguous: it was not simply a matter of Great Russian chauvinism, or even of Russification. Dance troops, national choirs and orchestras, peasant costumes and customs – folk *mores* and 'folkways' in general – received financial support from Moscow and the republican governments. But the régime encouraged these overt manifestations of 'nationality' on the firm understanding that they did not menace the unity of the Soviet state or threaten the party's leading rôle. 'Friendship of the peoples' could function only under the carapace of absolute fealty to socialism.[82] Alternative loyalties which imperiled the USSR's territorial integrity or struck at the heart of the party's claim to ideological predominance (regardless of how the ideology was defined at any particular moment) were never tolerated.

And only in one area was radicalism completely repudiated: Moscow's alarm at the manifold implications of de-legalization, de-schooling and social flux rudely interrupted dreams that families, schools or the law would soon 'wither away'. Shulgin's prognoses threatened planned economic growth, Pashukanis's theories undermined the Kremlin's struggles to establish control over the 'quicksand society' while the disintegration of the family placed a heavy financial burden on the state – central and republican organizations had to look after the growing number of waifs and strays. Loosening filial ties also jeopardized industrialization. Unattached workers and peasants with no responsibilities – or responsibilities left behind at

[82] See R. Conquest, ed., *Soviet Nationalities Policy in Practice* (The Bodley Head, London, 1967); Hosking, *Soviet Union*, ch. 9.

the last construction site – could and did behave like nomadic Gypsies; hence the massive labour turnover characteristic of the first piatiletka. Marriage, on the other hand, tended to root workers in one locality, allowing enterprise directors to deal peremptorily with labour while simultaneously shifting the costs of child-rearing to the community.[83] Finally, strong and stable families replicated key elements of Stalinist ideology throughout society – patriarchal authority and the idealization of the vozhd' as 'the father of his people' mutually reinforced social discipline and the political order. Indeed, Timasheff's thoughts on the matter were anticipated in Trotsky's elaboration of 'Thermidorian reaction'. 'The triumphal rehabilitation of the family', noted Trotsky in 1936,

> is caused by the material and cultural bankruptcy of the state... the leaders are forcing people to glue together the shell of the broken family, and not only that, but to consider it, under threat of extreme penalties, the sacred nucleus of triumphant socialism. It is hard to measure with the eye the scope of this retreat... The most compelling motive for the present cult of the family is undoubtedly the need of the bureaucracy for a stable hierarchy of relations, and for the disciplining of youth by means of 40,000,000 points of support for authority and power.[84]

In any event, if these institutions withered away, why not, as Marx prophesied in 1848 and Lenin predicted in 1917, let the state wither away too?[85] 'Withering away' ran counter to state-building, an inherent feature of post-NEP modernization.

State and society

If successive changes were not produced by fixed ideological precepts neither were they linear and accumulative (the gradual perfection of the totalitarian Leviathan), nor were they caused by a single agency. The cultural revolution was, in many instances, a period of

---

[83] From the mid-1930s onwards childless couples or those with only one offspring were encouraged to adopt orphans.

[84] L. Trotsky, *The Revolution Betrayed: What is the Soviet Union and Where is it Going?* (trans. M. Eastman, Harcourt & Brace, New York, 1937) pp. 151–3.

[85] 'When, in the course of development, class distinctions have disappeared, and all production has been concentrated in the hands of a vast association of the whole nation, the public power will lose its political character. Political power, properly so called, is merely the organized power of one class for oppressing another': K. Marx & F. Engels, *Manifesto of the Communist Party* (Moscow, 1986) p. 54. 'The suppression of the bourgeois state by the proletarian state is impossible without a violent revolution. The abolition of the proletarian state, i.e., of the state in general, is impossible except through the process of "withering away"': V. I. Lenin, *The State and Revolution* (Moscow, 1972) p. 22.

experimentation driven forward by a jostling alliance of grass roots militants, lower ranking apparatchiki, non-party specialists and Politburo radicals temporarily united by a shared enthusiasm for social transformation.[86] Moreover, though Stalin and the Kremlin élite played a vital rôle as enablers or initiators, not everything was under their direct jurisdiction nor met with their full approval. For the most part they set out broad guide-lines. They involved themselves in detail when some crucial principle seemed to be at issue or when matters spun out of control,[87] but they rarely wholly revoked past policies. Bubnov's educational reforms addressed the immediate imperatives of collectivization and industrialization, but while the ruinous consequences of Narkompros's prescriptions quickly persuaded leaders to espouse classroom discipline, formal pedagogy in higher education and conservatism in the curriculum, it remains the case that after 1931 more children and adolescents attended more schools and technical institutes than ever before. If the centre promulgated vydvizhenie, responsibility for policy implementation rested elsewhere, with the nomenklatura: declining standards in the engineering profession, therefore, were an unintended by-product of proletarianization and democratization. In consequence the régime viewed the old technical intelligentsia more favourably after 1931, but white-collar personnel lifted from obscure backgrounds continued to pursue their careers and workers still found their way into technical institutes and universities.[88] Similarly, while the dire effects of sexual liberation and declining family values soon frightened Moscow into reaction, the stress on parental custodianship and filial loyalty survived the years 1936–8, the period when devotion to the party-state supposedly transcended all other allegiances.[89] In both

[86] For a fine exposition of this interpretation in the field of public housing see S. F. Starr, 'Visionary town planning during the cultural revolution', in Fitzpatrick, *Cultural Revolution*.

[87] In January 1936, for example, *Pravda* mentioned that in summer 1934 Kirov, Stalin and Zhdanov had been labouring over a new textbook on party history. In October 1931 Stalin personally intervened in the internal debates wracking the historical profession. In a letter to the journal *Proletarskaia revoliutsiia* he critcized 'archive rats' for relying on 'written documents alone' in their researches into Lenin's pre–revolutionary career. See J. D. Barber, *Soviet Historians in Crisis 1928–32* (Macmillan, London, 1981); id., 'Stalin's letter to the editors of *Proletarskaya revolyutsiya*', *Soviet Studies* (1, 1976); Enteen, in Fitzpatrick, *Cultural Revolution*.

[88] See K. E. Bailes, *Technology and Society under Lenin and Stalin. Origins of the Soviet Technical Intelligentsia 1917–1941* (Princeton University Press, 1978) chs. 2–3; N. Lampert, *The Technical Intelligentsia and the Soviet State. A Study of Soviet Managers and Technicians 1928–1935* (Macmillan, London, 1979) chs. 4–6.

[89] See R. W. Thurston, 'The Soviet family during the Great Terror 1935–41', *Soviet Studies* (3, 1991) p. 561. Three books published in 1937 for mass consumption – *For Love and Happiness in our Family*, *The Family and Marriage in their Historical Development* and *A Book for Parents* – made it clear that while parents and children owed enormous responsibilities to the state, political commitment should never be allowed to destroy family life.

instances women still had numerous opportunities to escape from domesticity, and after 1934 the Pavlik Morozov phenomenon (children denouncing their parents as enemies of socialism) never again attracted significant official support – not even at the height of the Ezhovshchina.[90]

Ideology and society

Whatever difficulties researchers face over causation, motivation and the ideological balance sheet there is no doubt that the 1930s were basic to the making of Soviet society. The onslaught against religion and ultramontane ethnic identities helped to foster Soviet patriotism. Undermining family values weakened social forms resistant to modernization. Restructuring family values buttressed the political order. De-legalizing social relationships created space for the arbitrary exercise of power during the most hectic period of socialist construction. Vyshinskii's articulation of socialist legality epitomized the primacy of the party-state over the individual. Throughout society radicalism expedited transformation, conservatism assisted restabilization. Pride of place in the scheme of social change, however, should be given to education.

In the 1920s advocates of a 'hard line' in cultural policy – for the most part concentrated in the trade unions, lower party organizations and Komsomol – criticized Narkompros for failing to revolutionize the pedagogical system. For them democratization, secularization and the universalization of provision were not enough. Schools and institutes needed to proletarianize their intake and restructure the curriculum.[91] Hardliners were supported by some on the Left who feared the consequences of leaving matters as they were – staff trained under the *ancien régime* could all too easily undermine socialism – and some in Vesenkha and the economic commissariats; proponents of vocationalization who begrudged wasting money on the humanities. A third group objected to current policies on strictly Leninist grounds: de-schooling would mark an important step towards the withering away of the state while refashioning Soviet man along 'productivist' lines – in the future individuals would look

---

[90] In 1932 the young Pavlik Morozov denounced his father as a kulak. He was killed by enraged relatives. The press treated the child as a martyr and praised his devotion to socialism.
[91] See Fitzpatrick, *Education & Social Mobility*; id., 'The "soft line" on culture and its enemies: Soviet cultural policy 1922–1927', *Slavic Review* (2, 1974); Lapidus, in Fitzpatrick, *Cultural Revolution*.

to their work for spiritual as well as material fulfilment.[92]

Towards the end of the 1920s millenarial dreams, productivist theories and the obsession with fundamental reform combined with élite disputes over the broad direction of policy to unleash militancy. By 1931, however, Stalin's alliance with the radicals had served its purpose; the initial breakthrough in industry and agriculture was complete and the Right Opposition defeated. Thereafter central controls were tightened. By 1940 the entire system had been remodelled, fitted to a polity which had become hierarchical, authoritarian and conservative and dedicated to reproducing these qualities in the population at large. But ideological instruction overlaid traditional values. Children, university undergraduates and technical trainees attended compulsory lectures and classes in 'scientific communism' which emphasized socialism in one country, the importance of planning, the rôle of government and the doctrine of 'sharpening class struggle' – as communism became ever more imminent the danger from internal and external enemies increased, necessitating the continual strengthening of state power. These legitimating myths were expounded in the *History of the Communist Party of the Soviet Union (bolsheviks): Short Course*, first published in 1939 and required reading for all pupils, teachers and students for the rest of the Stalin period.

Massification and atomization

It is here that totalitarian theories have much to offer. Although many analysts conceived the rôle of ideology in a crude one-dimensional fashion, totalitarianism has been sensitive to the manner in which Stalinism shaped perceptions of the world. Education and the mass media – the press, posters, radio and cinema – completely controlled by the régime, structured the meanings which Soviet citizens could ascribe to phenomena. What one could read, write, listen to, look at, love or hope for, was quite flagrantly manipulated by the state, with real consequences for people's sense of identity.[93] Atomization helped to destroy old allegiances and beliefs; massification promoted the formation of new ones at the state's behest, giving rise to a heady brew compounded of romanticism, optimism and

[92] The most vigorous exponent of the productivist ethos was Aleksei Gastev (1882–1941), a tireless propagandist for NOT – the 'scientific organization of work' – and an admirer of F. W. Taylor, an early twentieth-century American engineer who advocated the fullest possible harmonization of worker and machine. Lenin too was fascinated by 'Taylorism'. During the Civil War he believed that its 'refined brutality' could be put to the service of the workers' state. See S. A. Smith, 'Bolshevism, Taylorism and the technical intelligentsia; the Soviet Union 1917–41', *Radical Science Journal* (13, 1983).
[93] For an examination of some of these themes see V. Bonnell, 'The representation of politics and the politics of representation', *Russian Review* (3, 1988).

materialism laced with fear of the 'enemy'. Consider this evocative passage from a child's primer, published in 1931, glorifying the first piatiletka. The chapter is headed 'New people: a fragment from a book to be written fifty years hence':

> Socialism is no longer a myth, a phantasy of the mind. We ourselves are building it.
> But the task of building socialism is not easy.
> We are surrounded on all sides by enemies.
> Like the builders at Dneprostroi, we have raised protecting walls around us. But any minute the water may break through the walls, rush into the enclosure, overturn and destroy everything that we have done.
> And that is why the work must go on so rapidly and with such concentration.
> More quickly must be erected the stone dams of factories and mills. More quickly, because time does not wait.
> All the figures have grown, all the tasks have multiplied. Every day the papers spur on the laggers. In every enterprise shock brigades are at work. One factory sends a challenge to another: which will do the task faster, which will do it better?
> Millions of workers are striving to fulfil the Five-Year Plan successfully; every one hopes that life with be better afterwards.
> Yes, life will be better afterwards, if we will it.[94]

And it is here, in the realm of massification and atomization, that the notion of 'cultural revolution' is at its weakest. While it is true that contemporaries occasionally used the term – Averbakh, for example – it is nevertheless a construct of Western academics, a simulacrum of China's quite different history.[95] What happened in Russia between 1928–31 did not emerge 'from below'; it was articulated 'from above', by the Stalinist clique. Even if cultural militancy resonated with particular groups (disaffected workers, Komsomolites, etc.) Moscow easily reined in rank-and-file activists once radicalism had served its purpose. Russia's real 'cultural revolution' occurred in the ten years or so after 1917. In fact, Stalin's rise signalled the end of a period of daring iconoclasm – 'proletarian culture', new art movements and experimental life-styles were dead or in decline by the late 1920s.[96]

---

[94] M. Ilin, *New Russia's Primer: The Story of the Five-Year Plan* (trans. G. S. Counts & N. P. Lodge, Houghton Mifflin, Boston, 1931) pp. 156–8.
[95] Mao's faction of the Chinese communist party only regained control of the Cultural Revolution via the intervention of the People's Liberation Army. Nothing like that happened in Stalin's Russia.
[96] See A. Gleason, et al., eds., *Bolshevik Culture: Experiment and Order in the Russian Revolution* (Indiana University Press, 1985); Stites, *Revolutionary Dreams*.

Tradition and meritocracy

Despite the open propagation of traditional values after the first piatiletka, however, this was not a traditional society. It was highly mobile, not static. Hundreds of thousands of men and women stepped from behind the bench or the plough to become overlookers, engineers, soviet apparatchiki and local party officials after attending likbez, rabfak and technical courses. The assiduous and fortunate were quickly integrated into the nomenklatura system and promoted into industrial administration, central government or the central party apparatus. A few subsequently ascended to the highest positions: Andrei Gromyko was taught to read by the party,[97] for example, and Khrushchev began his career as a technical student. By the time Stalin died at least thirty ministers and deputy ministers had started out as 1930s vydvizhentsy.[98] This was in sharp contrast to the old Leninist élite; most of whom were drawn from the tsarist middle class and educated in law or the humanities.

But on the other hand society was not fully meritocratic – males monopolized key positions – nor did the new apparatchiki constitute a social class, at least not in classical Marxist terms. They led privileged and comfortable lives but excepting personal belongings they had no property rights: they did not own the means of production nor did they draw incomes from rents. Equally, though apparatchiki formed a bureaucratic stratum they were never a bureaucratic 'class': though salaried they had no tenure and promotion was neither orderly nor predictable.[99] Rise could occur with dizzying rapidity. In 1931, for instance, while still a provincial technical student, the young Viktor Kravchenko was summoned to Ordzhonikidze's office. 'Well, comrade,' remarked the commissar's secretary after the interview,

> I congratulate you. Your stock has certainly gone up! Here are tickets for the Bolshoi Theatre and for the Moscow Art Theatre. Your expenses in the hotel will be taken care of. And here's a thousand rubles for pocket money. A gift from Comrade Ordzhonikidze. Have a good time and if you need anything, just ring me.[100]

---

[97] Gromyko (1909–89) joined the party in 1931. After a spell as ambassador to the USA and Cuba he was Minister of Foreign Affairs from 1957 to 1985.
[98] Data is available for fifty-seven of the 115 ministers and their deputies. Many others graduated from technical institutes during the NEP. Of the total sixty-five per cent were proletarian by social origin or had worked in industry for a while.
[99] For a discussion of the vexed question of 'class' in the Soviet context see D. Lane, *The End of Social Inequality? Class, Status and Power under State Socialism* (Allen & Unwin, London, 1982); id. *Politics and Society in the USSR* (2nd ed., Martin Robertson, London, 1978).
[100] V. Kravchenko, *I Chose Freedom: The Personal and Political Life of a Soviet Official* (Robert Hale, London, 1947) p. 85.

But fall could be no less swift. A few years later Kravchenko, by then a qualified engineer, witnessed the public humiliation of dozens of specialists and apparatchiki, thrown out of their jobs and homes by howling workers egged on by NKVD operatives. Some doubtless found other posts, some disappeared for good in 1937–8, others were plucked from the Gulag to serve the state during the Great Fatherland War. To some extent vydvizhentsy could bequeath their success – their children entered universities and technical institutes relatively easily – but all were at the mercy of Stalin, purge commissions, the secret police or the central committee, and in the final analysis their collective defences were weak: only mutual protection or the prompt denunciation of potential rivals could stave off ruin, and often only for a time.

These confusing and contradictory features of Stalinist society were not without precedent: centrally instigated social mobility, insecurity of tenure, arbitrariness and brutality were commonplaces of Russia's past. For over three hundred years the tsars struggled to discipline and mobilize the population. Ivan the Terrible's Oprichnina acted like the NKVD. Peter the Great consciously strove to build a 'service state' where ability would count for more than nobility: his 'Table of Ranks' subjugated society to the régime (rank followed one's position in the bureaucracy, not the other way around), but he was not immune to capriciousness, vindictiveness and millenarial fantasies.[101] In the early nineteenth century Alexander I chose Mikhail Speranskii (1772–1839), the son of a poor village priest, as his closest adviser. After a spell in disgrace he became an important figure under Nicholas I, a ruler who patronized a network of 'military colonies', settlements in which the close supervision of everyday life rivalled the prognostications of twentieth-century productivists. Nicholas also founded the 'Third Section', a political police instructed to inquire into 'all and every matter' which might disturb 'the tranquillity of His Majesty's Empire'. Half a century later, Alexander III snatched from obscurity a provincial railway manager who impressed him by his ability to make the trains run on time: promoted to be Minister of Finances in 1892, Sergei Witte was ennobled by Nicholas II in 1903 and sacked the same year – only to return as prime minister in 1905 before being dismissed once more in 1906, this time for good.

---

[101] Peter personally participated in the bloody massacre of the Kremlin guard. In a move which chimed well with Stalinist notions of order and hierarchy, his initial plans for St Petersburg envisaged allocating housing space strictly in accordance with rank (the higher one's rank, the closer one's residence to the Imperial Presence) and the absence of streets: instead the entire city would be criss-crossed with canals, forcing the people to become 'maritime' – like the English and Dutch. As is well known Peter also forced the Court to ape Western manners and dress.

State–society relations, therefore, were not entirely different from those obtaining under the tsars. What distinguishes the Stalin period from all earlier epoches is quantity and sweep – the sheer scale of mobility, arbitrariness and brutality. The earthquake of the first piatiletka and its aftershocks refashioned Russian life more fundamentally and affected non-Russian populations more profoundly than did tsarism, the Revolution or the Civil War. Peasants left for the towns in swarms; droves of working men and women traded old lives for new; millions rather than thousands moved upwards across the board; thousands rather than hundreds lost their jobs and lives if they fell foul of plebeian apparatchiki or Stalin's burgeoning 'Caliban state'.

Ideology and high culture

Like many later vydvizhentsy Witte's marriage was a source of embarrassment,[102] his manner coarse, his inclinations conservative and his social pretensions considerable. It is all too easy to belittle the ambitions and insecurities of parvenus. In May 1936, for example, a conference of executives' wives convened in the Kremlin: Stalin and the Politburo watched with approval as flunkeys demonstrated flower-arranging and the correct placing and use of silverware. It is easier still to mock the banalities of official culture. After 1934 schools and universities inculcated a solemn regard for literary realism and the 'classics', a fear and loathing of freshness and the automatic tendency to dismiss experimentation as mere cleverness. This often cost writers their lives, but even the most acceptable were troubled – long after their deaths. Pushkin's bawdy verse never saw the light of day and approved texts were regularly bowdlerized – asterisks replaced lines considered too *risqué* by Glavlit. In concert halls audiences listened to tedious recitations by military choirs, portentous works based on sentimental folk ditties or dreary replications of dead musical formulae. Plebeian apparatchiki and their spouses sat rigidly through ballets commissioned for tsars, princesses and royal mistresses which they vigorously applauded without understanding or appreciation. Galleries exhibited statues of naked, overmuscled workers breaking the chains of oppression – but with genitalia of modest proportions ludicrously concealed behind figleaves. Enormous canvases displayed implausible scenes of proletari-

---

[102] Witte's wife was never accepted at Court. Many vydvizhentsy, and some established party leaders, suffered because of their spouses. In the late 1940s, for example, Molotov continued to dance attendance on the vozhd', even though his Jewish wife was incarcerated in the Gulag. Molotov was born on 9 March. Immediately after Stalin's death, according to one story, Khrushchev and Malenkov asked him what he would like for a birthday present. 'Give me back Polina', he replied. Another source has him dispatching a private aircraft to rescue her a few days later.

an heroism set against impossible landscapes. Interspersed with these were endless images of Stalin and Lenin haloed by storm-clouds, battles and collapsing empires.[103]

But all this needs to be set in context. In the first place, the régime feared art – prose and poetry in particular – precisely because it respected it. More than in any other European country, literature in nineteenth-century Russia was political. In the 1840s Vissarion Belinskii, a seminal figure in Russian intellectual history, came to believe that writers should serve the people.[104] Thereafter many viewed themselves as the people's tribune, the nation's conscience and the storm petrels of revolution. They drew no distinction between artistic creativity, social criticism and political opposition. Even literary theory owed much to the past – the doctrine of socialist realism directly echoed the articulation of social realism by Belinskii's followers.

Secondly, by censoring and controlling access to high culture, the party-state was acting no differently to the *ancien régime*: Nicholas I fidgeted over Pushkin,[105] just as Zhdanov took a neurotic interest in Soviet poets, novelists and musicians. Stalin personally censored Mandelstam and Shostakovich ironically recalled how Tikhon Khrennikov became head of the Composers' Union in 1948:

> First, I was told, Stalin studied the applications of all the candidates for the post of administrator, and then called for their photographs. He spread them out on the desk and after some thought poked his finger at Khrennikov's face. 'Him.' And he was right. Stalin had a wonderful instinct for such people.[106]

Thirdly, cultural production has rarely occurred without overt ideological intent. If monumentalist Stalinist architecture – Moscow University or the city's metro – reflected current aspirations so did King's College Chapel in Cambridge; the structure is more a hymn to

---

[103] For a recent survey of Soviet painting, interior design, sculpture and architecture from the mid-1920s to the 1950s see M. C. Brown, *Art Under Stalin* (Phaidon, Oxford, 1991).

[104] Belinskii (1811–48) – philosopher, critic and journalist – was the son of a poor army surgeon and the first major nineteenth-century radical to emerge from the lower social stratum. Since much of his literary criticism contained a strong political imperative he found himself in constant trouble with the censors.

[105] Due to Pushkin's public expressions of sympathy for the Decembrists, Nicholas appointed himself the poet's personal censor. Pushkin only narrowly escaped further persecution.

[106] D. D. Shostakovich, *Testimony: The Memoirs of Shostakovich* (ed. S. Volkov, trans. A. W. Bouis, Hamish Hamilton, London, 1979) p. 196. Khrennikov (b.1913) graduated from the Moscow Conservatoire in 1936 and became a deputy to the Supreme Soviet in 1941.

Henry VIII's than to God's power. If Soviet writers and composers served the personality cult, most artists in other countries and other times served despotism: Shakespeare's *Richard the Third* fabricated history in the interests of the Tudor tyranny; Milton's *Samson Agonistes* is panegyric to Cromwellian republicanism; Mozart wrote scores to suit the tastes of Habsburg emperors. Visual artefacts – the most ancient form of propaganda – have always falsified: 'red corners' were ideological constructs,[107] but so are icons, religious friezes and stained glass windows. As in Stalin's Russia, seventeenth-century French painters depicted the 'Sun King' in clothes he never wore, opening exhibitions he never visited, welcoming ambassadors he never met and reviewing armies he never commanded. And no portrait of the 'Virgin Queen' could be exhibited unless it followed prescribed rules of composition – half-profile, staring blankly from the canvas.[108] To help artists achieve the authorized image clerks supplied officially approved templates and tracings.

Finally, though socialist realism, official prudery and the Zhdanovshchina provided vulgarians, philistines and bureaucratic busy-bodies with ample opportunity to ply their trades, the hunger for improvement was real. Vydvizhentsy and newly-literate workers and peasants hankered after 'refinement', and the educational system implanted a respect (however ponderous and unimaginative) for 'classical' art, literature and music which long outlived Stalin. In the early 1980s this writer overheard two Leningrad railwaymen bickering over Pushkin. Westerners familiar with the Soviet Union will have had similar experiences. But if we eavesdropped on workers in French car factories, British supermarkets or the Chicago stockyards, we would be unlikely to be rewarded with discussions of Molière, Byron or Whitman.

Suggestions for further reading

V. S. Dunham, *In Stalin's Time: Middleclass Values in Soviet Fiction* (Cambridge University Press, 1976). An unusual study examining the culture and literary tastes of the 'upwardly mobile' Stalinist apparatchiki.

H. Günther, ed., *The Culture of the Stalin Period* (Macmillan, London, 1990). Comprises sections on popular culture and every-

---

[107] Small areas in Soviet factories and offices with a red flag, busts of Lenin and Stalin and a scattering of propaganda tracts.

[108] Just as Louis XIV's ministers and bureaucrats fostered the notion of celestial monarchy, so Elizabeth I's courtiers nurtured the idea of impregnable virginity. Both cults were utilized for a variety of political, social and ideological purposes.

day life, art, literature, architecture and film with contributions from a range of European and American specialists.

N. Lampert & G. T. Rittersporn, eds., *Stalinism: Its Nature and Aftermath. Essays in Honour of Moshe Lewin* (Macmillan, London, 1992). Includes useful articles on Soviet peasants and literature (Alec Nove), urban social mobility (Hans-Henning Schröder), construction workers (Jean-Paul Depretto), foremen (Lewis Siegelbaum), and the parallels drawn between Stalin, Ivan the Terrible and Peter the Great (Maureen Perrie).

A. Kemp-Welch, *Stalin and the Literary Intelligentsia 1928–1939* (Macmillan, London, 1991). A fine monograph based on previously unpublished Soviet archives which links literature and literary policy to social and economic change.

S. Fitzpatrick, ed., *Cultural Revolution in Russia 1928–1931* (Indiana University Press, 1978). Seminal work espousing the 'cultural revolution' interpretation; contributors include Sheila Fitzpatrick (class war), Gail Lapidus (education), George Enteen (Soviet historians), Fredrick Starr (town planning), Robert Sharlet (law), and Moshe Lewin (the first piatiletka).

N. S. Timasheff, *The Great Retreat: The Growth and Decline of Communism in Russia* (Dutton, New York, 1946). The pioneer study of changes in cultural and social policy under Stalin during the 1930s.

A. Werth, *Russia: The Post-War Years* (Robert Hale, London, 1971). Contains vivid accounts of the Zhdanovshchina – the author was a newspaper correspondent who knew many of the intellectuals, artists and high party officials involved.

CONCLUSION: HISTORY AND STALIN'S RUSSIA

History is a pack of tricks we play upon the dead.

Voltaire.

Tout comprendre, c'est tout pardonner

'Nero, too, was a product of his epoch,' wrote Trotsky from his exiled fastness,

> yet after he perished his statutes were smashed and his name was scraped off everything. The vengeance of history is more terrible than the vengeance of the most powerful General Secretary. I venture to think that this is consoling.[1]

This book was written when Trotsky's prediction finally came true, and in a manner which probably would not have surprised him. The state which Stalin helped to construct has gone forever, and Stalin and all his works are being repudiated in the lands over which his name once held sway. In consequence we might ask, since so many millions perished so violently and, it now seems, so pointlessly between the late 1920s and early 1950s, whether we should play tricks upon the dead by seeking to conjure manifest injustice into balanced and judicious explanation. 'Are there really no crimes', objected one exasperated reader of the manuscript of this book, 'towards which History will not exercise its indulgence?'

This is a basic problem for all historians, but it is one which haunts those who work on the Soviet Union during these thirty-odd years with unusual vehemence, and it would be foolish to deny its harrowing potency. But we need to remind ourselves of the purpose of academic history. It is not to establish a mythic truth. Nor is it to point the moral tale. Nor is it to praise winners and condemn losers, or *vice versa*. Hard though it is and imperfect though the attempt must always be, historians should to try to see all round a problem; to understand and make comprehensible old policies, old factions and past lives. And understanding – that effort to suspend disbelief and enter into the world of men and women for whom we may now have no particular sympathy – requires more than a modicum of empathy. It is comparatively easy to respond to the dispossessed: the quivering

[1] L. Trotsky, *Stalin: An Appraisal of the Man and his Influence* (trans. C. Malamuth, Hollis & Carter, London, 1947) p. 383.

family standing by the bloody corpse of the murdered 'kulak', the black slave in the ante-bellum South, the exploited child labourer, the victims of imperial pride or religious bigotry. Understanding the oppressors, however – the NKVD operative, the Mississippi slave-owner, the money-grabbing Lancashire capitalist, the Roman patriarch or the interrogators of the Holy Inquisition – is probably an unattractive proposition, even though we are not required to share their view of the world. We are obliged, however, to realize that it was *their* view of *their* world – whether held sincerely, from fear, in the hope of advancement, or out of weakness or insouciance – located in times and circumstances far removed from our own. And once we have made that imaginative leap we are no longer free to talk easily of the crimes and follies of this or that epoch, or to engage in the glib luxury of alloting praise or blame. Praise and blame become harder to dispense as we ponder conflicting passions and choices. To the everlasting chagrin of moralists, politicians and pundits, the world becomes stranger, more complicated and less amenable to manipulation when we recognize the singularities of the past, see things otherwise, begin to think for ourselves, and falter before judging. And this is where we should start from.[2]

The successes of history
Over the last fifty years or so, and bearing in mind the limits imposed by the pre-glasnost' source base, Western historians have enjoyed some undoubted successes. Much fine work has been produced by academics struggling to map out the USSR's over-arching framework. Questions surrounding Stalin's rise, the rôle of ideology, the nomenklatura system, the functioning of the governmental machine, the purges or the hypertrophic development of the party-state have all attracted considerable attention, and they continue to do so. Stalinist foreign policy – even more than domestic policy a matter of immediate concern to bourgeois democracies – has been pretty thoroughly examined. 'High politics' in general has been well served by the profession.

The labours of those who chart the economic aspects of the Great Breakthrough and its aftermath – de-kulakization, collectivization and industrialization – are no less significant. Though precise figures are still not available (and perhaps never will be) we know something of the broad economic effects of 'revolution from above' and the impact of the command–administrative system. Moreover, in recent years social historians have advanced our knowledge of a

---

[2] For forceful – and sometimes hysterical – rejections of views like this see the meditations of Robert Conquest, Geoffrey Hosking, Michael Howard, Leszek Kolakowski, Martin Malia, Richard Pipes and Adam Ulam on the occasion of the Russian Revolution's seventy-fifth anniversary in *The Times Literary Supplement* (6 November 1992).

whole range of topics associated with state-building, purging and economic transformation. By looking 'from below' instead of 'from above' they have often confirmed generalizations propounded by earlier researchers or given them a new twist. Sometimes, by wrenching attention away from high politics, personalities and macro-economics, they have elaborated entirely different interpretive frameworks. But notwithstanding these successes, for a number of reasons we are still largely in the dark.

The failures of history

If history is a kind of conjuring trick, researchers in some fields might have resources enough to mesmerize and persuade their readers, but this is not the case for those who exercise their talents on Stalin's Russia. The traumas experienced by Soviet citizens between the late 1920s and 1953 were so momentous and varied in their impact, profoundly affecting the lives of all ethnic groups – not just Russians, or even Slavs, but also the multifarious peoples of Central Asia, the Caucasus, Siberia and the far-flung borderlands – that no historian can claim possession of anything approaching a full deck of cards. To change the metaphor what we have are intimations of colossal landscapes; fleeting after-images of immense social, economic and political earthquakes which are often no more than hints of some vast and booming *terra incognita*.

The main cause of this, of course, has been the régime's absolute control of primary sources. In the second place, for over sixty years native academics – Russians, Ukrainians, Uzbeks, Georgians, etc. – have been cut off from world-wide intellectual developments. The intellectual map of Europe and America is not the same as it was in 1930, but Soviet scholars were never – and never could be – fully cognizant of the momentous changes which have taken place. History in particular suffered greatly. Since Marxism–Leninism is and was an historicist doctrine, one which overtly and aggressively interprets past and present in terms of each other, the scope for intellectual creativity was always extraordinarily narrow. Russia's best researchers tended to 'migrate backwards' into medieval or ancient history – areas where official dogma was less in evidence. The main reason why so few Soviet works have been cited in this book is because the vast majority of them are, quite simply, not worth reading.[3] In consequence the 'vanguard' of Soviet history has always been located in the West. Only now has it become possible for native academics to engage in intellectual debate without fear of repression.

---

[3] With one exception. After Khrushchev's further denunciation of Stalin at the twenty-second party congress in 1961 a series of articles and books appeared, based on party archives, discussing collectivization and de-kulakization. See R. W. Davies, *Soviet History in the Gorbachev Revolution* (Macmillan, London, 1989) ch. 1.

We have yet to see what will emerge, but it is almost certain that Russian and other scholars living in the territories of the former Soviet Union will reclaim their own history. No longer will foreigners play the leading rôle.

The West's vanguard rôle has, in some senses, been beneficial – without it worthwhile academic history would not have occurred. But on the other hand political considerations all too often over-determined the direction of research. Since the USSR's very existence was always controversial, academics found it extraordinarily difficult to escape from agendas set by others. Merely to advance history – to ask new questions – invariably entangled scholars in quarrels with pro- and anti-Soviet lobbies, and the kind of questions asked were often a reflection of these quarrels. It *is* important to investigate Stalin's rôle, the rationality of planning or the impact of the purges, for example, but there are other matters of no less significance which have scarcely been touched upon. Most writing has been homocentric: scant attention has been paid to women, even by social historians studying the working class or the peasantry. Equally, the nationalities have been viewed almost exclusively in the context of state-building, modernization, ideology or the purges – objects of policy rather than subjects worthy of investigation in their own right. And the study of popular culture is only in its infancy; a vast range of source material – oral, visual and written – awaits exploitation.

In short, too much writing is still ahistorical. By and large to this day the academic community – in the West and in the lands of the old régime – still fails one of the prime tests of the historian's craft: to disengage from partisan strife and to see Stalin, Stalinism and Stalinist society as products of their time. The Cold War annexed history because it annexed the historical imagination. The liberation of both from the baleful ideologies of East and West is long overdue. Every historian stands to gain from the USSR's collapse, but changes will not come automatically: in order to free themselves academics will have to forget old quarrels and abandon old habits of thought. The history of Stalin's Russia is only just beginning.

Suggestions for further reading

V. Andrle, 'Demons and devils advocates: problems in historical writing on the Stalin era', in N. Lampert & G. T. Rittersporn, eds., *Stalinism: Its Nature and Aftermath. Essays in Honour of Moshe Lewin* (Macmillan, London, 1992). Discusses 'ideographic' and 'nomothetic' approaches to Stalinism (descriptions of unique events and attempts to 'normalize' the past), the problem of moral judgement and the rôle of metaphor in historical texts.

M. Reiman, 'The Russian Revolution and Stalinism: a political problem in its historiographic context', in J. W. Strong, ed., *Essays on Revolutionary Culture and Stalinism: Selected Papers from the Third World Congress for Soviet and East European Studies* (Slavica, Columbus, 1990). Criticizes post-facto rationalizations of historical actors' motives and argues in favour of de-idealizing Lenin, Stalin and the Russian Revolution.

T. H. von Laue, 'Stalin among the moral and political imperatives, or how to judge Stalin', *Soviet Union/Union Soviétique* (1, 1981); id., 'Stalin in focus', *Slavic Review* (3, 1983); id., 'Stalin reviewed', *Soviet Union/Union Soviétique* (1, 1984). Three articles by an established historian of Russia which add up to a powerful indictment of the Anglo-American historical community's failure to see Stalin and Stalinism in context.

INDEX